The
Long Lost
Friend

© MEGHAN C. CURRY

About the Editor

Daniel Harms (Upstate New York) holds two master's degrees, one in anthropology and one in library and information science. His major area of research is magic from antiquity to the present, and he has been published in the *Journal for the Academic Study of Magic* and the *Journal of Scholarly Publishing*. Harms is also the author of two books on horror fiction and folklore. Visit him online at DanHarms.wordpress.com.

To Write to the Editor

If you wish to contact the author or would like more information about this book, please write to the author in care of Llewellyn Worldwide Ltd. and we will forward your request. Both the author and publisher appreciate hearing from you and learning of your enjoyment of this book and how it has helped you. Llewellyn Worldwide Ltd. cannot guarantee that every letter written to the author can be answered, but all will be forwarded. Please write to:

Daniel Harms
⅘ Llewellyn Worldwide
2143 Wooddale Drive
Woodbury, MN 55125-2989
Please enclose a self-addressed stamped envelope for reply,
or $1.00 to cover costs. If outside the U.S.A., enclose
an international postal reply coupon.

Many of Llewellyn's authors have websites with additional information and resources. For more information, please visit our website at http:// www.llewellyn.com

FOREWORD BY JOSEPH H. PETERSON

The Long Lost Friend

A 19TH CENTURY AMERICAN GRIMOIRE

JOHN
GEORGE
HOHMAN

Edited by
DANIEL
HARMS

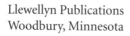

THE COMPLETE ANNOTATED EDITION

Llewellyn Publications
Woodbury, Minnesota

FIRST EDITION
First Printing, 2012

Cover owl art © Michael Halbert
Cover design by Kevin R. Brown
Editing by Connie Hill
Interior border art by Llewellyn Art Department

Llewellyn is a registered trademark of Llewellyn Worldwide Ltd.

Library of Congress Cataloging-in-Publication Data

Hohman, Johann George.
  [Lange verborgene Freund. English]
  The long-lost friend : a 19th century American grimoire / John George Hohman ; foreword by Joseph Peterson. — The complete annotated ed. / edited by Daniel Harms.
        p.   cm.
  Includes bibliographical references and index.
  ISBN 978-0-7387-3254-1 (alk. paper)
  1. Medicine, Magic, mystic, and spagiric—United States—History—19th century.
  2. Alternative medicine—United States—History—19th century. I. Harms, Daniel.
  II. Title.
  R133.H5813   2012
  615.5—dc23   2012003884

Llewellyn Publications
A Division of Llewellyn Worldwide Ltd.
2143 Wooddale Drive
Woodbury, MN 55125-2989
www.llewellyn.com

Printed in the United States of America

Other Books by Daniel Harms

The Cthulhu Mythos Encyclopedia

The Necronomicon Files
with John Wisdom Gonce

Disclaimer

Please note that the remedies within this book might be ineffective, toxic, or harmful. Although notes on their general efficacy are included for the purposes of scholarship, these should not be seen as comprehensive. The author(s) and publisher are not liable for any usage of these recipes. Please consult your physician before using any of these remedies, and bear in mind individuals may respond differently to the same treatment due to medical history, drugs being taken, and other factors.

Acknowledgements

The material from Charms A24–A58 is reproduced here with the permission of the New York Historical Society. The material from Charms S1-S69 is reproduced with the permission of the Edward G. Miner Library at the University of Rochester Medical Center. The quotations from the 1846 edition are from the collections of the American Antiquarian Society in Worcester, MA.

Thanks to Chris R. Bilardi, Bobby Derie, Jennifer Jones, Bret Kramer, Lorraine Melita, Jutta Roth, Franklin Townsend, Krystal Williams, the Berks County Genealogical Society, the Franklin and Marshall Special Collections, the Bucks County Historical Society, the Dauphin County Historical Society, the Historical Society of Berks County, the Millersville University Special Collections, the Society for the Academic Study of Magic listserv, and the Interlibrary Loan department at SUNY Cortland.

Special thanks to Meghan Curry for all her support and frustration, Lise Weaver and Raine Ford for their assistance with herbs, Joe Peterson for his keen eye on the text, Ralf Oderwald for his comments on the German, and Giovanni Engel for proofing the German text.

Contents

FOREWORD

Joseph Peterson

This well-researched new edition of *The Long Lost Friend* by esoteric scholar Dan Harms is most welcome.

Of the "five best books on magic" (in an earlier America) Hohman's book was ranked at the top.[1] It's easy to see why. Well known as a primary text of Hoodoo practitioners, and deeply rooted in centuries-old northern European traditions, its importance and influence spread worldwide.

Although often characterized as a collection of magic spells, it could properly be considered a wide-ranging self-sufficiency guide, although with many religious and magical elements. *Long Lost Friend* includes tips for dealing with common problems, providing charming illustrations of daily life in earlier days. Prominent among these concerns are medical and veterinary problems, theft, and protection from various dangers, including weapons.

There are a number of reasons for its viral popularity: it is inexpensive, the tips are simple to try, and most if its magical elements are innocuous religious invocations, free of sinister elements. It is also bold in its claims—simply carrying a copy is said to protect the owner from various dangers, without "practicing" or even reading the text. Having a copy in your house (often hidden in a wall), is said to protect it from fires or other disasters.

No doubt its popularity also profited from the fair amount of mystique attached to Catholic "practical" prayers. Although it may

seem innocuous today, this kind of "black book" literature was forbidden and often severely punished in the Protestant world.[2] This phenomenon occurred over a wide geography and timeline—in fact it engendered much of the "grimoire" literature.

In spite of its importance and many editions, this text has gotten very little critical analysis or scholarly treatment. Until now, the most significant publication dealing with it at length was Carleton Brown's 1904 article in *The Journal of American Folklore*, which is quite dated. Since Brown's study, significant findings have been made, such as the identity of the mysterious "Gypsy" work alluded to in Hohman's preface. Brown also relied heavily on Charles Leland's *Gypsy Sorcery*, which is now widely regarded as unreliable.

Dan Harms has critically analyzed the various editions and variations, starting with the earliest German texts. His extensive introduction and frequent footnotes shed light on the many obscurities in *Long Lost Friend*. Dan has collected extensive information on the mysterious author, along with the text's provenance, history, legend, and influence. All and all, this is the most comprehensive and reliable edition yet to appear.

Despite efforts by centuries of rationalists, skeptics, and authorities whose livelihoods were threatened by popular self-help publications like this, practices that are essentially magical show little sign of disappearing. Self-reliance is powerful. When people maintain a sense of control in their lives, they are freed from absolute reliance on various religious, medical, and government leaders for personal protection and well being. Whether from tradition, social convention, or because "you never know" we continue drinking to someone's health, blessing someone who sneezes, and practice countless other everyday rituals.

In fact, instead of being remnants of an outdated way of thinking, magical practices continue to adapt with the times, evolving and expressing themselves in new ways. A recent illustration of this magical thinking was recently seen using Facebook as a magical vehicle:

God has seen YOU struggling with something. God says its over. A blessing is coming your way. If you believe in God, send this message on; please do not ignore it, you are being tested. God is going to fix two things (BIG) tonight in your favor. If you believe in God, drop everything and repost.[3]

In the sixteenth century, the Swiss physician Paracelsus revolutionized medicine by rejecting blind adherence to traditional treatments, and emphasizing an experimental approach. Hohman suggested: Rather than rely on it, put it to the test—and perhaps question some of our fanatical acceptance, trust, and reliance on conventional methods as well.

INTRODUCTION

Der Lang Verborgene Freund, or *The Long Lost Friend,*[4] is perhaps the most influential and well known of all the grimoires, or books of magic,[5] to originate in the New World. Originally published in Reading, Pennsylvania, circa 1820, it has been reprinted in dozens of editions, and its influence over one state has grown to international proportions. The book has become a practical manual of spellcraft in traditions ranging from the "powwowing" cures of the German immigrants to Pennsylvania, to Hoodoo, conjure, and Santeria. Countless copies have been carried onto the battlefield to protect the user from violent death, and the book is still used as a talisman against all manner of horror. Indeed, the book might be the most influential American work that has eluded the literary canon, and an essential document of the occult tradition in North America.

To uncover how the *Friend* became so prominent, we must begin with the people among whom it found its genesis: the Pennsylvania Dutch.

I. The Pennsylvania Dutch

The use of the term "Pennsylvania Dutch" is misleading, as it implies to modern readers that the people to which it applies came from the Netherlands. Many scholars have substituted the phrase "Pennsylvania German" instead. Even this, however, is slightly misleading, as many of their ancestors came not from Germany itself, but from the German-speaking regions of present-day France and Switzerland.

Also, many descendants of these immigrants reject the term "Pennsylvania German" in favor of calling themselves "Dutch." For these reasons, "Pennsylvania Dutch" is the term I will be using here.

The coming of Francis Daniel Pastorius to Pennsylvania in 1683 marked the beginning of a long period of German immigration to the colony. Pastorius (1651–c. 1720) not only founded Germantown near Philadelphia, but he also promoted the new land and brought about good relations with their neighbors from other parts of Europe.[6] Major immigrant waves came around 1750 and 1840, but trickles continued throughout the eighteenth and nineteenth centuries. The majority came from the Palatinate region of southwest Germany, though other areas of Germany and adjacent parts of France and Switzerland contributed to the population. They came for a variety of reasons—fleeing warfare, seeking religious freedom, or seeking economic prosperity. Most of those who arrived settled in eastern Pennsylvania, slowly moving west to find more available land.

Most of the settlers were Protestant, of the Lutheran or Reformed faiths. Nonetheless, the colony's founder, Quaker William Penn (1644-1718), had guaranteed freedom of religion to all monotheists who inhabited the land, and the ability to hold office to any who believed in Jesus Christ. This mandate of religious freedom made the colony an attractive site of emigration for those of many small sects, including the Moravians, the Amish, the Mennonites, and the Dunkards. A small number of German Catholics had also emigrated; though initially welcomed, by the time *The Long-Lost Friend* was published, they were regarded with increasing suspicion.[7] Later commentators have asserted that some of the colony's inhabitants were in fact polytheistic, a question with which we will deal later.

Literacy was very important to German settlers; although few went on to higher education, local schools often taught the basics of reading and arithmetic to the children. Most German households had books—in fact, books are one of the few items that the settlers are known to have brought with them on their cramped overseas travels.[8] The most prominent works were the Bible and other religious tracts, though other genres flourished, including stories of robbers

and *Eulenspiegel*, a simple-minded peasant who nonetheless gets the better of others on a regular basis.[9] A small publishing industry sprang up for German speakers, publishing newspapers (such as *Der Unpartheyische Readinger Adler (The Impartial Reading Eagle)*, later *Der Readinger Adler* and *Reading Adler (The Reading Eagle)*, which began publication in 1797 and continued for over a century, as well as broadsides, pamphlets, and books.

The most important genre of books for our purposes was the *Hausvaterliteratur*, a term literally meaning "House-Father-Literature," of which the *Friend* might be considered the most prominent American example. Such books were aimed at an independent land-owner of little means who might have had crops, livestock, and possibly a servant or two, but with a shortage of free cash and little access to medical services for either animals or humans. Even though the genre was dying out in Germany by 1800, the need for such books would have been acutely felt in the New World, as the settlers were more spread out from their neighbors and towns than they had been in Europe, and medical assistance was often unavailable.

The character of such works varies considerably, with some being herbal cures or home remedies, while others were based upon principles of sympathetic magic or even included incantations and charms. The settlers appear to have set boundaries between these types of recipes. Many of the charms of more secular character appear in written sources published by local houses. On the other hand, the magic often turns up in handwritten account books, the flyleaves of other books, or scribbled on a small piece of paper, often in cipher.[10]

The written charms in these works, along with oral traditions, became mainstays of Pennsylvania Dutch healing practices. In an age with few doctors and no health insurance, medical care in Germany was rarely conducted via trained medical specialists. Those Germans who immigrated to the New World found the situation exacerbated, with most health services and resources available only in the English language.[11] A strong tradition of household self-sufficiency combined with a dearth of physicians among the German-speaking population of rural Pennsylvania led to medical practice based upon a mixture

of medically trained clergy, pharmacies, herbalists, midwives, home remedies, popular literature, and visits to the brauchers, or healers.

A *Braucher*, from the German for "try" or "use" (plural: *brauch-erei*), was a healer who employed both material and spiritual means of curing. The practice later became known as powwowing, to reflect the purported power of Native American healing, though most of the indigenous inhabitants of Pennsylvania Dutch country were long gone and little of their healing lore had passed on to the settlers. Some individuals specialized in one particular illness, such as a charm to stop bleeding, while others took on the full gamut of ailments with a variety of treatments. Some of these individuals, such as Anna Maria Jung, or "Mountain Mary," and Johann Peter Seiler, gained prominent reputations, while others no doubt worked in relative obscurity.[12]

Did the presence of powwowers mean that followers of Pagan traditions had come to live in Pennsylvania? Some authors have insisted that many of the settlers were in fact practitioners of a pre-Christian Pagan tradition, coming to Pennsylvania to escape persecution, and that powwowing is a reflection of this belief. Although Pennsylvania was home to mystics and spiritual seekers aplenty, no evidence has appeared to indicate that believers in Pagan faiths lived there until the twentieth-century revival of European Pagan beliefs. Magic has never been the property of one system of belief, and a look at any collection of powwowing charms will confirm their essential Christian, and often Catholic, nature. It is true that a few charms from the Friend likely date back to pre-Christian times, but even these have been Christianized to fit into the belief system of those who used them.

Pagan or Christian, other curers were present in the area, but John George Hohman, the author of the *Friend*, does not mention his competitors. Those who do appear in the text are either deceased, such as the late Dr. William Stoy, or no longer present, such as the healing pastor mentioned in the introduction. He speaks obliquely of at least one other in the trade—the seller of a letter intended to cure rheumatism—but nonetheless keeps quiet about the person's nature or whereabouts. We do, however, know of one other curer: Hohman's wife. Hohman mentions in his book her cure for "mortification" in

1812—in fact, the earliest date for a cure provided in *The Long-Lost Friend*. We have no other evidence of her involvement, save that she did not wish to have the book published, so we are left to wonder whether she filled in for her husband at short notice, if both were curers of equal stature, or—based solely on the dates provided—whether she brought him to charming.

II. John George Hohman

The Long-Lost Friend breaks with the grimoire tradition in one important respect: whereas most magical works throughout history have deliberately obscured the names of their authors, this one trumpets itself as the work of one Johannes Georg (or John George or Georg) Hohman (or Homan or Hohmann or Homann). The fragmentary nature of the documentation, plus the ubiquity of the "John Homan" name in the Reading area, make researching the author's background particularly difficult. The best information can be found in the works of folklorists Wilbur Oda and Ned Heindel, which I follow here.

Much data regarding Hohman's early life remains unknown, as no work in German archives or records has been done. Based on suppositions based on his publication schedule (see below), some have placed Hohman's date of birth in October of 1778. This is likely inaccurate, for reasons we will explore below.

On October 12, 1802, Hohman, his wife, Anna Catherina, and their son, Philip, arrived in Philadelphia with one basket on the ship *Tom*, captained by F. P. C. Permeir, from Hamburg.[13] Their previous dwelling place is unknown, but they might have been refugees of the Napoleonic Wars that had recently ended with the French occupation of German territory.

Hohman and his family were redemptioners, individuals who were lent the money to travel to the New World on the condition that the sum be paid within thirty days after arrival. Many redemptioners had friends or family in the New World who would repay the price of passage. Those who had neither—the Hohmans seem to have fallen

into this category—became servants to whomever was willing to meet the bill.[14] Different accounts have circulated as to the identity of Hohman's contract holder. According to an account by the son of a local farmer, Nicholas Buck, Hohman and his family supposedly worked for a farmer named Fretz in Bedminster Township, until Hohman's contract was sold to the elder Buck. Hohman bought himself and his family out of servitude via the sale of *Taufscheine*, hand-written and richly illustrated birth certificates.[15] The Registry of Redemptioners indicates otherwise, however. On October 19, 1802, Hohman was indentured to Adam Frankenfield or Frankenfiehl of Springfield Township in Bucks County for three and a half years, to pay the $84 for his passage.[16] The farmer promised him suits and twenty dollars upon his release from service. Hohman's wife was employed by Samuel Newbold in Springfield Township, New Jersey,[17] meaning the two would remain separated for quite some time.

Over the years, Hohman seems to have moved about eastern Pennsylvania; his *Himmelsbrief* places him near Hellertown in 1811,[18] yet another 1811 publication lists him as living in District Township, Berks County,[19] and an advertisement in 1813 gives his residence as Nockamixon Township, Bucks County.[20]

Hohman's religious background has been a matter for speculation. Local folklore holds that Hohman attended the Catholic Church of the Holy Sacrament at Churchville (now Bally),[21] and he claimed ecclesiastical license for his printing of *Der kleine Catholische Catechismus "(The Small Catholic Catechism)"* in 1819.[22] In addition, he appears as a sponsor to the christening of Maria Catherina DeBender on June 11, 1821, at St. Peter's Catholic Church, though it was not unheard of for sponsors at baptisms to be non-Catholic.[23] If this was the case, however, he seems not to have minded doing business with Protestants, as a publication from 1815 includes a hymn intended for a confirmation near the Mertz Church, a Lutheran sanctuary, near Dryville,[24] and the *Taufscheine* he sold were almost exclusively used among Reformed and Lutheran believers.[25] Nonetheless, Hohman's religious interests could hardly have been orthodox, not only due to

his use of powwowing, but also his publication of apocryphal scriptures such as the *Gospel of Nicodemus*.

As is becoming apparent, our main source of information regarding Hohman is his publications. Hohman's first publication, dating to 1802,[26] was a single-page edition of the *Himmelsbrief*, or "Heaven's Letter," a single-page charm describing a heaven-sent document calling the faithful to observe the Sabbath. It was meant to be hung in the home for protection against various disasters. Hohman added his own poem—or rather, one composed out of fragments of others—to the letter, calling upon the reader to trust in God, attend church, and give alms to the poor.[27] Thus, almost a decade before *The Long-Lost Friend* was published, Hohman was clearly interested in religious topics.

Hohman was best known for his ballads and hymns, as the period's most prolific publisher of musical broadsides.[28] He was already printing songs at the offices of the *Readinger Adler* in 1805.[29] The first of these to survive is the *Wahre Geschichte oder Lebensbeschreibung des immer in der Welt herum wandernden Juden*, a work on the legend of the Wandering Jew, issued in Easton, Pennsylvania, by Christian Jacob Hütter in 1810.[30] Following that, Hohman issued a wide range of publications. His other works include the aforementioned Catholic catechism, apocryphal gospels, and works of mystical or medicinal nature.

It is the latter on which we will concentrate.

As early as 1813, Hohman was publishing charm-books. An entry in the account books of John Ritter and Company, publishers of the *Readinger Adler,* records Hohman's order of a thousand copies of a "Kunst-stuecke" dated December 23, 1812. Oda suggests that this might be a publication entitled *Verschiedene Sympathetische und Geheime Kunst-Stücke* (*Various Sympathetic and Secret Tricks*), an edition of which appeared from the Reading publisher Heinrich Sage in 1815. The book that appeared from Ritman in 1813, however, was *Der Freund in der Noth, oder: Geheime Sympathetische Wissenschaft, welche nie zuvor in Druck erschienen*, or "The Friend in Distress, or Secret Sympathetic Science, which never before appeared in print." The typography of this work indicates John Ritter and Company was

indeed its publisher.[31] Based on the surviving copies, though, this work is the same as the surviving portions of the *Verschiedene ... Kunst-Stuecke*, so it is likely that Hohman placed a new title on the book when it was reprinted by Sage two years later.

The work, which does not list an author, claims to be a Spanish manuscript found by an old hermit in the Swiss canton of Graubunden. It includes thirty-five magical charms emphasizing protection against fire-arms (likely a key concern during the War of 1812) and covering such topics as invisibility, blood-stilling, and fever. Variants of some of these appear in *The Long-Lost Friend* charms (e.g., items 119, 143, 151), but there is little evidence that Hohman used material from the *Freund in der Noth* in his later book.

Nonetheless, for our purposes, it is the title here that is more noteworthy. Assuming Hohman was not simply reprinting a previously existing *Freund in der Noth*, his title was likely inspired by Tobias Hirte's *Der Freund in der Noth, oder Zweyter Theil, des Neuen Auserlesenen Gemeinnützigen Hand-Büchleins,* (*The Friend in Need, or the second part of the new select handbook to the public benefit*) printed in Philadelphia in 1793.[32] As with *The Long-Lost Friend*, Hirte's work also covered many remedies for common household ailments and difficulties. Brendle and Unger state that Hohman used Hirte's work for much of the material in his later release, *Die Land-und Haus-Apotheke* (*The Land and House Medicine Chest*).[33] Although other works were referred to as "friends," it is likely that Hohman created his own "Freund" due to the inspiration of one, or both, of these works.[34]

On February 9, 1813, Hohman advertised *Der Freund in der Noth* in *Der Readinger Adler*, which came out from the same publisher, for the price of a quarter dollar. He states that he has been sick for some time and is still not entirely well, this making it necessary to publish the book. He makes much note therein of the "Twenty-five Letters," or SATOR square, claiming that its presence in a house prevents destruction by lightning or fire.[35] This same charm would later be incorporated into the *Friend*.

Hohman's most prominent work before *The Long-Lost Friend* was *Die Land- und Haus-Apotheke, oder getreuer und gründlicher Unter-*

richt, für den Bauer und Stadtmann, Enthaltend die allerbesten Mittel, sowohl für die Menschen als für das Vieh besonders für die Pferde (The Land and House Medicine Chest, or True and Thorough Lessons, for the Farmer and Town Man, containing the very best remedies, for both man and animals, also for the horses), published at Carl Bruckman's press in Reading in 1818. An article published in *Der Readinger Postbothe und Berks, Schuylkill und Montgomery Caunites Adverteiser* (The Reading Mailman and Berks, Schuylkill and Montgomery Counties Advertiser) on November 23, 1816, solicits subscribers for the book.

As the same issue of the *Readinger Postbothe* reveals, Hohman seems to have come under some fire, at least from one publisher who charged him without name as publishing books on magic. The letter reveals his state of mind and echoes comments he would later make in the introduction to *The Long-Lost Friend* in a few years:

Aufgepasst ihr Leute! Wer gern von mir Johann George Homann, ein Buch kaufen will, der sehe zu, dass er keine Lügen- und Hexen-Bücher bekommt: Denn ein gewisser Drucker in Pennsylvanien, verachtet alle übrigen Vieh-Doctor-Bücher, und absonderlich meines! Er nennet zwar meinen Namen nicht; aber einiger, der dem Drucker sein Adverteisment nur ein wenig mit Bedacht liesset der wird sagen, das es so gemeint ist; die Ursache aber ist, weil der Drucker selbst Vieh-Docter-Bücher zu verkaufen hat ... Ich sage dem Publikum dass ich mein Bücher vor einigen Prediger, Doctor, Färber, &c. sehen, und untersuchen lassen kann—Sie werden Wahrheit, aber keine Lügen- und Hexen-Geschichten darinn finden.

So viel von mir für diesmal, von
Johann Georg Homan
Den 23sten November, 1816.

Listen, everyone! Whoever happily wishes to buy a book from me, Johann George Homann, take heed, that he receives no books of lies and charms: for a certain publisher in Pennsylvania

holds all other livestock doctor books, and, strangely, mine, in contempt! Admittedly, he does not give my name; but anyone who reads the publisher's warning with only a little care can tell it means me, which is dirty; but the reason is because the publisher himself sells livestock doctor books... I tell the readers that I can let some preachers, doctors, dyers, &c., examine my books. The truth will be revealed, that no lies and charm histories are found in them.[36]

Hohman published the apocryphal Gospel *Die Evangelium Nicodemi* (*The Evangelist Nicodemus*) in 1819, and in its introduction he might have already mentioned *The Long-Lost Friend*. The book in question is not named, but Hohman completed the introductions for the books within two weeks of each other.

Es sind noch viele Bücher unbekannt, wie ich selber eins habe und bezeugen kann, dass ich schon grosse Thaten mit gethan habe, und dass daher ein sehr nützliches Buch ist. [There are still many books that are not well-known, of which I myself have one and to which I can attest, with which I already have done great things, and that therefore is a very useful book.]

Hohman had finished the *Friend* on July 31, 1819. The book was published by early February of the following year, as the first mention of it in print is Hohman's ad for the *Friend* and the *Evangelium* in the February 12 issue of the *Readinger Postbothe und Berks, Schuykil und Montgomery Caunties Adverteiser*. After discussing the book's virtues, Hohman tells us that the price is three shillings (roughly 72 cents) and available in the newspaper's bookstore.[37] Given this location, it is likely that the unknown publisher responsible for the book was Carl A. Bruckman, the publisher of the *Postbothe*.

Some have maintained that Hohman made a prosperous career for himself out of his publishing, but he seems to have been poor for most of his stay in America. He was unable to begin paying off his first publication in 1805 until four months after the printing,[38] indicating that his publishing was less than successful. His levels of tax payments during his time at Reading were lower than those of his townsmen. The introduction to *Der Freund in der Noth* in 1813 indicates that he was sick for a long period. After much talk about his service to his fellow man in the book's introduction, written in 1819, he admits that he is publishing it because he needs money. The book does not seem to have been lucrative, as in 1826 his holdings and goods were seized, and later auctioned on Christmas Eve of that year, due to nonpayment of debts to Jacob K. Boyer, from whom he had bought land in 1819. After a quick and unexpected rise in tax rates in the following year, Hohman's payments drop once again, even being reduced near the end of his life due to poverty.[39]

Even after the release of *The Long-Lost Friend*, Hohman could find no success. Further, his wife died on September 11, 1832, as announced in *Der Readinger Adler*. Hohman continued his publications, though most of these were hymns and popular ballads. His last book, *Der Fromme zu Gott in der Andacht* (*The Pious of God in Silent Worship*), a compilation of an apocryphal account of Christ's early years; and several songs, including one of Hohman's own creation, appeared in 1846.

Hohman's date of death remains uncertain. Scouring the records for the area and period for an individual of similar age has turned up a reference in the *Der Readinger Adler* to a John Homan who passed on April 19, 1845, at the age of 66 years, 6 months, and some days.[40] This, however, would appear to be Johann or John Homan, a hatter who was born in America on October 1, 1778, and who fought in the War of 1812.[41] The exact fate of John George Hohman remains a mystery, but he left an indelible imprint upon the history of American magic through the publication and distribution of *The Long-Lost Friend*.

III. Legitimizing the Book

Hohman found himself in a precarious situation on a number of fronts. First, he was likely a Catholic in an area that was primarily Lutheran and Reformed, selling a work that included Catholic prayers, historical figures, and other trappings. His audience was acutely sensitive to the idea of books of evil magic—in fact, Hohman himself had been charged with this at the time he was soliciting subscriptions to the *Land and House Medicine Chest*. Physicians were gaining ground on the clientele of charmers, declaring such folk magic to be dangerous superstition. Finally, there was the admonition, common within the magical literature, that the contents of such books be kept secret from the general public. He could not be guaranteed a friendly audience; in fact, he likely assumed that many who picked up the book would be openly hostile to his project. Thus, Hohman relied upon a number of strategies to ensure that his readers would purchase and support the book.

The most prominent strategy is perhaps the first in the rhetorical arsenal of practitioners of magic throughout time—that the remedies have been tried and worked. Hohman seems to have acquired a number of clients over the years who were beneficiaries of his healing practices, and he provides a long list of these individuals, including locations, times, and conditions healed. Nonetheless, Hohman apparently had some qualms about their willingness to support him, as he notes that he is quite happy to take them before a judge if need be to back up his claims. The claims of the medical community can be swept aside quickly, as Hohman has a method that works and theirs is more dubious.

Another legitimizing force to which Hohman could appeal was the religious faith of his time, whether his own or that of his neighbors. As such, the introduction includes a biblical passage, with the variants from both the Lutheran and Catholic Bibles. He also refers to two members of the clergy, one of each denomination, who either believed in or themselves used remedies such as those used in the book. Hohman not only justifies his practice in a Christian framework, but he uses it to launch the attack against his foes: God would not have let such works be circulated if it was not His will. In fact, not using these charms to effect a cure when it could benefit a person is a sin. Hohman's final strategy is perhaps the most breathtakingly audacious—not only are these charms holy, but their efficacy proves the existence of God, thereby serving as a valuable weapon against the doctrine of atheism.

Also critical were those who felt the charms and remedies should be kept secret. We do not know how prevalent such individuals might have been, but today's braucherei emphasize the importance of a transmission of the knowledge or power to cure. To circumvent such concerns, Hohman played upon a common trope of the authors of grimoires throughout time—the coupling of hidden information with its revelation, a cycle that is a common element surrounding the mythology of many grimoires. The notorious *Key of Solomon*, according to the introduction in some copies, was originally revealed by the biblical king to his son Reboam, who then hid it in an ivory box in his father's grave.[42] Closer to Hohman's time, the *Egyptian Secrets* proclaimed itself to contain "the hidden secrets and mysteries of life unveiled" for the purpose of protecting men from witches,[43] and a hermit supposedly discovered *Der Freund in der Noth* in a Swiss cavern. Even though he put his own name upon the book, Hohman presented himself in line with this tradition, as a man merely bringing vital and "long-hidden" knowledge to the public.

Hohman had one final justification he could use—one drawing upon the principles of the country in which he now lived:

The publication of books (provided they are useful and morally right) is not prohibited in the United States, as is the case in other countries where kings and despots hold tyrannical sway over the people. I place myself upon the broad platform of the liberty of the press and of conscience, in regard to this useful book...

IV. Medicine and Charming in *The Long-Lost Friend*

After he had justified his project's existence, Hohman could turn to his main purpose for the book: providing remedies to a wide variety of conditions. Whereas others from his time might have seen illness and misfortune in terms of polluting vapor, called miasma, or God's punishment, Hohman never articulates a clear etiology of disease in his work. Misfortune of all varieties seems to be due to either unexplained causes or the work of witches. The latter term deserves some attention.

In this work, "witches" should not be read in the modern sense of practitioners of Pagan faith, but instead as individuals believed to use malevolent power against the persons, livestock, and property of those nearby. People and animals fell ill, cows' milk dried up, butter refused to churn, and guns missed their mark at the will of a witch.[44] Any one of these, in a rural agricultural society could be devastating to a household.

Accusations of witchcraft in Pennsylvania were rarely handled through the legal system. Of the two cases of witchcraft that had arrived in court during Penn's time as governor, one ended after the accusation was "found trifling," and the other came to a close with the defendants found "Guilty of having the Common fame of a witch, but not guilty" of witchcraft itself.[45] Given the lack of recourse to the courts, and the post-Enlightenment medical attitude that witchcraft did not exist, people believing they were bewitched routinely turned to magic to help them.

Hohman not only had faith in witches, but also thought they posed enough threat that he included two charms—Items 137 and 178—intended to bring about their destruction.[46] Nonetheless, Hohman's main concern is not the cause of illness, but how it might be alleviated.

The modern reader will differentiate among three types of recipes in this book:

    1. those that seem to work on strictly material grounds, based on the medicinal or chemical properties of various substances;

2. those that employ natural magic, relying upon the powers inherent in certain objects; and

3. charms, involving spoken or written words, touching the patient, hand motions, and performing particular actions at different times, often within a religious context.

The question that we should ask first, then, is if these were categories that Hohman himself recognized. This would indeed seem to be the case; Hohman's *Land and House Medicine Chest* avoids the third category entirely and shies away from the second. Hohman was well aware of these charms, so it is likely that this choice was intentional. As such, Hohman's work is an important document relating how medicine was practiced on the ground, not in the more sanitized version available in many printed works from the period. As such, the charms provide the most interesting aspect of the book.

Most of these charms have a linguistic component, whether that is verbal or written. These reveal that the religious mindset of *The Long-Lost Friend* is predominantly Catholic, with frequent references to the Virgin Mary and the saints, and calls for conventional prayers such as the Ave Maria. It would be remiss to consider the readers of the book to be Catholic because of this; a long-standing tradition exists of German works of magic justifying themselves via reference to Catholicism, including stories of various books of magic being found in abandoned monasteries.

Despite this orientation, however, the *Friend* contains much material that is not orthodox. For example, we have a number of charms that include non-canonical elements, such as the mythical "Saint Itorius" (Charm 23), that exist outside the realm of accepted theology. Within the spells, we often find Biblical figures and occurrences in mysterious situations, permutations, and conjunctions. One charm apparently features the prophet Daniel, the infant Jesus, and an adult Saint Peter, thereby effectively combining figures from three different periods in a single incantation. We might also find Jesus being born in Jerusalem, or crossing the Red Sea (instead of the Sea of Galilee).

In addition, the book contains phrases that seem completely non-sensical to us. Items 24 ("*Dullix, ix, ux*"), 36 ("*Potmat sineat*"), and 131 ("*Ito, alo Massa Dandi Bando*"). Referred to as *nomina barbara*, or "barbarous names," the origin of such phrases likely varies considerably. Some might be derived from phrases in German, Latin, or Hebrew which have lost their original meaning through recopying, often by those unfamiliar with the original tongue or who were attempting to retain the original rhyme scheme. Others might be onomatopoeia, words created for their poetic effect, or simple nonsense phrases. We might even see more corrupted versions of common magical phrases (such as Item 33's substitution of "Abaxacatabax" for "Abracadabra"). Sorting out which explanation is true for a particular passage is likely a matter for specialists in these tongues who can find such phrases in their original context. One such example from the *Friend* is Yoder's etymology for "Zing, zing, zing" in Item 67, which ties it to the German phrase "draw out the poison."

These linguistic aspects of the charms are often accompanied with a set of ritual gestures—rubbing or touching the body, making crosses over an afflicted area, or taking a broader action by taking a person, animal, or object, on a particular path, to a particular place, or through a particular item. It is in these that Hohman's interpretation comes to the fore, as he attempts to string together this collection of charms from diverse sources with an overall framework.

If we were to distill Hohman's advice regarding the charms, it might appear as follows: The crosses are to be made with the whole hand, or merely the thumb, three times over the afflicted part of the body. Each also stands for one component of the Holy Trinity. If the curer's hand is to touch the afflicted's body, that part of the body must be bare. Spoken charms must be said three times, with the second time several hours after the first, and the third on the following day. He also assures us that the cures for humans will also work equally well for beasts. He also gives more specific instructions; for example, the powwower should be walking about to facilitate any spell to immobilize thieves.

This emphasis upon charms does not mean Hohman places complete faith in their efficacy, however. In charm 101, Hohman admits that the charm might not work in every case it is employed. Nonetheless, he finds them to be largely effective, noting when his own experience has found them so.

V. Hohman's Sources

Uncovering the sources of a magical work is always a perilous task, and even in the case of *The Long-Lost Friend* it is not unproblematic. Magical practice combines both a deep respect for, and a need to maintain, traditional formulae, rituals, and actions that can reach back hundreds or thousands of years. Such charms are circulated both orally and in writing time and time again, undergoing transformations based on the practitioner, their levels of literacy of various sorts, and their preferences. The charms and recipes themselves are combined, separated, and recombined in endless permutations as they pass through the repertoires of different practitioners. At the same time, magic's nature as a performative social act opens it up to countless cycles of reinterpretation, appropriation, additions, deletions, and metamorphoses based upon the materials and circumstances at hand and the experience and preferences of the individual practitioner.

Thus, it is important not to become too devoted to the idea of the "origins" of such a book as *The Long-Lost Friend*. For example, we know that the book's first edition was most likely published in 1820. At the same time, however, we know that one particular charm, Item 33, has variants dating back to the third century. Archaeologists have found the SATOR square, used in Items 123 and 148, in archaeological sites dating back to the first century.[47] Nonetheless, our natural tendency would be either to emphasize those charms that are nearly two millennia old, or to declare the book's publication date as the most important factor.

Further, Hohman's own discussions of his sources are another source of puzzlement. For some, he is quite clear on their origins, or at least he seems to be at first. Others are attributed to "secret

writings" of some sort, which leaves us at something of a loss. A vibrant tradition of both printed and manuscript works of charms existed at the time Hohman wrote, so it is quite possible that many of his recipes came from some of these works. Nonetheless, it might be the case that Hohman invented some of these recipes, or heard them orally, with the label of "secret writings," whether originating with him or the tellers, granted to give the formulae greater authority. Given the time that separates us from that milieu and the disappearance of many possible sources, we might never know some of the sources for Hohman's charms. Nonetheless, we do have some clues as to where Hohman found some of his recipes.

One source that can be mostly rejected is that implied by the title later given to some editions of the book "Pow-Wows," or the medicinal practices of the Native Americans. Most of the incantations in Hohman's book include explicitly Christian elements, and most of the herbs referenced within are actually transplants to the New World from the Old, with few contributions from the Native American pharmacopeia.[48] Elsewhere in Pennsylvania other settlers were adopting Native American cures,[49] but they seem absent from The *Long-Lost Friend*. It might be that a specialist on Native American medicine and curing practices might be able to find some traces of these arts in Hohman's book, but I think this is unlikely.

Another possibility that has seen some adherents is that Hohman derived parts of his book from the *Aegyptische Geheimnisse*, or *Egyptian Secrets*, attributed to Albertus Magnus. Two major obstacles might suggest themselves. First, the book was first published in Brabant in 1816, which would leave it only three years to reach him in the New World. Second, most of the charms the two share in common are either found in the works mentioned below, or discrepancies exist between the two sources (e.g. the "Trotter-head" incantation in Item 121, directed toward a spirit called "Bettzaierle" in Magnus).

The most prominent source—and one to which Hohman refers explicitly in his introduction—is the *Romanusbüchlein*, or "Romanusbook," a collection of charms of unknown authorship. Though saints, lawyers, and other individuals of the name "Romanus" have been pro-

posed as authors, none seems to fit the bill. Although the work was to become popular in Germany throughout the nineteenth century, in Hohman's time it was barely a few decades old, with the first confirmed publication date being 1788,[50] though it had appeared with other treatises published before then. Hohman relies heavily on this work in the latter parts of *The Long-Lost Friend*—as Don Yoder points out[51]—not only does he use the charms verbatim, but he often lists them in the same order as the other work does.

Another authority to whom Hohman refers is Albertus Magnus, the thirteenth-century theologian. Shortly after Albertus' death, a series of works on the magical properties of stones, animals, and plants appeared, which came to be known as the *Liber Aggregationis*, or *The Book of Aggregations*.[52] The book became popular as time went on and saw translations into several languages. Numerous German language editions were available in the eighteenth century. Hohman takes a few passages directly from this work for his own, though it is unclear as to what exact edition he employed and why he chose the passages he selected.

One uncredited source for the recipes was Hohman himself, as some of the charms derive from *The Land and House Medicine Chest* (1818), which is described above. His editorial reasons for choosing these particular recipes remain a mystery.

Hohman did not draw exclusively on the magical literature for his sources, however. Charm 103, to cure the bite of a rabid dog, purports to come from "the Senate of Pennsylvania." This is a reference to an actual recipe submitted to that body on March 5, 1802, by one Valentine Kettring of Dauphin County. Hohman's source was not the records of the Senate itself, it appears, but rather an article on the topic from the popular magazine *Niles' Weekly Register*, from the October 11, 1817 issue,[53] as Kettring's name appears as "Kettering" in both the *Register* and *The Long-Lost Friend*.

Another nonmagical source for Hohman, this one uncredited, was Theodor Zwinger's *Theatrum botanicum, das ist, Vollkommenes Kraüter-buch (Theater of Plants, that is, the Complete Herb Book*, with its second edition revised by his son Friedrich and published in 1744.

This encyclopedia of herbs included a section on home remedies for each, from which Hohman took several of his recipes.

The ordering of charms from these different sources gives us some idea of Hohman's editorial practices. Most of the charms from the same sources are lumped together, though their order might not be entirely faithful to the original order. This might indicate that Hohman was compiling the book systematically from front to back. Further, the large proportion of *Romanus-book* material later in the book might indicate that Hohman was seeking a quick means to increase the page count of his book. Not having Hohman's own word on the topic, however, it is impossible to be certain.

VI. Editions

Following the original edition circa 1820, dozens of editions of *The Long-Lost Friend* were published, and the book has been available ever since. The most complete roster appears in Heindel's work;[54] the reader is referred to that work for a mostly complete list of editions.

1828—*Der lang verborgene Freund, oder getreuer und christlicher Unterricht für jedermann,* ... —Published in Ephrata, likely by Joseph Baumann, this was Hohman's own second edition, which would later form the basis of many later editions and translations. This edition is notable for the removal of Charms 12–19 and 178, as well as the inclusion of newspaper cures as Charms A1–A4. Hohman gives us no statement upon why this change was made. Charm 178 might result in a person's death, and Charms 13–16 and 18–19 involve the death of an animal, but Hohman includes other charms of the latter sort elsewhere in the book.

1829—*Der lang verborgene Freund, oder getreuer und christlicher Unterricht für jedermann,* ... —This edition was published in Chambersburg, Pennsylvania, likely from the press of Heinrich Ruby. It merely reproduces the text of the 1820 edition, not incorporating the changes from that of 1828. As such, it might represent the first pirated edition of the text.

1837—*Der lange verborgene Schatz und Haus-Freund: oder, Getreuer und christlicher Unterricht für Jedermann* ... —This was the first falsely attributed edition of Hohman's book, published in Skippacksville by one "J. S........s." Contrary to others' reports, this is not simply a reprint of a previous edition, but it revises the order of the recipes and includes sixty-nine new charms, most of which were taken from Paul Bolmer's *Eine Sammlung von Neuen Recepten und Erprobten Kuren für Menschen und Vieh* (*A Collection of New Recipes and Proven Cures for Men and Beasts*),[55] along with a new preface. The presence of Charms 12–19 argues for the 1820 edition being used as the source for this copy.

1839—*Albertus Magnus, oder Der lange verborgene: Schatz und haus-freund und Getreuer und Christlicher Unterricht für Jedermann*... —A reprint of the 1837 pirated edition with only minor differences. It is attributed to Albertus Magnus, possibly to draw upon the success of the *Egyptian Secrets*. No subsequent works in this particular line seem to have appeared.

1840—*Der lang verborgene Freund, oder getreuer und Christlicher Unterricht für jedermann*... —What might be considered a third German edition, including the dropsy cures listed as A5–A6.

1846—*The long secreted friend, or, A true and Christian information for every body.* The first English edition of Hohman's work. This Harrisburg imprint, claiming to be Hohman's own work, was the first English edition. This translation, riddled with typographical and grammatical errors, was never republished.

1850—*The long lost friend, or, Faithful & Christian instructions containing wonderous and well-tried arts & remedies, for man as well as animals*... This publication, issued from an unknown press in Harrisburg, was likely made from the 1840 edition. It includes the first exclusively English-language charms, items A8 and A9, for lockjaw and wasp stings.

1853—*Der lang verborgene Freund: enthaltend wunderbare und probmässige Mittel und Künste fur Menschen und Vieh.* This version includes an additional treatise on charming, *Dr. G. F. Helfenstein's vielfältig erprobter Hausschatz der Sympathie.*

1856—*The Long Lost Friend: A Collection of Mysterious & Invaluable Arts & Remedies, for Man as Well as Animals, with Many Proofs of Their Virtue and Efficacy in Healing Diseases, &c.* An English translation, with recipes for windgall and windbroken horses.

c. 1860 [?]—*The Long Lost Friend, Containing Mysterious and Invaluable Arts and Remedies, for Man as Well as Animals, with Many Proofs of Their Virtue and Efficacy in Healing Diseases.* The longest edition of Hohman's basic text, this edition adds Items A24–A58.

1863—*The Long-Hidden Friend, or True and Christian Information for Every Man ...* —This appears to be a second English translation of Hohman's original 1820 publication, thus containing the charms that Hohman omitted in the 1828 edition but omitting the appended recipes and Item 112.

c. 1900—*John George Hohman's pow-wows: or Long lost friend: a collection of mysterious and invaluable arts and remedies for man as well as animals, with many proofs of their virtue and efficacy in healing diseases, etc.* Issued by Philadelphia's Royal Publishing Company, this might be the first edition to include the phrase "Pow-wows" in the title.

1904—"The Long-Hidden Friend." Carleton Brown's republication of the 1863 translation in *The Journal of American Folklore* is the only scholarly edition of Hohman's book to this date.

1924—*John George Homan's Pow-Wows or Long Lost Friend ...* A publication of the Chicago publisher L. W. De Laurence. The son of a Pennsylvania Dutch woman, De Laurence (1868–1936) was known for issuing pirated editions of various grimoires, including *The Sixth and Seventh Books of Moses* and *The Key of Solomon.* His publications gained a broader circulation in African-American communities and on the African continent itself. His version claimed to be the sixty-fourth published, insisting that "the de Laurence Company as publisher does not hold itself responsible for the truth or terrors it may contain."[56]

1971—*John George Hohman's Pow-Wows, or Long Lost Friend, A Collection of Mysterious and Invaluable Arts and Remedies for Man as Well as Animals.*

This edition from Health Research of Pomeroy, Washington, includes thirty-three pages on card tricks from Professor Hoffman's *Modern Magic: A Practical Treatise on the Art of Conjuring*. As card tricks appear nowhere in Hohman, this material seems to have been included simply as filler.

VII. Local Influence

Even the incomplete list above highlights the great interest that *The Long-Lost Friend* garnered. As time went on, the book became a common stock in trade across the Pennsylvania Dutch country, slowly moving into other areas in which German settlers were prominent, including Maryland, West Virginia, Kentucky, South Carolina, and Arkansas. In the first years of this century, Baltimore author Letitia Wrenshall found a powwower in the mountains of Maryland using what she describes as a book of spells dating from 1820, with several examples being given identical to those in Hohman's book. That practitioner, and one other with whom she talked, was unwilling to sell her copy for any amount.[57] South Carolina powwower Lee Gandee spoke of traveling to a nearby town, after beginning his practice, to consult a family's copy of *The Long-Lost Friend*, only to find that a local minister had borrowed it before he arrived.[58]

While this diffusion was going on, the book itself acquired a considerable reputation in folklore. According to some traditions, possession of the book, or even touching a copy, would lead to crows, including one transformed witch, roosting on the roof of the owner's house.[59] Others believed that a braucher could not perform magic without a copy nearby.[60] One owner claimed that her cherished copy had passed through water and fire, speaking to its protective efficacy.[61] The book itself seemed to be surrounded by an unspoken secrecy. Folklorist Earl Robacker heard one of his Pennsylvania Dutch consultants mention a "long-lost friend" before his wife enjoined him to be quiet. Robacker continued to inquire of his informants, finding that none of them would reveal what it was. Only after he found a copy by chance in a catalogue did he realize that it was the title of a book.[62]

Elsewhere, he notes that copies were often difficult to collect, as few owners would actually admit to owning one.[63] Folklorist Barbara Reimensnyder relates the tale of a friend who was asked to leave a bookstore in Norristown after requesting a copy of the book.[64]

In 1970, Richard Shaner was cleaning his uncle's house when he found a German copy of the book amongst the possessions. He found papers inside that indicated that the book was seen as a source of remedies, though he does not elaborate.[65]

The book's continued use in remedies did lead to one stand-off with authorities. On October 22, 1951, state police removed a young boy, Elmer Zimmerman, Jr., from the care of his parents. Despite their son having a serious head wound from a traffic accident, his parents kept him from receiving medical care for several hours. The family was reported to have been ousted from the Mennonites due to beliefs centering upon *The Long-Lost Friend*. (It should be noted that Hohman's book includes no cures for head injuries.)

Nonetheless, this was not the most troubling legal case in which the *Friend* was involved.

VIII. The Rehmeyer Murder

The murder of Nelson Rehmeyer is still a controversial topic in Pennsylvania history. Though numerous articles and two books—Arthur Lewis' *Hex* and J. Ross McGinnis' *Trials of Hex*—have been written on this topic, many of their sources have had a clear interest in either promoting or downplaying the sensational ties to witch belief on which it seems to have been based. I have used the two books above as my main sources. The matter of the trial itself has yet to see a serious historical study, so scrutiny might reveal some of the facts below are inaccurate or misinterpreted.

John Blymire, or Blymyer, was supposedly the fourth in a line of brauchers living near York, Pennsylvania. He himself took up the healing trade part-time, and his clients credited him with some success. Nonetheless, Blymire was an unlucky man, with bouts of illness, a poor employment record, a failed marriage, and even a brief stay in

a mental hospital in 1923. He made trips to many different brauchers throughout the region, spending a great deal of time and money to find a solution to his ills.

The last braucher whom Blymire visited was Emma Noll (or Knopp) of Marietta. The unwitcher showed Blymire a vision of the purported witch in his hand. Her prescribed remedy, as described later, was to take a lock of hair and a copy of *The Long-Lost Friend* from the man. By taking a part or possession of the magician, his power could be overcome.

None of what has occurred so far is out of the ordinary when it comes to beliefs about witchcraft. Both textbooks and popular depictions portray witchcraft being responded to in formal trials. Though their role was certainly important, many witchcraft accusations were made among neighbors and dealt with locally through a corpus of folk beliefs and the assistance of individuals thought to have supernatural power over the witches. One who is believed to be bewitched might interact with several different practitioners of unwitching, until the misfortune is overcome. Emotions often run high among the participants in these social dramas, but they rarely result in violence. Such informal actions against witchcraft have been prevalent in a wide variety of times and places, and do not necessarily reflect negatively on the people of York County at the time.[66] Nonetheless, these actions do occasionally result in tragic consequences, as was the case for Emma Noll's choice of witch, Nelson Rehmeyer.

Rehmeyer dwelt outside Shrewsbury in the valley known as Rehmeyer's Hollow. A potato farmer and devout Socialist of impressive size, he was also a powwower who saw many clients in his small, two-story house. His wife and two daughters had departed from him four years before the murder, but they were still on friendly terms. (His wife would later claim that she left him due to his obsession with powwowing, though that did not stop her from seeking his help when she or her children were ill.) Rehmeyer was a familiar figure to John Blymire, whose parents had taken him to Nelson to be cured at the age of five, and John had worked briefly at the Rehmeyer farm when he was ten years old. The farmer had also been one of the powwowers

from whom Blymire sought help, working with him for three sessions before Blymire decided to go elsewhere. The two had only seen each other on occasion, and they were never at odds before Emma Noll's diagnosis.

At this time, Blymire's two accomplices entered the picture. The first was John Curry, only fourteen years old, who met Blymire when working at a cigar factory in York. Curry seems to have filled the role of Blymire's assistant in his cures, and Blymire had convinced the young man that he, too, was likely cursed. The two had taken on the case of the Hess family, whose farm near Hametown had seen a number of misfortunes that Blymire attributed to witchcraft. The family's eighteen-year-old son, Wilbur Hess, was devoted to freeing his family from the curse. Emma Noll later named Rehmeyer as the witch responsible for the trouble for both Curry and Hess. All these parties accepted the statement as fact, even though no one but Blymire had any contact with Rehmeyer previously.

After seeking to overcome Rehmeyer remotely in a contest of wills from his home in York, Blymire undertook direct action. On the evening of November 26, 1928, he set out with John Curry to visit Rehmeyer. They did not find him at home, so they walked to the house of his wife, who said he was visiting a neighbor. Returning to Nelson Rehmeyer's home around midnight, they found him still awake. He admitted the two and they spent some time talking to him before the three of them went to bed. Blymire's motivations are unclear—was he trying to mentally dominate his foe, or did he intend a physical confrontation that never came to pass? No matter the cause, Blymire and Curry departed in the morning after Rehmeyer cooked them breakfast, with neither hair nor book.

On the following night, Blymire and Curry returned to the hollow with Wilbur Hess and several pieces of rope. Rehmeyer allowed the men in, and they began to search for the book. When Rehmeyer tried to stop them, the trio attacked him, using a chair, the rope, a piece of wood, and their bare hands. No small man, Rehmeyer fought off all three for some time but eventually died after numerous blows from the three conspirators.

26

At this point, the group seems to have become distracted. No mention is made of them taking hair; Blymire indicated at the trial that he thought burying Rehmeyer would serve just as well. In addition, they were unable to find Rehmeyer's copy of the *The Long-Lost Friend*. No such book was found in Rehmeyer's effects, in fact, and the historic record is unclear as to whether he actually ever had a copy.[67] Blymire and his accomplices searched the house, but never seem to have entered the basement where Rehmeyer did much of his curing. In the end, they took what little money—between one and three dollars—the braucher had hidden about his house, poured water around him to cover up their fingerprints, set Rehmeyer's body on fire, and fled. Blymire later claimed to have seen a curious shadow standing in the road as they ran into the night.

Contrary to popular crime dramas, the human body is quite difficult to burn, and the fire on Rehmeyer's body quickly extinguished itself. Concerned neighbors visited the farm two days later, discovering Rehmeyer's remains largely intact. It took little effort to track down the perpetrators, and the police quickly arrested Blymire, Curry, and Hess.

The trials of the three men began on January 7, 1929. The case's sensationalistic aspects brought reporters from across the country, catapulting York County into the national consciousness. Newspaper stories portrayed southeast Pennsylvania as an outpost of medieval Europe, filled with ignorance and superstition. The journalists were either unaware or chose to ignore the fact that books such as *The Long-Lost Friend* could be easily purchased at stores in New York City and other large cities.

The prosecution attempted to present the crime as the unintended result of a simple robbery, likely to avoid complicating the case. It is true that the trio had taken money from the scene of the crime, and that the disorganized nature of the crime left the matter open to interpretation. (For example, Blymire and Curry seem to have been unconcerned that both Rehmeyer and his wife could have identified them, but Curry maintained that they nonetheless wore gloves to make sure they left no fingerprints.) Some locals believed that Rehmeyer had a hidden stash of money, making a robbery theory more

plausible. Nonetheless, it seems unlikely that the three murderers—two of whom had no criminal records whatsoever, and one of whom had just met the other two—would have suddenly decided to commit a robbery. A more compelling reason must have existed, and witchcraft fears certainly would have been sufficient.

In the end, both Blymire and Curry received life sentences for first-degree murder, which were later commuted, and Hess went to jail for ten to twenty years on a second-degree murder charge. Many commentators raised the issue of whether evidence of witchcraft was excluded at the trial that could have softened the jurors, but the matter was raised at each of the three trials. The first-degree murder sentences seem harsh to me, as no evidence was provided that the killing was premeditated. This is especially the case for Curry, who was scarcely fourteen. Nonetheless, a man had died, so an acquittal was unlikely in any case.

The most lasting effect of this case was the impact that it had on the practice of braucherei among the Pennsylvania Dutch. Given the attention paid to it during the trial, local and state officials felt that its presence should be addressed, removed, and ignored, as appropriate. Those powwowers who survived kept a low profile and seemed to have emphasized the transmission of oral knowledge rather than the book itself. By the time David Kriebel began his fieldwork among the powwowers in 1999, oral charms from the book remained staples of practice, but actual copies were almost never seen.[68] Rehmeyer had taken any good name the book might have once had in his native country to the grave with him.

IX. Broader Influence

Despite its notoriety in Pennsylvania, the book had traveled beyond the German-American population into a broader marketplace. It was through the catalogues of de Laurence and other spiritual suppliers that *The Long-Lost Friend* became part of the literature of Hoodoo. Hoodoo, or conjure, is a magical tradition combining African, European, and American remedies that became popular among African-

Americans in the late nineteenth and early twentieth centuries. As practitioners became more concentrated in urban areas, they drew more upon the products created by such entrepreneurs as de Laurence, which included *The Long-Lost Friend*.

As a consequence of this, the *Friend's* influence extended to locations far from the German-American population of Pennsylvania. In 1907, a New Zealand newspaper published an account of many of Hohman's charms found in the neighborhoods of Chicago's South Side.[69] Examples of incantations from Hohman turn up from time to time in the works of Harry Middleton Hyatt, who extensively interviewed practitioners of conjure across the South.[70] Hortense Powdermaker's ethnographic work in "Cottonville," a locale in Mississippi, turned up "Doctor A.," who employed *The Long-Lost Friend* alongside the *Egyptian Secrets* in his healing work. He was only willing to sell his copy of the *Friend* to the ethnographer after he was promised the purchaser was a good Christian.[71] Tom Pimpton, a "spirit controller" who took on ghosts during treasure hunting in Louisiana, gained his power from the *Friend*, along with the *Sixth and Seventh Books of Moses* and the *Petit Albert*, all of which he claimed to have ordered through the Sears and Roebuck catalogue.[72]

The book has remained quite popular among practitioners of Hoodoo, becoming popular in many of the local shops to whom practitioners turn for books and supplies for their businesses. James Foster noted that many shops in Harlem and Brooklyn stocked *The Long-Lost Friend* in 1957. A Chicago shopkeeper told Loudell Snow in 1973 that a person only needed three books to stay healthy—the Bible, an almanac, and *The Long-Lost Friend*.[73] These trends have continued into the digital age: the proprietor of a popular online spiritual supply shop has listed Hohman's book as one of her two top sellers.[74]

The book's reputation has also extended into the realm of popular culture. In the realm of fiction, the *Friend* appears frequently in Manly Wade Wellman's tales of Silver John, a balladeer and folklorist who travels the mountains fighting evil with his wits, his silver-stringed guitar, and incantations from the book.[75] Poet Jesse Glass published a short work of erasure poetry using Hohman's book as

its source material.[76] More recently, Pennsylvania author Brian Keene has written two horror novels in which the *Friend* appears, helping to provide the tools the protagonists need to ward off supernatural evils.[77]

The *Friend* has even appeared on the big screen in *Apprentice to Murder* (1988), a highly fictionalized version of the Rehmeyer murder with Donald Sutherland as the chief powwower. The *Friend* is never explicitly mentioned, but the powwowers in the film all own copies of the book, even brandishing them before them to ward off evil as if holding off vampires with a crucifix. Spoken and written charms from the actual book are sprinkled throughout the script.

More recently, *The Long-Lost Friend* has come to prominence in two religious contexts. The first is modern Paganism. Noted Wiccan author Silver RavenWolf has suggested using the book's magic in Pagan practice,[78] and Robin Artisson quotes from and modifies a copy of Hohman's "three springs" charm in his work on his own brand of traditional British witchcraft.[79] The other, Chris R. Bilardi, eschews this approach in favor of one that places powwowing squarely in a Christian belief system.[80] Wherever one might stand on the issue of the "proper" use of Hohman's incantations, their embrace across the religious spectrum speaks clearly of the significance and influence of his work.

X. A Personal Note

No doubt some readers hope that I spent my childhood in a centuries-old house just outside Reading or Berks, with a grandmother who whispered tales of the tattered copy of *The Long-Lost Friend* kept in a locked chest in the attic. In fact, my Pennsylvania Dutch credentials are a quarter-German heritage and a few years living in Pittsburgh and Altoona—in other words, practically nothing. My interest in the book has had its roots elsewhere.

I found out about the science fiction and horror writer H. P. Lovecraft in middle school. Lovecraft led me to his fictional book the *Necronomicon*, and the many hoax editions thereof, which led me

to grimoires, which led me to *The Long-Lost Friend*. I spent at least one family trip to Dutch country seeking the book in gift shops, all in vain. In graduate school, I finally found Carleton Brown's 1904 edition published in *The Journal of American Folklore*, and I managed to track down two or three more versions. The book struck me as a wonderful juxtaposition of practical household recipes and prayers for all manner of supernatural ends. It soon became obvious that this was one of the few books of magic that originated in the United States— most such books, until the latter part of the twentieth century, were cheap reprintings of European works.

As my research into the *Friend* and magic continued, I came across more fascinating information. On one hand, scholars such as Don Yoder, Wilbur Oda, and Ned Heindel had uncovered a great deal about the book's background and its relation to the culture as a whole. The murder of Nelson Rehmeyer, in which the book was claimed to play an important role, also caught my attention. My research into other fields of charms turned up parallels between the book's spells and others dating back to Classical or Anglo-Saxon times. Each source held a small piece that I painstakingly assembled into a larger view of the book, placing it into a context that spanned thousands of years and many different cultures.

When I looked at the discussion of the book, however, I was aghast. Many claimed that the book was a result of Native American, Egyptian, or Druidic lore, when in fact the book was reflective of practices in German-speaking areas of Europe. Few pointed out that the *Friend* existed in many different editions, with charms and recipes excised and added. Even academics treated the book in isolation, separate from comparable books of magic and folklore from Hohman's homeland and the studies in magic that had been done since. Publishers of the *Friend* did little to alleviate this situation, merely reprinting the book again and again with no notes or introduction that might educate the readers as to the book's significance.

I said to myself, "If only someone would publish an edition of the *Friend* that explained all this." As has happened with so many other writing projects, "someone" became "I" in a short time, and I was

soon delving into archives in Pennsylvania Dutch country and tracking down obscure German books, in order to assemble a complete edition of Hohman's work.

That's roughly the truth, as the writing and research processes are hardly that clear cut. They are more a mixture of opportunities and hunches, details recalled and forgotten, and long periods working on other projects while the present one waits for time and attention. Nonetheless, it covers the important points.

In case anyone is wondering, I cannot vouch for any of the charms or recipes in this book. I haven't even been able to talk anyone into trying the beer recipe. I would strongly advise against expecting it to stop bullets or anything of the sort.

Some of you might be reading a copy of this book that you did not purchase. If that is the case, I would suggest you buy your own copy, in order that publishers will be encouraged to put out more works such as this to everyone's benefit. I am baffled when I encounter people with thousands of dollars of electronics who insist they cannot afford a paperback.

In this project, I have sought to compile the material that I would have wanted to know when I first read the book, in a way that is useful for scholars, practitioners, and the curious. If I happen to make a little money off of it, then I can only say I find myself in company with Mr. Hohman himself.

Dan Harms

Upstate New York

A Note on the Text

For this work, multiple examinations of multiple editions of the *Friend* were made, including both German and English editions. It soon became clear that numerous variants existed between the text, ranging from typos to wholesale omissions of charms and reorganizations of the text.

The German herein represents the original German as published in 1820, with all of its variant spellings. The English represents the

translation first published in 1850, which has been reprinted numerous times in the next century and a half. Given the corruption of every text I have examined, I have perused several different ones to create a corrected edition that nonetheless is, I believe, faithful to the intent of each one. The English text of the charms omitted in the German editions after 1820 has been taken from the 1863 translation as reprinted by Brown in 1904. (Although this translation is reputed to be more accurate than that of 1850, close examination proves this is not the case.) The 1846 edition attributed to Hohman itself was also examined, but the text is so corrupt as to be unusable. I have indicated where that edition has variants that might be significant or interesting in the endnotes.

Most of the English within does not constitute a new translation, but a reprint of the most popular edition of the text. Such a text has considerable history in its own right. I have made a note of where I have found a significant difference between the English and German texts. The material in Appendix S represents my own translation.

The order of the charms in this edition follows the 1820 German edition, with the charms in the appendix added in the order of their initial appearance. Hohman changed the ordering and content for his 1828 edition, which served as the basis of the most popular English edition. As such, some readers of other editions might believe charms are missing on first examination. Nonetheless, this is the most complete edition of the *Friend* ever published.

Works Cited

Albertus. *Albertus Magnus. Being the Approved, Verified, Sympathetic and Natural Egyptian Secrets; or, White and Black Art for Man and Beast.* Chicago: Egyptian Pub. Co., 1930.

Artisson, Robin. *The Horn of Evenwood: A Grimoire of Sorcerous Operations, Charms, and Devices of Witchery.* Los Angeles: Pendraig Publishing, 2007.

Ashforth, Adam. *Madumo, a Man Bewitched.* Chicago: University of Chicago Press, 2000.

Bilardi, C. R. *The Red Church or the Art of Pennsylvania German Braucherei.* Sunland, CA: Pendraig Publishing, 2009.

Birch, Edith. "Barrick Mariche: Mountain Mary." *Historical Review of Berks County* 4, no. 1 (1938): 6–10.

Bolmer, Paul. *Eine Sammlung Von Neuen Rezepten Und Erprobten Kuren Für Menschen Und Thiere*. Deutschland: Gedruckt für den Käufer, 1831.

Bötte, Gerd-J, Karl John Richard Arndt, Reimer C. Eck, Werner Tannhof, Annelies Müller, and Oswald Seidensticker. *The First Century of German Language Printing in the United States of America: A Bibliography Based on the Studies of Oswald Seidensticker and Wilbur H. Oda*. 2 vols. Göttingen: Niedersächsische Staats- und Universitätsbibliothek Göttingen, 1989.

Brendle, Thomas Royce, and Claude W. Unger. *Folk Medicine of the Pennsylvania Germans: The Non-Occult Cures*. Pennsylvania-German Society, 45, 2. Norristown, PA: Soc., 1935.

Brenner, Scott Francis. *Pennsylvania Dutch, the Plain and the Fancy*. Harrisburg, PA: Stackpole Co., 1957.

Buck, William J. *Local Sketches and Legends Pertaining to Bucks and Montgomery Counties, Pennsylvania*. Philadelphia, PA: Printed for the author, 1887.

Burkhart, Larry L. *The Good Fight: Medicine in Colonial Pennsylvania*. Edited by Stuart Bruchey, Garland Studies in Historical Demography. New York: Garland Publishing, 1989.

Burr, George Lincoln, *Narratives of the Witchcraft Cases, 1648–1706*. New York: Barnes and Noble, 1946.

Cowen, David L. "The Impact of the Materia Medica of the North American Indians on Professional Practice." In *Botanical Drugs of the Americas in the Old and New Worlds: Invitational Symposium at the Washington-Congress, 1983 = Amerikanische Pflanzliche Arzneien in Der Alten Und Neuen Welt: Einladungs-Symposium Anlässlich Des Kongresses in Washington, 1983*, edited by Wolfgang Hagen Hein. Stuttgart: Wissenschaftliche Verlagsgesellschaft, 1984.

Davies, Owen. *Grimoires: A History of Magic Books*. Oxford: Oxford University Press, 2009.

Draelants, Isabelle, and Albertus. *Le Liber De Virtutibus Herbarum, Lapidum Et Animalium: (Liber Aggregationis); Un Texte À Succès Attribué À Albert Le Grand*, Micrologus' Library, 22. Firenze: SISMEL, Ed. del Galluzzo, 2007.

Favret-Saada, Jeanne. *Deadly Words: Witchcraft in the Bocage*. Cambridge [Eng.]: New York: Cambridge University Press, 1980.

Gandee, Lee R. *Strange Experience; the Autobiography of a Hexenmeister*. Englewood Cliffs, NJ: Prentice-Hall, 1971.

Glass, Jesse. *Man's Wows*. Madison, WI: Black Mesa Press, 1983.

Harms, Daniel. "The Role of Grimoires in the Conjure Tradition." In *Journal for Academic Study of Magic* no. 5 (2008) p. 40–68, 2008.

Heindel, Ned D. *Hexenkopf: History, Healing & Hexerei.* Easton, PA: Williams Township Historical Society, 2005.

Hohman, Johann Georg. *John George Homan's Pow-Wows, or, Long Lost Friend: A Collection of Mysterious and Invaluable Arts and Remedies for Man as Well as Animals; with Many Proofs of Their Virtue and Efficacy in Healing Diseases, the Greater Part of Which Was Never Published until They Appeared in Print for the First Time in the United States in the Year of Eighteen Hundred and Twenty.* Chicago: De Laurence, 1924.

Homan, John Geo. "Schöne Bücher." *Der Readinger Adler*, 1813, 3.

Homan, John George. "Bekanntmachung." *Der Readinger Postbothe und Berks, Schuykil und Montgomery Caunties Adverteiser*, 1820, 3.

Homann, John George. "An Das Publikum." *Der Readinger Postbothe und Berks, Schuykill und Montgomery Caunties Adverteiser*, November 23, 1816, 2.

Hyatt, Harry Middleton. *Hoodoo–Conjuration–Witchcraft–Rootwork: Beliefs Accepted by Many Negroes and White Persons, These Being Orally Recorded among Blacks and Whites.* Hannibal, MO: Printed by Western Pub.; distributed by American University Bookstore, Washington, 1970.

Keene, Brian. *Dark Hollow.* New York: Enfield–Leisure Books, Publishers Group UK, 2008.

———. *Ghost Walk.* New York; Enfield: Dorchester; Publishers Group UK [distributor], 2008.

Knab, T. J. *A War of Witches: A Journey into the Underworld of the Contemporary Aztecs.* Boulder, CO: WestviewPress, 1995.

Kriebel, David W. *Powwowing among the Pennsylvania Dutch: A Traditional Medical Practice in the Modern World*, Publications of the Pennsylvania German Society: Pennsylvania State University Press, 2007.

Kulikoff, Allan. *From British Peasants to Colonial American Farmers.* Chapel Hill, NC: University of North Carolina Press, 2000.

Lambert, Margo M. "Francis Daniel Pastorius: An American in Early Pennsylvania, 1683–1719/20." PhD diss.

M'Jimsey, Joseph A. "Cure of the Hydrophobia." *Niles' Weekly Register*, October 11, 1817, 100–01.

"Modern American Charms." *Otago Witness*, April 3, 1907, 71.

Montgomery, Morton L., J. H. Beers, and Co. *Historical and Biographical Annals of Berks County, Pennsylvania, Embracing a Concise History of the*

County and a Genealogical and Biographical Record of Representative Families, Comp. By Morton L. Montgomery. Chicago: J. H. Beers & Co., 1909.

Nolt, Steven M. *Foreigners in Their Own Land: Pennsylvania Germans in the Early Republic*. University Park, PA: Pennsylvania State University Press, 2002.

Oda, Wilbur H. "John George Homan." *Historical Review of Berks County* 13 (1948): 66–71.

———. "John George Homan: Man of Many Parts." *The Pennsylvania Dutchman* 1, no. 16 (1949): 1.

Philadelphia, Mayor of. *Registry of Redemptioners,*1785.

Powdermaker, Hortense. *After Freedom: A Cultural Study in the Deep South*. New York: Viking Press, 1939.

Quinter, Edward H., and Charles L. Allwein. *Most Blessed Sacrament Church, Bally, Pennsylvania: Originally Known as St. Paul's Chapel of Goshenhoppen, Berks County, Pennsylvania*. Bally, PA: Most Blessed Sacrament Church, 1976.

RavenWolf, Silver. *Hexcraft: Dutch Country Pow-Wow Magick*, Llewellyn's Practical Magick Series. St. Paul, MN: Llewellyn Publications, 1995.

Reimensnyder, Barbara L. *Powwowing in Union County: A Study of Pennsylvania German Folk Medicine in Context*. New York: AMS Press, 1989.

Robacker, Earl F. *Arts of the Pennsylvania Dutch*. New York: Castle Books, 1965.

———. "Long-Lost Friend." *New York Folklore Quarterly* (1956): 25–31.

Saxon, Lyle, Edward Tallant, and Robert Dreyer. *Gumbo Ya-Ya: A Collection of Louisiana Folk Tales*. Gretna, LA: Pelican Publishing, 1987.

Shaner, Richard H. "Recollections of Witchcraft in the Oley Hills." *Pennsylvania Folklife* 21, no. Folk Festival Supplement (1972): 39–43.

Snow, Loudell F. *Walkin' over Medicine*. Boulder, CO: Westview Press, 1993.

Solomon, and S. L. MacGregor Mathers. *The Key of Solomon the King (Clavicula Salomonis)*. York Beach, ME: Samuel Weiser, 2000.

Spamer, Adolf, and Johanna Nickel. *Romanusbüchlein; Historisch-Philologischer Kommentar Zu Einem Deutschen Zauberbuch*. Berlin: Akademie-Verlag, 1958.

Starr, Frederick. "Some Pennsylvania German Lore." *The Journal of American Folklore* 4, no. 15 (1891): 321–26.

Weaver, William Woys. *Sauer's Herbal Cures: America's First Book of Botanic Healing, 1762–1778*. New York: Routledge, 2001.

Weiser, Frederick S. "Piety and Protocol in Folk Art: Pennsylvania German Fraktur Birth and Baptismal Certificates." *Winterthur Portfolio* 8, (1973): 19–43.

Wellman, Manly Wade. *After Dark*. Garden City, NY: Doubleday, 1980.

———. *The Hanging Stones*. Garden City, NY: Doubleday, 1982.

———. *The Lost and the Lurking*. Garden City, NY: Doubleday, 1981.

———. *The Old Gods Waken*. Garden City, NY: Doubleday, 1979.

———. *The Voice of the Mountain*, Doubleday Science Fiction. Garden City, NY: Doubleday, 1984.

Wellman, Manly Wade, and John Pelan. *Owls Hoot in the Daytime and Other Omens*. San Francisco: Night Shade Books, 2003.

Wrenshall, Letitia Humphreys. "Incantations and Popular Healing in Maryland and Pennsylvania." *The Journal of American Folklore* 15, no. 59 (1902): 268–74.

Yoder, Don. *Discovering American Folklife: Studies in Ethnic, Religious, and Regional Culture*, American Material Culture and Folklife. Ann Arbor, MI: UMI Research Press, 1990.

———. "European Chapbook Literature in Pennsylvania German Culture." In *The Harold Jantz Collection: Proceedings of a Conference to Introduce the Collection to Specialists in German-American Literary Relations*, edited by Leland R. Phelps, 92–110. Durham, NC: Duke University. Center for International Studies, 1981.

———. "Hohman and Romanus: Origins and Diffusion of the Pennsylvania German Powwow Manual." In *American Folk Medicine: A Symposium*, edited by Wayland Debs Hand, UCLA Conference on American Folk Medicine, Los Angeles Center for the Study of Comparative Folklore and Mythology University of California at Los Angeles. Medical History and Science Society for the History of Medical, 235–48. Berkeley: University of California Press, 1976.

———. *The Pennsylvania German Broadside: A History and Guide*. University Park, PA: Penn State University Press for the Library Co. of Philadelphia and the Pennsylvania German Society, 2005.

Yronwode, Catherine. "Hoodoo: African-American Magic." http://www.luckymojo.com/hoodoohistory.html.

Note: *Hohman's Der Freund in der Noth* will be released summer 2012, in an edition translated and annotated by Patrick Donmoyer.

PREFACE TO THE FIRST EDITION
OF THIS USEFUL BOOK

The author should have preferred writing no preface whatever to this little book, were it not indispensably necessary, in order to meet the erroneous views some men entertain in regard to works of this character. The majority, undoubtedly, approve of the publication and sale of such books, yet some are always found who will persist in denouncing them as something wrong. This latter class I cannot help but pity, for being so far led astray; and I earnestly pray everyone who might find it in his power to bring them from off their ways of error. It is true, whosoever taketh the name of JESUS in vain, committeth a great sin. Yet, is it not expressly written in the fiftieth Psalm, according to Luther's translation: "Call upon me in the day of trouble; I will deliver thee, and thou shalt glorify me."[81] In the Catholic translation, the same passage is found in the forty-ninth Psalm, reading thus: "Call upon me in the day of thy trouble, and I will deliver thee, and thou shalt glorify me."

Where is the doctor who has ever cured or banished the panting or palpitation of the heart, and hideboundness?[82] Where is the doctor who ever banished a wheal?[83] Where is the doctor who ever banished the mother-fits?[84] Where is the doctor that can cure mortification when it once seizes a member of the body? All these cures, and a great many more mysterious and wonderful things are contained in this book; and its author could take an oath at any time upon the fact of his having successfully applied many of the prescriptions contained herein.

I say: any and every man who knowingly neglects using this book in saving the eye, or the leg, or any other limb of his fellow-man, is guilty of the loss of such limb, and thus commits a sin, by which he may forfeit to himself all hope of salvation. Such men refuse to call upon the Lord in their trouble, although He especially commands it. If men were not allowed to use sympathetic words, nor the name of the MOST HIGH, it would certainly not have been revealed to them; and what is more, the Lord would not help where they are made use of. God can in no manner be forced to intercede where it is not his divine pleasure.

Another thing I have to notice here: there are men who will say, if one has used sympathetic words in vain, the medicines of doctors could not avail any, because the words did not effect a cure. This is only the excuse of physicians; because whatever cannot be cured by sympathetic words, can much less be cured by any doctor's craft or cunning. I could name at any time that Catholic priest whose horse was cured with mere words; and I could also give the name of the man who did it. I knew the priest well; he formerly resided in West-moreland county.[85] If it was desired, I could also name a Reformed preacher who cured several persons of the fever, merely by writing them some tickets for that purpose; and even the names of those persons I could mention. This preacher formerly resided in Berks County. If men but use out of this book what they actually need, they surely commit no sin; yet woe unto those who are guilty that any-one loses his life in consequence of mortification, or loses a limb, or the sight of the eye! Woe unto those who misconstrue these things at the moment of danger, or who follow the ill advice of any preacher who might teach them not to mind what the Lord says in the fiftieth Psalm. "Call upon me in the day of trouble: I will deliver thee, and thou shalt glorify me." Woe unto those who, in obeying the direction of a preacher, neglect using any means offered by this book against mortification, or inflammation, or the wheal.[86] I am willing to follow the preacher in all reasonable things, yet when I am in danger and he advises me not to use any prescriptions found in this book, in such a

case I shall not obey him. And woe also unto those who use the name of the Lord in vain and for trifling purposes.[87]

I have given many proofs of the usefulness of this book, and I could yet do it at any time.[88] I sell my books publicly, and not secretly as other mystical works are sold.[89] I am willing that my books should be seen by everybody, and I shall not secrete or hide myself from any preacher. I, Hohman, too, have some knowledge of the Scriptures, and I know when to call and pray unto the Lord for assistance. The publication of books (provided they are useful and morally right) is not prohibited in the United States, as is the case in other countries where kings and despots hold tyrannical sway over the people. I place myself upon the broad platform of the liberty of the press and of conscience, in regard to this useful book, and it shall ever be my most heartfelt desire that all men might have an opportunity of using it to their good, in the name of Jesus.

Given at Rosenthal,[90] near Reading, Berks county, Pennsylvania, on the 31st day of July, in the year of our Lord, 1819.

JOHN GEORGE HOHMAN

Author and original publisher of this book.

NOTE

There are many in America who believe neither in a hell nor in a heaven; but in Germany there are not so many of these persons found. I, Hohman, ask: Who can immediately banish the wheal, or mortification?[91] I reply, and I, Hohman, say: All this is done by the Lord. Therefore, a hell and a heaven must exist; and I think very little of any one who dares deny it.[92] [93]

TESTIMONIALS,

Which go to show at any time, that I, Hohman, have successfully applied the prescriptions of this book.

BENJAMIN STOUDT, the son of a Lutheran schoolmaster, at Reading,[94] suffered dreadfully from a wheal in the eye. In a little more than 24 hours,

this eye was as sound as the other one, by the aid I rendered him with the help of God, in the year 1817.

HENRY JORGER, residing at Reading,[95] brought to me a boy who suffered extreme pain, caused by a wheal in the eye, in the year 1814. In a little more than 24 hours, I, with the help of God, have healed him.

JOHN BAYER, son of Jacob Bayer,[96] now living near Reading, had an ulcer on his leg, which gave him great pain. I attended him, and in a short time the leg was well. This was in the year 1818.

LANDLIN GOTTWALD, formerly residing in Reading,[97] had a severe pain in his one arm. In about 24 hours I cured his arm.

CATHARINE MECK, at that time in Alsace township,[98] suffered very much from a wheal in the eye. In a little more than twenty-four hours the eye was healed.

MR. SILVIS, of Reading,[99] came to my house while engaged at the brewery of my neighbor.[100] He felt great pain in the eye, caused by a wheal. I cured his eye in a little more than 24 hours.

ANNA SNYDER, of Alsace township,[101] had a severe pain in one of her fingers. In a little more than twenty-four hours she felt relieved.

MICHAEL HARTMAN, JR., living in Alsace township,[102] had a child with a very sore mouth. I attended it, and in a little more than twenty-four hours it was well again.

JOHN BINGEMANN, at Ruscombmanor, Berks County,[103] had a boy who burnt himself dreadfully. My wife came to that place in the fall of the year 1812.[104] Mortification had already set in—my wife used sympathy for it, and in a short time the mortification was banished. The boy was soon after perfectly cured and became well again. It was about the same time that my wife cured John Bingemann's wife of the wild-fire, which she had on a sore leg.[105]

SUSANNA GOMBER[106] had a severe pain in the head. In a short time I relieved her.

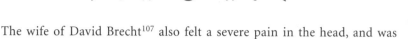

The wife of David Brecht[107] also felt a severe pain in the head, and was relieved by me in a short time.

JOHN JUNKINS' daughter and daughter-in-law,[108] both suffered very much from pain in the head; and his wife too had a sore cheek,[109] on which the wild-fire had broken out severely. The headache of the daughter and the daughter-in-law was banished by me; and the wild-fire of the wife was cured in some seven or nine hours—the swelled cheek burst open and healed very fast. The woman had been laid up several days already on account of it. The family of Junkins live at Nackenmixen,[110] but Brecht and Gomber reside in and near Reading. Nackenmixen is in Bucks county. The four[111] last mentioned were cured in the year 1819.

The daughter of John Arnold[112] scalded herself with boiling coffee; the handle of the pot broke off while she was pouring out coffee, and the coffee ran over the arm and burnt it severely. I was present and witnessed the accident. I banished the burning; the arm did not get sore at all, and healed in a short time. This was in the year 1815. Mr. Arnold lived near Lebanon,[113] Lebanon county, Pennsylvania.

☞ If any one of the above-named witnesses, who have been cured by me and my wife through the help of God, dares to call me a liar, and deny having been relieved by us, although they have confessed that they have been cured by us—I shall, if it is at all possible, compel them to repeat their confession before a Justice of the Peace.[114]

JACOB STOUFFER, at Heckak, Bucks County,[115] had a little child who was subject to convulsions every hour. I sold him a book containing the 25 letters;[116] and he was persuaded by his neighbor, Henry Frankenfield,[117] to try these 25 letters. The result was that the child was instantaneously free from convulsions, and perfectly well. These letters are also to be found in this book.

A letter to cure rheumatism,[118] sold at from one to two dollars, and did not even give directions how to make use of it; these depending on verbal communications. John Allgaier of Reading,[119] had a very sore finger. I used sympathy to banish the wild fire, and to cure the finger. The very

43

next morning the wild fire was gone; he scarcely felt any pain, and the finger began to heal very fast. This was in 1819.

This book is partly derived from a work published by a Gypsy,[120] and partly from secret writings, and collected with much pain and trouble, from all parts of the world, at different periods, by the author, John George Hohman,[121] I did not wish to publish it; my wife, also, was opposed to its publication; but my compassion for my suffering fellow-men was too strong, for I had seen many a one lose his entire sight by a wheal, and his life or limb by mortification. And how dreadfully has many a woman suffered from mother-fits! And I therefore ask thee again, oh friend, male or female,[122] is it not to my everlasting praise, that I have had such books printed? Do I not deserve the rewards of God for it? Where else is the physician that could cure these diseases? Besides that I am a poor man in needy circumstances, and it is a help to me if I can make a little money with the sale of my books.

Hohman

The Lord bless the beginning and the end of this little work, and be with us, that we may not misuse it, and thus commit a heavy sin! The word misuse means as much as to use it for anything unnecessary. God bless us! Amen. The word Amen means as much as that the Lord might bring to pass in reality what had been asked for in prayer.[123]

The Long
Lost Friend,
Annotated
& Edited by
Daniel Harms

ARTS AND REMEDIES

1. A good remedy for Hysterics,[124] *(or Mother-Fits,) to be used three times.*[125]

Put that joint of the thumb which sits in the palm of the hand, on the bare skin covering the small bone which stands out above the pit of the heart,[126] and speak the following at the same time:

Matrix,[127] patrix,[128] lay thyself right and safe,

Or thou or I shall on the third day fill the grave. † † †

2. Another remedy for Hysterics, and for Colds.

This must be strictly attended to every evening, that is: whenever you pull off your shoes or stockings, run your finger in between all the toes, and smell it. This will certainly effect a cure.[129]

3. A certain remedy to stop Bleeding—which cures, no matter how far a person be away, if only his first name is rightly pronounced[130] *when using it.*

Jesus Christ, dearest blood!

That stoppeth the pain, and stoppeth the blood.

In this help you,[131] (first name) God the Father, God the Son, God the Holy Ghost. Amen.

4. A remedy to be used when any one is falling away,[132] *and which has cured many persons.*

Let the person in perfect soberness[133] and without having conversed with any one, make water in a pot before sunrise; boil an egg in this

47

urine, bore three small holes in this egg with a needle, and carry it to an ant-hill made by big ants;[134] and the person will feel relieved as soon as the egg is devoured.[135]

5. Another remedy to be applied when any one is sick; which has effected many a cure where doctors could not help.

Let the sick person, without having conversed with any one,[136] make water in a bottle before sun-rise,[137] close it up tight, and put it immediately in some box or chest, lock it and stop up the key-hole; the key must be carried in one of the pockets for three days, as nobody dare have it except the person who puts the bottle with urine in the chest or box.

6. A good remedy for Worms, to be used for Men as well as for Cattle.

> Mary, God's mother, traversed the land,
> Holding three worms close in her hand;
> One was white, the other was black, the third was red.[138]

This must be repeated three times, at the same time stroking the person or animal with the hand; and at the end of each application strike the back of the person or the animal, to wit: at the first application once, at the second application twice, and at the third application three times; and then set the worms a certain time, but not less than 3 minutes.[139]

7. A good remedy against Calumniation or Slander.[140]

If you are calumniated or slandered to your very skin, to your very flesh, to your very bones, cast it back upon the false tongues. † † †

Take off your shirt, and turn it wrong side out,[141] and then run your two thumbs along your body, close under the ribs, starting at the pit of the heart down to the thighs.[142]

8. A good remedy for the Fever.

Good morning, dear Thursday![143] Take away from (name) the 77-fold fevers![144] Oh! thou dear Lord Jesus Christ, take them away from him! **† † †**

This must be used on Thursday for the first time, on Friday for the second time, and on Saturday for the third time; and each time thrice. The prayer of faith[145] has also to be said each time, and not a word dare be spoken to any one until the sun has risen. Neither dare the sick person speak to any one till after sunrise;[146] nor eat pork,[147] nor drink milk, nor cross a running water,[148] for nine days.

9. A good remedy for the Colic.

I warn ye, ye colic fiends![149] There is one sitting in judgment, who speaketh: just or unjust. Therefore beware, ye colic fiends! **† † †**

10. To attach a Dog to a person, provided nothing else was used before to effect it.

Try to draw some of your blood, and let the dog eat it along with his food, and he will stay with you. Or scrape the four corners of your table while you are eating, and continue to eat with the same knife after having scraped the corners of the table. Let the dog eat those scrapings, and he will stay with you.[150]

11. To make a Wand[151] for searching for Iron, Ore, or Water.[152]

On the first night of Christmas.[153] between 11 and 12 o'clock, break off from any tree a young twig of one year's growth, in the three highest names, (Father, Son and Holy Ghost), at the same time facing toward sunrise. Whenever you apply this wand in searching for anything, apply it three times. The twig must be forked, and each end of the fork must be held in one hand, so that the third and thickest part of it stands up, but do not hold it too tight. Strike the ground with the thickest end, and that which you desire will appear immediately, if there is any in the ground where you strike.[154] The words to be spoken when the wand is thus applied, are as follows:

Archangel Gabriel,[155] I conjure thee in the name of God, the Almighty, to tell me, is there any water here or not? Do tell me! † † †

If you search for iron or ore, you have to say the same, only mention the name of what you are searching for.

12. A very good remedy for Palpitation of the Heart, and for persons who are Hide-bound.[156] [157]

Palpitation and hide-bound, be off (name) ribs,
Since Christ, our Lord, spoke truth with his lips.

13. To make sure to Hit in Shooting.

Take the † heart of a † field-mouse,[158] and put a little of it † between the ball and the powder, and you will hit what you wish.[159] You must use the three highest names when you begin to load, and you must not finish the words till you finish loading.

14. Another, Good and Safe for Shooting.

Put some blood of a young mule (just foaled)[160] in the barrel, between the powder and the lead, and you will be sure to hit.[161]

15. To make one answer when he is asleep—also to hinder the barking of a dog.

If you lay the heart and right foot of a barn owl on one who is asleep, he will answer whatever you ask of him, and tell what he has done. Put the two even halves under the armpits, and no dog will bark at you.[162]

16. Another, to Prevent the Barking of a Dog.

Whoever wears a dog's heart[163] on his left side[164] no dog will bark at him; they are all dumb before him.[165]

17. Another, for the same.

Put the plant, called houndstongue,[166] under the big toes, and all dogs will be dumb before you.[167]

18. To Make a Black Horse White.

The water in which a mule-foal[168] is boiled makes a black horse white, if it is rubbed or washed with it.[169]

19. A Precaution.

Whoever carries the right eye of a wolf fastened inside of his right sleeve, remains free from all injuries.[170]

20. How to obtain things which are desired.

If you call upon another[171] to ask for a favor, take care to carry a little of the fivefinger-grass[172] with you, and you shall certainly obtain that you desired.[173]

21. A sure way of catching Fish.

Take rose seed and mustard seed, and the foot of a weasel, and hang these in a net, and the fish will certainly collect there.[174]

22. A safe remedy for various Ulcers, Biles, and other Defects.

Take the root of iron-weed,[175] and tie it around the neck; it cures running ulcers;[176] it also serves against obstructions in the bladder (stranguary) and cures the piles, if the roots are boiled in water with honey, and drank; it cleans and heals the lungs and effects a good breath. If this root is planted among grape vines or fruit trees,[177] it promotes the growth very much. Children who carry it, are educated without any difficulty; they become fond of all useful arts and sciences, and grow up joyfully and cheerfully.[178]

23. A very good remedy for Mortification[179] and Inflammation.

Sanctus Itorius[180] res, call the rest. Here the Mother of God came to his assistance, reaching out her snow-white hand, against the hot and cold brand. † † †

Make three crosses with the thumb.[181] Every thing which is applied in words, must be applied three times, and an interval of several hours

must intervene each time, and for the third time it is to be applied the next day, unless where it is otherwise directed.[182]

24. To prevent wicked or malicious persons[183] from doing you an injury—against whom it is of great power.[184]

Dullix, ix, ux. Yea, you can't come over Pontio; Pontio is above Pilato.[185] † † †

25. A very good remedy to destroy Bots or Worms in Horses.

You must mention the name of the horse, and say: "If you have any worms, I will catch you by the forehead. If they be white, brown, or red, they shall and must now all be dead."[186] You must shake the head of the horse three times, and pass your hand over his back three times to and fro.[187] † † †

26. To cure the Pollevil[188] in Horses, in two or three applications.[189]

Break off 3 twigs from a cherry tree;[190] one towards morning, one towards evening, and one towards midnight. Cut three small pieces off the hind part of your shirt, and wrap each of those twigs in one of these pieces; then clean the pollevil with the twigs and lay them under the eaves.[191] The ends of the twigs which had been in the wound must be turned toward the north;[192] after which you must do your business on them, that is to say, you must s—t on them; then cover it leaving the rags around the twigs.[193] After all this the wound must again be stirred with the three twigs, in one or two days, and the twigs placed as before.[194]

27. A good remedy for bad Wounds and Burns.

The word of God, the milk of Jesus' Mother, and Christ's blood, is for all wounds and burnings good. † † † [195]

It is the safest way in all these cases to make the crosses with the hand or thumb three times over the affected parts; that is to say, over all those things to which the three crosses are attached.

28. A very good remedy for the Wild-fire.[196]

Wild-fire and the dragon,[197] flew over a wagon,[198]
The wild-fire abated, and the dragon skeated.[199] [200]

29. To stop pains or smarting in a Wound.

Cut three small twigs from a tree—each to be cut off in one cut—rub one end of each twig in the wound, and wrap them separately in a piece of white paper, and put them in a warm and dry[201] place.

30. To destroy Warts.[202]

Roast chicken-feet[203] and rub the warts with them, then bury them under the eaves.[204]

31. To banish the Whooping Cough.

Cut three small bunches of hair from the crown of the head of a child that has never seen its father; sew this hair up in an unbleached rag and hang it around the neck of the child having the whooping cough. The thread with which the rag is sewed must also be unbleached.[205]

32. Another remedy for the Whooping Cough, which has cured the majority of those who have applied it.[206]

Thrust the child having the whooping-cough three times through a black-berry bush, without speaking or saying anything.[207] The bush, however, must be grown fast at the two ends, and the child must be thrust through three times in the same manner, that is to say, from the same side it was thrust through in the first place.[208]

33. To banish Convulsive Fevers.[209]

Write the following letters on a piece of white paper, sew it in a piece of linen or muslin, and hang it around the neck until the fever leaves you:

A b a x a C a t a b a x[210]
A b a x a C a t a b a x
A b a x a C a t a b a
A b a x a C a t a b
A b a x a C a t a
A b a x a C a t
A b a x a C a
A b a x a C
A b a x a
A b a x
A b a
A b
A

34. *A very good remedy for the Colic.*

Take half a gill of good old rye whiskey,[211] and a pipe full of tobacco;[212] put the whiskey in a bottle, then smoke the tobacco and blow the smoke into the bottle, shake it up well and drink it. This has cured the author of this book, and many others.

Or take a white clay pipe which has turned blackish from smoking, pound it to a fine powder, and take it. This will have the same effect.

35. *A good remedy for the Tooth-ache.*

Stir the sore tooth with a needle until it draws blood; then take a thread and soak it with this blood. Then take vinegar and flour, mix them well so as to form a paste, and spread it on a rag, then wrap this rag around the root of an apple tree,[213] and tie it very close with the above thread, after which the root must be well covered with ground.[214]

36. *How to banish the Fever.*

Write the following words upon a paper and wrap it up in knot-grass,[215] (*breiten Wegrich*) and then tie it upon the navel of the person who has the fever:

Potmat sineat,[216]
Potmat sineat,
Potmat sineat.

37. A good remedy to stop Bleeding.

This is the day on which the injury happened. Blood, thou must stop, until the Virgin Mary bring forth another son.[217] Repeat these words three times.[218]

38. How to walk and step securely in all cases.[219]

Jesus walketh with (name[220]). He is my head; I am his limb[221]. Therefore walketh Jesus with (name). † † †

39. A very good Plaster.

I doubt very much whether any physician in the United States can make a plaster equal to this. It heals the white swelling,[222] and has cured the sore leg of a woman who for 18 years had used the prescriptions of doctors[223] in vain.

Take two quarts of cider, one pound of bees-wax, one pound of sheep-tallow, and one pound of tobacco;[224] boil the tobacco in the cider till the strength is out, and then strain it and add the other articles to the liquid, stir it over a gentle fire till all is dissolved.[225]

40. To make a good Eye water.

Take four cents worth of white vitriol,[226] four cents worth of prepared spicewort (calamus root[227]), four cents worth of cloves,[228] a gill of good whiskey, and a gill of water. Make the calamus fine, and mix all together; then use it after it has stood a few hours.

41. To stop Bleeding.[229]

Count backwards from fifty inclusive till you come down to three. As soon as you arrive at three, you will be done bleeding.[230]

42. A very good remedy for the White Swelling.[231]

Take a quart of unslaked lime, and pour two quarts of water on it; stir it well and let it stand overnight. The scum that collects on the lime water must be taken off, and a pint of flax-seed oil[232] poured in, after which it must be stirred until it becomes somewhat consistent; then put it in a pot or pan, and add a little lard and wax, melt it well, and make a plaster, and apply it to the parts affected—the plaster should be renewed every day, or at least every other day, until the swelling is gone.

43. A remedy for Epilepsy, provided the subject had never fallen into fire or water.

Write reversedly or backwards upon a piece of paper: "IT IS ALL OVER!" [233] This is to be written but once upon the paper, then put it in a scarlet-red cloth, and then wrap it in a piece of unbleached linen, and hang it around the neck, on the first Friday of the new moon.[234] The thread with which it is tied must also be unbleached.[235] † † †

44. A remedy to relieve Pain.

Take a rag which was tied over a wound for the first time,[236] and put it in water together with some copperas;[237] but do not venture to stir the copperas until you are certain of the pain having left you.

45. Remedy for Burns.

"Burn, I blow on thee!" It must be blown on three times in the same breath, like the fire by the sun. † † †

46. A good remedy for the Tooth-ache.[238]

Cut out a piece of greensword (sod) in the morning before sunrise, quite unbeshrewdly,[239] from any place, breathe three times upon it, and put it down upon the same place from which it was taken.

47. A remarkable passage from the book of Albertus Magnus.[240]

It says: If you burn a large frog[241] to ashes and mix the ashes with water, you will obtain an ointment that will, if put on any place covered with hair, destroy the hair and prevent it from growing again.

48. Another passage from the work of Albertus Magnus.[242]

If you find the stone which a vulture[243] has in his knees, and which you may find by looking sharp, and put it in the victuals of two persons who hate each other, it causes them to make up and be good friends.

49. To cure Fits or Convulsions.[244]

You must go upon another person's land, and repeat the following words: "I go before another court[245]—I tie up my 77-fold fits."[246] Then cut three small twigs off any tree on the land, in each twig you must make a knot.[247] This must be done on a Friday morning before sunrise, in the decrease of the moon[248] unbeshrewedly.[249] † † † Then over your body where you feel the fits you make the crosses. And thus they must be made in all cases where they are applied.[250]

50. Cure for the Head-ache.

Tame thou flesh and bone, like Christ in Paradise; and who will assist thee, this I tell thee, (name,) for your repentance-sake. † † † This you must say three times, each time pausing for three minutes, and your head-ache will soon cease. But if your head-ache is caused by strong drink, or otherwise will not leave you soon, then you must repeat those words every minute. This, however, is not often necessary in regard to headache.[251]

51. To remove Bruises and Pains.

Bruise, thou shalt not heat;
Bruise, thou shalt not sweat;
Bruise, thou shalt not run,
No more than Virgin Mary shall bring forth another son.[252] † † †

52. *How to make Cattle return to the same place.*

Pull out three small bunches of hair, one between the horns, one from the middle of the back, and one near the tail, and make your cattle eat it in their feed.[253]

53. *Another method of making Cattle return home.*

Take a handful of salt, go upon your fields and make your cattle walk three times around the same stump or stone, each time keeping the same direction, that is to say, you must three times arrive at the same end of the stump or stone at which you started from, and then let your cattle lick the salt from the stump or stone.

54. *To mend Broken Glass.*

Take common cheese and wash it well, unslaked lime, and the white of eggs, rub all these well together until it becomes one mass, and then use it. If it is made right, it will certainly hold.

55. *To prevent the Hessian Fly[254] from Injuring the Wheat.*

Take pulverised charcoal, make lye of it,[255] and soak the seed-wheat in it; take it out of the lye, and on every bushel of wheat sprinkle a quart of urine; stir it well, then spread it out to dry.

56. *To prevent Cherries from ripening before Martinmas.[256]*

Engraft the twigs upon a mulberry tree,[257] and your desire is accomplished.

57. *Stinging Nettle[258]—good for banishing fears and fancies, and to cause fish to collect.*

Whenever you hold this weed in your hand together with Millifolia,[259] you are safe from all fears and fancies that frequently deceive men. If you mix it with a decoction of the hemlock,[260] and rub your hands with it, and put the rest in water that contains fish, you will find the fish to collect around your hands.[261] Whenever you pull your

hands out of the water, the fish disappear by returning to their former places.[262]

58. Heliotrope, (sun-flower[263])—a means to prevent Calumniation.[264]

The virtues of this plant are miraculous, if it be collected in the sign of the lion, in the month of August, and wrapped up in a laurel leaf, together with the tooth of a wolf. Whoever carries this about him will never be addressed harshly by any one, but all will speak to him kindly and peaceably. And if any thing has been stolen from you, put this under your head during the night, and you will surely see the whole figure of the thief.[265] This has been found true.[266]

59. To heal a Sore Mouth.

If you have the scurvy, or quinsey[267] too,
I breathe my breath three times into you.

✝ ✝ ✝

60. Swallow-wort.[268]

A means to overcome and end all fighting and anger, and to cause a sick man to weep when his health is restored, or to sing with a cheerful voice when on his death-bed; also a very good remedy for dim eyes, or shining of the eyes. This weed grows at the time when the swallows build their nests, or eagles breed. If a man carries this about him, together with the heart of a mole, he shall overcome all fighting and anger. If these things are put upon the head of a sick man, he shall weep at the restoration of his health, and sing with a cheerful voice when he comes to die.[269] When the swallow-wort blooms, the flowers must be pounded up and boiled, and then the water must be poured off into another vessel, and again be placed to the fire and carefully skimmed; then it must be filtered through a cloth and preserved, and whosoever has dim eyes, or shining eyes, may bathe his eyes with it, and they will become clear and sound.

61. A very good and certain means of destroying the Wheal in the Eye.

Take a dirty plate;[270] if you have none, you can easily dirty one, and the person for whom you are using sympathy shall in a few minutes find the pain much relieved. You must hold that side of the plate or dish, which is used in eating, towards the eye. While you hold the plate before your eye, you must say:

> Dirty plate I press thee,
> Wheal in the eye do flee.[271]

> † † †

62. To make Chickens lay many Eggs.

Take the dung of rabbits, pound it to powder, mix it with bran, wet the mixture till it forms lumps, and feed your chickens with it, and they will keep on laying a great many eggs.

63. Words to be spoken while making Divinatory Wands.[272]

In making divinatory wands, they must be broken as before directed,[273] and while breaking and before using them, the following words must be spoken:

> Divining wand, do thou keep that power,
> Which God gave unto thee at the very first hour.[274]

> † † †

64. How to destroy a Tape Worm.[275]

Worm, I conjure thee by the living God, that thou shalt flee this blood and this flesh, like as God the Lord will shun that judge who judges unjustly, although he might have judged aright. † † †

65. A good remedy for Consumption.

Consumption, I order thee out of the bones into the flesh, out of the flesh upon the skin, out of the skin into the wilds of the forest.[276] † † †

60

66. *How to cure a Burn.*

Three holy men[277] went out walking,
They did bless the heat and the burning;
They blessed that it might not increase;
They blessed that it might quickly cease![278]

✝ ✝ ✝

67. *To cure the Bite of a Snake.*

God has created all things, and they were good;
Thou only, serpent, art damned,
Cursed be thou and thy sting.

✝ ✝ ✝

Zing, zing, zing![279]

68. *Security against Mad Dogs.*

Dog, hold thy nose to the ground,
God has made me and thee, hound!

✝ ✝ ✝

This you must repeat in the direction of the dog; and the three crosses you must make towards the dog, and the words must be spoken before he sees you.[280]

69. *For the Hollow Horn[281] in Cows.*

Bore a small hole in the hollow horn, milk the same cow, and squirt her milk into the horn; this is the best cure. Use a syringe to squirt the milk into the horn.[282]

70. *A good remedy for the Bots[283] in Horses.*

Every time you use this, you must stroke the horse down with the hand three times, and lead it about three times, holding its head towards the sun, saying: "The Holy One sayeth: Joseph passed over a field and there he found three small worms; the one being black, another being brown, and the third being red; thus thou shalt die and be dead."[284]

71. *To remove Pain and heal up Wounds with Three Switches.*

With this switch and Christ's dear blood,
I banish your pain and do you good![285]

† † †

Mind it well: you must in one cut, sever from a tree, a young branch pointing toward sunrise, and then make three pieces of it, which you successively put in the wound. Holding them in your hand, you take the one towards your right side first. Everything prescribed in this book must be used three times, even if the three crosses should not be affixed. Words are always to have an interval of half an hour, and between the second and third time should pass a whole night, except where it is otherwise directed.[286] The above three sticks, after the end of each has been put into the wound as before directed, must be put in a piece of white paper, and placed where they will be warm and dry.

72. *Remedy for Fever, Worms, and the Colic.*

Jerusalem, thou Jewish city,
In which Christ, our Lord, was born,[287]
Thou shalt turn into water and blood,
Because it is for (name,) fever, worms, and colic good.[288]

† † †

73. *How to cure Weakness of the Limbs.*

Take the buds of the birch tree, or the inner bark of the root of the tree at the time of the budding of the birch, and make a tea of it, and drink it occasionally through the day. Yet after having used it for two weeks, it must be discontinued for a while, before it is resorted to again; and during the two weeks of its use, it is well at times to use water for a day, instead of the tea.

74. *Another remedy for Weakness.*

Take Bittany[289] and St. John's-wort,[290] and put them in good old rye whiskey. To drink some of this in the morning before having taken any

thing else,[291] is very wholesome and good. A tea made of the acorns of the white oak[292] is also very good for weakness of the limbs.

75. A good method of destroying[293] Rats and Mice.

Every time you bring grain into your barn, you must, in putting down the three first sheaves, repeat the following words: "Rats and mice, these three sheaves I give to you, in order that you may not destroy any of my wheat." The name of the kind of grain must also be mentioned.

76. To cure any Excrescence or Wen on a Horse.

Take any bone which you accidentally find, for you dare not be looking for it, and rub the wen of the horse with it; always bearing in mind that it must be done in the decreasing moon, and the wen will certainly disappear. The bone, however, must be replaced as it was lying before.[294]

77. To make Horses that refuse their Feed to eat again—especially applicable when they are afflicted in this manner on the public roads.

Open the jaws of the horse, which refuses his feed, and knock three times on his palate. This will certainly cause the horse to eat again without hesitation, and to go along willingly.

78. How to prepare a good Eye-Water.

Take one ounce of white vitriol[295] and one ounce of sugar of lead,[296] dissolve them in oil of rosemary, and put it in a quart bottle, which you fill up with rose water.[297] Bathe the eyes with it night and morning.[298]

79. How to cause male or female thieves to stand still, without being able to move backward or forward.[299]

In using any prescriptions of this book in regard to making others stand still, it is best to be walking about; and repeat the following three times:

63

"Oh Peter, oh Peter, borrow the power from God: what I shall bind with the bands of a Christian hand, shall be bound;[300] all male and female thieves,[301] be they great or small, young or old,[302] shall be spell-bound by the power of God, and not be able to walk forward or backward, until I see them with my eyes and give them leave with my tongue, except it be that they count for me all the stones that may be between heaven and earth, all rain-drops, all the leaves and all the grass in the world. This I pray for the repentance of my enemies."
† † † Repeat your articles of faith[303] and the Lord's prayer.

If the thieves are to remain alive, the sun dare not shine upon them before their release. There are two ways of releasing them, which will be particularly stated: The first is this, that you tell him in the name of St. John[304] to leave: the other is as follows: "The words which have bound thee, shall give thee free."[305] † † †

80. *To cure the Sweeney[306] in Horses.*

Take a piece[307] of old bacon, and cut it into small pieces, put them in a pan and roast them well, put in a handful of fish-worms, a gill of oats, and three spoonsful of salt into it; roast the whole of this until it turns black, and then filter it through a cloth; after which you put a gill of soft soap, half a gill of rye whiskey, half a gill of vinegar, and half a gill of the urine of a boy to it; mix it well, and smear it over the part affected with sweeney, on the third, the sixth, and the ninth day of the new moon, and warm it with an oaken board.

81. *How to make Molasses.*

Take pumpkins,[308] boil them, press the juice out of them, and boil the juice to a proper consistence. There is nothing else necessary. The author of this book, John George Hohman, has tasted this molasses, thinking it was the genuine kind, until the people of the house told him what it was.

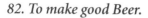

82. To make good Beer.

Take a handful of hops, five or six gallons of water,[309] about three table-spoonsful of ginger,[310] half a gallon of molasses;[311] filter the water, hops and ginger into a tub containing the molasses.[312]

83. Cure for the Epilepsy.[313]

Take a turtle dove,[314] cut its throat, and let the person afflicted with epilepsy drink the blood.[315]

84. Another way to make Cattle return home.

Feed your cattle out of a pot or kettle used in preparing your dinner, and they will always return to your stable.

85. A very good remedy to cure Sores.

Boil the bulbs (roots) of the white lily[316] in cream, and put it on the sore in the form of a plaster. Southernwort[317] has the same effect.

86. A good cure for Wounds.

Take the bones of a calf, and burn them until they turn to powder, and then strew it into the wound. This powder prevents the flesh from putrifying, and is therefore of great importance in healing the wound.

87. To make an Oil out of Paper, which is good for sore eyes.

A man from Germany informed me, that to burn two sheets of white paper would produce about three drops of oil or water, which would heal all sores in or about the eye if rubbed with it. Any affection of the eyes can be cured in this way, as long as the apple of the eye is sound.[318]

88. To destroy Crab-Lice.

Take capuchin powder,[319] mix it with hog's lard, and smear yourself with it. Or, boil cammock,[320] and wash the place where the lice keep themselves.

89. To prevent the worst kind of paper from blotting.

Dissolve alum in water, and put it on the paper,[321] and I, Hohman, would like to see who cannot write on it, after it is dried.

90. A very good remedy for the Gravel.

The author of this book, John George Hohman, applied this remedy, and soon felt relieved. I knew a man who could find no relief from the medicine of any doctor; he then used the following remedy, to wit: he ate every morning seven[322] peach stones[323] before tasting anything else, which relieved him very much; but as he had the gravel very bad, he was obliged to use it constantly. I, Hohman, have used it for several[324] weeks. I still feel a touch of it now and then, yet I had it so badly that I cried out aloud every time I had to make water. I owe a thousand thanks to God and the person who told me of this remedy.[325]

91. A good remedy for those who cannot keep their water.[326]

Burn a hog's bladder to powder, and take it inwardly.

92. To remove a Wen during the crescent moon.[327]

Look over the wen directly towards the moon, and say: "Whatever grows, does grow; and whatever diminishes, does diminish." This must be said three times in the same breath.[328]

93. To destroy Field-Mice and Moles.

Put unslaked lime in their holes, and they will disappear. [329]

94. To remove a Scum or Skin from the Eye.[330]

Before sunrise on St. Bartholomew's day,[331] you must dig up four[332] or five roots of the dandelion weed,[333] taking good care to get the ends of the roots; then you must procure a rag and a thread that have never been in the water; the thread, which dare not have a single knot in it, is used in sewing up the roots into the rag, and the whole is then to be hung before the eye[334] until the scum disappears. The tape[335] by which it is fastened must never have been in the water.

95. *For Deafness, roaring or buzzing in the ear, and for Tooth-ache.*[336]

A few drops of refined camphor-oil put upon cotton, and thus applied to the aching tooth, relieves very much. When put in the ear, it strengthens the hearing, and removes the roaring and whizzing in the same.[337]

96. *A good way to cause children to cut their teeth without pain.*

Boil the brain of a rabbit, and rub the gums of the children with it, and their teeth will grow without pain to them.[338]

97. *For Vomiting and Diarrhoea.*[339]

Take pulverized cloves and eat them together with bread soaked in red wine,[340] and you will soon find relief. The cloves may be put upon the bread.

98. *To Heal Burns.*

Pound or press the juice out of male fern,[341] and put it on the burnt spots, and they will heal very fast. Better yet, however, if you smear the above juice upon a rag, and put that on like a plaster.

99. *A very good cure for weakness of the limbs, for the purification of the blood, for the invigoration of the head and heart, and to remove giddiness, &c. &c.*[342]

Take two drops of the oil of cloves in a table-spoonful of white wine, early in the morning, and before eating anything else. This is also good for the mother-pains, and the colic. The oil of cloves which you buy in the drug stores will answer the purpose. These remedies are also applicable to cure the cold when it settles in the bowels, and to stop vomiting. A few drops of this oil poured upon cotton and applied to the aching teeth, relieves the pain.[343]

100. For Dysentery and Diarrhoea.[344]

Take the moss off of trees,[345] and boil it in red wine,[346] and let those who are affected with these diseases, drink it.[347]

101. Cure for the Tooth-Ache.[348]

Hohman, the author of this book, has cured the severest tooth-ache more than sixty times with this remedy; and out of the sixty times he applied it, it failed but once in affecting a cure. Take blue vitriol[349] and put a small piece of it in the hollow tooth, yet not too much; spit out the water that collects in the mouth, and be careful to swallow none. I do not know whether it is good for teeth that are not hollow, but I should judge it would cure any kind of toothache.

102. Advice to Pregnant Women.

Pregnant women must be very careful not to use any camphor; and no camphor should be administered to those women who have the mother-fits.[350]

103. Cure for the Bite of a Mad Dog.

A certain Mr. Valentine Kettering, of Dauphin County,[351] has communicated to the Senate of Pennsylvania, a sure remedy for the bite of any kind of mad animals. He says that his ancestors had already used it in Germany 250 years ago, and that he had always found it to answer the purpose, during a residence of fifty years[352] in the United States.[353] He only published it from motives of humanity. This remedy consists in the weed called Chick-weed.[354] It is a summer plant, known to the Germans and Swiss by the names of Gauchheil,[355] Rother Meyer, or Rother Huehnerdarm. In England it is called Red Pimpernel, and its botanical name is Angelica Phonicea. It must be gathered in June, when in full bloom, and dried in the shade, and then pulverized. The dose of this for a grown person is a small tablespoonful,[356] or in weight a drachm and a scruple, at once, in beer or water. For children the dose is the same, yet it must be administered at three different times. In applying it to animals, it must be used green, cut to pieces, and mixed with bran or other feed.

For hogs, the pulverised weed is made into little balls by mixing it with flour and water. It can also be put on bread and butter, or in honey, molasses, &c. The Rev. Henry Muhlenberg[357] says, that in Germany 30 grains of this powder are given four times a day, the first day, then one dose a day for a whole week;[358] while, at the same time, the wound is washed out with a decoction of the weed, and then the powder strewed in it. Mr. Kettering says that he in all instances administered but one dose, with the most happy results. This is said to be the same remedy through which the late Doctor William Stoy[359] effected so many cures.

104. A very good means to increase the growth of Wool on Sheep, and to prevent disease among them.

William Ellis, in his excellent work on the English manner of raising sheep,[360] relates the following: I knew a tenant who had a flock of sheep that produced an unusual quantity of wool. He informed me,[361] that he was in the habit of washing his sheep with buttermilk just after shearing them, which was the cause of the unusual growth of wool; because it is a known fact that buttermilk does not only improve the growth of sheep's wool, but also of the hair of other animals. Those who have no buttermilk may substitute common milk, mixed with salt and water, which will answer nearly as well to wash the sheep just sheared. And I guarantee that by rightly applying this means, you will not only have a great increase of wool, but the sheep-lice and their entire brood will be destroyed. It also cures all manner of scab and itch, and prevents the sheep from catching cold.[362]

105. A well-tried Plaster to remove Mortification.

Take six hen eggs and boil them in hot ashes until they are right hard, then take the yellow of the eggs and fry them in a gill of lard[363] until they are quite black, then put a handful of rue[364] with it, and afterwards filter it through a cloth.[365] When this is done, add a gill of sweet oil to it. It will take most effect where the plaster for a female is prepared by a male, and the plaster for a male prepared by a female.[366]

106. *A very good Plaster.*

Take wormwood,[367] rue, medels,[368] sheepripwort,[369] pointy plantain,[370] in equal proportions, a larger proportion of beeswax and tallow, and some spirits of turpentine, put it together in a pot, boil it well, and then strain it, and you have a very good plaster.

107. *A good remedy for the Poll-Evil in Horses.*[371]

Take white turpentine,[372] rub it over the poll-evil with your hand, and then melt it with a hot iron so that it runs into the wound. After this, take neatsfoot oil[373] or goose grease, and rub[374] it into the wound in the same manner, and for three days in succession, commencing on the last Friday of the last quarter of the moon.

108. *To stop Bleeding.*

I walk through a green forest;
There I find three wells,[375] cool and cold;
    The first is called courage,
    The second is called good,[376]
    And the third is called, stop the blood.[377]
† † †

109. *Another way to stop Bleeding, and to heal Wounds, in man as well as animals.*[378]

On Christ's grave there grow three roses; the first is kind, the second is valued among the rulers,[379] and the third says:[380] blood thou must stop, and wound thou must heal.[381] Every thing prescribed for man in this book, is also applicable to animals.[382]

110. *For the Scurvy and Sore Throat.*

Speak the following, and it will certainly help you: Job[383] went through the land, holding his staff close in the hand, when God the Lord did meet[384] him, and said to him: Job, what art thou grieved at? Job said: Oh God, why should I not be sad? My throat and my mouth are rotting away. Then said the Lord to Job: In yonder valley there is a well,

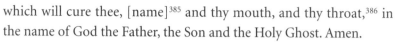

which will cure thee, [name][385] and thy mouth, and thy throat,[386] in the name of God the Father, the Son and the Holy Ghost. Amen.

This must be spoken three times in the morning, and three times in the evening; and where it reads "which will cure," you must blow three times in the child's mouth.[387]

111. For gaining a Lawful Suit.

It reads, if any one has to settle any just claim by way of a lawsuit, let him take some of the largest kind of sage and write the names of the 12 apostles on the leaves, and put them in his shoes before entering the courthouse,[388] and he shall certainly gain the suit.

112. For the Swelling of Cattle.

To Desh[389] break no Flesh, but to Desh![390] While saying this run your hand along the back of the animal. † † †

NOTE—The hand must be put upon the bare skin in all cases of using sympathetic words.

113. An easy method of Catching Fish.

In a vessel of white glass must be put: 8[391] grains of civit (musk),[392] and as much castorium;[393] 2 ounces of eel-fat, and 4 ounces of unsalted butter; after which the vessel must be well closed, and put in some place where it will keep moderately warm,[394] for nine or ten days, and then the composition must be well stirred with a stick until it is perfectly mixed.

APPLICATION.—1. In using the hooks—Worms or insects used for baiting the hooks, must first be moistened with this composition, and then put in a bladder or box, which may be carried in the pocket.

2. In using the net[395]—Small balls formed of the soft part of fresh bread must be dipped in this composition, and then by means of thread fastened inside of the net before throwing it into the water.

3. Catching fish with the hand—Besmear your legs or boots with this composition before entering the water, at the place where the fish are expected, and they will collect in great numbers around you.

114. A very good and safe Remedy for Rheumatism.

From one to two dollars have often been paid for this recipe alone, it being the best and surest remedy to cure the rheumatism. Let it be known therefore: Take a piece of cloth, some tape and thread, neither of which must ever have been in water; the thread must not have a single knot in it, and the cloth and tape must have been spun by a child not quite[396] or at least not more than seven years of age.[397] The letter given below must be carefully sewed in the piece of cloth, and tied around the neck, unbeshrewedly,[398] on the first Friday in the decreasing moon;[399] and immediately after hanging it around the neck, the Lord's prayer and the articles of faith[400] must be repeated.[401] What now follows must be written in the before-mentioned letter:

"May God the Father, Son, and Holy Ghost grant it, Amen. Seek immediately and seek; thus commandeth the Lord thy God, through the first man whom God did love upon earth.[402] Seek immediately, and seek; thus commandeth the Lord thy God, through Luke, the Evangelist, and through Paul, the Apostle. Seek immediately, and seek; thus commandeth the Lord thy God, through the twelve messengers. Seek immediately, and seek; thus commandeth the Lord thy God, by the first man, that God might be loved. Seek immediately, and convulse; thus commandeth the Lord thy God, through the Holy Fathers, who have been made by divine and holy writ. Seek immediately, and convulse; thus commandeth the Lord thy God, through the dear and holy angels, and through his paternal and divine Omnipotence, and his heavenly confidence and endurance. Seek immediately, and convulse; thus commandeth the Lord thy God, through the burning oven which was preserved by the blessing of God.[403] Seek immediately, and convulse; thus commandeth the Lord thy God, through all power and might, through the prophet Jonah who was preserved in the belly of the whale for three days and three nights, by the blessing of God. Seek immediately, and convulse; thus commandeth the Lord thy God, through all the power and might which proceed from divine humility, and in all eternity; whereby no harm be done unto † N † nor unto any part of his body, be they the raving convulsions,[404] or the yellow convulsions,[405] or the white convulsions, or the red convulsions,[406] or the

black convulsions,[407] or by whatever name convulsions may be called; these all shall do no harm unto thee ✝ N ✝ nor to any part of thy body, nor to thy head, nor to thy neck, nor to thy heart, nor to thy stomach, nor to any of thy reins,[408] nor to thy arms, nor to thy legs, nor to thy eyes, nor to thy tongue, nor to any part or parcel of thy body. This I write for thee ✝ N ✝ in these words, and in the name of God the Father, the Son, and the Holy Ghost, Amen.—God bless it. Amen."

Note. If any one writes such a letter for another, the Christian name of the person must be mentioned in it; as you will observe, where the N stands singly in the above letter, there must be the name.

115. A good way to destroy Worms in Bee-Hives.

With very little trouble and at an expense of a quarter dollar, you can certainly free your bee-hives from worms for a whole year. Get from an apothecary store the powder called Pensses Blum,[409] which will not injure the bees in the least. The application of it is as follows: For one beehive you take as much of this powder, as the point of your knife will hold, mix it with one ounce of good whiskey, and put it in a common vial, then make a hole in the bee-hive and pour it in thus mixed with the whiskey, which is sufficient for one hive at once. Make the hole so that it can be easily poured in. As said before, a quarter dollar's worth of this powder is enough for one hive.[410]

116. Recipe for making a paste to prevent gun barrels from rusting, whether iron or steel.

Take an ounce of bear's fat, half an ounce of badger's grease, half an ounce of snake's fat, one ounce of almond oil, and a quarter of an ounce of pulverized indigo, and melt it all together in a new vessel over a fire, stir it well, and put it afterwards into some vessel. In using it, a lump as large as a common nut must be put upon a piece of woolen cloth and then rubbed on the barrel and lock of the gun, and it will keep the barrel from rusting.

117. To make a Wick which is never consumed.

Take an ounce of asbestos[411] and boil it in a quart of strong lye[412] for two hours; then pour the lye and clarify what remains by pouring rain water on it three or four times, after which you can form a wick from it[413] which will never be consumed by the fire.

118. A Morning Prayer, to be spoken before starting on a journey, which will save the person from all mishaps.

I, [here the name is to be pronounced], will go on a journey to-day; I will walk upon God's way, and walk where God himself did walk, and our dear Lord Jesus Christ, and our dearest Virgin with her dear little babe, with her seven rings[414] and her true things. Oh thou! my dear Lord Jesus Christ, I am thine own, that no dog may bite me, no wolf bite me, and no murderer secretly approach me: Save me, oh my God, from sudden death![415] I am in God's hands, and there I will bind myself. In God's hands I am by our Lord Jesus' five wounds, that any gun or other arms may not do me any more harm than the virginity of our Holy Virgin Mary was injured by the favour of her beloved Jesus.[416] After this say three Lord's prayer[s], the Ave Maria,[417] and the articles of faith.[418]

119. A safe and approved means to be applied in cases of Fire and Pestilence.

Welcome! Thou fiery fiend! do not extend further than thou already hast. This I count unto thee as a repentant act, in the name of God the Father, the Son, and the Holy Ghost.

I command unto thee, fire, by the power of God, which createth and worketh every thing, that thou now do cease,[419] and not extend any further; as certainly as Christ was standing on the Jordan's stormy banks being baptized by John, the holy man.[420]

This I count unto thee as a repentant act in the name of the holy Trinity.

I command unto thee, fire, by the power of God, now to abate thy flames; as certainly as Mary retained her virginity before all ladies who retained theirs,[421] so chaste and pure; therefore, fire, cease thy wrath.

This I count unto thee, fire, as a repentant act, in the name of the most holy Trinity.

I command unto thee, fire, to abate thy heat, by the precious blood of Jesus Christ, which he has shed for us, and our sins and transgressions.[422]

This I count unto thee, fire, as a repentant act, in the name of God the Father, the Son, and the Holy Ghost.

Jesus of Nazareth, a king of the Jews, help us from this dangerous fire, and guard this land and its bounds from all epidemic disease and pestilence.

REMARKS

This has been discovered by a Christian Gypsy King of Egypt[423] — Anno 1740, on the 10th of June,[424] six Gypsies were executed on the gallows in the Kingdom of Prussia. The seventh of their party was a man of eighty years of age, and was to be executed by the sword, on the 16th of the same month. But fortunately for him, quite unexpectedly a conflagration broke out, and the old Gypsy was taken to the fire to try his arts; which he successfully done to the great surprise of all present, by bespeaking the conflagration in a manner that it wholly and entirely ceased and disappeared in less than ten minutes.[425] Upon this, the proof having been given in day time, he received pardon and was set at liberty. This was confirmed and attested by the government of the King of Prussia, and the General Superintendent at Koenigsberg,[426] and given to the public in print. It was first published at Koenigsberg in Prussia, by Alexander Bausman, anno 1745.[427]

Whoever has this epistle in his house,[428] will be free from all danger of fire, as well as from lightning. If a pregnant woman carries this letter about her, neither enchantment or evil spirits can injure her or her child. Further, if anybody has this letter in his house, or carries it about his person, he will be safe from the injuries of pestilence.

While saying these sentences one must pass three times around the fire. This has availed in all instances. [429]

120. *To prevent Conflagration.*

Take a black chicken[430] in the morning or evening, cut its head off and throw it upon the ground; cut its stomach out, yet leave it all together; then try to get a piece of a shirt which was worn by a chaste virgin during her terms,[431] and cut out a piece as large as a common dish from that part which is bloodiest. These two things wrap up together, then try to get an egg which was laid on Maundy Thursday. These three things put together in wax; then put them in a pot holding eight quarts, and bury it under the threshold of your house, with the aid of God, and as long as there remains a single stick of your house together, no conflagration will happen. If your house should happen to be on fire already in front and behind you, the fire will, nevertheless, do no injury to you, nor to your children. This is done by the power of God, and is quite certain and infallible.[432] If fire should break out unexpectedly, then try to get a whole shirt in which your servant maid had her terms, or a sheet on which a child was born, and throw it into the fire, wrapped up in a bundle, and without saying anything. This will certainly stop it.[433]

121. *To prevent Witches from bewitching Cattle, to be written and placed in the stable; and against Bad Men and Evil Spirits, which nightly torment old and young people, to be written and placed on the bedstead.*

"Trotter Head,[434] I forbid thee my house and premises,[435] I forbid thee my horse and cow stable, I forbid thee my bedstead, that thou mayest not breathe upon me:[436] breathe into some other house, until thou hast ascended every hill, until thou hast counted every fence post, and until thou hast crossed every water—And thus dear day may come again into my house, in the name of God the Father, the Son, and the Holy Ghost.[437] Amen."[438]

This will certainly protect and free all persons and animals from witchcraft.

122. To prevent Bad People[439] from getting about the Cattle.

Take wormwood,[440] gith,[441] five-finger weed,[442] and asafetida,[443] three cents worth of each;[444] the straw of horse-beans,[445] some dirt swept together behind the door of the stable, and a little salt.[446] Tie these all up together with a tape, and put the bundle in a hole about the threshold over which your cattle pass in and out, and cover it well with lignum vitae wood.[447] This will certainly be of use.[448]

123. To Extinguish Fire without Water.

Write the following words on each side of a plate,[449] and throw it into the fire,[450] and it will be extinguished forthwith:

S A T O R
A R E P O
T E N E T
O P E R A
R O T A S [451] [452]

124. Another Method of stopping Fire.

Our Dear Sarah[453] journeyed through the land, having a fiery, hot brand in her hand. The fiery brand heats; the fiery brand sweats. Fiery brand stop your heat; fiery brand stop your sweat.

125. How to Fasten or Spell-bind anything.

You say: "Christ's cross and Christ's crown, Christ Jesus' coloured blood, be thou every hour good. God, the Father, is before me, God, the Son, is beside me; God, the Holy Ghost, is behind me. Whoever now is stronger than these three persons, may come by day or night, to attack me."[454] † † † Then say the Lord's prayer three times.

126. Another way of Fastening or Spell-binding.

After repeating the above, you speak:[455] "At every step, may Jesus walk with [name]. He is my head, I am his limb; therefore Jesus be with [name].[456]

127. A Benediction to prevent Fire.

"The bitter sorrows and the death of our dear Lord Jesus Christ shall prevail. Fire, and wind, and great heat, and all that is within the power of these elements, I command thee through the Lord Jesus Christ, who has spoken to the winds and the waters, and they obeyed him. By these powerful words spoken by Jesus, I command, threaten, and inform thee, fire, flame, and heat, and your powers as elements, to flee forthwith. The holy, rosy blood of our dear Lord Jesus Christ, may rule it. Thou, fire and wind, and great heat, I command thee, as the Lord did by his holy angels command the great heat in the fiery oven, to leave those three holy men, Sadrach and his companions Mesach and Obed Rego,[457] untouched, as was done accordingly. Thus thou shalt abate, thou fire, flame and great heat, the Almighty God having spoken in creating the four elements, together with heaven and earth: Fiat, Fiat, Fiat! that is: It shall be, in the name of God, the Father, the Son, and the Holy Ghost. Amen." [458]

128. How to Relieve Persons or Animals after being Bewitched.

Three false tongues have bound thee,[459] three holy tongues[460] have spoken for thee. The first is God, the father, the second is God, the son, and the third is God, the holy ghost. They will give you blood and flesh, peace and comfort. Flesh and blood are grown upon thee, born on thee, and lost on thee. If any man trample on thee with his horse, God will bless thee, and the holy Ciprian;[461] has any woman trampled on thee, God and the body of Mary shall bless thee; if any servant[462] has given you trouble, I bless thee through God and the laws of heaven; if any servant maid or woman has led you astray,[463] God and the heavenly constellations shall bless thee. Heaven is above thee, the earth is beneath thee, and thou art between. I bless thee against all tramplings by horses.[464] Our dear Lord Jesus Christ walked about in his bitter afflictions and death; and all the Jews that had spoken and promised, trembled in their falsehoods and mockery.[465] Look, now trembleth the Son of God, as if he had the itch,[466] said the Jews. And then spake Jesus: I have not the itch, and no one shall have it. Whoever

will assist me to carry the cross, him I will free from the itch, in the name of God, the father, the son, and the holy ghost. Amen.[467] [468]

129. Against Evil Spirits and all manner of Witchcraft.

I.

N. I. R.

I.

SANCTUS SPIRITUS

I.

N.[469] I. R.

I.

All this be guarded, here in time, and there in eternity. Amen.

You must write all the above on a piece of white paper, and carry it about you.[470] The characters or letters above, signify: "God bless me here in time, and there eternally."[471]

130. Against Mishaps and Dangers in the house.

Sanct Matheus, Sanct Marcus, Sanct Lucas, Sanct Johannis.[472]

131. To protect Houses and premises against Sickness & Theft.

Ito, alo Massa Dandi Bando, III.[473] Amen. J. R. N. R. J.[474]

Our Lord Jesus Christ stepped into the hall, and the Jews searched[475] him everywhere. Thus shall those who now speak evil of me with their false tongues, and contend against me, one day bear sorrows, be silenced, dumbstruck, intimidated, and abused,[476] for ever and ever, by the glory of God. The glory of God shall assist me in this. Do thou aid me J. J. J. for ever and ever. Amen.[477]

132. A Direction for a Gypsy[478] Sentence, to be carried about the person, as a Protection under all circumstances.

Like unto the prophet Jonas, as a type of Christ, who was guarded for three days and three nights in the belly of a whale,[479] thus shall the Almighty God, as a father, guard and protect me from all evil. J. J. J.[480]

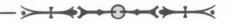

133. *Against Danger and Death, to be carried about the person.*

I know that my Redeemer liveth, and that he will call me from the grave, &c.[481] [482]

134. *Against Swellings.*

"Three pure Virgins went out on a journey, to inspect a swelling and sickness. The first one said: It is hoarse.[483] The second said: It is not. The third said: If it is not, then will our Lord Jesus Christ come." This must be spoken in the name of the Holy Trinity. [484]

135. *Against Adversities and all manner of Contentions.*

Power, hero, Prince of Peace, J. J. J.[485] [486]

136. *How to Treat a Cow after the Milk is taken from her.*

Give to the cow three spoonsful of her last[487] milk, and say to the spirits in her blood:[488] [489] "Ninny[490] has done it, and I have swallowed her in the name of God, the Father, the Son, and the Holy Ghost. Amen."—Pray what you choose at the same time.[491]

137. *Another method of treating a Sick Cow.*

 J. The cross of Jesus Christ poured out milk;
 J. The cross of Jesus Christ poured out water;
 J. The cross of Jesus Christ has poured them out.

These lines must be written on three pieces of white paper, then take the milk of the sick cow and these three pieces of paper, put them in a pot, and scrape a little of the skull of a criminal;[492] close it well, and put it over a hot fire, and the witch will have to die. If you take the three pieces of paper, with the writing on them, in your mouth, and go out before your house, speak three times, and then give them to your cattle, you shall not only see all the witches, but your cattle will also get well again.[493]

138. *Against the Fever.*

Pray early in the morning, and then turn your shirt around the left sleeve, and say: "turn thou, shirt, and thou, fever, do likewise, turn. [Do not forget to mention the name of the person having the fever.] This I tell thee, for thy repentance sake, in the name of God, the Father, the Son, and the Holy Ghost. Amen." If you repeat this for three successive mornings, the fever will disappear.[494]

139. *To Spell-bind a Thief so he cannot stir.*

This benediction must be spoken on a Thursday morning, before sunrise, and in the open air:[495]

"Thus shall rule it God, the Father, the Son, and the Holy Ghost, Amen. Thirty-three Angels[496] speak to[497] each other, coming to administer in company with Mary. Then spoke dear Daniel,[498] the holy one: Trust, my dear woman, I see some[499] thieves coming who intend stealing your dear babe; this I cannot conceal from you. Then spake our dear lady to Saint Peter:[500] I have bound with a band, through Christ's hand; therefore my thieves are bound even by the hand of Christ, if they wish to steal mine own, in the house, in the chest, upon the meadow or fields, in the woods, in the orchard, in the vineyard, or in the garden,[501] or wherever they intend to steal.[502] Our dear lady said: Whoever chooses may steal; yet if any one does steal, he shall stand like a buck, he shall stand like a stake,[503] and shall count all the stones upon the earth, and all the stars in the heavens. Thus I give thee leave, and command every spirit to be master over every thief,[504] by the guardianship of Saint Daniel, and by the burden of this world's goods. And the countenance shall be unto thee, that thou canst not move from the spot,[505] as long as my tongue in the flesh shall not give thee leave. This I command thee by the holy virgin Mary, the Mother of God, by the power and might by which he has created heaven and earth, by the host of all the angels, and by all the Saints of God, the Father, the Son, and the Holy Ghost, Amen." If you wish to set the thief free, you must tell him to leave in the name of Saint John.[506]

140. Another way to Still-bind Thieves.

Ye thieves, I conjure you, to be obedient like Jesus Christ, who obeyed his heavenly father[507] unto the cross, and to stand without moving out of my sight, in the name of the Trinity. I command you by the power of God and the incarnation of Jesus Christ, not to move out of my sight, † † † like Jesus Christ was standing on Jordan's stormy banks to be baptized by John.[508] And furthermore, I conjure you, horse and rider, to stand still and not to move out of my sight, like Jesus Christ did stand when he was about to be nailed to the cross to release the fathers of the church from the bounds of hell.[509] Ye thieves, I bind you with the same bonds with which Jesus our Lord has bound hell; and thus ye shall be bound; † † † and the same words that bind you, shall also release you.[510] [511]

141. To effect the same in less time.

Thou horseman and footman, you are coming under your hats;[512] you are scattered! With the blood of Jesus Christ, with his five holy wounds, thy barrel, thy gun, and thy pistol are bound; sabre, sword, and knife, are enchanted and bound, in the name of God, the Father, the Son, and the Holy Ghost. Amen.

This must be spoken three times. [513]

142. To Release Spell-bound Persons.

You horseman and footman, whom I here conjured at this time, you may pass on in the name of Jesus Christ, through the word of God and the will[514] of Christ; ride ye on now and pass.[515]

143. To Compel a Thief to return Stolen Goods.

Early in the morning before sunrise, you must go to a pear tree,[516] and take with you three nails out of a coffin,[517] or three horse-shoe nails that were never used, and holding these towards the rising sun, you must say:

"Oh thief, I bind thee by the first nail, which I drive into thy skull and thy brain, to return the goods thou hast stolen, to their former place; thou shalt feel as sick and as anxious to see men, and to see the place you stole from, as felt the disciple Judas after betraying Jesus. I bind thee by the other nail, which I drive into your lungs and liver, to return the stolen goods to their former place; thou shalt feel as sick and as anxious to see men, and to see the place you have stolen from, as did Pilate in the fires of hell. The third nail I shall drive into thy foot, oh thief, in order that thou shalt return the stolen goods to the very same place from which thou hast stolen them. Oh thief, I bind thee, and compel thee, by the three holy nails which were driven through the hands and feet of Jesus Christ, to return the stolen goods to the very same place from which thou hast stolen them." † † † The three nails, however, must be greased with the grease from an executed criminal or other sinful person.[518]

144. A Benediction for all purposes.

Jesus, I will arise;[519] Jesus, do thou accompany me; Jesus do thou lock my heart into thine, and let my body and my soul be commended unto thee. The Lord is crucified. May God guard my senses that evil spirits may not overcome me, in the name of God, the Father, the Son, and the Holy Ghost. Amen.[520]

145. To Win every Game one engages in.

Tie the heart of a bat[521] with a red silken string to the right arm,[522] and you will win every game at cards you play.[523]

146. Against Burns.

Our dear Lord Jesus Christ going on a journey, saw a fire-brand burning: it was Saint Lorenzo[524] stretched out on a roast. He rendered him assistance and consolation; he lifted his divine hand, and blessed the brand; he stopped it from spreading deeper and wider. Thus may the burning be blessed in the name of God, the Father, the Son, and the Holy Ghost. Amen.[525]

147. Another Remedy for Burns.

Clear out brand, but never in; be thou cold or hot, thou must cease to burn. May God guard thy blood and thy flesh, thy marrow and thy

bones, and every artery[526] great or small—they all shall be guarded and protected in the name of God, against inflammation and mortification, in the name of God the Father, the Son, and the Holy Ghost. Amen.[527][528]

148. To be given to Cattle, against Witchcraft.

S A T O R
A R E P O
T E N E T
O P E R A
R O T A S[529]

This must be written on paper and the cattle made to swallow it in their feed.[530]

149. How to tie up and heal Wounds.

Speak the following: "This wound I tie up in three names, in order that thou mayest take from it, heat, water, falling off of the flesh, swelling, and all that may be injurious about the swelling, in the name of the holy trinity." This must be spoken three times; then draw a string three times around the wound, and put it under the corner of the house towards the east, and say: "I put thee there, † † † in order that thou mayest take unto thyself the gathered water, the swelling, and the running, and all that may be injurious about the wound. Amen." Then repeat the Lord's prayer and some good hymn.[531][532]

150. To take the Pain out of a Fresh Wound.

Our dear Lord Jesus Christ had a great many biles and wounds, and yet he never had them dressed. They did not grow old, they were not cut,[533] nor were they ever found running.[534] Jonas was blind,[535] and I spoke to the heavenly child, as true as the five holy wounds were inflicted.[536][537]

151. A Benediction against Worms.[538]

Peter and Jesus went out upon the fields; they ploughed three[539] furrows, and ploughed up three worms. The one was white, the other was

black, and the third one was red. Now all the worms are dead, in the name † † †.[540] Repeat these words three times.[541] [542]

152. *Against every Evil Influence.*
Lord Jesus, thy wounds, so red, will guard me against death.[543]

153. *To retain the Right in Court and Council.*[544]
Jesus Nazarenus, Rex Judeorum.[545]

First carry these characters with you, written on paper, and then repeat the following words: "I, (name) appear before the house of the judge. Three dead men look out of the window; one having no tongue, the other having no lungs, and the third was sick, blind and dumb." [546] —This is intended to be used when you are standing before a court in your right, and the judge not being favorably disposed towards you.[547] While on your way to the court, you must repeat the benediction already given above.[548]

154. *To stop Bleeding at any time.*
As soon as you cut yourself, you must say: "Blessed wound, blessed hour, blessed be the day on which Jesus Christ was born,[549] in the name † † † Amen." [550]

155. *Another way to Stop Blood.*
Write the name of the four principal waters of the whole world, flowing out of Paradise, on a paper, namely: Pison, Gihon, Hedekiel, and Pheat,[551] and put it on the wound. In the first book of Moses, the second chapter, verses 11, 12, 13, you will find them. You will find this effective.[552] [553]

156. *Another similar Prescription.*
Breathe three times upon the patient, and say the Lord's prayer three times until the words, "upon the earth," and the bleeding will be stopped.[554]

157. Another still more certain way to stop.

If the bleeding will not stop, or if a vein has been cut, then lay the following on it, and it will stop that hour. Yet if any one does not believe this, let him write the letters upon a knife and stab an irrational animal, and he will not be able to draw blood. And whosoever carries this about him, will be safe against all this enemies:

I. m. I. K. I. B. I. P. a. x. v. ss. Ss. vas

I. P. O. unay Lit. Dom. mper vobism.[555] [556]

And whenever a woman is going to give birth to a child, or is otherwise afflicted, let her have this letter about her person; it will certainly be of avail.[557]

158. A peculiar sign[558] to keep back men and animals.

Whenever you are in danger of being attacked, then carry this sign with you: "In the name of God I make the attack. May it please my Redeemer to assist me. Upon the holy assistance of God I depend entirely;[559] upon the holy assistance of God and my gun I rely very truly.[560] God alone be with us. Blessed be Jesus."[561]

159. Protection of one's House and Hearth.

Beneath thy guardianship, I am safe against all tempests and all enemies, J. J. J.

These three J's signify Jesus three times.[562] [563]

160. A Charm—to be carried about the person.

Carry these words about you, and nothing can hit you: Annania, Azaria, and Misael,[564] blessed be the Lord, for he has redeemed us from hell, and has saved us from death, and he has redeemed us out of the fiery furnace, and has preserved us even in the midst of the fire;[565] in the same manner may it please him, the Lord that there be no fire:

I.

N. I. R.

I.[566] [567]

161. To Charm Enemies, Robbers and Murderers.

God be with you, brethren; stop, ye thieves, robbers, murderers, horse-men, and soldiers, in all humility, for we have tasted the rosy blood of Jesus. Your rifles and guns[568] will be stopped up with the holy blood of Jesus; and all swords and arms are made harmless by the five holy wounds of Jesus. There are three roses upon the heart of God: the first is beneficent,[569] the other is omnipotent, and the third is his holy will.[570] You, thieves, must therefore stand under it, standing still as long as I will. In the name of God the Father, Son, and Holy Ghost, you are conjured and made to stand. [571]

162. Protection against all kinds of Weapons.

Jesus, God and man, do thou protect me against all manner of guns, firearms, long or short, of any kind of metal. Keep thou thine fire, like the Virgin Mary, who kept her fire[572] both before and after her birth. May Christ bind up all firearms after the manner of his having bound up himself in humility, while in the flesh. Jesus, do thou render harmless all arms and weapons, like unto the husband of Mary the mother of God, he having been harmless likewise. Furthermore, do thou guard the three holy drops of blood which Christ sweated on the Mount of Olives.[573] Jesus Christ! do thou protect me against being killed, and against burning fires. Jesus, do thou not suffer me to be killed, much less to be damned, without having received the Lord's supper. May God the Father, Son, and Holy Ghost, assist me in this. Amen.[574]

163. A Charm against Fire-arms.

Jesus passed over the Red Sea,[575] and looked upon the land; and thus must break all ropes and bands, and thus must break all manner of fire-arms, rifles, guns, or pistols, and all false tongues be silenced.[576] May the benediction of God on creating the first man, always be upon me; the benediction spoken by God, when he ordered in a dream that Joseph and Mary together with Jesus[577] should flee into Egypt,[578] be upon me always, and may the holy † be ever lovely and beloved in my right hand. I journey through the country at large where no one

is robbed, killed, or murdered—where no one can do me any injury, and where not even a dog could bite me, or any other animal tear me to pieces. In all things let me be protected, as also my flesh and blood, against sins and false tongues which reach from the earth up to heaven, by the power of the four Evangelists, in the name of God the Father, God the Son, and God the Holy Ghost, Amen. [579]

164. Another for the same.

I, [name,] conjure ye guns, swords, and knives, as well as all other kinds of arms, by the spear that pierced the side of God, and opened it so that blood and water could flow out,[580] that ye do not injure me, a servant of God, in the † † †. I conjure ye by Saint Stephan, who was stoned by the virgin,[581] that ye cannot injure me who am a servant of God, in the name of [582] † † †. Amen. [583]

165. A Charm against shooting, cutting or thrusting.

In the name of J. J. J. Amen. I, [name,[584]] Jesus Christ is the true salvation; Jesus Christ governs, reigns, defeats and conquers every enemy, visible or invisible; Jesus, be thou with me at all times, for ever and ever, upon all roads and ways, upon the water and the land, on the mountain and in the valley, in the house and in the yard, in the whole world wherever I am, stand, run, ride or drive; whether I sleep or wake, eat or drink, there be thou also, Lord Jesus Christ, at all times, late and early, every hour, every moment; and in all my goings in or goings out. Those five holy red wounds, oh Lord Jesus Christ,[585] may they guard me against all fire-arms, be they secret or public, that they cannot injure me, or do me any harm whatever, in the name of † † †. May Jesus Christ with his guardianship and protection shield me, (name[586]), always from daily commission of sins, worldly injuries and injustice, from contempt, from pestilence and other diseases, from fear, torture and great suffering, from all evil intentions, from false tongues and old clatter brains; and that no kind of fire-arms can inflict any injury to my body, do thou take care of me † † †. And that no band of thieves, nor Gypsies, highway robbers, incendiaries, witches and other evil

spirits may secretly enter my house or premises, nor break in; may the dear Virgin Mary, and all children who are in heaven with God in eternal joys, protect and guard me against them; and the glory of God the Father shall strengthen me, the wisdom of God the Son shall enlighten me, and the grace of God the Holy Ghost shall empower me from this hour unto all eternity. Amen. [587]

166. To Charm Guns and other Arms.

The blessing which came from heaven at the birth of Christ, be with me (name[588]). The blessing of God at the creation of the first man, be with me; the blessing of Christ on being imprisoned, bound, lashed, crowned so dreadfully and beaten, and dying on the cross, be with me; the blessing which the Priest spoke over the tender, joyful corpse of our Lord Jesus Christ,[589] be with me; the constancy of the Holy Mary and all the Saints of God,[590] of the three holy kings, Casper, Melchior, and Balthasar,[591] be with me; the holy four Evangelists, Matthew, Mark, Luke, and John, be with me; the Archangels St. Michael,[592] St. Gabriel, St. Raphael, and St. Uriel,[593] be with me; the twelve holy messengers of the Patriarchs and all the Hosts of Heaven, be with me; and the inexpressible number of all the Saints, be with me. Amen.

Papa, R. tarn, Tetregammaten Angen.[594]

Jesus Nazarenus, Rex Judeorum[595] [596]

167. To prevent being Cheated, Charmed, or Bewitched, and to be at all times blessed.

Like unto the cup, and the wine, and the holy supper, which our dear Lord Jesus Christ gave unto his dear disciples on Maundy Thursday, may the Lord Jesus guard me in day time and at night, that no dog may bite me, no wild beast tear me to pieces, no tree fall on me, no water rise against me, no fire-arms injure me, no weapons, no steel, no iron cut me, no fire burn me, no false sentence fall upon me, no false tongue injure me, no rogue enrage me, and that no fiends, no witchcraft and enchantment can harm me. Amen. [597]

168. Different Directions to effect the same.

The Holy Trinity guard me, and be and remain with me[598] on the water and upon the land, in the water or in the fields,[599] in cities or villages, in the whole world wherever I am. The Lord Jesus Christ protect me against all my enemies, secret or public;[600] and may the Eternal Godhead also guard me, through the bitter sufferings of Jesus Christ; his holy rosy blood, shed on the cross, assist me, J. J. Jesus has been crucified, tortured, and died. These are true words; and in the same way must all words be efficacious which are here put down, and spoken in prayer by me. This shall assist me that I shall not be imprisoned, bound, or overcome by any one.[601] Before me all guns and other weapons shall be of no use or power. Fire-arms, hold your fire in the almighty hand of God. Thus all fire-arms shall be charmed.[602] † † † When the right hand of the Lord Jesus Christ was fastened to the tree of the cross; like unto the son of the heavenly father who was obedient unto death, may the eternal Godhead protect me by the rosy blood, by the five holy wounds on the tree of the cross; and thus must I be blessed and well protected, like the cup and the wine, and the genuine true bread, which Jesus Christ gave to his disciples on the evening of Maunday Thursday. J. J. J. [603]

169. Another Similar Direction.

The grace of God and his benevolence be with me (N.) I shall now ride or walk out; and I will gird about my loins with a sure ring. So it pleases God, the heavenly father, he will protect me, my flesh and blood, and all my arteries and limbs, during this day and night which I have before me; and however numerous my enemies might be, they must be dumbstruck, and all become like a dead man, white as snow, so that no one will be able to shoot, cut, or throw at me, or to overcome me, although he may hold rifle or steel against whosoever else evil weapons and arms might be called, in his hand. My rifle shall go off like the lightning from heaven, and my sword shall cut like a razor. Then went our dear lady Mary upon a very high mountain; she looked down into a very dusky valley, and beheld her dear child standing amidst the Jews, harsh, very harsh, because he was bound so harsh,

because he was bound so hard; and therefore may the dear Lord Jesus Christ save me from all that is injurious to me. **† † †** Amen. [604]

170. *Another Similar Direction.*

There walk out during this day and night, that thou mayest not let any of my enemies, or thieves, approach me,[605] if they do not intend to bring me what was spent from the holy altar. Because God, the Lord Jesus Christ, is ascended into heaven in his living body. O Lord, this is good for me this day and night. **† † †** Amen. [606]

171. *Another one like it.*

In the name of God I walk out. God the father be with[607] me,[608] and God the Holy Ghost be by my side. Whoever is stronger than these three persons, may approach my body and my life;[609] yet whoso is not stronger than these three, would much better let me be. J. J. J.[610]

172. *A very Safe and reliable Charm.*

The peace of our Lord Jesus Christ be with me, [name[611]] Oh shot, stand still! in the name of the mighty prophets Agtion and Elias[612], and do not kill me! oh shot, stop short! I conjure you by heaven and earth, and by the last judgment, that you do no harm unto me, a child of God. **† † †** [613]

173. *Another one like it.*

I conjure thee, sword, sabre, or knife, that mightest injure or harm me, by the priest of all prayers, who had gone[614] into the temple at Jerusalem, and said; an edged sword shall pierce your soul that you may not injure me, who am a child of God. J. J. J. [615]

174. *A Very Effective Charm.*

I, (name,) conjure thee, sword or knife, as well as all other weapons, by that spear which pierced Jesus' side and opened it to the gushing out of blood and water[616], that he keep me from injury as one of the servants of God. **† † †** Amen. [617]

175. A Good Charm against Thieves.

There are three lilies standing upon the grave of the Lord our God: the first one is the courage[618] of God, the other is the blood of God, and the third one is the will of God.[619] Stand still, thief! No more than Jesus Christ stepped down from the cross, no more shalt thou move from this spot:—this I command thee, by the four evangelists and elements of heaven, there in the river, or in the shot, or in the judgment, or in the sight. Thus I conjure you by the last judgment to stand still and not to move, until I see all the stars in heaven, and the sun rises again. Thus I stop thy running and jumping, and command it in the name of † † †. Amen.

This must be repeated three times.[620]

176. How to Recover Stolen Goods

Take good care to notice through which door the thief passed out,[621] and cut off three small chips from the posts of that door, then take these three chips to a wagon, unbeschrewedly[622] however, take off one of the wheels and put the three chips into the stock of the wheel, in the three highest names, then turn the wheel backwards[623] and say: Thief, thief, thief! Turn back with the stolen goods; thou art forced to do it by the Almighty power of God: † † † God the father calls thee back, God the son turns thee back so that thou must return, and God the holy ghost leads thee back until thou arrive at the place from which thou hast stolen. By the almighty power of God the Father[624] thou must come, by the wisdom of God the Son thou hast neither peace nor quiet until thou hast returned the stolen goods to their former place, by the grace of God the Holy Ghost thou must run and jump and canst find no peace or rest until thou arrivest at the place from which thou hast stolen. God the Father binds thee, God the Son forces thee, and God the Holy Ghost turns thee back.—(You must not turn the wheel too fast.[625]) Thief, thou must come, † † † thief, thou must come, † † † thief, thou must come, † † †. If thou art more almighty, thief, thief, thief, if thou art more almighty than God himself, then you may remain where you are.[626] The ten commandments force thee, thou shalt not steal, and therefore thou must come. † † † Amen.[627]

177. A well-tried Charm.

Three holy drops of blood have passed down the holy cheeks of the Lord God, and these three holy drops of blood are placed before the touch-hole.[628] As surely as our dear lady was pure from all men, as surely shall no fire or smoke pass out of this barrel. Barrel, do thou give neither fire, nor flame, nor heat.[629] Now I will walk out, because the Lord God goeth before me, God the Son is with me, and God the Holy Ghost is about me forever.[630] [631]

178. A Charm for Bad People.[632]

It is said, that if you suspect a person for badness, and he sits down in a chair, and you take a shoemaker's wax-end,[633] that has not been used, and stick one end of it on the underside of the chair, and you sit on the other end of it, he will immediately make water, and in a short time die.

179. Another well-tried Charm against Fire-Arms.

Blessed is the hour in which Jesus Christ was born; blessed is the hour in which Jesus Christ was born;[634] blessed is the hour in which Jesus Christ has arisen from the dead; blessed are these three hours over thy gun, that no shot or ball shall fly toward me, and neither my skin, nor my hair, nor my blood, nor my flesh, be injured by them, and that no kind of weapon or metal[635] shall do me any harm, so surely as the Mother of God shall not bring forth another son. † † †. Amen. [636]

180. A Charm to gain advantage of a man of superior strength.

I, [name,[637]] breathe upon thee. Three drops of blood I take from thee; the first out of thy heart, the other out of thy liver, and the third out of thy vital powers; and in this I deprive thee of thy strength and manliness.

Hbbi[638] Massa[639] danti Lantien. I. I. I [640] [641]

181. *A Recipe for destroying Spring-Tails or Ground Fleas.*[642]

Take the chaff upon which children have been laying in their cradles, or take the dung of horses,[643] and put that upon the field, and the spring-tails or ground-fleas will no longer do you any injury.

182. *To prevent anyone from Killing Game.*

Pronounce the name, as for instance Jacob Wohlgemuth,[644] shoot whatever you please; shoot but hair and feathers with and what you give to poor people. † † † Amen.[645]

183. *A Benediction for and against all Enemies.*

The cross of Christ be with me;[646] the cross of Christ overcomes all water and every fire;[647] the cross of Christ overcomes all weapons; the cross of Christ is a perfect sign and blessing to my soul. May Christ be with me and my body during all my life, at day and at night. Now I pray, I, [name,] pray God the Father for the soul's[648] sake, and I pray God the Son for the Father's sake, and I pray God the Holy Ghost for the Father's and the Son's sake, that the holy corpse of God may bless me against all evil things, words, and works. The cross of Christ open unto me future bliss; the cross of Christ banish all evil from me; the cross of Christ be with me, above me, before me, behind me, beneath me, aside of me, and everywhere, and before all my enemies, visible and invisible, these all flee from me as soon as they but know or hear. Enoch and Elias, the two prophets,[649] were never imprisoned, nor bound, nor beaten,[650] and came never out of their power: thus no one of my enemies must be able to injure or attack me in my body or my life, in the name of God the Father, the Son, and the Holy Ghost. Amen. [651]

184. *A Benediction against Enemies, Sickness and Misfortunes.*

The blessing which came from heaven, from God the Father, when the true living Son was born, be with me at all times; the blessing which God spoke over the whole human race, be with me always. The holy cross of God, as long and as broad, as the one upon which God suffered his blessed, bitter tortures, bless me to-day and forever. The

three holy nails which were driven through the holy hands and feet of Jesus Christ, shall bless me to-day and forever. The bitter crown of thorns which was forced upon the holy head of Christ, shall bless me to-day and forever. The spear by which the holy side of Jesus was opened, shall bless me to-day and forever. The rosy blood protect me from all my enemies, and from everything which might be injurious to my body or soul, or my worldly goods. Bless me, oh ye five holy wounds, in order that all my enemies may be driven away and bound, while God has encompassed all Christendom. In this shall assist me God the Father, the Son, and the Holy Ghost. Amen.—Thus must I, (N.[652]) be blessed as well and as valid as the cup and the wine, and the true, living bread which Jesus gave his[653] disciples on the evening of Maunday Thursday. All those that hate you must be silent before me; their hearts are dead in regard to me; and their tongues are mute, so that they are not at all able to inflict the least injury upon me, or my house, or my premises:[654] And likewise, all those who intend attacking and wounding me with their arms and weapons, shall be defenseless, weak, and conquered before me. In this shall assist me the holy power of God, which can make all arms or weapons of no avail. All this in the name of God the Father, the Son, and the Holy Ghost. Amen.[655]

185. THE TALISMAN.

It is said that any one going out hunting and carrying it in his game bag, cannot but shoot something worthwhile, and bring it home.

An old hermit once found an old, lame huntsman in a[656] forest, laying beside the road, and weeping. The hermit asked him the cause of his dejection. Ah me, thou man of God, I am a poor unfortunate being; I must annually furnish my lord with as many deer, and hares, and partridges[657] as a young and healthy huntsman could hunt up, or else I will be discharged from my office; now I am old and lame, besides game is getting scarce, and I cannot follow it up as I ought to, and I know not what will become of me.—Here the old man's feelings overcame him, and he could not utter another word. The hermit, upon this, took out a small piece of paper, upon which he wrote some words with a pencil, and handing it to the huntsman, he said: there,

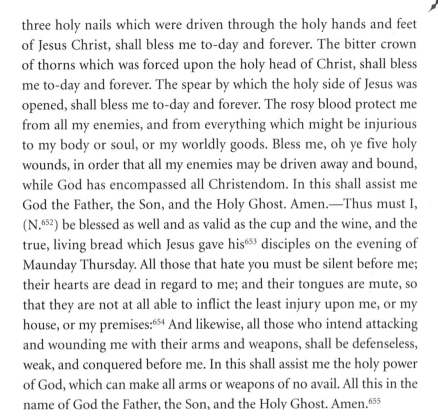

95

old friend, put this in your game-bag whenever you go out hunting, and you shall certainly shoot something worthwhile, and bring it home too; yet be careful to shoot no more than you necessarily need, nor to communicate it to any one that might misuse it, on account of the high meaning contained in these words.[658] The hermit then went on his journey, and after a little the huntsman also arose, and without thinking of anything particular, he went into the woods, and had scarcely advanced a hundred yard,[659] when he shot as fine a roe-buck as he ever saw in his life.

This huntsman was afterwards and during his whole lifetime lucky in his hunting, so much so that he was considered one of the best hunters in that whole country. The following is what the hermit wrote on the paper:

Ut nemo in sense tentat, descendere nemo.

At precedenti spectatur mantica tergo.[660]

The best argument is to try it.[661]

186. To Compel a Thief to return Stolen Goods.

Walk out early in the morning, before sunrise, to a juniper tree,[662] and bend it with the left hand toward the rising sun, while you are saying: Juniper tree, I shall bend and squeeze[663] thee, until the thief has returned the stolen goods to the place from which he took them.— Then you must take a stone and put it on the bush, and under the bush[664] and the stone you must place the skull of a malefactor.[665] † † † Yet you must be careful in case the thief return the stolen goods, to unloose the bush and replace the stone where it was before.[666]

187. A Charm against Powder and Ball.

The heavenly and holy trumpet[667] blow every ball and misfortune away from me. I seek refuge beneath the tree of life which bears twelvefold fruits. I stand behind the holy altar of the Christian Church. I commend myself to the Holy Trinity. I, [name,] hide myself beneath the holy corpse of Jesus Christ. I commend myself unto the wounds of Jesus Christ, that the hand of no man might be able to seize me, or to bind me, or to cut me, or to throw me, or to beat me[668] or overcome me in any way whatever, so help me, [N.] [669]

188. ☛ *Whoever carries this book with him, is safe from all his enemies, visible or invisible;[670] and whoever has this book with him, cannot die without the holy corpse of Jesus Christ, nor drowned in any water, nor burn up in any fire, nor can any unjust sentence be passed upon him.[671] So help me.[672]*
  † † †

189. UNLUCKY DAYS.
To be found in each month:[673]

January 1, 2, 3, 4, 6, 11, 12.	July 17, 21.
February 1, 17, 18.	August 20, 21.
March 14, 16.	September 10, 18.
April 10, 17, 18.	October 6.
May 7, 8.	November 6, 10.
June 17.	December 6, 11, 15.

Whoever is born upon one of these days, is unfortunate and suffers from poverty; and whoever takes sick on one of these days, seldom recovers health; and those who engage or marry on these days, become very poor and miserable.[674] Neither is it advisable to move from one house to another, nor to travel, nor to bargain, nor to engage in a lawsuit, on one of these days.[675]

The Signs of the Zodiac must be observed by the course of the moon, as they are daily given in common almanacs.

If a cow calves in the sign of the Virgin, the calf will not live one year; if it happens in the Scorpion, it will die much sooner; therefore no one should be weened off in these signs, nor in the sign of the Capricorn or Aquarius, and they will be in less danger from mortal inflammation.[676]

This is the only piece extracted from a centennial almanac imported from Germany, and there are many who believe in it.[677]

HOHMAN.

190. In conclusion the following Morning Prayer is given, which is to be spoken before entering upon a Journey. It protects against all manner of bad luck.

Oh Jesus of Nazareth, King of the Jews, yea, a King over the whole world, protect me, (name,) during this day and night, protect me[678] at all times by thy five holy wounds, that I may not be seized and bound. The Holy Trinity guard me, that no gun, fire-arm, ball, or lead, shall touch my body; and that they shall be weak like the tears and the bloody sweat of Jesus Christ, in the name of God the Father, the Son, and the Holy Ghost. Amen.[679]

APPENDIX A: CHARMS FROM LATER EDITIONS OF THE LONG-LOST FRIEND

A1. The following Remedy for Epilepsy was published in Lancaster, (PA) papers, in the year 1828.

TO SUFFERING HUMANITY.

We ourselves know of many unfortunate beings who are afflicted with Epilepsy—yet how many more may be in the country who have perhaps already spent their fortunes in seeking aid in this disease, without gaining relief. We have now been informed of a remedy which is said to be infallible, and which has been adopted by the most distinguished physicians in Europe, and has so well stood the test of repeated trials, that it is now generally applied in Europe. It directs a bedroom for the sick person to be fitted up over the cow stable, where the patient must sleep at night, and should spend the greater part of his time during the day in it. This is easily done by building a regular room over the stable. Then care is to be taken to leave an opening in the ceiling of the stable, in such a manner that the evaporation from the same can pass into the room, while, at the same time, the cow may inhale the perspiration of the sick person. In this way the animal will gradually attract the whole disease, and be affected with arthritic attacks, and when the patient has entirely lost them, the cow will fall dead to the ground. The stable must not be cleaned during the operation, though fresh straw or hay may be put in; and, of course, the milk of the cow, as long as she gives any, must be thrown away as useless.

—Lancaster Eagle[680]

A2. A Salve to Heal up Wounds.

Take tobacco, green or dry; if green, a good handful; if dry, 2 ounces; together with this take a good handful of elder leaves,[681] fry them well in butter, press it through a cloth, and you may use it as a salve. This will heal up a wound in a short time.[682]

Or go to a white oak tree[683] that stands pretty much isolated,[684] and scrape off the rough bark from the eastern side of the tree, then cut off the thinner bark, break it into small pieces, and boil it until all the strength[685] is drawn out, strain it through a piece of linen, and boil it again, until it becomes as thick as tar; then take out as much as you need, and put to it an equal proportion of sheep tallow, rosin and wax, and work them together until they form a salve. This salve you put on a piece of linen, very thinly spread, and lay it on the wound, renewing it occasionally till the wound is healed up.

Or take a handful of parsley,[686] pound it fine,[687] and work it to a salve with an equal proportion of fresh butter. This salve prevents mortification and heals very fast.

A3. Peaches.

The flowers of the peach tree, prepared like salad, open the bowels, and are of use in the dropsy.[688] Six or seven peeled kernels of the peach stone, eaten daily, will ease the gravel;[689] they are also said to prevent drunkenness, when eaten before meals.

Whoever loses his hair, should pound up peach kernels, mix them with vinegar, and put them on the bald place.

The water distilled from peach flowers opens the bowels of infants and destroys their worms.[690]

A4. Sweet Oil.[691]

Sweet oil possesses a great many valuable properties, and it is therefore adviseable for every head of a family to have it at all times about the house, in order that it may be applied in cases of necessity. Here follow some of its chief virtues:

It is a sure remedy, internally as well as externally, in all cases of inflammation, in men and animals.

Internally, it is given to allay the burning in the stomach, caused by strong drink or by purging too severely, or by poisonous medicines. Even if pure poison has been swallowed, vomiting may be easily produced by one or two wine glasses of sweet oil, and thus the poison will be carried off, provided it has not already been too long in the bowels; and after the vomiting, a spoonful of the oil should be taken every hour until the burning caused by the poison is entirely allayed.

Whoever is bit by a snake, or by any other poisonous animal, or by a mad dog, and immediately takes warmed sweet oil, and washes the wound with it, and then puts a rag, three or four times doubled up, and well soaked with oil, on the wound every three or four hours, and drinks a couple of spoonsful of the oil, every four hours, for some days, will surely find out what peculiar virtues the sweet oil possesses in regard to poisons.

In Dysentery, sweet oil is likewise a very useful remedy, when the stomach has first been cleansed with Rhubarb[692] or some other suitable purgative, and then a few spoonsful of sweet oil should be taken every three hours. For this purpose, however, the sweet oil should have been well boiled and a very little hartshorn[693] be mixed with it. This boiled sweet oil is also serviceable in all sorts of bowel complaints and in colics; or when any one receives internal injury as from a fall, a few spoonsful of it should be taken every two hours: for it allays the pain, scatters the coadjulated blood, prevents all inflammation, and heals gently.

Externally, it is applicable in all manner of swellings; it softens, allays the pain, and prevents inflammation.

Sweet oil and white lead[694] ground together makes a very good salve, which is applicable in burns or scalds. This salve is also excellent against infection from poisonous weeds or waters, if it is put on the infected part as soon as it is noticed.

If sweet oil is put in a large glass, so as to fill it about one half full, and the glass is then filled up with the flowers of the St. Johnswort,[695] and well covered and placed in the sun for about four weeks, the oil proves then, when distilled, such a valuable remedy for all fresh wounds in men and animals, that no one can imagine its medicinal

powers who has not tried it. This should at all times be found in a well conducted household. In a similar manner, an oil may be made of white lilies, which is likewise very useful to soften hardened swellings and burns, and to cure the sore breasts of women.[696]

A5. Cure for Dropsy.

Dropsy is a disease derived from a cold humidity, which passes through the different limbs to such a degree that it either swells the whole or a portion of them. The usual symptoms and precursors of every case of dropsy are the swelling of the feet and thighs, and then of the face; besides this the change of the natural colour of the flesh into a dull white, with great thirst, loss of appetite, costiveness, sweating, throwing up of slimy substances, but little urine, laziness and aversion to exercise.

Physicians know three different kinds of dropsy, which they name:

1. Anasarca, when the water penetrates between the skin and the flesh over the whole body, and all the limbs, and even about the face, and swells them.

2. Ascites, when the belly and thighs swell, while the upper extremities dry up.

3. Tympanites, caused rather by wind than water. The belly swells up very hard, the navel is forced out very far, and the other members fall away. The belly becomes so much inflated, that knocking against it causes a sound like that of a large drum, and from this circumstance its name is derived.

The chief thing in curing dropsy, rests upon three points, namely:

1. To reduce the hardness of the swelling which may be in the bowels or other parts.

2. To endeavor to scatter the humours.

3. To endeavour to pass them off either through the stool or through the urine.

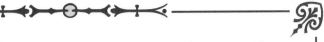

The best cure therefore must chiefly consist in this: To avoid as much as possible all drinking, and use only dry victuals; to take moderate exercise; and to sweat and purge the body considerably.

If any one feels symptoms of dropsy, or while it is yet in its first stages, let him make free use of the sugar of the herb called Fumatory,[697] as this purifies the blood; and the Euphrasy sugar[698] to open the bowels.

A6. A Cure for Dropsy.—(Said to be Infallible.)

Take a jug of stone or earthen ware, and put four quarts of strong healthy cider into it; take two handsful of parsley roots and tops, cut it fine; a handful of scraped horseradish, two table-spoonsful of bruised mustard seed, half an ounce of squills,[699] and half an ounce of juniper berries; put all these in the jug, and place it near the fire for 24 hours, so as to keep the cider warm, and shake it up often; then strain it through a cloth and keep it for use.

To a grown person give half a wine glass full three times a day, on an empty stomach. But if necessary you may increase the dose, although it must decrease again as soon as the water is carried off; and, as stated before, use dry victuals and exercise gently.

This remedy has cured a great many persons, and among others a woman of 70 years of age, who had the dropsy so badly, that she was afraid to get out of bed, for fear her skin might burst, and who it was thought could not live but a few days. She used this remedy according to the directions given, and in less than a week the water had passed off her, the swelling of her stomach fell, and in a few weeks afterwards she again enjoyed perfect health.

Or: Drink for a few days very strong Bohea tea,[700] and eat the leaves of it. This simple means is said to have carried away the water from some persons in three or four days, and freed them from the swelling, although the disease had reached the highest pitch.

Or: Take three spoonsful of rape seed,[701] and half an ounce of clean gum myrrh,[702] put these together in a quart of good old wine, and let it stand overnight in the room, keeping it well covered. Aged persons are to take two spoonsful of this an hour after supper, and the same

before going to bed; younger persons must diminish the quantity according to their age, and continue the use of it as long as necessary.

Or: Take young branches of spruce pine,[703] cut them into small pieces, pour water on them and let them boil a while, then pour it into a large tub, take off your clothes, and sit down over it, covering yourself and the tub with a sheet or blanket, to prevent the vapor from escaping. When the water begins to cool, let someone put in hot bricks; and when you have thus been sweating for a while, wrap the sheet or blanket close around you and go to bed with it. A repetition of this for several days will free the system from all water.

The following Valuable Recipes, not in the original work of Hohman, are added by the publishers.

A7. Cure for Dropsy.

Take of the broom-corn seed,[704] well powdered and sifted, one drachm. Let it steep twelve hours in a wine glass and a half of good, rich wine, and take it in the morning fasting, having first shaken it so that the whole may be swallowed. Let the patient walk after it, if able, or let him use what exercise he can without fatigue, for an hour and a half; after which let him take 2 oz. of olive oil; and not eat or drink anything in less than half an hour afterwards. Let this be repeated every day, or once in three days, and not oftener, till a cure is effected; and do not let blood, or use any other remedy during the course.

Nothing can be more gentle and safe than the operation of this remedy. If the dropsy is in the body, it discharges it by urine, without any inconvenience; if it is between the skin and flesh, it causes blisters to rise on the legs, by which it will run off; but this does not happen to more than one in thirty; and in this case no plasters must be used, but apply red cabbage leaves.[705] It cures dropsy in pregnant women, without injury to the mother or child. It also alleviates asthma, consumption, and disorders of the liver.

A8. Remedy for the Lock Jaw.

We are informed by a friend that a sure preventive against this terrible disease is to take some soft soap and mix it with a sufficient quantity

of pulverized chalk, so as to make it of the consistency of buckwheat batter; keep the chalk moistened with a fresh supply of soap until the wound begins to discharge, and the patient finds relief. Our friend stated to us that explicit confidence may be placed in what he says, that he has known several cases where this remedy has been successfully applied. So simple and so valuable a remedy, within the reach of every person, ought to be generally known.

—*N. Y. Evening Post.*

A9. For the Sting of a Wasp or Bee.

A Liverpool paper states as follows:—"A few days ago, happening to be in the country, we witnessed the efficacy of the remedy for the sting of a wasp mentioned in one of our late papers. A little boy was stung severely and was in great torture, until an onion[706] was applied to the part affected, when the cure was instantaneous. This important and simple remedy cannot be too generally known, and we pledge ourselves to the fact above stated."

A10. Diarrhoea Mixture.

Take one oz. Tinct. Rhubarb, one oz. Laudanum, one oz. Tinct. Cayenne pepper, one oz. Spirits of Camphor. DOSE—From ten to thirty drops for an adult.

A11. Soap Powders.

Take one pound of hard soap, cut it fine, and mix with it one pound of Soda Ash. This article is much used, and its preparation, we believe, is a "great secret."

A12. To Dye a Madder Red.

For each pound of cloth, soak half a pound of madder in a brass kettle overnight, with sufficient warm water to cover the cloth you intend to dye. Next morning, put in two ounces of madder compound[707] for every pound of madder. Wet your cloth and wring it out in clean water, then put it into the dye. Place the kettle over the fire, and bring it slowly to a scalding heat, which will take about half an hour; keep at

this heat half an hour, if a light red is wanted, and longer if a dark one, the color depending on the time it remains in the dye.

When you have obtained the color, rinse the cloth immediately in cold water. [708]

A13. To dye a fine Scarlet Red.

Bring to a boiling heat, in a brass kettle, sufficient soft water to cover the cloth you wish to dye; then add 1½ oz. cream of tartar for every pound of cloth. Boil a minute or two, add 2 oz. Lac Dye[709] and one oz. Madder Compound, (both previously mixed in an earthen bowl), boil five minutes; now wet the cloth in warm water, and wring it out and put it into the dye; boil the whole nearly an hour, take the cloth out and rinse it in clear cold water.

A14. To dye a Permanent Blue.

Boil the cloth in a brass kettle for an hour, in a solution containing five parts of alum and three of tartar for every 32 parts of cloth. It is then to be thrown into warm water, previously mixed with a greater or less proportion of Chemic Blue, according to the shade the cloth is intended to receive. In this water it must be boiled until it has acquired the desired color.

A15. To dye a Green.

For every pound of cloth add 3 ½ oz. of alum and one pound of fustic. Steep (not boil) till the strength is out; soak the cloth till it acquires a good yellow, then remove the chips, and add the Chemic Blue by degrees, till you have the desired color.

A16. Physic Ball for Horses.

Cape aloes, from 6 to 10 drachms; Castile soap, 1 drachm; spirit of wine, 1 drachm; syrup to form the ball. If mercurial physic be wanted, add from one-half a drachm to 1 drachm of calomel.

Previous to physicing a horse, and during its operation, he should be fed on bran mashes, allowed plenty of chilled water, and have exercise. Physic is always useful; it is necessary to be administered in

almost every disease; it improves digestion, and gives strength to the lacteals by cleansing the intestines, and unloading the liver; and if the animal is afterward properly fed, will improve his strength and condition in a remarkable degree. Physic, except in urgent cases, should be given in the morning, and on an empty stomach; and if required to be repeated, a week should intervene between each dose.

Before giving a horse a ball, see that it is not too hard or too large. Cattle medicine is always given as a drench.

A17. Physic for Cattle.

Take aloe, 4 drachms to 1 oz.; Epsom salts, 4 to 6 oz.; powdered ginger, 3 drachms. Mix and give in a quart of gruel. For calves, one-third of this will be a dose.

A18. Sedative and Worm Ball.

Powdered white hellebore, one-half drachm; linseed powder, one-half oz. If necessary, make into a ball, with molasses. This ball is a specific for Weed. Two ounces of Gargling Oil,[710] in one-half bottle of linseed oil, is an effectual remedy for Worms in horses and cattle.

A19. Astringent Ball for Looseness in Horses.

Opium, from ½ to 1 drachm; ginger 1½ drachms; prepared chalk, 3 drachms; flour, 2 drachms. Powder, and make into a ball with molasses.

A20. Mixture for Ulcers and all foul Sores.

Sulphate of zinc,[711] 1 oz.; corrosive sublimate,[712] 1 drachm; spirit of salt,[713] 4 drachms; water, 1 pint; mix.

A21. Yellow Water in Horses.

Take Venetian soap,[714] juniper oil, saltpetre, sal prunella,[715] sweet spirits of nitre,[716] of each one ounce; make it into a ball with pulverized licorice root, and give the horse two ounces at once, and repeat, if necessary. If attended with a violent fever, bleed, and give bran mashes, or: Take a gallon of strong beer, or ale, add thereto two ounces of

Castile soap, and one ounce of saltpetre; stir, and mix daily of this with his feed.

The following is also highly recommended in a German work:

Take pulverized gentian and calamus,[717] of each, one-half ounce; sulphate of potasso,[718] two ounces; tartar emetic,[719] liver of sulphur,[720] and oil of turpentine, one-eighth of an ounce each; mix it with flour and water, and give the above in the incipient stage of the disease.

The dose, if necessary, may be given daily for several days.

A22. A Valuable Recipe for Galls—Windgall in Horses.

An intelligent and experienced farmer, rising of seventy years of age, residing in Allen township, Cumberland county, has assured us that the following ointment, if applied two or three times a day, will cure the most obstinate wind-galls.

Take one pound of the leaves of stramonium (Jamestown weed[721]), bruised; two pounds of fresh butter or hog's lard, and one gill of the spirits of turpentine; put the whole of the ingredients into a clean earthen crock and place it with the contents over live coals for twenty or thirty minutes, stirring it occasionally; then strain it through a coarse cloth or canvass, and it forms a consistent ointment, with which anoint the wind-galls two or three times a day.

Fifty dollars had been offered for the above receipt, so says our informant, who kindly furnished it.

A23. Wind-Broken Horses.[722]

The excellent ball for broken-winded horses, that has made a perfect cure of over seven hundred, in less than nine months, after many other medicines being tried in vain.[723]

Take myrrh, elecampane,[724] and licorice root, in fine powder, three ounces each; saffron, three drachms; assafoetida, one ounce; sulphur squills,[725] and cinnabar of antimony,[726] of each two ounces; aurum mosaicum,[727] one ounce and a half; oil of aniseed, eighty drops. You may make it into paste with either treacle or honey, and give the horse the quantity of a hen's egg every morning for a week; and afterwards

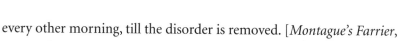

every other morning, till the disorder is removed. [*Montague's Farrier,* page 57.]

A24. Flax-Seed Lemonade.

Four tablespoonsful flax-seed (whole); 1 quart of boiling water poured upon the flaxseed; juice of two lemons leaving out the peel, sweeten to taste. Steep three hours in a covered pitcher. If too thick put in cold water with the lemon juice and sugar. Ice for drinking. It is admirable for colds.

A25. To Tell a Horse's Age.

After a horse is nine years old a wrinkle comes in the eyelid, at the upper corner of the lower lid, and every year thereafter he has one well-defined wrinkle for each year of his age over nine. If, for instance, a horse has three wrinkles he is twelve; if four thirteen. Add the number of wrinkles to nine and you will always get at it.

A26. To preserve Wood.

Petroleum has a strong preservative power converting soft, perishable woods to the durability of red cedar. It improves all farm implements, baskets, all wooden tools, as rakes, hoe handles, common water-pails or any wooden tool which is exposed to the weather. It may be found valuable, also for rustic work, rustic furniture or chairs left upon a piazza. Give them a good coat of this oil occasionally. It will harden the wood, give them a dark color and make them last longer.

A27. For Stings and Snake Bites.

Lean, fresh meat will remove the pain of the sting of a wasp almost instantly, and has been recommended for the cure of snake bites. It is said to have a marked effect in cases of erysipelas.

A28. Maine Cider receipt.

Here is a receipt for making cider that comes from the State of Maine: Make your cider carefully of good sound apples—of choice cider kinds. Put the cider into good sound barrels and let stand till clear,

then rack off into a whisky barrel. Fill the barrel chock full and bung it up tight. Then leave the barrel in this condition until the cider has the taste to your liking. Then draw off a bucketful or two and put in the barrel an ounce or so of sweet linseed oil. This will form a film over the cider and effectually keep out the air. After the oil is put in, and the air excluded, the cider will never get hard or sour or change its taste any more than if it was bottled. Cider treated in this way will keep the taste it had when the oil was put in for a year or more, or until the contents of the barrel are exausted.

A29. An excellent Liniment.

Alcohol, one ounce; spirits of turpentine, sulphuric ether,[728] chloroform, laudanum, and gum camphor, of each half an ounce; oil of olives, one-fourth of an ounce. This liniment is also good for internal pains, as colic, pain in the stomach, etc. Take from two to thirty drops in sweetened water, and repeat every twenty to thirty minutes until relieved.

A30. Soap for the Toilet.

Six pounds of sal-soda,[729] six pounds of lime, six pounds of clear sweet fat. Pour four gallons of boiling soft water over the lime and soda. Stir the mixture well and let it stand over night to settle. Strain off the water and add the fat and boil until it thickens. If it does not seem thin enough add another gallon of water to the lime and soda and add to the boiling mixture. When boiled enough add three ounces of glycerine oil and one pound of borax, pulverized, and any perfumery you may prefer. Wet a washtub and pour the boiling mixture in and let it get cold, then cut into bars and lay away to dry.

A31. To Kill Bedbugs.

With a brush paint the cords at the eyelet holes and all the crevices in the bedstead with oil of Cedar, and after one or two applications, housekeepers will be delighted to find that all the bugs have disappeared and there is nothing dangerous or unpleasant in the remedy.

110

A32. For Inflammatory Rheumatism.

Take half an ounce of pulverized saltpeter, put in half a pint of sweet oil, bathe the parts affected, and a sound cure will speedily be effected.

A33. Sham Champagne.

One lemon, sliced, one spoonful tartar acid, one ounce ginger root, one pound and a half sugar. Pour ten quarts of boiling water on the above ingredients. When blood-warm stir in two gills of home-made yeast, cover with a thin piece of gauze to keep out the flies and insects, and allow it to stand all day in the sun. When cold in the evening bottle, cork and wire it, then place it on the floor of the cellar. In forty-eight hours it will be ready for use, and will pay the trouble of making it.

A34. Valuable Remedy for Heaves.

Forty sumac buds, one pound of resin, one pint of ginger, half a pound of mustard, one pint of unslaked lime, one pound of epsom salt, four ounces of gum guiacum,[730] six ounces of cream of tartar. Mix thoroughly and divide into thirty powders, and give one every morning to the horse in his feed before watering.

A35. For Ear-ache.

Take a bit of cotton batting, put upon it a pinch of black pepper, gather it up and tie it, dip in sweet oil and insert into the ear. Put a flannel bandage over the head to keep it warm. It will give immediate relief.

A36. Antidote for Poison.

If a person swallows any poison whatever, or has fallen into convulsions from having overloaded his stomach, an instantaneous remedy, most efficient and applicable in a large number of cases, is a heaping teaspoonful of common salt, and as much ground mustard, stirred rapidly in a teacupful of water, warm or cold, and swallowed instantly. It is scarcely down before it begins to come up, bringing with it the remaining contents of the stomach; and lest there be any remnant of

the poison, however small, let the white of an egg or a teaspoonful of strong coffee be swallowed as soon as the stomach is quiet, because these very common articles nullify a large number of virulent poisons.

A37. Cure for Dyspepsia.

Milk and lime-water are now frequently prescribed by physicians in cases of dyspepsia and weakness of the stomach, and in some cases are said to prove beneficial.

A38. To clean Brass.

Whitning[731] wet with aqua ammonia[732] will cleanse brass from stains, and is excellent for polishing faucets and doorknobs of brass or silver.

A39. Buttermilk Pop.

Boil one quart of fresh buttermilk. Beat one egg, a pinch of salt, and a heaping tablespoonful of flour together, and pour into the boiling milk. Stir briskly and boil for two or three minutes, and serve while warm with sugar, or, still better, maple syrup. Although this is an old-fashioned and homely dish, eaten and relished by our grandparents before corn starch, sea-moss, farina, desiccated coconut and other similar delicacies were ever heard of, it is perhaps as nutritious as any of them, and often far more easily obtained.

A40. A Simple Treatment for Sciatica, Neuralgia, &c.

Heat a common flatiron, then cover it with some woolen fabric, which is moistened with vinegar and apply it at once to the painful spot. The application may be repeated two or three times a day. Generally, the pain disappears in twenty-four hours, and recovery ensues at once.

A41. To Lay Bricks.

Bricks should always be wet before being laid. A wall, twelve inches thick, of wet laid bricks is equivalent to one sixteen inches thick where the bricks have been put in dry.

A42. Cure for Consumption.

Make a tea of the common mullen sweetened with sugar and drink it freely. Young or old plants are good, dried in the shade and kept in clean bags. The medicine must be continued from three to six months, according to the nature of the disesase. It is very good for the blood vessels also. It strengthens and builds up the system instead of taking away the strength. It makes good blood and takes inflammation away from the lungs.

A43. Croup Remedy.

Give the child a teaspoonful of fresh lard warmed to the consistency of oil, but not hot. In a few minutes follow with another, until vomiting ensues. Bathe the feet in warm mustard water. Wring a flannel out of hot water and lay on across the chest, and lay a dry flannel over it; then wrap the child in a woolen blanket. In a short time it will perspire profusedly, and you can enjoy your rest for the remainder of the night.

A44. Plaster for Cracks, etc.

Whitning mixed with glue water or calcined plaster and water makes a good putty for filling cracks in plastered ceilings, walls, &c.

A45. Cold in the Head.

Dissolve a tablespoonful of borax in a pint of water; let it stand until it becomes tepid; snuff some up the nostrils two or three times during the day, or use the dry powdered borax like snuff, taking a pinch as often as required. At night have a handkerchief saturated with the spirits of camphor, and place it near the nostrils, so as to inhale the fumes while sleeping.

A46. Cure for Cold.

Boil two ounces of flaxseed in a quart of water, strain it, add two ounces rock-candy, half-pint syrup, juice of three lemons; mix well, put on the stove, let it come to a boil, then take it off, and as soon as cool bottle it; take a cupful before meals, the hotter you drink it the better it is.

A47. Loose but Sound Teeth.

Turkish myrrh diluted in water—at first a teaspoonful to a tumbler, and then gradually strengthened—and use as a wash four or five times a day, will generally give relief. There are only two causes for the above trouble, viz: calomel and soda, and the use of both must be stopped entirely.

A48. Asthma.

Iodide of potassium,[733] two drams; tincture of lobelia,[734] half an ounce; syrup of senega,[735] two ounces; camphorated tincture of opium, half an ounce; water sufficient to make four ounces. A teaspoonful every half hour until relieved. The above has proved very efficacious.

A49. To press Ferns and Leaves.

Ferns should be pressed in a large book, such as newspaper, as soon as picked, at any time when growing or at maturity. Writing or sized paper is not good for pressing any leaves, as it does not absorb the moisture.

A50. Canning Fruit Cold.

A lady has found that by filling up the cans with the fruit and then with the pure cold water, and allowing them to stand until all the confined air has escaped, the fruit will, if then sealed perfectly, keep indefinitely without any change or loss of its original flavor.

A51. Chicken Cholera.

A mixture made of equal parts of red pepper, alum, rosin, and sulphur, will cure chicken cholera. Feed a tablespoonful of this mixture in three pints of scalded meal daily, and the chickens will get well speedily.

A52. Prepared Glue.

In a half a pint of water in a wide mouthed bottle put eight ounces of best glue, place the bottle in water and heat until the glue is dissolved. Then stir in it slowly 2½ ounces of strong nitric acid. Cork tightly.

The glue thus prepared is always ready for use, and may be applied to mending other articles not exposed to the water.

A53. Cure for Hoarseness.
Spikenard root, sliced and bruised, and then steeped in a teapot containing equal parts of water and spirits, and the vapor inhaled, when sufficiently cooled, will relieve the soreness and hoarseness of the throat or lungs, when arising from a cough or cold.

A54. Pain in the Stomach.
A teaspoonful of vinegar, well salted, and covered with a good coating of cayenne pepper. Stir together in a tumbler until well mixed, swallow quickly, and you will experience little further inconvenience.

A55. For Boils.
The skin of a boiled egg is said to be one of the most efficacious remedies that can be applied to a boil.

A56. For Smooth Hands.
After washing and drying the hands pour into one hand a few drops of good cider vinegar; rub the hands together, wetting the whole surface, both sides, and dry it. Practice this and your hands will feel smooth.

A57. How to get Thin.
Take regularly three times a day in a little water 15 drops of hydrate of potassium[736]—always after meals—and a little moderation in eating will help.

A58. A Good Disinfectant.
Five pounds copperas, one-half pound of carbolic acid and five gallons of water. Apply one quart to a cesspool once a week.

APPENDIX S: ADDITIONAL CHARMS IN *DER LANGE VERBORGENE SCHATZ UND HAUS-FREUND*

Foreword

The author does not believe that it is necessary to recommend a useful book through a long preface, which every time the readers scroll past and usually read little. Nonetheless, in order to achieve the usual goal, and at the same time to teach the reader about the secret remedies and arts which are contained in this book, and maybe through it to teach to arouse many scruples of conscience, it is appropriate that a little foreword for the little work is required.

Many people are afraid to employ remedies, in cases of need, which are holy or as one ordinary is wont to say: high words are used. These principles and opinions, however, cannot be taken into consideration for use in the remedies in this book.—It exists indisputably in reality, that many, very many remedies and arts contained in this book in their use the names of holy people, holy things and the three holy names themselves occur. But can this be sin? Admittedly, the godly law says clearly: "Thou shalt not take the name of the Lord your God in vain." Yet this law cannot be taken into consideration in the use of remedies and arts to the welfare of men. Will nobody come up with the idea to use such remedies and arts, if he does not trouble to help those in need? It is said in the Fiftieth Psalm, which says the motto of this book: "Call upon me in need, and I will save you and you shall

117

praise my name." Consequently, there can be use of the high words without sin, but to the contrary, God must be agreeable, in accordance with the above written statement.

Go out into the world in this way, you dear little book. Trail all peaceful men, and bring the blessing and help which your contents pronounce; and delight your owner, lead him or her not to the path of vice but to salvation. This is your only purpose, to which you are written, and that he that wishes satisfaction, warm wishes.

The author
Written in Skippacksville, in Pennsylvania, in September 1837.

S1. Remedy against the weevil.
Brush the fruit boxes with resinous pine oil, and the weevils will vanish in a couple days after the treatment.

S2. A safe remedy, that the young maidens will be well disposed to one.
Wear on your left side in your shirts, sewn or fastened, a piece of the tail of a mouse and and two large peppercorns. This is certainly very good.

S3. Remedy to drive off the mosquitos.
Boil squash in water, and sprinkle the room with it, or smoke with squash leaves and hold the window to, so they will surely die.

S4. Remedy for the blight in wheat.
Take soap-boiler salt solution and moisten the wheat which will be sown. One may also use unslaked lime there.

S5. Remedy to drive off the fleas from the hound.
Wipe anise oil on a spot on the hound's body that it cannot lick, and, in short time, the fleas will vanish.

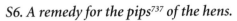

S6. A remedy for the pips[737] of the hens.

Cut a piece of bread in small pieces, dunk the same in vinegar, dry it a little afterwards, and give it to the chickens three times daily.

S7. Remedy for the swelling of cattle after the consumption of young clover.

Take tobacco waste, or otherwise common tobacco, pour common whiskey on it, and let it stand until it is as brown as beer. If a cow has become swollen with clover, take a piece of soap as big as a large walnut, put it in the cow's throat and pour a teacup full of the tobacco-extract on it. The swelling will vanish instantly.

S8. A heat-resistant cement to seal a stove.

One takes iron cable shavings, unslaked lime and salt. Bring these three things with the whites of eggs to a paste, and smear it on the cracks of the stove. One leaves the smeared patch to dry in the air. Do not heat the oven too much at first. One will find that this cement will last as long as the stove itself.

S9. Remedy to catch fleas.

Take a shoot of an elderberry bush, pull the green shell off, and free it from the skin. Wipe a feather in a little honey, and lay it in the evenings near yourself in the bed. On the next morning are the fleas on the honey firmly caught.

S10. For greater yields in bread baking.

Boil five pounds bran, and with the water decanted from it mix fifty-six pounds flour. Make the dough ordinarily, as if normal, and bake it in bread. Through this bran water one obtains a fifth part increase in bread. The bread is high quality and tasty, and the bran remains good for feed. With the baking of small quantities, one can use both, flour and bran, in ratio of a half, a third, or a quarter.

S11. Remedy for cracked, frozen limbs.

Get four cents of spermaceti oil, four cents of sweet almond oil and a piece of white wax melted with the bulk of a little soot. Smear the wounds with it, so the wound is healed completely in a few days.

S12. Remedy for the bite of a mad dog.

If one has the bad luck to be bitten by a mad dog, one can make himself the following remedy. Brush out the wound now and then, and very heavily, with salt water. Lay a piece of butter-smeared pimpernel bread, which one obtains in the apothecary, on it and eat it. When the bite is on a foot or hand, place it in freshly dug earth.

S13. Remedy for the dropsy.

Take one ounce blue lily bulbs, one ounce of cloves, and two ounces of small raisins. Boil these pieces in two pints water and a little wine. It is drunk and the remainder eaten. Already very many men were healed through this inexpensive remedy, and for that reason it cannot be recommended enough to all who are ailing of this dangerous evil.

S14. To make a safe remedy, that another can shoot or kill no game with their shotgun.

Take Cuculi Arambost,[738] pp. six cents' worth, stir this amongst fresh hares' fat and wipe this salve on the gun barrel, and he can never shoot a beast dead.

S15. Remedy that the guns of others constantly fail.

Pull your left pants pocket out, place both hands in a cross over it, so that the thumbs meet each other and speak, if another wants to pull the trigger, the following words.

Racce, Balce, Veluti, Arma

S16. Remedy for when the cows give blood instead of milk

Give the cows the following under their food each day:

1 bushel dried barley;
½ ounce chopped crinis fulvae[739]
1 cent's worth Sancta Simplex[740]

All of these are mixed well with each other.

S17. A very proven remedy for sunburn.
Fry a pound of white lily bulbs in hot ash, pound it in a mortar with four ounces of sugar candy as well. Make it into an ointment, and lay it on the burnt place.

S18. Remedy for the insects.
One spreads Bierhäfen[741] on the woodwork several times daily. Let it dry on top of it. The insects will pass by in a couple days.

S19. Remedy for consumption.
One boils scraped deer horn until it turns into jelly, and gives it to the patient to eat daily. This remedy, which was long kept secret, has been of service already to very many suffering from this illness, with great success.

S20. That a horse stands still against the will of the driver.
Very many secret remedies were already known up until now for this situation. Nonetheless, to give those people who do not believe in such supernatural remedies, or who shrink from making use of them, an opportunity to employ a natural method to bring this about, here follows a natural and unmistakable remedy. Mix the following items together:

½ ounce *Quarilaserum,*[742]
¼ ounce *Putandrum longum* and
¼ ounce *Succus leritarium.*[743]

Spread this over the road, where the horse should remain standing; and he will not move until the substance is taken away. But if the driver has the left ear of a mouse by him, it has no effect.

S21. Remedy if a horse does not come to its stable.

Stir the sheep excrement up, and put it on top of the horse. It will come to the stall in a short time.

S22. That the hair grows quickly and oneself on places where none is or the same has fallen out.

Take a half pound of pig's fat, a half ounce of lime juice, a quarter ounce of pulverized asafoetida and a quarter ounce of snail fat.

Mix all of these together well and smear the hairless places with the salve made from it.

S23. A remedy to still the blood.

Lay the two first fingers of the right hand on the wound, and say: Christ and Peter walked over the flood, there Christ took the rod and hit the flood, here stills the blood.

† † †

S24. Another for the same.

Likewise, lay the first two fingers of the right hand on the wound and say, Blood, stop, throughout me, that the wound will again be healed.

† † †

S25. A secret but natural remedy, if someone from a house or family goes away or is long absent, to learn whether he be living or dead.

For this the root Telepium item Grasula, as the Germans call it, Wundenkraut, Donnerkraut, Fette-Henne, or as Knableinskraut,[744] helps; but it is not an orchid or Specis Satiri, which often in herb books is called Knabenkraut,[745] It grows often on withered, infertile places, about a span high. It has green, thick, and fat leaves, light red blossoms and many knots on the roots.

If someone goes away from a house, whether it is the father, the son or the daughter, who has an interest at the house, and one knows not whether that person is living or dead, one must only break a stalk off of the abovementioned herb, without saying or doing anything fur-

ther. They must stick the same under the roof of the house in which the absentee belongs, between the lath and the shingles or bricks. If the absent person is dead, the herb stalk will soon wilt and wither. If that person is alive instead, so will it not only remain green, but grow further and put forth new shoots. This item is centuries old, proven by the original author (an Arab), and after that time many others found it infallible.

S26. A cure if a horse is stiff and frail, which is entirely without inconvenience, to free it from the same.

Take a pint of pig fat, put it in a pan and melt it, then pour it into another pot. Stir in a half pint of fresh milked cow's milk with it and give this to the horse. This cure should be used as soon as one finds out that the horse is taken with the illness above. Who observes this and can use or harness the horse finds it ordinary and undamaged.

S27. One of the best cures that ever was used, for a horse that is in danger of becoming blind.

Cut a piece of new linen, the size of a quarter. Pull through the same a needle with a strong thread, so that one can pull it together with it. Enclose within three living spiders, which must be taken from three corners of the house. Pull it together and make three knots in it. Afterward bind it at the front of the horse's head, so that it hangs just over the horse's eye. Leave it to hang until it falls off on its own. If the eye is not totally dead, it is cured with this infallible remedy.

S28. To cure a horse which is overheated.

If a horse is fallen over and overheated, then give it a half pint of flax-seed oil and a half pint of pig's fat mixed together, and wash the horse with fresh water.

S29. Remedy to avoid the swelling up and jumping of cows that have eaten clover.

Take tansy,[746] grated ivy[747] and alum, crush it well, and give it to the cattle each Wednesday and Friday morning, under salt, to eat.

S30. To cure a horse that receives wounds from pressure, or other sorts, in two or three days.

Boil a handful of the inner bark of the white oak and a little comfrey in three quarts good soapy water, until it is thickened to two quarts. Take it from the fire and pour it off into an earthenware pot, and put in four ounces alum. Let it stand until it is lukewarm, then stir it together well and wash the horse three times a day with it, by means of a sponge. Mix a little spikenard oil and coal oil together and smear the horse with it, each time after you wash it.

S31. A cure for the uterus[748] falling out of a cow.

If the uterus of a cow is falling out, then take a little pure ash, strew it over the same, and bring it again to its proper place. This will make it stay.

S32. A recipe to clean cider barrels.

First rinse the barrel out well with hot water, and then pour the water out. Put a pound of unslaked lime through the bunghole with nine or ten gallons boiled water. Close it up and pour it off. Rinse the barrel well with cold water and fill it with cold water, and let it remain for twenty four hours. Pour the water out, rinse the barrel once more and let the water completely run out. Pour in a quart of apple whiskey, rinse it well with it and leave it after that until you wish to use it. This one can do with all barrels that one is willing to fill with cider.

S33. A recipe to make good wine from cider.

Boil two barrels of cider until it is one barrel. Take care and remove the foam well during the boiling. Put it boiling hot in a barrel, close it up and leave it until the following month of March. Tap it on a clear day with a full moon, rinse the barrel out well with cold water, put a gallon of good Lisbon wine[749] and a gallon of good apple whiskey in, before you fill it up again. After that fill it up, close it up and lay it up. The older it is, the better it will be, but it has no regular wine taste until two years pass, but it is as well as a real drink during this time. If it is two years old like this, it is far better than the imported wine.

S34. A recipe to make good cider that does not ferment.

Place a washtub high enough, that you can place a bucket underneath. Put in the cider after that, and stir good sweet earth[750] in, in proportion of a gallon of earth to three barrels cider. After it has mixed continuously, then tap it down in the cleaned barrels, and leave it for two months. Tap it on a clear day with a full moon, rinse the barrels out well with cold water, and place in each barrel a pint of good apple whiskey. Fill the cider in again after that, close it up and leave it as long as you want. It is certain not to spoil. This unmistakable remedy is recommended not only because of its cheapness, but also because of its goodness.

S35. To make cider oil.

If you want to make cider oil, then place in the barrel, as soon as it is cleaned, two gallons of apple whiskey. Fill it up with cider, and if you tap it, as in the preceding items is said, place once again a gallon of whiskey in each barrel. Three gallons will make, casually speaking, about a barrel of cider oil.

S36. Another recipe to make good cider.

Take a clean hogshead, with a bottom. Bore holes in the bottom and place clean washed rye straw in the hogshead, about six inches high, along with two bushels of washed sand. After that place the cider inside and let it move through in a washtub. If the cider is prepared in this way, it is not fermented and strong while tasting sweet. The straw and the sand must be washed all days while the cider is made, because it otherwise will be sour and the cider will spoil.

S37. A remedy to make weevils flee.

Clean your barn out on the third day of the new moon before the harvest. Take a handful of hops and three handfuls Andorn or Marrubium,[751] an equal quantity of chamomile, and a full quart of fresh sheep dung. Place it all in a kettle full of water and boil it well. Lastly, place it in another piece of crockery, and sprinkle it through a strainer over your entire barn, and likewise in the corners where the weevils

keep. Without these, allow the woman to bake some cake in pig's fat on Shrove Tuesday. Preserve the fat until the harvest, when the fruit has gone home, and it is then smeared on the wagon and the forks. If you do these, you will not be plagued with either mice or weevils.

S38. A cure for the scabs.

Take the root of Indian Pen.[752] These plants grow in the woods, only alone in cold stone ground, have almost round but bent leaves, and carry white blooms in April. The root is of red gold colour, soft, and not deep under the surface of the earth. Pound the root a little, place it in a crockery and pour some strong vinegar with it. Let it stand some time, and after that lay it on the scab for approximately three hours. Take it off and wash the scab with your particular urine, then place a new compress on it and allow it to lay for the whole night. In the morning, as soon as you get up, take it off and wash the place again with urine and lay a fresh compress on. If your particular urine is not strong enough, take the urine of a boy who is still not seven years old. This cure does not fail to bring forth the desired success.

S39. A cure for the snakebite.

If you have been bitten by a snake, afterward as swiftly as possible, go to running water and wash the wound until the following is prepared. A handful of plantain leaves, of the small sort, must be mashed a little, and a small quantity of five-finger grass (cinquefoil) with it. Place it in a pan and place a pint of fresh-milked cow's milk, if such is to be had, and boil it well. Afterward put it on as warm as you can tolerate it. If the bite is from a very poisonous snake, then take a fresh compress an hour afterwards, and every two hours take a little fire-powder.[753]

S40. Another.

Boil about two pounds chestnut leaves with just as much ash leaves in fine soapy water. Lay it on your hand or foot as soon as it is sufficiently cooled. If it is a beast that bit, then bind a good bundle of the leaves on the wound.

S41. Yet another.

Take hogweed, divide it into two parts in wide pieces, and bind them on the wound.

S42. A cure for the poisonous herb which grows in meadows.[754]

Crush some soot out of the chimney to powder and stir it into a salve with sweet cream. Spread this salve on plantain leaves and lay it over the poisoned spot, and in twelve hours, the poison will be killed.

S43. A description of all illnesses of horses.

If you would find out the nature of the illness of your horse, then twist its upper lip in such a way that you can examine it entirely. If the same has a white and knotty appearance, thus this is a sign of worms. If it is red and knotty, then the horse has the bots. If the lip is red and full of veins, then the horse has the wind-colic. If the lip is red and not full of veins, then it has only the colic. I have tried to describe all the various cures in this book. The following rules may be observed, immediately after one knows the illness. Ride or lead the horse for a short time around, then take a strong dung fork handle and stick it through under the horse's stomach. Let another man at the opposite side take hold of it and thus rub the invalid horse under the behind parts, but not upwards under the breast. Keep on this way every time for three minutes. This operation may be resumed every hour until the illness of the horse is over.

If a horse has worms, then give it a full pint of flaxseed oil, and proceed as it is said above.

S44. A cure for the bots

Pour on that horse a half pint of sweet oil. This is the best remedy that can be used for the bots. A gill of spirits of turpentine is likewise good for the bots, but sweet oil is the absolutely best remedy.

S45. A cure for the Wind-Colic in horses.

Strike a black hen down with the thick end of a whip and tear it up as quickly as possible into pieces. If you cannot tear it, cut it open

and take the whole innards out. Stuff these in the horse's mouth and punch it with the handle of the whip in the neck. This is such a perfect cure for the wind-colic that the horse will never have it again.[755]

S46. *Another.*

Place a good handful of aspen bark in an iron pot with two quarts of water, and boil it until a quart remains. Pour it off in another piece of crockery and let it stand until it is warm as milk. Then may you give it to the horse and the rules given above are observed.

S47. *Another.*

Place a half pint of whiskey in a flask, with a little vinegar and a little scraped chalk. Blow the smoke from a burning cigar in the flask, hold the hand tightly over it and pour it. Repeat the same until the cigar is almost entirely burned, but give care and hold the hand tightly on the flask so that the smoke does not get out and shake it well. After it is as warm as fresh milk, give it to the horse.

S48. *A cure for the stomach and purification of the blood.*

Take gentian root, ginseng root, elder bark, elder root,[756] the bark of the sassafras root, horehound, burdock, of each half an ounce, and the rosin of pine wood as big as a hickory nut. Place them all together in a flask and pour a quart of good rye whiskey[757] in with it. When it has stood twenty-four hours then it is good for use.

An adult person of strong nature and physique can take a teaspoonful at a time from it, and it is easy to find out whether more or less is needed to work. It is to be taken three times a day, morning before eating, midday, and evening.

S49. *Another remedy for the purification of the blood and the strengthening of the stomach.*

Take nutmeg blossom, flower of sulphur,[758] cloves, cinnamon bark, of each half an ounce, eleven pennies' worth of saffron and about a half ounce of small snake's root.[759] Put these together in a flask and pour in a quart of good wine with it. Let it stand 24 hours and it is good to

use. A teaspoon full of it may be taken in the mornings before eating or even three times a day.

S50. A cure for the consumption.

Take the herbs heart-tongue, lungwort, liverwort, sarsaparilla root, and common speedwell, of each a small handful. Place the whole in a new, clean, earthenware pot with two quarts of good wine and boil it over a mild coal fire. The pot must be kept covered, but the mixture must be stirred for all of five minutes with a clean spoon of pine wood. When it starts to boil, leave it a half hour, then take it off and let it stand until it is as warm as fresh milk. Strain it through a pure linen cloth, place it in a flask and leave it well. An adult person may take a tablespoonful of it in the morning before eating, and afterwards the same dose every three hours. It is likewise good for the illness to take some common scurvy grass or watercress each day. With any of these remedies, food can be enjoyed with them, save pork and sharp vinegar.

S51. Another cure for the consumption.

Collect the roots and flowers of violets, in the month of May, and dry them in the shade. Then stuff it in a pipe and smoke it.

S52. Another cure for the consumption.

Take a fresh-laid hen's egg, on the third day in the new moon in the morning before eating. Break it in a glass and beat it well with a teaspoon of pine wood, then take a gill of good wine with it and drink it for seven or nine days. French clover (Haasenklee)[760] is also very good for the consumption, when a little of it is eaten each day.

S53. A cure for the stopping of the urine.

For any person who cannot stop their water, take a little five-finger grass (cinquefoil), some plantain leaves with the root, and a little sheep dung, and drink tea made from them. Tea made from nettles is likewise a good cure for the above-named complaint.

S54. A cure for warts or other growths.

On the third day of the waxing moon, in the evening, if you see the new moon for the first time, take the sufferer outside. Lay the finger of the right hand on the wart and glance to the moon, then speak as follows: "That which I see is increasing, and that which I now touch is decreasing." After you have repeated these three times, go back into the house.

S55. An instruction to make fire powder.

Take a quarter pound of ordinary gunpowder, a quarter pound of sulfur and a pound of alum. Put it all together in a mortar and pound it as fine as dust. Of this powder a man of strong body and nature can take as much as one can lay on a postage stamp,[761] in a small tablespoonful of strong vinegar. A weak person should take less proportionately. It is to be taken every two hours.

This powder is proven for the gangrene and is simultaneously good for St. Anthony's fire.

S56. One of the best compresses for Gangrene.

If this compress is used and some of the above powder is taken simultaneously, damage is not to be feared again.

Take a handful of oats and a handful of red cedar sprouts, with the small branches on which the needles are grown. Cut the latter fine and place it with the oats together in a pan and roast it in the same way as ordinary coffee is roasted. Grind all of it in a coffee mill, then place it again in the pan with a pint of sweet cream, and bake it to a paste. Break an egg in with it and stir it well into each other. Take it off the fire, paint it on a pure linen cloth and lay it on the wound as warm as you can endure it.

S57. How one can purify sweet oil.

Take however much shot as is required to load two shotguns otherwise. Place the same in a flask full of sweet oil, and it is as clear as water.

S58. An invaluable remedy to regain hearing if it is lost.

Take peppermint, some burnet saxifrage and the head of a rat. Singe the hair from the rat's head and boil it with the pepper in a full pint of March snow water. Then likewise place three heads of hops in, then mix it with a pint of flour and make a dough from it. Make however much peppermint (which beforehand must be cut up) in the dough as is possible, then bake a cake with it. In the evening, before you get into bed, split it in the middle, tie half on the left and the other on the right ear, and keep it on them until the following morning. Then may you take it off and place three drops of purified oil in each ear. The fat of a rattlesnake is likewise very good for deafness, it is accepted, when a snake is on hand which has not bitten, which cannot well be prevented, except if one shoots the head off before the animal is angered. The body is not poisonous, except if it is bitten. If you can get it prepared, then place a drop of the fat in each ear for nine days.

S59. Pills for Toothache.

Take some brown sugar in a pan, and fry it over the fire until it is a blister. Take however much ground pepper with it as there is sugar, place it on the fire and stir it together. After that make pills with it at a size that one can place one in a hollow tooth.

S60. A cure for the Pleurisy.

Take a small handful of hawthorn blooms, as much thistle blooms, a little catnip, a small handful of buds of a Peruvian balm tree (these buds must at the beginning of the month of March be cut), and, a little horehound. Place these together in a flask and place a quart of rye whiskey with it. This medicine has not its full power, until it is a year old, when it must be strained through a piece of new linen and placed in a clean flask. A strong person can take a teaspoon full each two hours until the nuisance is over.

S61. A proven cure for hysteria.

Take an ounce of bergamot, a similar quantity of catnip, about a soup spoon full of whiteness of dry chicken manure, and burn three groats

of corn to ash. Place the whole together in a flask and place a quart of spirits of rye whiskey with it, then place the flask nine days in the sun and shake it once each day. After this, strain it during the waning moon and place it once again in a flask. If it shows a sediment, then pour the schnapps out until it is completely clear. A woman who is plagued with hysteria can take between eighteen and thirty drops each two hours, and one gives a child who has the colic between one and seven drops according to its age. If the child is very small, this medicine can be given in the mother's milk.

S62. A remedy for the Vomiting at Childbirth.
Take a little catnip and give it to the birthing woman as tea to drink. This will stop the vomiting.

S63. A cure for a child with colic.
If a child is plagued with the colic so seriously that he in no way would be relieved, then take a little garden garlic, crush it, and press the juice through a pure linen cloth. Of this extract, mix a drop with a drop of spirit of rye whiskey for a very young child, and give it to the same in mother's milk. For a child three months old, three drops of each in the mother's milk may be given.

S64. A cure for the sore mouth of children.
Take the leaves of the red fall roses, white lilies, and sage, of each a handful, place all in a flask with a quart of good rye whiskey and let it stand for three days. If you wish to use it for the sore mouth of children, mix a teaspoonful of the above liquor with a half gill of March snow water and a teaspoonful of honey in a teacup. Stir it with a small piece of alum until the alum has shrunk as much as the point of a knife. After that, wind a clean linen cloth around your finger and wash the child's mouth once or twice a day with the given preparation. This will soon heal it.

S65. A remedy for the red dysentery or colic.

Take about an ounce of the inner bark of the white oak, a little of the herb mint,[762] an ounce of Knotengrass[763] and a gill of whortleberries. Place these all in a flask with a quart of alcoholic liniment and let it stand for three days. An adult may take a teaspoon full three times a day, but a soup spoon full of sweet oil must be taken in the morning a half hour before taking the medicine.

S66. To prepare an oil to which heals each type of wound.

Take a handful of white lilies, a handful of red fall rose leaves, and a gill of Peruvian balsam buds (the buds must have been picked early in the month of March), in a flask with a pint of good rye whiskey, a pint of brandy and an ounce of camphor. Put it in the sun for three days. Then take a pint of this liquid and mix it in a flask with a half gill of spirits of turpentine, a half ounce of spikenard oil, a soup spoonful of brown sugar and a half ounce of coal oil. Put the mixture in the sun for three days again and shake the flask each day. This gives an excellent oil for healing each and every kind of wound.

S67. To make a salve that overcomes all others.

Take three red corn grains and burn them entirely into fine powder, approximately three ounces of a man's excrement (the latter must be done on a shovel and burnt entirely to fine powder), a half ounce of dragon's blood, and an ounce of litharge of silver. Pound this all to a fine powder, then take a half gill of mullein blooms, a half gill of young elder branches, an equal quantity of parsley, a little comfrey root, some nightshade and a small handful of stinking Nachtschatten[764] flowers. Put all the herbs together in a cloth and crush them a little, then place them in a pan with two pounds of fresh unsalted butter and a half ounce of rosin. Fry it well, then take it out and strain it well through a cloth into a bowl. After that, place an ounce of beeswax with it, and let it stand for a little while. Last, stir the powder in with a spoon of pine wood, add one half ounce camphor and stir it well until it is cold. When you have a wound, then spread some of the above salve on a cloth from a linen shirt, lay it on. Leave it on for a half day,

then take it off. Wash the wound with some March snow water, mixed with some of the foregoing recipe for the aforementioned oil, warm it a little, place another plaster on it and go as before. This will rapidly heal it.

S68. Another remedy to heal wounds.

Take a pound of unslaked lime in a bowl with about a pint of March snow water, let it stand for twelve hours, then pour the sediment out in another crockery and take a little sweet oil or flaxseed oil with it. These make a very good ointment for burns. And if you take a half gill of the previously mentioned oil mixed in the next to last formula and wash the wound with it, then will you discover good effects from it.

S69. A marvelous remedy for frozen feet.

Take about 6 quarts chicken excrement, and stir in about two gallons of boiled water, in a bucket, then lay a little board above it, on which you put the feet. Cover them so until the mixture is so cold that you can place the feet in, then place them into it until it is entirely cold.

Works Cited

Abdullah, A. Z., S. M. Strafford, S. J. Brookes, and M. S. Duggal. "The Effect of Copper on Demineralization of Dental Enamel." *Journal of Dental Research* 85, no. 11 (2006): 1011–15.

Albertus. *Albertus Magnus. Being the Approved, Verified, Sympathetic and Natural Egyptian Secrets; or, White and Black Art for Man and Beast.* Chicago: Egyptian Pub. Co., 1930.

———. *Bewährte und Approbierte Sympathetische und Natürliche Ägyptische Geheimnisse für Menschen und Vieh, Städter und Landleute: Kleiner Wunder-Schauplatz der Geheimen Wissenschaften, Mysterien, Theosophie, Göttlichen und Morgenländischen Magie, Naturkräfte, Hermetischen und Magnetischen Philosophie, Kabbala und Anderen Höheren Kenntnissen, Divination, Offenbarung, Vision, Kombination und Schwer Begreiflichen Tatsachen; Nach Alten Hand- und Druckschriften und Erscheinungen der Neuzeit; Zugleich Als Beiträge zur Geschichte der Kultur und Literatur, des Mystizismus, der Religiösen Sekten, Geheimen Ordensverbindungen und Dahin Bezüglichen Kuriositäten; Teil 1 Bis 4.* Leipzig: Bohmeier, 2008.

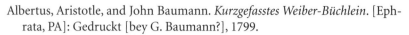

Albertus, Aristotle, and John Baumann. *Kurzgefasstes Weiber-Büchlein.* [Ephrata, PA]: Gedruckt [bey G. Baumann?], 1799.

Alfayé Villa, Silvia. "Nails for the Dead: A Polysemic Account of an Ancient Funerary Practice." In *Magical Practice in the Latin West: Papers from the International Conference Held at the University of Zaragoza, 30 Sept.–1 Oct. 2005,* edited by Richard Gordon and Francisco Marco Simón, 427–56. Leiden [etc.]: Brill, 2010.

Althaus, Georg. "An Eighteenth-Century Gypsy Charm." *Journal of the Gypsy Lore Society* Series 3, 38 (1959): 77–80.

Andrian-Werburg, Ferdinand. *Die Altausseer; Ein Beitrag zur Volkskunde des Salzkammergutes.* Wein: A. Hölder, 1905.

Bächtold-Stäubli, Hanns, Eduard Hoffmann-Krayer, and Gerhard Lüdtke. *Handwörterbuch des Deutschen Aberglaubens.* Berlin und Leipzig: W. de Gruyter & Co., 1927.

Bächtold, Hanns. "Volkskundliche Mitteilungen aus dem Schweizerischen Soldatenleben: Proben aus den Einsendungen Schweizerischer Wehrmänner." *Schweizerisches Archiv für Volkskunde* 19 (1915): 201–31.

Ballmer, D. *A Collection of New Receipts and Approved Cures for Man and Beast.* Shellsburg, PA: Frederick Goeb, 1872.

Barrett, William, and Theodore Besterman. *The Divining-Rod; an Experimental and Psychological Investigation.* New Hyde Park, NY: University Books, 1968.

Bartsch, Karl. *Sagen, Märchen und Gebräuche Aus Meklenburg.* Wien: Braumüller, 1879.

Baumgarten, P. Amand. *Aus der Volksmässigen Ueberlieferung der Heimat 1 zur Volkthümlichen Naturkunde.* [Linz: Oberösterr. Musealverein, 1862.]

Bergen, Fanny D., and William Wells Newell. *Current Superstitions Collected from the Oral Tradition of English Speaking Folk.* Teddington, Middlesex: Echo Library, 2007.

Best, Michael R., Frank Brightman, and Albertus. *The Book of Secrets of Albertus Magnus of the Virtues of Herbs, Stones and Certain Beasts, Also a Book of the Marvels of the World,* Series of Studies in Tudor and Stuart Literature. Oxford [Eng.: Clarendon Press, 1973.]

Bindewald, Theodor. *Oberhessisches Sagenbuch, aus dem Volkskunde Gesammelt.* Frankfurt a.M.: Heyder und Zimmer, 1873.

Birlinger, A. "Besegnungen Aberglauben." *Alemannia: Zeitschrift für Sprache, Litteratur und Volkskunde des Elsaszes Oberrheins und Schwabens.* 17 (1889): 239–47.

————. "Besegnungen aus dem Xvii Jahrhundert." *Alemannia: Zeitschrift für Sprache, Litteratur und Volkskunde des Elsaszes Oberrheins und Schwabens.* 14 (1886): 67–74, 233–34.

Birlinger, Anton. *Aus Schwaben Sagen, Legenden, Aberglauben, Sitten, Rechtsbräuche, Ortsneckereien, Lieder, Kinderreine, Neue Sammlung, von Anton Birlinger.* Wiesbaden: H. Killinger, 1874.

————. *Volksthümliches, Aus Schwaben. Herausgegeben von Dr. Anton Birlinger.* Freiburg im Breisgau: Herder, 1861.

Blaas, C. M. "Kleine Beiträge zur Mythologie." *Germania: Vierteljahrsschrift für Deutsche Alterthumskunde.* 22 (1877): 257–64.

Boecler, Johann Wolfgang. *Der Ehsten Abergläubische Gebrauche, Weisen und Gewohnheiten, von Johann Wolfgang Boecler, . . . Mit auf die Gegenwart Bezüglichen Anmerkungen Beleuchtet, von Dr. Fr. Kreutzwald.* St. Petersburg: Eggers, 1854.

Brendle, Thomas Royce, and Claude W. Unger. *Folk Medicine of the Pennsylvania Germans: The Non-Occult Cures,* Pennsylvania-German Society, 45,2. Norristown, PA: Soc., 1935.

Brenner, Scott Francis. *Pennsylvania Dutch, the Plain and the Fancy.* Harrisburg, PA: Stackpole Co., 1957.

Cohen, Stephanie. "Vinny 'Gorgeous' Winds up Doing Time for a 'Spell.'" *The New York Post,* December 21, 2007, 3.

Davies, Owen. "Healing Charms in Use in England and Wales 1700–1950." *Folklore* 107 (1996): 19–32.

Der Freund in der Noth, Oder Geheime Sympathetische Wissenschaft, Welche Nie Zuvor im Druck Erschienen. aus dem Spanischen Übersezt. Offenbach [?]: Calendar-Fabrike, 1790.

Der Hundertjährige Calender, Auf Das Gegenwärtige Jahr-Hundert Nach Christi Geburt, von 1799 Bis 1899; Enthaltend: Die Witterung, Frucht- und Unfruchtbarkeiten Eines Jeden Jahres, Monats und Tages, Nach der Sieben Planeten Eigenschaft; Die Berechnung des Sonnencirkels, Sontags-Buchstaben, Güldne Zahl und Epacten; Tabellen Über die Ostern, Bewegliche und Unbewegliche Festtage, Mondstabelle, Sonnen und Wetterzeiger; Die Unglückliche Tage; Die Vier Complexionen der Menschen; von den Kräuter, Thieren, Metallen und Mineralien; Der Zwölf Himmlischen Zeichen, und der Sieben Planeten Eigenschaft und Würkungen Bey Dem Menschlichen Körper; Nebst Verschiedene Bewährte Hülfsmittel Auf Allerley Fälle.—Baltimore—: Samuel Saur, 1799.

Dettling, A. "Aus Dem Arzneibuch des Landamanns Michael Schorno von Schwyz, + 1671." *Schweizerisches Archiv für Volkskunde* 15 (1911): 89–94, 177–84.

Dieterich, Albrecht Wünsch Richard. *Kleine Schriften.* Leipzig: Berlin, B.G. Teubner, 1911.

Dillinger, Johannes. *"Evil People": A Comparative Study of Witch Hunts in Swabian Austria and the Electorate of Trier.* Charlottesville: University of Virginia Press, 2009.

Dillman, J. "Alte Äberglaubische Mittel." *Zeitschrift des Vereins für rheinische und westfälische volkskunde* 6, no. 4 (1909): 288–94.

Dörler, Adolf F. "Die Tierwelt in der Sympathetischen Tiroler Volksmedizin." *Zeitschrift des Vereins für Volkskunde* 8 (1898): 38–48.

Draelants, Isabelle, and Albertus. *Le Liber De Virtutibus Herbarum, Lapidum Et Animalium: (Liber Aggregationis); Un Texte à Succès Attribué à Albert Le Grand,* Micrologus' Library, 22. Firenze: SISMEL, Ed. del Galluzzo, 2007.

Drechsler, Paul. *Sitte, Brauch und Volksglaube in Schlesien.* Leipzig: B. G. Teubner, 1903.

Earnest, Russell D., Corinne P. Earnest, and Edward L. Rosenberry. *Flying Leaves and One-Sheets: Pennsylvania German Broadsides, Fraktur, and Their Printers.* New Castle, DE: Oak Knoll Press, 2005.

Ebermann, Oskar. *Blut- und Wundsegen in Ihrer Entwicklung.* Berlin: Mayer & Müller, 1903.

Engelien, August, and Wilhelm Lahn. *Der Volksmund in der Mark Brandenburg: Sagen, Märchen, Spiele, Sprichwörter und Gebräuche.* Berlin: Schultze, 1868.

Evenden, William L. *Deutsche Feuerversicherungs-Schilder = German Fire Marks.* Karlsruhe: VVW, 1989.

Fogel, Edwin Miller. *Beliefs and Superstitions of the Pennsylvania Germans.* Edited by Marion Dexter Learned, Americana Germanica. Philadelphia: American Germanica Press, 1915.

Freudenthal, Herbert. *Das Feuer im Deutschen Glauben und Brauch.* Berlin; Leipzig: W. de Gruyter & Co., 1931.

Fry, Jacob. *The History of Trinity Lutheran Church, Reading, Pa, 1751–1894.* Reading, PA: The Congregation, 1894.

"Further Evidence in Hageman Case." *North American,* March 12, 1903.

Glock, J. Ph. "Lieder und Sprüche aus dem Elsenztal. aus dem Munde des Volks Gesammelt." *Alemannia: Zeitschrift für Sprache, Litteratur und Volkskunde des Elsaszes Oberrheins und Schwabens.* 25 (1898): 193–255.

Graves, Thomas E. "The Pennsylvania German Hex Sign: A Study in Folk Process." s.n., 1990.

Grimm, Jacob, and Leopold Kretzenbacher. *Deutsche Mythologie.* Graz: Akademische Druck- und Verlagsanstalt, 1968.

Haas, A. "Diebsglaube in Pommern." *Blätter für Pommersche Volkskunde* 4, no. 9 (1896): 139–41.

———. "Feuersegen." *Blätter für Pommersche Volkskunde* 3, no. 2 (1894): 26–28.

Haase, K. E. "Volksmedizin in der Grafschaft Ruppin und Umgegend." *Zeitschrift des Vereins für Volkskunde* 7 (1897): 53–74, 162–72, 287–92, 405–12.

Hale, Frank, and Joyce Marks Hale. *Descendants of the Jacob Meck Family, Berks Co. PA* n. p.: Frank & Joyce Marks Hale, 2001.

Hand, Wayland D. *Magical Medicine: The Folkloric Component of Medicine in the Folk Belief, Custom, and Ritual of the Peoples of Europe and America: Selected Essays of Wayland D. Hand.* Berkeley: University of California Press, 1980.

Handelmann, H. "Volksmedizin. Zauber- und Heilsprüche Udgl." *Am Ur-Quell* 1 (1890): 186–87.

Harden, Pam. *Brecht: Descendants of Kuntz Brecht.* Kutztown, PA: Berks County Genealogical Society, n. d.

Hardy, James. "Wart and Wen Cures." *The Folk-Lore Record* 1 (1878): 216–28.

Haupt, Herman. "Aus Karl Bernbecks Sammlungen zur Oberhessischen Volkskunde." *Hessische Blätter für Volkskunde* 1 (1902): 4–18.

Heilig, Otto. "Segen Aus Handschuhsheim." *Zeitschrift des Vereins für Volkskunde* 5 (1895): 293–98.

Heyl, Johann Adolf. *Volkssagen, Bräuche und Meinungen Aus Tirol.* Brixen: Katholisch-politischer Pressverein, 1897.

Hirzel, Paul. "Aberglauben im Kanton Zürich." *Schweizerisches Archiv für Volkskunde* 2 (1898): 257–79.

Hoffman, W. J. "Folk-Lore of the Pennsylvania Germans II." *The Journal of American Folklore* 2, no. 4 (1889): 23–35.

Höfler, Max. *Deutsches Krankheitsnamen-Buch.* München: Piloty & Loehle, 1899.

Hohman, Johann Georg. *Die Land- und Haus-Apotheke, oder, Getreuer und Gründlicher Unterricht für den Bauer und Stadtmann, Enthaltend die Allerbesten Mittel, Sowohl für die Menschen als für das Vieh Besonders für die Pferde. Nebst Einem Grossen Anhang von der Aechten Färberey.* Reading [PA]: Gedruckt bey Carl A. Bruckmann, 1818.

Horst, Georg Conrad. *Zauber-Bibliothek: Oder, von Zauberei, Theurgie und Mantik, Zauberern, Hexen und Hexenprocessen, Dämonen, Gespenstern und Geistererscheinungen.* Freiburg i.Br.: Aurum-Verlag, 1979.

Hovorka, Oskar, and Adolf Kronfeld. *Vergleichende Volksmedizin: Eine Darstellung Volksmedizinischer Sitten und Gebräuche, Anschauungen und Heilfaktoren, des Aberglaubens und der Zaubermedizin.* Stuttgart: Strecker & Schröder, 1908.

Hoyt, A. B. "Case of Asthma Treated by Iodide of Potassium." *The Boston Medical and Surgical Journal* 53, no. 16 (1855): 325–26.

Hurt, Ray Douglas. *American Agriculture: A Brief History.* West Lafayette, IN: Purdue University Press, 2002.

Huss, Karl, and Alois John. *Die Schrift "Vom Aberglauben" von Karl Huss Nach dem in der Fürstlich Metternichschen Bibliothek Zu Königswart Befindlichen Manuskripte Herausgegeben,* Beiträge zur Deutsch-Böhmischen Volkskunde, 9,2. Prag: Calve, 1910.

Isidore, and Stephen A. Barney. *The Etymologies of Isidore of Seville.* Cambridge; New York: Cambridge University Press, 2006.

Jäckel, A. "Aphorismen über Volkssitte, Aberglauben und Volksmedicin in Franken, Mit Besonderer Rücksicht auf Oberfranken." *Abhandlungen der Naturhistorischen Gesellschaft zu Nürnberg* 2 (1861): 148–258.

John, Alois. *Sitte, Brauch und Volksglaube im Deutschen Westböhmen, von Alois John.* Prag: J. G. Calve, 1905.

John, Ernst. *Aberglaube, Sitte und Brauch im Sächsischen Erzgebirge: E. Beitr. zur Dt. Volkskunde.* Annaberg: Graser, 1909.

Juvenal, and Persius. *Juvenal and Persius. With an English Translation by G.G. Ramsay.* Cambridge: Harvard University Press, 1965.

Kaindl, Raimund Friedrich. "Ein Deutsches Beschwörungsbuch: Aus der Handschrift Herausgegeben." *Zeitschrift für Ethnologie* 25 (1893): 22–45.

Kell, Katharine T. "Tobacco in Folk Cures in Western Society." *The Journal of American Folklore* 78, no. 308 (1965): 99–114.

Kirlin, Joseph L. J. *Catholicity in Philadelphia from the Earliest Missionaries Down to the Present Time.* Philadelphia: J. J. McVey, 1909.

Kleeberger, C. *Volkskundliches Aus Fischbach I. D. Pfalz.* Kaiserslautern: H. Kayser, 1902.

Knoop, Otto. *Volkssagen, Erzählungen, Aberglauben, Gebräuche und Märchen Aus Dem Östlichen Hinterpommern.* Posen: J. Jolowicz, 1885.

Köhler, Johann August Ernst. *Volksbrauch, Aberglauben, Sagen und Andere Alte Ueberlieferungen im Voigtland: Mit Berücksichtigung des Orlagau's und des Pleissnerlandes: Ein Beitrag zur Kulturgeschichte des Voigtlandes.* Leipzig: Fleischer, 1867.

Kriebel, David W. *Powwowing among the Pennsylvania Dutch: A Traditional Medical Practice in the Modern World,* Publications of the Pennsylvania German Society: Pennsylvania State University Press, 2007.

Kuhn, Adalbert. *Sagen, Gebräuche und Märchen Aus Westfalen: und Einigen Andern, Besonders den Angrenzenden Gegenden Norddeutschlands.* Leipzig: F. A. Brockhaus, 1859.

Lambelet, M. "Prièures Et Recettes." *Schweizerisches Archiv für Volkskunde* 15 (1911): 184–85.

Lambing, Andrew Arnold. *A History of the Catholic Church in the Dioceses of Pittsburg and Allegheny from Its Establishment to the Present Time.* New York: Benziger Bros, 1880.

Lick, D. E., and Thomas Royce Brendle. "Plant Names and Plant Lore among the Pennsylvania-Germans." *The Pennsylvania-German Society* 33, no. 3 (1923): 1–300.

Liebrecht, Felix des *Gervasius von Tilbury Otia Imperialia in Einer Auswahl Neu Herausgegehen.* Hannover: Rümpler, 1856.

Löbe, J. "Aberglaube und Volksmittel aus dem Altenburgschen." *Mitteilungen der Geschichts- und Altertumsforschenden Gesellschaft des Osterlandes* 7 (1874): 441–57.

Lommer, Victor. *Volksthümliches Aus Dem Saalthal.* Orlamünde: Heyl, 1878.

Losch, Friedrich. "Deutsche Segen, Heil- und Bannsprüche." *Württembergische Vierteljahrshefte für Landesgeschichte* 13 (1890): 157–259.

Mahr, August C. "A Pennsylvania Dutch 'Hexzettel'." *Monatshefte für Deutschen Unterricht* 27, no. 6 (1935): 215–25.

Mannhardt, Wilhelm, and Walter Heuschkel. *Wald- und Feldkulte.* Berlin: Gebrüder Borntraeger, 1875.

Manz, Werner. "Volksglaube aus dem Sarganserland." *Schweizerisches Archiv für Volkskunde* 24 (1922–23): 292–308.

———. "Volksglaube aus dem Sarganserland." *Schweizerisches Archiv für Volkskunde* 25 (1924–25): 65–69.

Maria de Jesús de Agreda, Madre, and George John Blatter. *City of God, the Coronation; the Divine History and Life of the Virgin Mother of God, Manifested to Mary of Agreda for the Encouragement of Men.* Hammond, IN: W. B. Conkey, 1914.

Marzulli, John. "Hit List? Nah, Just a Silly Li'l Curse, Sez Mob Boss." *Daily News*, December 21, 2007, 36.

Menčik, Ferdinand. "Ein Erprobter Feuersegen." *Zeitschrift des Vereins für Volkskunde* 8 (1898): 345.

Merrifield, Ralph. "Witch Bottles and Magical Jugs." *Folklore* 66, no. 1 (1955): 195–207.

Meyer, Elard H. *Deutsche Volkskunde mit 17 Abbildungen und 1 Karte.* Strassburg: K. J. Trübner, 1898.

Meyer, Elard Hugo. *Badisches Volksleben im Neunzehnten Jahrhundert.* Strassburg: K. J. Trübner, 1900.

Milnes, Gerald. *Signs, Cures, & Witchery: German Appalachian Folklore.* Knoxville: University of Tennessee Press, 2007.

Montague, Peregrine. *The Family Pocket-Book or, Fountain of True and Useful Knowledge. Containing the Farrier's Guide; ... The Good Housewife's Daily Companion; ... Compiled ... By Peregrine Montague.* London: printed for George Paul, 1762.

Oda, Wilbur H. "John George Homan." *Historical Review of Berks County* 13 (1948): 66–71.

Ohrt, F. *Danmarks Trylleformler.* København: Gyldendal, 1917.

Owens, J. G. "Folk-Lore from Buffalo Valley, Central Pennsylvania." *The Journal of American Folklore* 4, no. 13 (1891): 115–28.

Paden, William D., and Frances Freeman Paden. "Swollen Woman, Shifting Canon: A Midwife's Charm and the Birth of Secular Romance Lyric." *PMLA: Proceedings of the Modern Language Association* 125, no. 2 (2010): 306–21.

Penn, William. "A Further Account of the Province of Pennsylvania, by William Penn, 1685." In *Narratives of Early Pennsylvania, West New Jersey and Delaware, 1630–1707*, edited by Albert Cook Myers, 259–78. New York: C. Scribner's Sons, 1912.

Peterson, Joseph H. *The Lesser Key of Solomon: Lemegeton Clavicula Salomonis: Detailing the Ceremonial Art of Commanding Spirits Both Good and Evil.* York Beach, ME: Weiser Books, 2001.

Pliny, and W. H. S. Jones. *Natural History, Libri XXVIII—XXXII.* Cambridge, Mass.: Harvard University Press, 1975.

Pócs, Éva. "Miracles and Impossibilities in Magic Folk Poetry." In *Charms, Charmers and Charming: International Research on Verbal Magic*, edited by Jonathan Roper, 27–53. Hampshire, England; New York: Palgrave Macmillan, 2009.

Pollinger, Johann. *Aus Landshut und Umgebung: Ein Beitrag zur Heimat- und Volkskunde.* München: Oldenbourg, 1908.

Prahn, H. "Glaube und Brauch in der Mark Brandenburg." *Zeitschrift des Vereins für Volkskunde* 1 (1891): 178–97.

Randolph, Vance. *Ozark Magic and Folklore.* New York: Dover Publications, 1964.

Roan, Donald. "Deivels-Dreck (Asafoetida) Yesterday and Today." *Pennsylvania Folklife* 14, no. 2 (1964): 30–33.

Roediger, Else. "Allerlei Aus Bärwalde, Kr. Neustettin, Pommern." *Zeitschrift des Vereins für Volkskunde* 13 (1903): 98–99.

Roper, Jonathan. *English Verbal Charms*, Ff Communications, No. 288. Helsinki: Suomalainen Tiedeakatemia, 2005.

Schönwerth, Franz Xaver von. *Aus der Oberpfalz—Sitten und Sagen*. Augsburg: Rieger, 1859.

Schramek, Josef. *Der Böhmerwaldbauer: Eigenart, Tracht und Nahrung, Haus- und Wirtschaftsgeräte, Sitten, Gebräuche und Volksglaube. Nebst Einem Anhange: Der Böhmerwaldholzhauer*, Beiträge zur Deutsch-Böhmischen Volkskunde, XII. Bd. Prag: J. G. Calve (R. Lerche), 1915.

Sello, G. "Ein Fiebersegen Kurfürst Joachims I von Brandenburg." *Zeitschrift für Deutsches Alterthum und Deutsche Literratur* 23 (1879): 433–35.

Serenus Sammonicus, Quintus. *Liber Medicinalis*. Paris: Presses universitaires de France, 1950.

Seyfarth, Carly. *Aberglaube und Zauberei in der Volksmedizin West-Sachsens*. Leipzig: Wilhelm Heims, 1913.

Shoemaker, Henry W. *Gipsies and Gipsy Lore in the Pennsylvania Mountains: An Address [to the] Civic Club, Huntingdon, Pennsylvania, December 5, 1924*. Altoona, PA: Times Tribune, 1924.

Spamer, Adolf, and Johanna Nickel. *Romanusbüchlein; Historisch-Philologischer Kommentar zu einem Deutschen Zauberbuch*. Berlin: Akademie-Verlag, 1958.

Spier, Jeffrey. "Medieval Byzantine Magical Amulets and Their Tradition." *Journal of the Warburg and Courtauld Institutes* 56 (1993): 25–62.

Staricius, J. *Geheimnissvoller Heldenschatz, oder der Vollständige Egyptische Magische Schild*, 1750.

Steele, Robert. "Dies Aegyptiaci." *Proceedings of the Royal Society of Medicine* 12(Supplement) (1919): 108–21.

Steve Miller Band. *Abracadabra*. Los Angeles: Capitol Records, 1982.

Stoll, Otto. "Zur Kenntnis des Zauberglaubens, der Volksmagie und Volksmedizin in der Schweiz." *Jahresberichte der Geographisch-Ethnographischen Gesellschaft in Zürich* 9 (1908–09): 37–207.

Strack, Hermann Leberecht. *Das Blut im Glauben und Aberglauben der Menschheit. Mit Besonderer Berücksichtigung der "Volksmedizin" und des "Jüdischen Blutritus,"* Schriften des Institutum Judaicum in Berlin, Nr. 14. München: Beck, 1900.

Thäter, Johannes. *Selbstbiographie Eines Alten Schulmeisters: Nach dem Tode des Verfassers für Seine Freunde Herausgegeben*. Nürnberg: Sebald, 1866.

Von Zingerle, Oswald. "Segen und Heilmittel Aus Einer Wolfsthurner Handschrift des XV. Jahrhunderts." *Zeitschrift des Vereins für Volkskunde* 1 (1891): 315–24.

Weinitz, Franz. "Zwei Segen." *Zeitschrift des Vereins für Volkskunde* 21 (1911): 339–40.

Weinreich, Otto. "Eine Bewährter Feuersegen." *Hessische Blätter für Volkskunde* 9 (1910): 139–42.

Winstedt, E. O. "German Gypsies and Fire." *Journal of the Gypsy Lore Society* Series 3, 12 (1933): 58–60.

Wirsung, Christof, and Peter Uffenbach. *Ein New Artzney Buch Darinn Fast Alle Eusserliche unnd Innerliche Glieder dess Menschlichen Leibs Sampt Ihren Kranckheiten und Gebrechen von dem Haupt an Biss zu der Fussolen und Wie Man Dieselben Durch Gottes Hülff und Seine Darzu Geschaffene Mittel auff Mancherley Weiss Wenden und Curieren Soll.* Ursel: Durch Cornelium Sutorium, 1605.

"Witnesses Heard in Hageman Case." *North American*, March 13, 1903.

Wolf, Johann Wilhelm. *Beiträge zur Deutschen Mythologie.* Leipzig; Göttingen 1852.

Wolff, Theodor. "Volksglauben und Volksgebräuche an der Oberen Nahe." *Zeitschrift des Vereins für rheinische und westfälische Volkskunde* 2 (1905): 277–309.

Wossidlo, Richard. *Erntebräuche in Mecklenburg.* Hamburg: Quickborn, 1927.

Wuttke, Adolf, and Elard Hugo Meyer. *Der Deutsche Volksaberglaube der Gegenwart.* Berlin: Wiegandt & Grieben, 1900.

Yoder, Don. "Hohman and Romanus: Origins and Diffusion of the Pennsylvania German Powwow Manual." In *American Folk Medicine: A Symposium*, edited by Wayland Debs Hand, UCLA Conference on American Folk Medicine, Los Angeles Center for the Study of Comparative Folklore and Mythology University of California, Division California University at Los Angeles. Medical History and Science Society for the History of Medical, 235-48. Berkeley: University of California Press, 1976.

Yronwode, Catherine. ""Pow-Wows": The European Influence on Hoodoo." http://www.luckymojo.com/powwows.html.

Zwinger, Theodor. *Theodori Zuingeri Theatrum Botanicum, das ist, Vollkommenes Kraüter-Buch Worinnen Allerhand, Erdgewächse, Bäume, Stauden und Kräuter, Welche in Allen Vier Theilen der Welt, Sonderlich aber in Europa, Hervorkommen Neben Ihren Sonderbaren Eigenschaften, Tugenden, und Vortresslichen Wirkungen, auch Vielen Herrlichen Ausneymitteln und Derer Gebrauche, Wider Allerley Krankheiten an Menschen und Vieh: Mit Sonderbarem Fleiss auf eine Gantz Neue Beliebte Art und Weise, Dergleichen in Andern Kräuterbuchern Nicht zu Finde, Beschrieben, auch mit Schönen Nach der Natur Gezeichneten Figuren Gezieret und Neben den Ordentlichen, So Wohl Kraüter-Als Krankenheit Registern, Mit Nützlichen Di ... [Illegible]*

Vorgestellet Find: Allen Aertzten, Wundärtzten, Apotheckern, Gärtner, Hausvätern und Hausmiitern, Sonderlich aber Denen auf Dem Lande Wohnenden Kranken und Presthaftes Personen Höchstnützuch und Vorträglich: Itzo auf das Neue. Basel: In Veriegung Hans Jacob Bischoffs, 1744.

Der lange Verborgene Freund

Der lange
Verborgene Freund,
oder:
Getreuer und Christlicher
Unterricht für jedermann,
enthaltend:
Wunderbare und probmäßige
Mittel und Künste,
Sowohl für die Menschen als das Vieh.
Mit vielen Zeugen bewiesen in diesem Buch, und wovon das Mehrste noch wenig bekannt ist, und zum allerersten Mal in America in Druck erscheint.

Herausgegeben
Von

Johann Georg Hohman,
Nahe bey Reading, in Elsaß Taunschip, Berks Caunty,
Pennsylvanien.

Reading:
Gedruckt für den Verfasser.
1820.

VORREDE:
ZUR ERSTEN AUSGABE DIESES BÜCHLEINS.

Der Verfasser hätte gern keine Vorrede zu diesem Büchlein geschrieben; aber wegen irriger Meynung etlicher Menschen kann ich, es nicht unterlassen. Viele sagen, es ist recht, daß ihr so Bücher verkaufet, und drucken lasset. Der kleinste Theil sagt, es wäre nicht recht. Solche Menschen bedaure ich sehr, daß sie auf solchen Irrwegen gehen; und ich bitte daher jedermann, wer es am besten kann, solche Menschen von ihren Irrwegen abzuführen. Es ist wahr, wer den Namen Jesus vergeblich mißbrauchet, der thut eine große Sünde. Steht nicht ausdrücklich im 50sten Psalm: "Rufe mich an in der Noth, so will ich dich erretten, und du sollst mich preisen. Das ist in der Lutherischen Bibel; in der Katholischen steht es im 49sten Psalm: "Rufe mich an am Tage der Trübsal, so will ich dich erretten, und du sollst mich preisen. Wo ist ein Doctor, das das Herzgesperr' und Anwachsen vertrieben hat? Wo ist ein Doctor, der noch eine Schußblatter vertrieben hat? Wo ist ein Doctor, der die Mutterkrankheit vertrieben hat? Wo ist ein Doctor, der den kalten Brand heilen kann, wenn er stark an einem Gliede ist? Dies alles zu heilen, und noch viel mehr heimliche Sachen, sind in diesem Buche enthalten; und der Verfasser von diesem Buch kann einige Zeit seinen Eid nehmen, daß er schon viele Proben aus dem Buch gemacht hat. Ich sage: einiger Mensche versündiget sich hart; er kann sich den Himmel entziehen, wenn er schuld ist, daß sein Nebenmensch ein Auge oder ein Bein, oder sonst ein Glied verliert, wenn ihm mit diesen Büchlein geholfen werden könnte.—Solche

Menschen verwerfen dies, was uns der Herr befiehlt, daß man ihn in der Noth anrufen solle. Wenn wir mit Worten und mit den höchsten Namen nicht brauchen dürften, so wäre es den Menschen auf der Welt nicht offenbaret, und der Herr thäte auch nicht helfen, wenn jemand brauchen würde. Gott kann auf keine Art gezwungen werden, wenn es sein göttlicher Wille nicht ist. Eins muß ich auch noch anführen: es giebt auch Menschen, die sagen, wenn man mit Worten gebraucht hat, nachher helfen die Doctors' Sachen nichts; denn es half mit Worten nichts. Das ist den Doctors nur ihre Ausrede. Denn wenn etwas nicht mit Worten geheilet werden kann, so kann es gewiß noch weniger ein Doctor heilen. Einige Zeit kann ich den Katholischen Pfarrer mit Namen nennen, und kann auch dem Manne seinen Namen nennen, der dem Pfarzer seinen Gaul mit Worten geheilet hat. Den Pfarrer habe ich gekannt; er wohnte sonst in Westmoreland Caunty. Ich kann auch den Reformirten Pfarrer mit Namen nennen, wenn es verlangt wird, und auch die Leute, denen er Zettel dafür geschrieben hat; und die Gichter sind mit diesem Zettel geheilet worden. Der Pfarrer wohnte sonst in Berks County. Wenn die Leute nur aus diesem Büchlein brauchen, was nothwendig ist, so haben sie keine Sünde, aber wehe denen, die schuld sind; wenn sie durch kalten Brand das Leben lassen müßen, oder sonst ein Glied verlieren, oder das Augensicht! Wehe denen, die in der Noth dies verdrehen, oder einigem Prediger in diesem Stück folgen, das nicht zu beobachten, was der Herr im 50sten Psalm spricht: Rufe mich an in der Noth, so will ich dich erretten, und du sollst mich preisen. Wehe denen, die in diesem Stück folgen einigem Prediger, aus diesem Buch nichts für den kalten oder heißen Brand oder Schutzblatter zu brauchen! Ich will dem Prediger sonst in allen billigen Sachen folgen; aber wenn ich in der Noth bin, und soll aus diesem Buch nichts brauchen in diesem Fall kann ich ihm nicht folgen. Aber wehe auch denen, die den Namen Gottes vergeblich um nichtswerthe Sachen mißbrauchen!

Ich habe viele Proben aus dem Buch gemacht, und kann es auch noch bey einigem thun. Ich verkaufe meine Bücher öffentlich und nicht heimlich, wie schon Kunstbücher verkauft worden sind. Ich bin willens, meine Bücher bey jedermann sehen zu lassen, und werde

mich vor keinen Prediger heimlich verbergen oder viekriechen. Ich, Hohman, kann auch ein wenn die Schrift versteben, wenn ich den Herrn, um Beystand anrufe, und zu ihm bete.—Büchen drucken ist in den Vereinigten Staaten nicht verboten, wenn es nutzbare und gute Bücher sind, welches der Fall in andern Ländern ist, wo Könige und Despoten uber das Volk tyrannisch herrschen. Ich nehme zu diesem nützlichen Buch die Press- und Gewissens-Freyheit, welche bey uns in diesem Lande herrscht, zur Richtschnur. Deswegen wünsche ich allen von Herzen, in Namen Jesu, dieses gute Buch mit Nutzen zu gebrauchen.

Gegeben im Rosenthal, nahe bey Reading, Berks Caunty, Pennsylvanien, am 31sten July, im Jahr unsers Herrn Jesu Christ 1819.

Johann Georg Hohman,
Verfasser und Herausgeber von diesem Buch.

Anmerkung.

Mancher in America glaubt an keine Hölle oder Himmel. In Deutschland giebt es solcher Leute nicht so viel. Ich Hohman, frage: Wer vertreibt gleich die Schußblatter, kalten Brand? Wer stopft das Blut? Ich antworte, und ich, Hohman, sage: Dies thut der Herr. So muß Hölle und Himmel seyn. Und auf solche Leute halte ich nichts.

Zeugnisse,

Welche zu einiger Zeit beweisen können, daß ich, Hohman, für sie aus diesem Buch gebraucht habe.

Benjamin Staubt, Lutherischer Schulmeisters Sohn von Reading, litt sehr große Schmerzen, wegen einer Schußblatter am Auge; in ein wenig mehr, als 24 Stunden, war dies Auge so gut, als das andere; durch mich Hülfe bekommen und durch Gott, im Jahr 1817.

Henrich Jorger, wohnhaft jetzt in Reading, brachte zu mir einen Buben im Jahr 1814, welcher erstaunliche Schmerzen hatte, auch wegen einer

Schußblatter am Auge: in ein wenig mehr, als 24 Stunden, habe ich und der liebe Gott ihm geholfen.

John Bayer, Sohn von Jacob Bayer, wohnt jetzt bey Reading, hatte ein Geschwür am Bein, er litt sehr große Schmerzen daran. Ich bediente ihn, und in kurzer Zeit war sein Bein geheilet. Es war im Jahr 1818.

Landlin Gottwalt, jetzt in Reading wohnhaft, hatte heftige Schmerzen an einem Arm. In ungefähr vier und zwanzig Stunden war schier gar der Arm geheilet.

Catharina Meck, damals in Elsass Taunschip, litt große Schmerzen am Auge, wegen einer Schußblatter; in ein wenig mehr, als 24 Stunden, war das Auge geheilet.

Herr Silvis von Reading, war bey mir, als er bey meinem Nachbar in der Brennerey schaffte. Er litt große Schmerzen am Auge, wegen einer Schuß-blatter. Ich heilte das Auge in ein wenig mehr, als 24 Stunden.

Anna Schneider, in Elsaß Taunschip, hatte große Schmerzen an einem Finger; in ein wenig mehr, als 24 Stunden, habe ich ihr geholfen.

Michael Hartman, jun. wohnt in Elsaß Taunschip, hat ein Kind, das hatte einen sehr wehen Mund. Ich bediente ihm. In ein wenig mehr, als 24 Stun-den, habe ich ihm geholfen.

Johann Bingemann, in Ruscombmaner, hatte einen Buben, welcher sich sehr verbrannt hatte. Meine Frau kam von ungefähr, im Spätjahr, dort hin. Es war im Jahr 1812. Der kalte Brand war schon daran. Meine Frau brauchte dafür, und der kalte Brand wurde in kurzer Zeit vertrieben. Der Bube wurde bald darauf wieder gesund hergestellt, und war geheilet.

Um die nämliche Zeit stillte meine Frau seiner Frau einer starken Rothlauf an einem wehen Bein.

Susanna Gomber hatte auch Schmerzen, die groß waren, am Haupt. In kurzer Zeit habe ich ihr geholfen.

David Brecht seine Frau hatte auch große Schmerzen am Haupte. In kurzer Zeit habe ich ihr geholfen.

Dem Johann Junken seine Tochter und Sohnesfrau hatten beyde auch heftige Schmerzen am Haupte, und die Frau hatte noch beyseits einen wehen Backen, wo erstaunlich der Rothlauf an war. Das Kopfweh war bey der Tochter und Frau, durch mich, weg, und der Rothlauf in etlichen 7 oder 9 Stunden vergangen. Ihr Bakken brach auf, und heilte sehr stark. Die Frau hatte deswegen schon etliche Tage im Bett gelegen. Junckens Familie wohnt in Nackenmixen; Brecht und Gomber aber wohnen in und ohnweit Reading. Nackenmixen liegt bey dem Heckack, Bucks County. Die vier Letztgemeldeten erhielten Hülfe im Jahr 1819.

Dem Arnold seine Tochter brannte sich mit heißem Kaffee. Der Hänkel brach von der Kanne während dem Ausschenken, und der Kaffee fuhr an den Arm, und verbrannte ihn ziemlich hart.—Ich war gegenwärtig, und sah es. Ich nahm den Brand heraus; der Arm wurde nicht wehe, und heilte in ganz kurzer Zeit. Meister Arnold wohnt ohnweit Libanon, Libanon Caunty. Sein Vorname heißt Johannes.

Sollte einer von obigen gemeldeten Zeugen, welche durch mich oder durch meine Frau, und durch Gott, Hülfe bekommen haben, mich einen Lügner nennen, daß wir ihnen nicht geholfen hatten, da sie es uns ja selber bekannten, daß wir ihnen geholfen hätten; so werde ich sie nöthigen, es vor einem Friedensrichter noch einmal zu bekennen, wenn es möglich ist; welches wir großtentheils glauben, dass wir es thun kennen. Dem obengemeldeten Arnold seine Tochter hatten den Arm verbrannt ungefähr im Jahr 1815.

Jacob Staufer, am Heckack, Bucks Caunty, hatte ein kleines Kind, das hatte jede Stunde die Gichter. Ich verkaufte ihm ein Buch, wo die 25 Buchstaben inne waren. Auf Zureden seines Nachbars Henrich Franckenfeld brauchte er die 25 Buchstaben. Sogleich wurde das Kind von den Gichtern befreyet, und ward gesund. Obengemeldete Buchstaben sind auch in diesem Buch.

Ein Brief von dem Rheumatismus wurde für $ 1 bis 2 verkauft, und war nicht einmal in demselben gemeldet, wie man es brauchen sollte, und musste sich deswegen aufs Sagen verlassen. Der John Algaier in Reading hatte auch einen sehr wehen Finger. Ich brauchte ihm für den Rothlauf, und für dem Finger zu heilen. Den andern Morgen war der Rothlauf weg, der

Finger that ihm gar nicht viel mehr weh, und fieng stark an zu heilen. Es war im Jahr 1819.

Dieses Buch ist theils aus einem Buch gezogen, welches von einem Zigeuner herausgegeben worden, theils aus heimlichen Schriften mühsam in der Welt zusammen getragen, durch mich, den Autor Johann Georg Hohman, in verschiedenen Jahren. Ich hätte es nicht abdrucken lassen; meine Frau wehrte auch dagegen: aber mein Mitleiden mit meinen Nächsten war zu groß, weil schon Mancher durch Schussblatter sein ganzes Gesicht, und durch kalten Brand sein Leben oder Bein verloren hat. Wie hart hat manche Frau an der Mutterkrankheit zu leiden! Ich frage dich nochmals, Freund oder Freundin, ist es nun nicht ein ewiges Lob für mich, daß ich solche Bücher habe drucken lassen? Verdiene ich deswegen bey Gott keinen Lohn? Wo ist denn sonst ein Doctor, der obengemeldete Krankheit heilen kann? Ich bin sonst auch noch ein ziemlich armer Mann, und kann es ja auch noch nöthig brauchen, wenn ich ein wenig mit solchen Büchern verdiene.

Der Herr segne unsern Anfang und Ende in diesem Büchlein, und stehe uns bey, daß mir es nicht mißbrauchen, und deswegen nicht eine schwere Sünde begehen!—Das Wort missbrauchen heißt so viel, als für eine Sache zu brauchen, die nicht nöthig ist. Gott segne es! Amen.—Das Wort Amen heißt so viel, als daß es der Herr geschehen lassen soll, darum man bittet.

Hohman

MITTEL AND KÜNSTE.

1. Ein gutes Mittel für die Mutterkrankheit, welches drey mal gebraucht werden muß.

Leg das oberste Glied am Daumen, das bey der Hand ist, auf die bloße Haut über der Herzgrube, auf das Knöchlein, das heraus steht, uns sprich dieses dabei:

Bärmutter, Schermutter, leg dich nieder in der rechten Statt,
Sonst wird man mich oder dich am dritten Tag tragen in das Grab.
† † †

2. Noch ein Mittel für die Mutterkrankheit und für den Schnupfen.

Du mußt es für gewiß alle Abende thun; wann du deine Schuhe oder Strümpfe ausziehst, so fahre mit den Fingern durch alle Zähne, und riech daran. Es wird dir gewiß helfen.

3. Ein gewißes Mittel um das Blut zu stillen; es hilft, der Mensch mag so weit seyn, als er will, wenn man seinen Vornamen recht dabey spricht, wenn man für ihn braucht.

Jesus Christus, theures Blut!

Das stillet die Schmerzen, und stillet das Blut.

Das helf dir (N.) Gott der Vater, Gott der Sohn, Gott der heilige Geist. Amen.

4. Ein Mittel, wenn jemand abdorret, so kann man es erst brauchen; denn dieses hat schon Vielen, ja den Meisten geholfen.

Laß den Menschen nüchtern unbeschrauen vor Sonnenaufgang in ein Geschirr brunzen, koch ein Ey in dieser Brunze, mach drey kleine Löchlein mit der Nadel in das Ey, und trag dasselbe in einen Ameisenhaufen, den die großen Ameisen machen; so wird es besser, wie das Ey verzehret wird.

5. Wieder ein Mittel, wenn jemand krank ist, so kann man es thun; denn es hat schon Vielen geholfen, wo kein Doctor helfen konnte.

Laß den Kranken unbeschrauen vor Sonnen-Aufgang nüchtern in eine Bottel brunzen, stopfe sie gut zu, und mach, daß due dieselbe gleich in eine Riste thun kannst; stopfe auch das Schlüssel-Loch zu. Wenn es helfen soll, so mußt du den Schlüssel drey Tage in einer deiner Taschen bewahren; denn es darf ihn niemand haben, als derjenige der die Bottel mit der Brunze in die Kiste thut.

6. Ein gutes Mittel gegen die Würmer, sowohl für Menschen als Vieh zu brauchen.

> Maria, die Mutter Gottes, gieng über Land,
> Sie hatte drei Würmer in ihrer Hand;
> Der eine war weiß, der andere schwarz, der dritte war roth

Streich den Menschen, (oder das Vieh), den du bedienst. Bey jedem Brauchen schlag ihm auf den Rücken, nämlich beym ersten Brauchen einmal, beym zweyten Brauchen zweymal, beym dritten Brauchen dreymal; und setze den Würmern ihre Zeit, aber nicht weniger, als drey Minuten.

7. Ein gutes Mittel für das Beschrauen.

Bist du beschrauen bis auf deine Haut, bis auf dein Fleisch, bis auf den Bein, so schicke es den falschen Zungen wieder heim.

† † †

154

Das Hemd ausgezogen, und letz angethan, mit den zwey Daumen dreymal auf der Herzgrube angefangen, und unter den Rippen durchgefahren, bis and die Hüfte.

8. Ein gutes Mittel für das Fieber

Guten Morgen, du lieber Donnerstag, nimm dem N. die 77-lei Fieber ab! Ich du lieber Herr Jesu Christ, so nimm du es ihm ab!

† † †

Das brauche man am Donnerstage zum ersten Mal, am Freytage zum zweyten Mal; und am Samstage zum dritten Mal, und jeden Morgen dreymal. Man muß alle Mal den Glauben dazu beten, und darf auch mit niemand reden, bis die Sonne aufgegangen ist. Der Kranke darf auch mit keinem sprechen, und kein Schweinefleisch essen und keine Milch trinken in neun Tagen, und auch während den neun Tagen über kein fließend Wasser gehen.

9. Ein Mittel für die Darmgichter.

Ich warne euch, ihr Darmgichter! Es ist Einer im Gericht; er spricht: Gerecht oder ungerecht. Drum hütet euch, ihr Darmgichter. † † †

10. Ein Mittel, um zu machen, daß ein Hund bleibt, wenn jemand noch nichts gebraucht hat, daß er bleiben soll.

Mach, daß du Blut von dir bekommst; gieb es dem Hunde in etwas zu fressen: so bleibt er. Oder schabe von den vier Tischecken oben am Tisch. Iß aber immer mit dem Messer, mit dem du die Tischecken abgeshabt hast. Gieb das Abgeschabte dem Hunde zu fressen; so bleibt er auch.

11. Ein Winkelruthe zu machen, um Eisen, Erz oder Wasser und dergleichen zu suchen.

Die erste Christnacht, zwischen 11 und 12 Uhr, brich einen jungen Schoß, welcher in einem Jahr gewachsen ist, in den drey höchsten Namen, gegen Sonnenaufgang. Wenn du die Ruthe brauchest, daß du etwas suchest, so brauche sie drey Mal: nämlich nimm die Ruthe, es

muß aber eine Gabel seyn, und nimm in jede Hand ein Theil davon, so daß das eine dicke Theil in die Höhe steht; halt die Ruthe aber nicht ganz fest, schlag das dritte Theil gegen den Grund: so ist das, was du verlangst, auf der Stelle da. Die Worte, die du sagen mußt, wann du die Ruthe brauchest, sind diese:

Du Erzengel Gabriel, ich beschwöre dich bey Gott, dem Allmächtigen, ist hier Wasser oder nicht, so sag es.

✝ ✝ ✝

Suchest du Eisen, dann mußt du auch so sagen; nur mußt du es mit Namen nennen, was du suchest.

12. Ein sehr gutes Mittel für das Herzgesperr' und Anwachsen.

Herzgesperr' und Angewächs, welche von N. Rippen, wie Christus, der Herr, gewichen ist von seiner Krippen.

✝ ✝ ✝

13. Ein gutes Mittel, um sicher im Schießen zu treffens.

Nimm das ✝ Herz von einer ✝ Fledermaus, und lade ein wenig ✝ zwischen die Kugel und das Pulver, so kannst du treffen, was du willst. Die drey höchsten Namen mußt du sagen, wann du anfängst zu laden. Du darfst aber mit dem Sprechen nicht eher fertig seyn, als bis du mit dem Laden zu Ende bist.

14. Ein anderes Mittel, das auch gut ist, um sicher zu schießen.

Thue Blut von einem Maulwurf in den Lauf, zwischen das Pulver und Bley; so wirst du sicher treffen.

15. Mittel, um jemand auszufragen, wann er schläft, und das Anbellen der Hunde zu verhindern.

Wenn man das Herz und den rechten Fuß eines Steinkäuzleins auf jemand legt, der schläft, dann sagt er alles, was man ihn fragt, und was er gethan hat. Thut man die beiden ebengenannten Theile unter die Achseln, so wird man von keinem Hunde angebellt, sondern er verstummt.

16. Noch ein anderes Mittel, um das Anbellen der Hunde zu verhindern.

Wer ein Hundsherz auf der linken Seite trägt, den wird kein Hund anbellen, sondern sie werden alle vor ihm verstummen.

17. Abermal ein Mittel, um das Anbellen der Hunde zu verhindern.

Thue die Pflanze, genannt Hundszunge, unter deine großen Zehen, so verstummen vor dir alle Hunde.

18. Mittel, um ein schwarzes Pferd weiß zu machen.

Das Wasser, darin ein Maulwurf gesotten ist, macht ein schwarzes Pferd weiß, wenn es damit gestrichen oder gewaschen wird.

19. Mittel, um sich gegen Schaden zu sichern.

So man von einem Wolf das rechte Auge in dem rechten Ermel angebunden bey sich trägt, dann geschieht einem kein Schaden.

20. Mittel, um etwas zu erhalten, darum man anhält.

Fünf-Finger-Kraut, davon ein wenig bey sich getragen, wenn jemand von einem Herrn oder Beamten etwas zu erhalten wünscht, dann wird er es gewiß bekommen. Der Saft diese Krautes ist sehr gut für die rothe Ruhr.

21. Mittel, um Fische zu fangen.

Nimm Rosenkörner und Senfkörner, und den Fuß eines Wiesleins und häng es in das Netz, so werden sich gewiß die Fische versammeln.

22. Eisenkraut Veneris. Ein gutes Mittel für mancherley Geschwüre und Auswüchse, und sonstige Leiben.

Die Wurzel von diesem Kraut an den Hals gelegt, heilet die Schlieren oder Geschwüre an demselben, dient auch für due Harnwinde und heilet die Feigwarzen, wenn sein Saft mit Honig in Wasser gekocht, getrunken wird; mach subtil und rein die Dinge, die in der Lunge sind, und macht einen guten Athem; denn es heilet die Lunge. Wenn es

gelegt wird in ein Haus, oder in Weinreben, oder in einem Feldgarten, so wächst es in Menge. Seine Wurzel ist allen denen gut, die Reben pflanzen oder bauen und Bäume ziehen wollen. Junge Kinder, die solches bey sich tragen, lassen sich gut ziehen, lieben alle guten Künste, und werden lustig und fröhlich.

23. Ein sehr gutes Mittel für den kalten und heißen Brand.

Sanct Itorius res, ruf den Rest. Da kam die Mutter Gottes ihm zum Trost; sie reichte ihm ihre schneeweiße Hand, für den heißen und kalten Brand.

† † †

Mach drey Kreuze drüber mit dem Daumen. Alles muß drey mal gebraucht werden, was mit Worten gebraucht wird, und allezeit ein paar Stunden gewartet werden, wenn man eins gebraucht hat, und zum dritten Mal braucht man am andern Tage. Das einzelne N. bedeutet den Vornamen, zwey N. N. aber bedeuten den Vor- und Zunamen desjenigen, für den man braucht. Das ist die Bedeutung der einzelnen N. N. durch das ganze Buch. Ein jeder nehme es wohl in Acht.

24. Ein gutes Mittel für böse Leute, denn für diese ist es kräftig gut.

Dullix, ix, ux. Ja, du kannst nicht über Ponzio; Ponzio ist über Pilato.

† † †

25. Ein sehr gutes Mittel, um die Würmer zu tödten bey den Pferden.

Du mußt dem Pferde seinen Namen nennen, und sagen: Hast due die Würmer, so krig ich dich bey der Stirn. Sie mögen seyn weiß, braun oder roth, so sollen sie alle seyn des Tods.

Du mußt den Gaul beym Kopfe drey Mal schütteln, und am Rücken drey Mal hin und her fahren.

† † †

26. Ein gutes Mittel, den Bolibel in zwey oder drey Malen zu heilen.

Drehe drey Aestchen von einem Kirschbaum, das erste gegen Morgen, das andere gegen Abend, und das dritten gegen Mitternacht. Schneide

drey Stückchen hinten von deinem Hemd, und wickle in ein jedes dieser Stückchen ein Aestchen; alsdann den Bolibel damit ausgekehrt, und hernach unter die Dachtraufe gelegt. Die Enden von dem Aestchen, die in der Wunde herum gerührt waren, werden gegen Mitternacht gelegt, und alsdann auf die Aestchen gehofirt, das heißt, due mußt darauf deine Nothdurst verrichten; alsdann decke es zu, und merk es mit dem Läpchen an dem Aestchen. Hernach muß damit im Bolibel herumgefahren werden, nämlich mit den drey Aestchen.

27. Ein herrliches Mittel für böse Wunden und Brandschäden.

Gottes Wort und Jesu Muttermilch und Christi Blut, ist für alle Wunden und Brandschäden gut.

Es ist das Sicherste, wenn man bey allen Stükken die drey Kreuze mit der Hand oder mit dem Daumen darüber macht. Es sind damit alle Stükke gemeint, wobei die drey Kreuze stehen.

28. Ein sehr gutes Mittel für den Rothlauf, sowohl bey Wunden als auch sonst bei einem wehen Gliede, woran der Rothlauf ist, zu brauchen.

Rothlaufen und der Drach' flogen mit einander über den Bach. Das Rothlaufen vergant; der Drach' verschwand.

† † †

29. Ein Mittel, um Schmerzen zu stillen.

Schneide drey Stöcklein—du mußt aber jedes in einem Schnitt abschneiden—rühre sie in der Wunde herum, wickele sie in ein wenig weiß Papier, und stecke sie an einem warmen Ort.

30. Ein Mittel, um die Warzen zu vertreiben.

Brate Hinkelfüße, und reibe die Warzen damit; hernach grabe sie unter die Dachtraufe.

31. Ein Mittel, um den blauen Husten zu vertreiben.

Schneide drey Büschlein Haare oben vom Wirbel eines Kindes, das seinen Vater sein Lebtage nicht gesehen hat, häng es dem Kinde an, das

den blauen Husten hat, in einem ungebleichten Lappen. Der Faden darf auch nicht gebleicht seyn, mit dem es genähet und angehängt wird.

32. Ein anderes Mittel, den blauen Husten zu vertreiben; welches den Mehrsten geholfen hat, die mit demselben befallen waren.

Stecke dasjenige Kind, das den blauen Husten hat, drey Mal durch einen Bläckbeerstock, ohne beschrauen; der Stock muss aber auf zwey Seiten angewachsen seyn, und du musst es den nämlichen Weg durch den Stock drey Mal stecken, nämlich auf derselben Seite durchstecken, wo du es zum ersten Mal durchgesteckt hast.

33. Ein Mittel, das Kämp-Fieber zu vertreiben

Hänge die folgenden Buchstaben geschrieben, in einen Lappen genäht, an den Hals, bis daß das Fieber sich von selbst verliert:

Abaxa Catabax
Abaxa Catabax
Abaxa Cataba
Abaxa Catab
Abaxa Cata
Abaxa Cat
Abaxa Ca
Abaxa C
Abaxa
Abax
Aba
Ab
A

34. Mittel für die Colik.

Nimm ein halbes Tschill guten Kornbranntewein, stopfe eine Pfeife voll Tobak, rauche die ganze Pfeife voll Rauch all' in den Branttewein, und nimm denselben ein. Dies Mittel hat dem Verfasser von diesem Buch und vielen Andern schon geholfen. Oder zerklopfe eine weisse irdene Pfeife, die schwarz geraucht ist. Dies thut die nämliche Wirkung, wenn man das Geklopfte einnimmt.

35. Ein gutes Mittel für Zahnschmerzen.

Für das Zahnweh nimm eine Nadel, und storre den wehen Zahn damit, daß du Blut bekommst; nimm einen Faden, mach ihn voll Blut von dem wehen Zahn, nimm Essig und Mehl und mach es durch einander, und thue es auf einen Lappen; dann wickele den Lappen um eine Apfelbaumwurzel, winde ihn mit einen Faden sehr fest, und wirf die Wurzel wohl mit Erde zu.

36. Ein gutes Mittel, das Fieber zu vertreiben.

Schreib folgende Worte auf einen Zettel, und wickele den Zettel in breiten Wegrich, und binde es demjenigen auf den Nabel, der das Fieber hat.

Potmat sineat,

Potmat sineat,

Potmat sineat.

37. Ein gutes Mittel, das Blut zu stillen.

Heuf ist der Tag, dass der Schaden geschah. Blut, du sollst stille stehen bis die Jungfrau Maria einen andern Sohn thut gebären.

38. Ein gutes Mittel, alle Tritte und Schritte fest zu machen.

Geht Jesus mit N. N. Er ist mein Haupt; ich bin sein Glied. Drum geht Jesus mit N. N.

† † †

39. Ein sehr gutes Pflaster.

Ich zweiflele sehr, daß solches ein Doktor in America machen kann. Es heilet die Weit-Schwellen, und hat einer Frau ihr wehes Bein geheilt, welche achtzehn Jahre vergebens bey den Doktoren Hülfe suchte.

Nimm zwey Quart Seider,

- ein Pfund Immenwachs,

- ein Pfund Schaaf-Unschlit und

- ein Pfund Rauchtobak.

Alles dieses durch einander gekocht und durchgeseihet.

40. Ein Mittel, gutes Augenwasser zu machen.

Nimm für vier Cents Callinenstein,

- - vier Cents präparirten Kalmen,
- - vier Cents Gewürznägellein,
- ein Tschill Kornbranntewein und
- ein Tschill Wasser.

Dieses alles sein zerstoßen und dann gebraucht. Man muss es aber vorher ins Wasser thun, ehe man es braucht.

41. Ein gutes Mittel, das Blut zu stillen.

Fange an von 50 bis auf 3 zurück zu zählen. Wann du bis an drei kommt dann bist du fertig.

42. Ein anderes sehr gutes Mittel für die Weit-Schwellen

Nimm ein Quart ungelöschten Kalk und zwey Quart Wasser, und gieße es auf den Kalk; dann rühre es um, und laß es über Nacht stehen. Das Häutchen muß von dem Kalk abgenommen, und ein Peint Oel ins Kalkwasser gegossen werden; hernach wird es umgerührt, bis es ein wenig dick wird; alsdann nimm Schweinefett und Wachs, thue alles in eine Pfanne, schmelze es gut, mach Pflaster davon, und lege täglich, oder nur alle zwey Tage, ein frisches auf.

43. Ein Mittel für die fallende Krankheit, wenn man noch nicht ins Feuer oder Wasser gefallen ist.

Man schreibt auf einen Zettel rückwärts: Es ist alles vollbracht! Es wird unbeschrauen angehängt am ersten Freitage im neuen Licht. Das geschriebene wird in ein rothes Scharlachtüchlein gethan und alsdann ein leinenes Tüchlein darüber. Das leinen Tüchlein und der Faden müßen aber ungebleicht sein, und der Faden darf keinen Knoten haben.

† † †

Dieses wird nur einmal auf den Zettel geschrieben.

44. Ein Mittel, Schmerzen zu nehmen.

Nimm den ersten Lumpen, den du das erste Mal um eine Wunde gebunden hast, und leg ihn in Wasser, wo ziemlich Kupferrost hinein gethan ist; rühre aber den Kupferrost nicht eher an, bis due keine Schmerzen mehr zu befürchten hast.

45. Ein Mittel für den Brand

Brand, ich blase dich. Er wird, wie das Feuer von der Sonne, dreimal in einem Athem geblasen.

† † †

46. Eine gute Cur für Zahnweh.

Stich einen Wasen des Morgens vor Sonnenaufgang ganz unbeschrauen auf einigen Platze aus, hauche drey mal darauf und setze ihn geschwind wieder an seinen Platz, aber gerade wie er gestanden.

47. Ein wunderbarliches Stück aus dem Buch Alberti Magni.

Es heißt darin, wenn man einen großen Frosch zu Asche brennt, und dieselbe unter Wasser thut, dann sollen auf einem Platze, wo Haare waren, keine mehr wachsen, wenn derselbe damit bestrichen wird.

48. Noch ein anderes Stück aus dem Buche Alberti Magni.

Wenn man den Stein, den ein Geyer in seinen Knieen hat, findet, und den man findet, wenn man recht darauf sieht, und thut denselben in die Speise zweyer Feinde, so stellt er den Frieden unter ihnen wieder her.

49. Ein Mittel für die Gichter.

Ich gehe auf ein anderes Gericht, das heißt, du gehest auf eines andern Mannes sein Land. Ich knöpfe meine 77erlei Gichter. Du nimmst drey Schüße; in jeden Schuß knöpfst du einen Knopf, Freytags vor Sonnenaufgang, im Abnehmen unbeschrauen.

† † †

Ueber deinen Körper, wo die Gichter sind, machst du die Kreuze. So macht man es bey allen Stücken die man braucht.

50. Ein Mittel für Kopfweh.

Zahmen Bein und Fleisch, wie Christus, im Paradies; der dazu hilft, das sage ich dir N. zur Buße.

† † †

Das sagst du dreymal, jedesmal drey Minuten ungefähr von ein-ander; dann wird sich dein Kopfweh bald legen.

Sollte es aber seyn, daß das Kopfweh durch starkes Getränke ent-standen wäre, oder sonst nicht gleich vergehen wollte, so mußt du alle Minuten den Spruch sagen; welches letztere mit Kopfweh nicht oft der Fall ist.

51. Ein Mittel, Wunden und Schmerzen zu vertreiben.

Wund', du sollst nicht hitzen;
Wund', du sollst nicht schwitzen;
Wund', du sollst nicht wässern,
So wenig, als die Jungfrau Maria einen andern Sohn thut gebären

† † †

52. Ein Stück, daß das Vieh gern wieder nach Haus kommt.

Rupfe vorn zwischen den Hörnern in kleines Zöpfchen Haare aus, mitten vom Rücken eins, und hinten beym Schwanz in der Kutt' eins, und gieb es dem Vieh in Brod zu fressen.

53. Noch ein anderes Stück, daß das Vieh gern wieder nach Haus kommt.

Nimm eine Hand voll Salz, geh auf dein Land, laß das Vieh um einen Stein oder Stumpfen drey mal herum gehen, aber allezeit den nämli-chen Weg, daß heißt, daß du alle drey Mal an das nämliche Ende des Steins oder Stumpfens kommst, an dem du das erste Mal angefangen hast; hernach gieb dem Vieh das Salz auf dem Stein oder Stumpfen zu lecken.

54. Ein Mittel, Glas gut zu leimen.

Nimm gemeinen Käse, wasche ihn wohl aus, und ungelöschten Kalk und Eyerklar, rühre es rechtschaffen durch einander, und gebrauche es. Wenn es recht gemacht wird, so hält es gewiß.

55. Ein gutes Mittel, die Hessenläuse aus dem Waizen zu vertreiben.

Mache Kohlen fein, und aus den feingemachten Kohlen eine Lauge, wälze den Samenwaizen darin herum, dann nimm eine Quart Brunze, thue sie auf ein Buschel Waizen, und laß ihn ein wenig abtrocknen. Wann du die Brunze auf den Waizen gießt, so rühre ihn schön darin herum.

56. Ein Mittel, um zu machen, daß die Kirschen erst um Martini zeitig werden.

Zweige die Reifer auf den Stock eines Maulbeerbaums, so ist dein Verlangen erfüllt.

57. Brenneßel,

Ein Mittel, Furcht und Phantasie zu vertreiben, und zu machen, daß sich die Fische versammeln.

So du dieses Kraut in deiner Hand hältst, mit dem Kraut Millifolia, das ist, Garbe; so bist du sicher vor aller Furcht und Phantasie, wodurch sonst ein Mensch oftmals bethöret wird. Wenn es gemischt wird mit den Saft der Hauswurzel und die Hände damit gesalbt werden, und das Uebrige ins Wasser gelegt wird, darin Fische sind, so versammeln sich die Fische bey den Händen und auch in den Rissen. Wann du die Hand wieder aus dem Wasser heraus ziehst, so verlieren sich die Fische, und kommen wieder an ihren vorigen Ort zurück.

58. Sonnenwirbel.

Ein Mittel, um böse Nachreden zu verhindern, und die Untreue einer Frau zu entdecken.

Die Tugend dieses Krautes ist wunderbarlich, so es gesammelt wird im Zeichen des Löwen, im Monat August, und gewickelt wird in ein

Lorbeerblatt, mit einem Wolfszahn. Trägt es jemand bey sich, zu dem mag niemand etwas Widriges reden, als nur allein friedsame Worte; und so einem ist etwas genommen worden, und man legt solches in der Nacht ihm unter das Haupt, so wird er dessen Gestalt und alle seine Eigenschaften sehen, der es gethan hat. Wenn erwähntes Ding etwa an einen Ort gelegt wird, wo viele Frauen sind, nämlich in eine Kirche, so kann diejenige, die unter ihnen die Ehe gebrochen hat, nicht eher vom Platze gehen, bis es wieder hinweg genommen ist. Das ist bewährt.

59. Ein Mittel für einen wehen Mund.

Hast du die Mundfäul' oder Bräun', so blas' ich dir drey mal meinen Athem ein.

✝ ✝ ✝

60. Die Schetwurzel

Ein Mittel, allen Krieg und Hader zu überwinden und zu enden, und zu machen, daß ein Kranker, wenn er geneset, weint, und wenn er stirbt, mit fröhlicher Stimme singt; wie auch für dunkele Augen oder Scheinen der Augen ein sehr gutes Mittel.

Zu der Zeit, wann die Schwalben Nester machen, oder die Adler nisten, wächset dieses Kraut. So es jemand bey sich trägt, mit einem Maulwurfsherz, der überwindet und endet allen Krieg und Hader. Wenn diese Dinge auf das Haupt eines Kranken gelegt werden, und soll er wieder genesen, so weint er; soll er aber sterben, so singt er mit fröhlicher Stimme. Wann die Schwelwurzeln blühen, soll man sie stoßen und sieden; hernach das Wasser in ein Geschirr thun, und es wieder ans Feuer setzen und wohl schäumen. So es dann einen Sud gethan hat, so siehe es durch ein Tuch, und behalte es. Wer nun dunkele Augen oder Scheinen der Augen hat, der streiche es darin, und seine Augen werden ihm klar und gut werden.

61. Ein sehr gutes und gewisses Stück, einige Schußblatter am Auge zu heilen.

Nimm einen schmutzigen Teller—hast du keinen, so mach einen; denn der, wo du für brauchst, hat in einer Minute schon nicht mehr so große Schmerzen. Du mußt die Seite des Tellers gegen das Auge halten, davon man ist. Wahrend der Zeit, daß du den Teller vor das Auge hältst, mußt du sagen:

Schmutziger Teller, ich druck' dich;
Schußblatter, duck dich.

† † †

62. Ein Mittel, um zu bewirken, daß die Hinkel viel Eyer legen.

Nimm Hasendreck, stoß ihn fein, menge ihn unter Kleye, mach die Kleye naß, daß sie klumpig wird, und gieb es den Hühnern allezeit zu fressen; so legen sie viel Eyer.

63. Was man sprechen muß, wenn man Winkels oder Glücksruthen macht.

Wenn man Winkel- oder Glücksruthen macht, so bricht man sie, wie vorn gemeldet, und sagt, während man sie macht, und ehe man sie braucht: Glücksruthe, behalt deine Macht, behalt deine Kraft, wozu dich Gott verordnet hat.

† † †

64. Ein Mittel, den Wurm zu vertreiben.

Wurm, ich beschwöre dich bey dem lebendigen Gott, daß du sollst meiden dieses Blut und dieses Fleisch, gleichwie Gott, der Herr, den Richter wird meiden, der das Urtheil unrecht spricht, und es doch hätte recht sprechen können.

† † †

65. Ein gutes Mittel für die Schwindsucht.

Schwindsucht, ich gebiete dir aus dem Bein ins Fleisch, aus dem Fleisch in die Haut, aus der Haut in den weiten Wald.

† † †

66. Ein Mittel, den Brand zu stillen.

Es giengen drey heilige Männer über Land;
Sie segneten die Hiße und den Brand;
Sie segneten ihn, daß er nicht einfrißt;
Sie segneten ihn, daß er ihn ausfrißt.

✝ ✝ ✝

67. Ein Mittel für den Schlangenbiß.

Gott hatt' Alles erschaffen, und alles war gut;
Alles du allein, Schlange, seyest verflucht;
Verflucht sollst du seyn und dein Gift.

✝ ✝ ✝

Zing, zing, zing!

68. Ein Mittel für böse Hunde.

Hund, halt deinem Mund auf die Erden,
Mich hat Gott erschaffen, dich hat er lassen werden.

✝ ✝ ✝

Dies macht du nach der Gegend, wo ungefähr der Hund ist; denn du mußt die drey Kreuze machen nach dem Hunde zu, und er darf dich nicht erst sehen, und du mußt auch erst den Spruch sagen.

69. Ein Mittel für hohle Küh-Hörner.

Bohre ein Loch in das Horn, das hohl ist, und melke von der nämlichen Kuh Milch, und spritze sie in das Horn. Dies ist die allerbeste Kur.

70. Ein sehr gutes Mittel für die Batz.

Bey jedem Brauchen streichst du das Pferd drey Mal, und führst es auch drey Mal herum gegen der Sonne mit dem Kopf, und sagst: Der Heilige sagt: Joseph gieng über einen Acker; da fand er drey Würmlein; das eine war schwarz, das andere war braun, das dritte war roth: sollst sterben, gehen todt.

✝ ✝ ✝

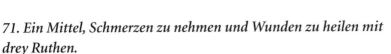

71. Ein Mittel, Schmerzen zu nehmen und Wunden zu heilen mit drey Ruthen.

Mit dieser Ruth' und Christi Blut,
Nehm' ich den Schmerz und Eiterwuth.

† † †

Merke es wohl: du mußt einen jungen Schuß (ein Hötzchen) nach Sonnenaufgang un einem Schnitt abschneiden, und aus diesem jungen Schuß drey Hölzerchen machen; dann mußt du sie in der Wunde herum rühren, eins nach dem andern. Wann du sie in der Hand hast, so nimm das auf der rechten Seite zuerst. Bey allen Stükken in diesem Buch, muß jedes drey Mal gebraucht werden, wenn auch die drey Kreuze nicht dabey stehen. Was mit Worten gebraucht wird, jedes eine halbe Stunde von einander; das letzte Mal übernacht. Obengemeldete Hölzer wickele in weis Papier, und stecke sie an einem warmen Ort.

72. Ein herrliches Mittel für Feibel und Darmgichter:

Jerusalem, du Jüdische Stadt,
Die Christus, der Herrn, geboren hat,
Du sollst werden zu Wasser und zu Blut;
Das ist dem N. für Feibel, Würmer und Darmgichter gut.

† † †

73. Ein Mittel für Schwachheit der Glieder.

Von Birken die Knospen, oder die mittelste Rinde von den Wurzeln genommen, das heißt, wann die Birken Knospen haben, das giebt auch einen sehr guten Thee für Schwachheit der Glieder; nur ist zu merken, daß wenn man vierzehn Tage vom Birken-Thee getrunken hat, man alsdann wieder eine Weile warten muß, ehe man wieder davon trinkt, und während den vierzehn Tagen, dass man von dem Thee trinkt, muß man ein paar Tage damit abwechseln, und anstatt den Thee Wasser trinken.

74. Noch ein anderes Mittel für Schwachheit der Glieder.

Nimm Bedonien und Johanniskraut, und thue es in guten Kornbranntewein. Davon des Morgens nüchtern getrunken, das ist sehr

heilsam und gut. Von Weiß-Eicheln einen Thee gemacht, ist auch sehr gut für Schwachheit der Glieder.

75. Ein gutes Mittel für große und kleine Mäuse.

Bey jeder Frucht, die du in die Scheuer bringest, mußt du sagen, so bald du die drey ersten Garben in dieselbe thust: Ratten und Mäuse, die drey Garben geb' ich euch, daß ihr keinen von meinem Waizen beißt. Du mußt von jeder Sorte Frucht den Namen nennen, die du brauchst.

76. Ein Mittel, einiges Gewächs an einem Gaul vertreiben zu können.

Du nimmst einen Knochen, wo du ihn findest, darfst ihn aber nicht suchen, und reibst damit dem Pferde das Gewächs; es muß aber im abnehmenden Licht geschehen. Das Gewächs wird alsdann ganz gewiß vergehen. Leg aber den Knochen wieder, wie er gelegen.

77. Ein Mittel, um zu machen, daß Pferde wieder fressen, besonders anwendbar, wann sie auf der Landstraße sind, und mit diesem Uebel befallen werden.

Mach dem Pferd, das nicht fressen will, das Maul auf und schlag ihm drey Mal inwendig an den Gaumen. Das hilft gewiß, daß es sogleich wieder fressen und weiter gehen wird.

78. Ein Mittel, gutes Augenwasser zu machen.

Nimm für 11 Pens weißen Vitriol und eine Unze Bley-Zucker, löse dieses auf mit Rosmarien-Oel, und thue es in eine ziemlich große Bottel; alsdann fülle sie mit Rosenwasser auf.

79. Ein Mittel, um zu machen, daß Diebe oder Diebinnen müßen stehen bleiben, und weder vor- noch rückwärts gehen können.

Es ist am besten, daß man überall um Sachen, die man aus diesem Buch für das Stehenbleiben braucht, herum geht.

O Petrus, o Petrus! nimm von Gott die Gewalt: Was ich binden werde mit dem Band der Christen-Hand, alle Diebe oder Diebinnen,

sie mögen seyn groß oder klein, jung oder alt, so sollen sie von Gott gestellet seyn, und keiner keinen Tritt mehr weder vor oder hinter sich gehen, bis ich sie mit meinen Augen sehe, und mit meiner Zunge Urlaub gebe, sie zählen mir denn zuvor alle Stein', die zwischen Himmel und Erde seyn, alle die Regentropfen, alles Laub und Gras. Dieses bitt' ich meinen Feinden zur Buss'.

† † †

Bete den Glauben und das Vater unser.—Dieses vom Stehen machen bleiben, sagt man drey Mal hinter einander. Wenn der Dieb soll leben bleiben, so darf auf ihn die Sonne nicht scheinen, bis du ihn hast los gemacht; welches du auf zweyerley Art thun mußt, wo es nicht doppelt gemeldet ist, wie man den Dieb los macht. Das erste ist: heiß ihn in Sanct Johannis Namen fortgehen; das andere heißt: mit welchen Worten ihr seyd gestellt, mit diesen seyd ihr los. Wenn's nur einer ist, oder ein Weibsbild, sagt man du.

† † †

80. Ein sehr gutes Mittel für Schweining der Pferde.

Nimm ein Pfund alten Speck, schneide ihn klein, thue ihn in eine Pfanne, brate ihn sehr aus, thue eine Hand voll Fischwürmer, ein Tschill Haber und drey Löfel voll Salz dazu, brate alles recht schwarz, und seihe es durch ein Tuch; hernach thue ein Tschill Schmierseife, ein halbes Tschill Kornbranntewein, ein halbes Tschill Essig und ein halbes Tschill Buben-Brunze darunter, rühre es durch einander, und schmiere damit das Glied überzwerg, den dritten, sechsten und neunten Tag nach dem neuen Licht, und wärme es ein mit einem eichenen Bord.

81. Ein gutes Mittel, Molaßes zu machen.

Nimm Kirbsen, (oder Kürbiß) koch sie, drück die Brühe heraus, nimm die Brühe und koch sie. Du brauchst sonst nichts dazu. Der Verfasser dieses Buch, Johann Georg Hohman, hat von diesem Molaßes gegessen, und er meinte, es wäre vom rechten Molaßes gewesen, bis es die Leute ihn sagten. Man kocht obengemeldete Kirbsen-Brühe so lange, bis sie so dick ist, wie Molaßes.

82. *Anweisung, wie man gutes Bier macht.*

Nimm eine Hand voll Hopfen, fünf oder sechs Gallons Wasser, ungefähr drey Eßlöffel voll gelben Ingwer (oder Imber) und eine halbe
Gallon Molaßes; und alle das andere, nämlich den Imber, &c., thust du
ins Wasser, und seihest es in einen Zuber auf den Molaßes; dann ist es
gutes Bier.

83. *Ein gutes Mittel für die fallende Krankheit.*

Nimm eine Turteltaube, schneid ihr den Hals ab, und gieb dem, der
die fallende Krankheit hat, das Blut ein.

84. *Noch ein anderes Mittel, dass das Vieh wieder nach Haus kommt.*

Gieb dem Vieh aus deinem Kochhafen zu fressen, so kommt es allezeit
wieder nach Haus.

85. *Ein sehr gutes Mittel, Schweren zu heilen.*

Koch weiße Lilien-Zwiebeln in süßen Rahm, und leg es pflasterweise
auf die Schweren. Die nämliche Wirkung thut auch das Eberkraut.

86. *Ein Mittel, Wunden zu heilen.*

Nimm Kalbsknochen, brenn sie, daß du Pulver daraus machen kannst,
und streie davon in die Wunde. Dies Pulver läßt kein faules Fleisch in
der Wunde werden; es ist eine überaus gute Sache zum Heilen.

87. *Ein Mittel, aus Papier Oel zu machen, das sehr dienlich für die Augen seyn soll.*

Es berichtete mich ein Deutschländer: weißes Papier, zwey Bogen, am
Licht zu verbrennen; dann gäbe es drey Tropfen-Wasser, die alle Fehler
am Auge wegnähmen, wenn man es damit schmiere; und man könnte
auch einiges Auge damit heilen, wenn nur der Augapfel noch ganz
wäre.

88. Ein Mittel, Filzläuse zu vertreiben

Nimm Kapuziner-Pulver, menge es unter Schweinefett, und schmiere dich damit.—Noch ein anderes: Steide Ochsenkranz, und wasche die Stelle damit, wo sich das Ungeziefer aufhält.

89. Ein Mittel, um zu machen, daß das allerschlechteste Papier nicht fließt, wann man darauf schreiben will.

Man muß das Papier in gestoßenen Alaun tunken; und ich, Hohman, will hernach ein wenig Wasser auf den Alaun gießen, und alsdann das Papier damit naß machen. Dann will ich sehen, ob man nicht darauf schreiben kann.

90. Ein sehr gutes Mittel für den reißenden Stein.

Der Verfasser dieses Buchs, Johann Georg Hohman, brauchte dieses Mittel, und er bekam Hülfe. Ein anderer Mann konnte nirgends bey den Doctoren Hülfe erlangen: er bediente sich alsdann dieses Mittels, nämlich: er aß alle Morgen nüchtern sieben Pfirschingsteine, und er erhielt Hülfe; weil er aber den reißenden Stein sehr stark hatte, so mußte er es immer thun. Ich, Hohman, habe es aber nur etliche Wochen gethan. Ich spüre dann und wann noch ein wenig davon; aber ich hatte es so stark, daß ich die mehrste Zeit laut jammerte, wann ich das Wasser ließ.—Dem lieben Gott und dem Weibsbild sey es tausend Mal gedankt, daß ich das Mittel von ihr erfahren habe.

91. Ein gutes Mittel für denjenigen, der sein Wasser nicht halten kann.

Nimm eine Schweinsblase, brenn sie zu Pulver, und nimm es ein.

92. Ein Mittel, um ein Gewächs zu vertreiben im zunehmenden Mond.

Brauch dieses: Sieh gerade über das Gewächs nach dem Mond, und sag: Was zunimmt, nimmt zu; was abnimmt, nimmt ab. Dieses mußt du drey Mal in einem Athem sagen.

93. Ein gutes Mittel, die Scherrmäuse oder Maulwürfe zu vertreiben.

Thue ungelöschten Kalk in die Löcher, so vergehen sie.

94. Ein gutes Mittel, Fell von den Augen zu bringen.

Grabe die Wurzel Bissebet auf Bartholomäus vor Sonnenaufgang, acht oder fünf Wurzeln; mach, daß du über dem Graben das Ende von der Wurzel bekommst; mach, daß du einen Lappen bekommst, und einen Faden, der noch nicht im Wasser war; und gieb ja Acht, daß der Faden keinen Knoten bekommt, mit dem die Wurzel in den Lappen genähet wird; häng es an, bis das Fell vergangen ist. Der Bändel, mit dem es angehängt wird, darf auch nich im Wasser gewesen seyn.

95. Ein gutes Mittel für übles Gehör und Sausen der Ohren, wie auch für Zahnweh.

Baumwolle mit etlichen Tropfen distilirten Kampfer-Oel angefeuchtet, und hernach auf den schmerzhaften Zahn gelegt; das lindert sehr die Schmerzen. Wenn man es in die Ohren thut, so starkt es das Gehör, und vertreibt das Sausen und Brausen in denselben.

96. Ein gutes Mittel, um zu machen, daß den Kindern die Zähne wachsen ohne Schmerzen.

Siede das Gehirn eines Hasen, und reib den Kindern das Zahnfleisch damit; so wachsen ihnen die Zähne ohne Schmerzen.

97. Ein Mittel für das Erbrechen und den Durchlauf der Menschen.

Nimm Nägelein, mach sie sein; nimm Brod, weich es in rothen Wein ein, und iß es; so wird es bald besser.—Kannst die Nägelein aufs Brod thun.

98. Ein Mittel, Brandschaden zu heilen.

Fahnenkraut geklopft, und mit dem Saft die Stelle geschmiert, die man sich verbrannt hat; das heilt ziemlich schnell. Es ist aber am besten,

wenn man den obengemeldeten Saft auf einen Lappen streicht, und ihn dann auflegt.

99. *Eine besonders gute Kur für schwache Glieder des Leibes, Reinigung des melancholischen Geblüts, Stärkung des Hauptes und Herzens, den Schwindel, u. s. w.*

Morgens nüchtern zwey Tröpflein in einem Löffel voll weißen Wein eingenommen; es ist auch wider Gebresten der Mutter gut, und vertreibet auch das Bauchgrimmen. Dieses sind also die Näglein, welche in den Stohren gekauft werden, Es ist dies auch gut für den kalten Magen, und es stärket und erwärmet denselben, und stillet das Erbrechen. Ein paar Tropfen in ein wenig Baumwolle gegossen, und auf die schmerzhaften Zähne gelegt, stillet die Schmerzen. Das Nägleinöl wird auf diese Weise distilirt: Nimm ein gutes Theil Gewürz-Näglein, stoße sie zu einem dicken Pulver, gieße eine halbe Unze Wasser darüber, laß es also vier Tage in warmen Sand stehen, distilire es hernach aus einem zinnenen oder kupfernen Kolben, und sondere das Oel mit Baumwolle oder Separirglas davon ab.

100. *Ein sehr gutes Mittel für die rothe Ruhr und den Durchlauf.*

Gebrauch für diese Plage: Moos von Bäumen, siede es in rothem Wein, und gieb es demjenigen zu trinken, der mit dieser Krankheit befallen ist.

101. *Ein sehr gutes Mittel für Zahnschmerzen.*

Der Verfasser diese Buchs, Hohman, hat sich mehr als sechzig Mal die allerheftigsten Zahnschmerzen mit diesem Mittel vertrieben; und unter den sechzig Malen, daß er es brauchte, hat es nur einmal nicht geholfen. Nimm nämlich blauen Vitriol. Wann die Schmerzen anfangen, so stecke ein Stückchen davon in den wehen Zahn, speye alles Wasser aus, aber nicht zu oft; sonst weiß ich nicht, ob es auch bey Zähnen hilft, die nicht hohl sind; aber ich denke, wenn man es auch an Zähne nimmt, die nicht hohl sind, es hilft auch.

102. Ein Warnungsmittel für schwangere Weiber.

Schwangere Weiber müßen sich besonders vor dem Kampfer hüten; auch muß man denjenigen Weibern keinen Kampfer geben, die den Geruch desselben nicht leiden können, wann sie die Mutterkrankheit haben.

103. Ein gutes Mittel für den Biß eines tollen Hundes.

Ein gewisser Herr Valentin Kettering, von Dauphin Caunty, hat dem Senat von Pennsylvanien ein Mittel bekannt gemacht, welches den Biß wüthender Thiere ohnfehlbar heilen soll. Er sagt, es sey bey seinen Vorfahren in Deutschland schon vor 250 Jahren, und von ihm selbst, seitdem er sich in den Vereinigten Staaten befindet, welches über 60 Jahre ist, gebraucht, und immer als untrüglich befunden worden. Er macht es blos aus Liebe zur Menschheit bekannt. Dieses Mittel besteht aus dem Kraut, welches er Chickweed nennt. Es ist eine Sommer-Pflanze, und bey den Schweizern und Deutschen unter den Namen: Gauchheil, rother Meyer oder rother Hühnerdarm, bekannt. In England nennt man es: rother Pimpernel; und in der Botanik heißt es: Anagellis Phönicea. Es muß in Junius, wann es in voller Blüthe ist, gesammelt, im Schatten getrocknet, und dann zu Pulver gemacht werden. Hievon ist die Dosis für ein erwachsene Person, ein kleiner Eßlöffel voll, oder an Gewicht ein Drachme, und ein Scrupel auf einmal in Bier oder Wasser; für Kinder ist die Dosis eben so groß; allein es wird zu drey verschiedenen Zeiten gegeben. Wenn es für Thiere grün gebraucht werden soll, so schneide und vermische man es mit Kleye oder anderm Futter. Wenn man es Schweinen geben will, so mache man das zu Pulver gemachte Kraut mit Teig zu kleinen Kugeln. Man kann es auch auf Butterbrod, Honig oder Molaßes, u. s. w. essen.

Der Ehrwürdige Henrich Mühlenberg sagt, daß man von dem Pulver diese Krautes in Deutschland 30 Grau schwer des Tages viermal gebe, und so eine Woche lang mit einer geringern Dosis fortfahre, und die Wunde mit der gekochten Brühe dieses Krautes wasche, und auch Pulver hinein streue. Herr Kettering sagt, daß er immer nur eine Dosis mit den glücklichsten Erfolg gegeben habe.

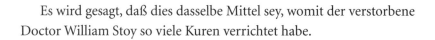

Es wird gesagt, daß dies dasselbe Mittel sey, womit der verstorbene Doctor William Stoy so viele Kuren verrichtet habe.

104. Ein sehr gutes Mittel, den schnellen Wachsthum der Schaaf-Wolle zu befördern, und viele Krankheiten der Schaafe, zu verhüten.

William Ellies, in seinem vortrefflichen Buch über die Englische Schaafszucht, erzählt folgendes: Ich kenne einen Pächter, der hatte eine Heerde Schaafe, die viele und grobe Wolle trug. Dieser nahm wahr, daß er deswegen viele Wolle erhalten, weil er, sobald ein Schaaf geschoren war, dasselbe über und über mit Buttermilch gewaschen. Denn man muß wissen, daß von der Buttermilch nicht nur den Schaafen alle in die Wolle, sondern auch jedem Thier die Haare stark wachsen. Wer übrigens keine Buttermilch bey den der Hand hat, der kann auch andere Milch nehmen, und sie mit Salz und Wasser vermischen, und die eben geschornen Schaafe damit einreiben. Ich versichere, daß beym rechten Gebrauch dieses Mittels zugleich auch die Schaaf-Läuse mit ihrer Brut vertilgt werden. Es heilet auch alle Raute oder Krätze, hindert die anfallende Kälte, und die Wolle wächset davon schnell und dick.

105. Für den kalten Brand ein probates Pflaster

Nimm Fett, worin Küchlein gebacken sind, ein Tschill voll; sechs Eyer in glühender Asche gesotten, bis sie recht hart sind; nimm den Dotter von den Eyern, brate sie in obengemeldetem Fett, bis sie recht schwarz sind; brate eine Hand voll Rauten mit, und seihe es hernach durch ein Tuch. Wann alles fertig ist, dann kühle es mit einem Tschill voll Baumöl ab. Das beste ist, wenn es soll recht seyn, daß das Pflaster für eine Mannsperson von einer Weibsperson, und das für eine Weibsperson von einer Mannsperson gemacht werde.

106. Ein Mittel, recht gutes Pflaster zu machen.

Nimm Wermuth, Rauten, Medeln, Schaafrippen, spitzigen Wegrich und Immenwächs, von einem so viel als vom andern, vom Immenwachs aber ein wenig mehr, und vom Unschlit, welches auch dazu muß,

und ein wenig Terpentin-Spirit. Dieses alles in einen Hafen gethan, gekocht und durchgeseihet; dann ist es fertig.

107. Noch ein anderes Mittel, gut für den Bolibel.

Nimm Terpentin, reib ihn, streiche ihn mit deiner Hand dem Pferde in die Wunde, und brat ihn mit einem heißen Eisen hinein, dann nimm Klauenoder Gänsfett, und brat es drey Tage nach einander in den Bolibel, den letzten Freytag im letzten Viertel.

108. Abermal ein Mittel, das Blut zu stillen.

Ich geh' durch einen grünen Wald,
Da waren drey Brunnen, die waren kühl und kalt;
    Der erst heißet Muth,
    Der zweyte heißet gut,
    Der dritte heißet still' das Blut.
    ✝ ✝ ✝

109. Noch ein gewisses Mittel, das Blut zu stillen und Wunden zu heilen, sowohl bey Menschen als Vieh.

Auf Christi Grab wachsen drey Rosen; die erst ist gütig, die andere ist nach Herrschen viel. Blut steh still, und Wunde heile.

Was für Menschen zu brauchen ist in diesem Buch, das kann auch für das Vieh gebraucht werden.

110. So ein Mensch die Mund- und Durchfäule hat, spreche man folgendes; es hilft gewiß.

Job zog über Land, der hatt den Stab in seiner Hand; da begegnete ihm Gott der Herr, und sprach zu ihm: Job, warum trauerst du so sehr. Er sprach: Ach Gott, warum sollt' ich nicht trauern? Mein Schlund und mein Mund will mir abfaulen. Da sprach Gott zu Job: Dort in jenem Thal, da fließt ein Brunn, der heilet dir N. N. dein' Schlund und dein' Mund, im Namen Gottes des Vaters, des Sohnes und des Heiligen Geistes. Amen.

Dieses sprich dreymal des Morgens und des Abends; und wann es heißt: "der heilet dir," so bläst man dem Kinde dreymal in den Mund.

111. Ein Mittel, einen rechtmäßigen Prozeß zu gewinnen.

Es heißt, wenn jemand eine rechtmäßige Sache auszumachen hätte bey der Law, und nähme vom allergrößten Salbey, und thäte die Namen der zwölf Apostel auf die Blätter schreiben, und legte solches in die Schuh; ehe er ins Courthaus gienge; so würde er alles gewinnen.

112. Ein Mittel für das Aufblähen des Viehs.

Zu Deisch brich nicht Fleisch, sondern zu Deisch. In währenden Sagen fahre über den Rückgrad mit deiner Hand.

† † †

Anmerkung

Für alles, was man braucht, legt man die Hand auf die bloße Haut, zu der Zeit, wann man braucht.

113. Noch ein Mittel, um auf eine leichte Art Fische zu fangen.

In eine Gefäß von weißem Glas wird gethan: Ziebeth und flüßiges Biebergail, von jedem neun Gran; Aalfett, vier Loth; ungesalzene frische Butter, acht Loth. Man vermache das Gefäß, stelle es neun oder zehn Tage an die Sonne, oder an eine gemäßigte Wärme, und rühre die Composition mit einem kleinen Span um, damit alles unter einander komme.

Gebrauch.

1. Wenn man sich der Angel bedient.

   Man befeuchtet mit dieser Composition die kleinen Thierchen oder Insecten, welche man an die Angel hängen will, und verwahrt sie dann in einer Blase, die man zu sich in die Tasche steckt.

2. Wenn man sich des Garns bedient.

   Man verfertigt Kügelchen aus der Grumme des neugebakkenen Brodes, und taucht sie in die Composition, befestigt sie dann mit Zwirn an verschiedenen Orten inwendig im Garn, und wirft dieses ins Wasser aus.

3. Wenn man die Fische blos mit der Hand fangen will.

Man bestreicht die Beine oder Stiefel mit der Composition, und geht so ins Wasser an einem Ort, wo man sie anzutreffen glaubt. Die Fische werden sich bald in großer Anzahl einfinden.

114. Ein sehr gutes und sicheres Mittel für den Rheumatismus.

Für das Stück allein ist schon ein bis zwey Thaler von Leuten bezahlt worden; es ist das sicherste und beste Mittel für den Rheumatismus. Es sey also hiemit zu wissen: Du mußt Tuch nehmen, das noch nicht im Wasser war, und der Bändel, mit dem es angehängt wird, so wie auch der Faden, mit dem es genähet wird, dürfen ebenfalls noch nicht im Wasser gewesen seyn; auch darf der Faden, mit dem es genähet wird, keinen Knoten bekommen. Der obengemeldete Bändel und Faden müßen von einem Kinde gesponnen seyn, das noch keine sieben Jahre alt, oder nicht älter als sieben Jahre ist. Angehängt wird es erstlich unbeschrauen am letzten Freytage im alten Licht, und du betest gleich dazu das Vater unser und den Glauben. Den Verfasser von diesem Brief ist auch gelehrt worden, daß wann der Brief fertig zusammen gelegt ist, drey Enden von demselben auf einer Seite bey einander seyn müßen.—Was nun folgt, wird nur in untengemeldetem Brief geschrieben:

Daß walte Gott der Vater, Sohn und Heiliger Geist. Amen. Gleich gesucht und gesucht; das gebeut dir Gott der Herr bey dem ersten Menschen, so Gott auf Erden geliebet möge werden. Gleich gesucht und gesucht; das gebeut dir Gott der Herr bey dem Evangelisten Lukas und dem heiligen Apostel Paulus. Gleich gesucht und gesucht; das gebeut dir Gott der Herr bey den zwölf Bothen. Gleich gesucht und gesucht; das gebeut dir Gott der Herr bey dem ersten Menschen, so Gott geliebet möge werden. Gleich gesucht und gegicht; das gebeut dir Gott der Herr bey den lieben heiligen Vätern, so in göttlicher, heiliger Schrift gemacht werden. Gleicht gesucht und gegicht; das gebeut dir Gott der Herr bey den lieben heiligen Engeln, und väterlichen, göttlichen Allmacht und himmlischen Vertrauen und Bleiben. Gleich gesucht und gegicht; das gebeut dir Gott der Herr bey dem feurigen Ofen, der durch Gottes Segen ist erhalten worden. Gleich gesucht und

180

gegicht; das gebeut dir Gott der Herr, bey aller Kraft und Macht, bey dem Propheten Jonas, der drey Tage und Nächte in's Wallfisches Bauch durch Gottes Segen ist erhalten worden. Gleich gesucht und gegicht; das gebeut dir Gott der herr bey aller der Kraft und Macht, so aus göttlicher Demüthigkeit gehen, und bis in alle Ewigkeit, also † N. † keinen Schaden thun an deinem ganzen Leib', es seyen gleich das reißende Gicht, oder das gelbe Gicht, oder weiß Gegicht, oder roth Gegicht, oder schwarz Gegicht, wie Gichter alle mit Namen genennet mögen werden, sie dir † N. † keinen Schaden thun an deinem ganzen Lieb', es sey gleich am Haupt, am Hals, am Herzen, am Bauch, an vielen Adern, Armen, Beinen, Augen, Zung', und an allen Adern an deinem ganzen Lieb' nichts schaden. Das schreibe ich dir † N. † mit diesen Worten: im Namen Gottes des Vaters, des Sohns und des Heiligen Geistes. Amen. Gott segne es. Amen.

Anmerkung.

Wenn jemand für einen Andern einen Brief schreibt, so muß der Vorname hinein geschrieben werden. Merke, wo das einzelne N. steht in obengemeldetem Brief für den Rheumatismas.

115. Ein gutes Mittel, die Bienenstöcke von Würmern zu befreyen.

Mit geringer Mühe und für einen Viertel-Thaler kann man ein ganzes Jahr die Bienen-Stöcke gänzlich von Würmern befreyen. Man kauft nämlich in der Apotheke, und das in allen Apotheken zu haben ist, dieses Pulver: Pensses Blum; welches den Immen im Geringsten nicht schadet. Der Gebrauch desselben ist also: Nimm für einen Immenstock eine kleine Messerspitze voll in guten Kornbranntewein, und thue solches in ein fingerdickes und grosses Gläschen; mach oben am Immenkord ein Loch, und schütte das in Branntewein eingeweichte Pulver hinein.

Niemand wird diesen Gebrauch für Immen, nämlich was hier gemeldet ist in diesem Buch für die Würmer, in keinem einzigen andern Buch finden, das noch zu einiger Zeit für die Immen herausgegeben wurde. Solch ein Gläschen voll wird auf einmal in einen Immenstock gethan; das Loch muß aber so gemacht werden, daß man es gut hinein schütten kann.—Für einen Viertel-Thaler von dem obenerwähnten Pulver ist für einen ziemlichen Immen-Stock hinlänglich.

116. Ein Mittel, eine Waffensalbe zu machen, welche jedes Gewehr, es sey von Stahl oder Eisen, für den Rost bewahrt.

Man nehme zwey Loth Bärenfett, ein Loth Dachsschmalz, ein Loth Schlangenfett, zwey Loth Mandelnöl und ein halbes Loth fein pulverisirten Indigo, welches alles in einem neuen Geschirr über dem Feuer zerlassen, wohl umgerührt, und hernach in einem Geschirr verwährt wird. Wann man es nun gebrauchen will, so nimmt man einer welschen Nuß groß auf einen wollenen Lappen, und bestreicht das Gewehr damit; so wird es vor allem Rost wohl bewahrt bleiben.

117. Ein Mittel, einen Tocht zu machen, der nie verbrennt.

Mann nimmt zwey Loth Aspect, und siedet es in einer Quart scharf gemachter Lauge zwey Stunden lang, dann die Lauge abgegossen, das Ueberbleibende aber durch drey- oder viermal aufgegossenes Regenwasser gereiniget, nachher in einem Mörsel wohl abgegossen, sodann einen Tocht davon gemacht, und an der Sonne getrocknet; so ist er fertig.

118. Morgengebet, welches, wenn man über Land gehet, sprechen muß, so alsdann den Menschen vor allem Unglück bewahret.

Ich, (hier nenne deinen Namen) heut' will ich ausgehen; Gottes Steg und Weg will ich gehen, wo Gott auch gegangen ist, und unser lieber Herr Jesus Christus, und unsere herzliche Jungfrau mit ihren herzlieben Kindlein, mit ihren sieben Ringen, mit ihren wahren Dingen. O du mein lieber Herr Jesu Christ, ich bin eigen dein, daß mich kein Hund beiß', kein Wolf beiß', kein Mörder beschleich; behüt' mich, mein Gott, vor dem jähen Tod'. Ich stehe in Gottes Hand; da bind ich mich; in Gottes Hand bin ich gebunden durch unsers Herr Gottes heilige fünf Wunden, daß mir alle und jede Gewehr' und Wassen so wenig schaden, als der heiligen Jungfrau Maria ihrer Jungfrauschaft mit ihrer Gunst, mit ihrem Gesponst Jesu. Bete drey Vater unser und drey Ave Maria und den Glauben.

119. Ein wahre und approbirte Kunst, in Feuersbrünsten und Pestilenz-Zeit nützlich zu gebrauchen.

Sey willkommen, du feuriger Gast! greif nicht weiter, als was du hast. Dies zähl' ich dir, Feuer, zu einer Buß', im Namen Gottes des Vaters, Sohnes und Heiligen Geistes.

Ich gebiete dir, Feuer, bey Gottes Kraft, die alles thut und alles schafft, du wollest stille stehen, und nicht weiter gehen; so wahr Christus stund am Jordan, da ihn taufte Johannes, der heilige Mann.

Das zähle ich dir, Feuer, zu einer Buß', im Namen der Heiligen Dreyfaltigkeit.

Ich gebiete dir, Feuer, bey der Kraft Gottes, du wollest legen deine Flammen; so wahr Maria behielt ihre Jungfrauschaft vor allen Damen, die sie behielt, so keusch und rein: d'rum stell', Feuer, dein Wüthen ein.

Dies zähl' ich dir, Feuer, zu einer Buß', im Namen der Allerheiligsten Dreyfaltigkeit.

Ich gebiete dir, Feuer, du wollest legen deine Gluth, bey Jesu Christi theures Blut, das Er für uns vergossen hat, für unsre Sünd' und Missethat.

Das zähle ich dir, Feuer, zu einer Buß', im Namen Gottes des Vaters, Sohns und Heiligen Geistes.

Jesus Nazarenus, ein König der Juden, hilf uns aus diesen Feuersnöthen, und bewahr' dies Land und Gränz' vor aller Seuch' und Pestilenz.

Anmerkungen.

Dieses hat ein Christlicher Zigeuner-König aus Egypten erfunden. Anno 1714, den 10ten Juny, wurden in dem Königreich Preußen sechs Zigeuner mit dem Strange hingerichtet; der siebente aber, ein Mann von achtzig Jahren, sollte den 16ten desselben Monats mit dem Schwerdt hingerichtet werden. Weil aber, ihm zum Glück, eine unversehene Feuersbrunst entstanden, so wurde der alte Zigeuner losgelassen, und zu dem Feuer geführt, allda seine Kunst zu probiren; welches er auch mit großer Verwunderung der Anwesenden gethan, die Feuersbrunst in einer halben Viertel-Stunde versprochen, daß solche ganz und gar

ausgelöschet und aufgehöret hat; worauf ihn dann, nach abgelegter Probe, weil er auch solches an Tag gegeben, das Leben geschenket und auf freyen Fuß gestellt worden. Solches ist auch von einer Königlich Preussischen Regierung, und dem General-Superintendenten zu Königsberg, für gut erkannt, und in öffentlichen Druck gegeben worden.

Zuerst gedruckt zu Königsberg, in Preußen, bey Alexander Baumann, Anno 1715.

Wer diesem Brief in seinem Hause hat, bey dem wird keine Feuersbrunst entstehen, oder kein Gewitter einschlagen; ingleichem so eine schwangere Frau diesen Brief bey sich hat, kann weder ihr noch ihrer Frucht eine Zauberey noch Gespenst schaden. Auch so jemand diesen Brief in seinem Hause hat, oder bey sich trägt, der ist sicher vor der leidigen Sucht der Pestilenz.

Wenn man den Spruch sagt, muß man dreymal um Feuer gehen. Es hat allezeit geholfen.

120. Feuersnot zu wenden.

Nimm ein schwarzes Huhn aus dem Neste des Morgens oder des Abends, schneide ihm den Hals ab, wirf es auf die Erde, schneide ihm den Magen aus dem Leibe, thue nichts daraus, laß es bey einander bleiben; darnach siehe, daß du ein Stück aus einem Hemde bekommst da ein Mägdlein, die noch eine reine Jungfrau ist, ihre Zeit innen hat; nimm davon eines Tellers breit, von dem da die Zeit am meisten darinnen ist. Diese zwey Stücke wickele zusammen, und gieb wohl Achtung, daß du ein Ey bekommst, das am grünen Donnerstage gelegt worden. Diese drey Stücke wickele zusammen, mit Wachs; darnach thue es in ein achtmäßig Häflein, decke es zu, und vergrab es unter deine Hausschwellen, mit Gottes Hülfe, so lange als ein Stecken am Haufe währet. Wenn es schon vor und hinter deiner Behausung brennt, so kann das Feuer dir und deinen Kindern keinen Schaden thun. Es ist mit Gottes Kraft auch ganz gewiß und wahrhaftig. Oder sollte unversehens ein schnelles Feuer ausbrechen, so siehe zu; daß du ein ganzes Hemd bekommst, da eine Magd ihre Zeit innen hat, oder ein Laylachen, darinnen eine Frau ein Kind geboren hat; wirf es also zusammengewickelt stillschweigend ins Feuer. Es hilft ganz gewiß.

121. Für Hexen, die das Vieh bezaubern, in den Stall zu machen, oder für böse Menschen oder Geister, die des Nachts alte und junge Leute plagen, an die Bettstätte zu schreiben, und die Menschen und das Vieh dadurch ganz sicher und befreyet sind.

Trotter Kopf, ich verbiete dir mein Haus und mein' Hof, ich verbiete dir meine Pferde und Kühstall, ich verbiete dir meine Bettstatt, daß du nicht über mich tröste: tröste in ein ander Haus, bis du alle Berge steigest, und alle Zaunstecken zählen, und über alle Wasser steigest. So komm' der liebe Tag wieder in mein Haus, im Namen Gottes des Vaters, Gottes des Sohnes und Gottes des Heiligen Geistes. Amen.

122. Für böse Leute in die Ställe zu machen, daß sie nicht zu dem Vieh können.

Nimm Wermuth, schwarzen Kümmel, Fünf-Fingerkraut und Teufelsdreck, von jedem für drey Cents; nimm Saubohnenstroh, die Zusammenkehrung hinter der Stallthür zusammengefaßt, und ein wenig Salz; alles in einem Bündchen in ein Loch gethan in den Schwellen, wo das Vieh ein- und ausgeht, und mit elfenbeinenem Holz zugeschlagen. Es hilft gewiß.

123. Eine Kunst, Feuer zu löschen ohne Wasser.

Schreib folgende Buchstaben auf eine jede Seite eines Tellers, und wirf ihn in das Feuer; sogleich wird es geduldig auslöschen.

S A T O R
A R E P O
T E N E T
O P E R A
R O T A S

124. Noch ein Mittel für den Brand.

Unsre liebe Sara zieht durch das Land; sie hat einen feurigen hitzigen Brand in ihrer Hand.—Der feurige Brand hitzet; der feurige Brand schwitzet. Feuriger Brand, laß du das Hitzen seyn; feuriger Brand laß du das Schwitzen seyn.

✝ ✝ ✝

125. Für das Bestmachen sprich:

Christi Kreuz und Christi Kron', Christus Jesus farbes Blut, sey mir allzeit und Stunden gut. Gott der Vater ist vor mir; Gott der Sohn ist neben mir; Gott der Heilige Geist ist hinter mir. Wer nun stärker ist, denn die drey Personen, der komm' bey Tag oder Nacht, und greif' mich an. † † † Bete drey Vater unser.

126. Noch eine andere Art, best zu machen.

Darnach sprich: Alle Tritt' und Schritt' geht Jesus mit N. Er ist mein Haupt, ich bin sein Glied; d'rum geht Jesus mit N. † † †

127. Ein gewisser Feuersegen, so allezeit hilft.

Daß walt' das bittere Leiden und Sterben unsers lieben Herrn Jesu Christi. Feuer und Wind und heiße Glut, was du in deiner elementischen Gewalt hast, ich gebiete dir bey dem Herrn Jesu Christi, welcher gesprochen hat über den Wind und das Meer, die Ihm aufs Wort gehorsam gewesen—durch diese gewaltige Wort', die Jesus gesprochen hat, thue ich dir, Feuer, besehlen, trohen und ankündigen, daß du gleich fliehen sollest, und deiner elementischen Gewalt, du Flamm' und Glut. Daß walt' das heilige rosensarbe Blut unsers lieben Herrn Jesu Christi. Du, Feuer und Wind, auch heiße Gluth, ich gebiete dir, wie Gott geboten hat dem Feuer durch seine heiligen Engel, der feurigen Gluth in dem Feuerofen, nis die drey heiligen Männer, Sadrach und seine Mitgesellen, Mesach und Abed Nego, durch Gottes Befehl dem heiligen Engel besohlen, daß sie sollen unversehrt bleiben, wie es auch geschehen: als sollest gleicher Weis', du Feuerflamme und heiße Gluth, dich legen, da der allmächtige Gott gesprochen, als er die vier Elemente, sammt Himmel und Erde, erschaffen hat. Fiat, Fiat, Fiat! das ist: Es werde im Namen Gottes des Vaters, des Sohnes und des Heiligen Geistes. Amen.

128. So ein Mensch oder Vieh verhext, wie ihm zu helfen.

Drey falsche Zungen haben dich geschlossen; drey heilige Zungen haben für dich gesprochen. Die erste ist Gott der Vater, die andere

ist Gott der Sohn; die dritte ist Gott der Heilige Geist. Die geben dir dein Blut und Fleisch, Fried' und Muth. Fleisch und Blut ist an dich gewachsen, an dich gebaren, sey an dir verloren. Hat dich überritten ein Mann, so segne dich Gott und der heilige Cyprian; hat dich überschritten ein Weib, so segne dich Gott und Maria Leib; hat dich bemühet ein Knecht, so segne ich dich durch Gott und das Himmelrecht; hat dich geführet eine Magd oder Dirn, so segne dich Gott und das Himmelgestirn. Der Himmel ist ob dir, das Erdreich unter dir; du bist in der Mitte. Ich segne dich vor das Verritten. Unser lieber Herr Jesu Christ, in seinem bittern Leiden und Sterben, trat; da zitterte alles, was da versprochen, die falschen Juden aus Spott. Schau zu, wie zittert der Sohn Gottes, als hätt' er den Ritter. Da sprach unser Herr Christus: Den Ritter ich nicht hab'; auch den wird niemand bekommen. Wer mir mein Kreuz hilft klagen und tragen, den will ich von Ritter absagen, im Namen Gottes des Vaters, des Sohnes und des Heiligen Geistes, Amen.

129. Für Gespenster und allerley Hexerey.

I.

N. I. R.

I.

Sanctus Spiritus

I.

N. I. R.

I.

Das alles bewahret sey, hier zeitlich und dort ewig. Amen.
Der Character, welcher dazu gehöret, heißet:
Gott segne mich hie zeitlich und dort ewiglich. Amen.

130. Für Unglück und Gefahr im Hause.
Sanct Mattheus, Sanct Marcus, Sanct Lucas, Sanct Johannis.

187

131. Für Haus und Hof, Bewahrung vor Krankheit und Dieberen.

Ito, alo Massa Dandi Bando, III. Amen.

J. R. N. R. J.

Unser Herr Jesus Christus trat in den Saal, da suchten ihn die Juden überall an. Also meine Tage müßen diejenigen, so mich mit ihren bösen Zungen fälschlich verkleinern, wider mich streiten, durch das Lob Gottes Leid tragen, stillschweigen, verstummen, verzagen und geschmähet werden, immer und allezeit. Gott Lob verleihen dazu. Hilf mir J. J. J. immer und ewiglich. Amen.

132. Eine Anweisung zum Beysichtragen für Zigeuner-Kunst, ein Bruch in Lebensgefahr, und welches allezeit den Menschen sicher stellt.

Gleichwie der Prophet Jonas, als ein Vorbild Christi, drey Tage und drey Nächte in des Wallfisches Bauch versorget gewesen, also wolle auch der allgewaltige Gott mich vor aller Gefahr väterlich behüten und bewahren. J. J. J.

133. Für Not und Tod, zum Beysichtragen.

Ich weiß, daß mein Erlöser lebet, und er wird mich hernach aus der Erde auserwecken, & c.

134. Für die Geschwulst.

Es giengen drey reine Jungfrauen, sie wollten eine Geschwulst und Krankheit beschauen. Die erste sprach: Es ist heisch. Die andere sprach: Es ist nicht. Die dritte sprach: Ist es dann nicht, so komm' unser Herr Jesu Christ. Im Namen der heiligen Dreyfaltigkeit gesprochen.

135. Für Widerwärtigkeit und allerhand Streit.

Kraft, Held, Friede-Fürst, J. J. J.

136. Wenn man einer Kuh die Milch genommen, wie ihr zu helfen.

Gieb der Kuh drey Löffel voll von der ersten Milch, und sprich zu den Blutmelen: Fragt dich jemand, wo du die Milch hingethan hast, so sprich: Nimmfrau ist's gewesen, und ich habe sie gegessen im Namen Gottes des Vaters, des Sohnes und des Heiligen Geistes. Amen. Bete dazu, was du willst.

137. Ein anderes.

J. Kreuz Jesu Christi Milch goß;

J. Kreuz Jesu Christi Wasser goß;

J. Kreuz Jesu Christi haben goß.

Diese Worte müssen auf drey Zettel geschrieben seyn; darnach nimm Milch von der kranken Kuh, und diese drey Zettel schabe etwas von einer Hirnschale eines armen Sünders, thue alles in einen Hafen, vermache es wohl, und siede es recht, so muß die Hexe crepiren. Man kann auch die drey Zettel abgeschrieben in das Maul nehmen, hinaus vor die Dachtraufe gehen, und dreymal sprechen, darnach dem Vieh eingeben; so wirst du nicht allein alle Hexen sehen, sondern es wird auch dem Vieh geholfen werden.

138. Für das Fieber

Bete erstlich früh, hernach kehre das Hemd um den linken Ermet zuerst, und sprich: Kehre dich um, Hemd; und du Fieber, wende dich. Und nenne den Namen dessen, der das Fieber hat. Das sage ich dir zur Buß', im Namen Gottes des Vaters, des Sohnes und des Heiligen Geistes. Amen. Sprich diese Worte drey Tage nach einander, so vergeht es.

139. Einen Dieb zu bannen, daß er still stehen muß.

Dieser Segen muß am Donnerstage, früh Morgens vor Sonnenaufgang unter freyem Himmel gesprochen werden.

Daß walte Gott der Vater und der Sohn und der Heilige Geist. Amen. Wohl drey und dreyßig Engel bey einander saßen; mit Maria kommen sie pflegen. Da sprach der liebe, heilige Daniel: Trauet, liebe Frau; ich sehe Dieb' hergehen, die wollen dir dein liebes Kind stehlen; daß kann ich dir nicht verhehlen. Da sprach unsere liebe Frau zu Sanct Peter; Bind, Sanct Peter, bind. Da sprach Sanct Peter: Ich hab' gebunden mit einem Band, mit Christi seiner Hand; als sind meine Dieb'

gebunden mit Christi selbst Händen, wenn sie mir wollen stehlen das Mein, in Haus, in Kasten, auf Wiesen und Aecker, im Holz oder Feld, in Baum- and Kraut- und Rebgarten, oder wo sie das Mein wollen stehlen. Unsere liebe Frau sprach: Es stehle, wer da wolle; und wenn einer stiehlt, so soll er stehen als ein Bock, und stehen als in Stock, und zählen alle die Stein, die auf Erden seyn, und alle Sterne, so am Himmel stehen. So geb' ich dir Urlaub, und gebiete dir allen Geist, daß er aller Dieb ein Meister weiß, bey Sanct Daniel zu einer Hurth, zu einer Bürde zu tragen der Erden Gut; und das Angesicht muß dir werden, daß du nicht ob der Stelle magst kommen, dieweil dich meine Augen nicht sehen, und dir meine fleischliche Zunge nicht Urlaub giebt. Das gebiete ich dir bey der heiligen Jungfrau Maria, Mutter Gottes, bey der Kraft und Macht, da Er erschaffen Himmel und Erden, bey aller Engelschaar und bey allen Gottes Heiligen, im Namen Gottes des Vaters, Gottes des Sohnes and Gottes des Heiligen Geistes. Amen.

Willst du ihm aber des Bannes entledigen, so heiß ihn in Sanct Johannis Namen fortgehen.

140. Ein anderes vergleichen.

Ihr Diebe, ich beschwöre euch, daß ihr sollt gehorsam seyn, wie Christus seinem himmlischen Vater gehorsam war, bis ans Kreuz, und müßet mir stehen, und nicht aus meinen Augen gehen, im Namen der heiligen Dreyfaltigkeit. Ich gebiete euch bey der Kraft Gottes und der Menschwerdung Jesu Christi, dass du mir aus meinen Augen nicht gehest, † † † wie Christus der Herr ist gestanden am Jordan, als ihn Sanct Johannes getauft hat. Diesem nach beschwöre ich euch, Roß und Mann, daß ihr mir stehet, und nicht aus meinen Augen gehet, wie Christus der Herr gestanden, als man ihn an den Stamm des heiligen Kreuzes genagelt, und hat die Altväter von der Höllen Gewalt erlöset.—Ihr Diebe, ich binde euch mit den Banden, wie Christus der Herr die Hölle gebunden hat, so seyd ihr gebunden; † † † mit welchen Worten ihr gestellt seyd, seyd ihr auch wieder los.

141. Eine sehr geschwinde Stellung.

Du Reuter und Fußknecht, kommst daher, wohl unter' deinem Hut; du bist gesprengt. Mit Jesu Christi Blut, mit den heiligen fünf Wunden, sind der dein Rohr, Flinten und Pistol gebunden; Säbel, Degen und Messer gebannet und verbunden, im Namen Gottes des Vaters, des Sohnes und des Heiligen Geistes. Amen.

Dieses muß dreymal gesprochen werden.

142. Wiederauflösung.

Ihr Reuter und Fußknecht', so ich euch hab' beschworen zu dieser Frist, reitet hin in dem Namen Jesu Christi, durch Gottes Wort und Christi Hort; so reitet ihr nun alle fort.

143. Wenn einem etwas gestohlen worden, daß so der Dieb wieder bringen muß.

Des Morgens früh, vor Sonnenaufgang, gehe zu einem Birnbaum, und nimm drey Nägel aus einer Todtenbahr, oder drey Hufnägel, die noch nie gebraucht, mit; halt die Nägel gegen der Sonne Aufgang, und sprich also.

O Dieb, ich binde dich bey dem ersten Nagel, den ich dir in deine Stirn und Hirn thu schlagen, daß du das gestohlene Gut wieder an seinen vorigen Ort musst tragen; es soll die so wider und so weh werden, nach dem Menschen und nach dem Ort, da du es gestohlen hast, als dem Jünger Judas war, da er Jesum verrathen hatte. Den andern Nagel, den ich dir in deine Lung' und Leber thu schlagen, daß du das gestohlene Gut wieder an seinen vorigen Ort sollst tragen; es soll dir so weh nach dem Menschen und nach dem Ort seyn, da dir es gestohlen hast, als dem Pilato in der Höllenpein. Den dritten Nagel, den ich dir, Dieb, in deinen Fuß thu schlagen, daß du das gestohlene Gut wieder an seinen vorigen Ort mußt tragen, wo du es gestohlen hast. O Dieb, ich binde dich, und bringe dich durch die heiligen drey Nägel, die Christum durch keine heiligen Hände und Füß' seyn geschlagen worden, daß du das gestohlene Gut wieder an seinen vorigen Ort mußt tragen, da du es gestohlen hast. † † † Die Nägel müßen aber mit Armensünderschmalz geschmiert werden.

144. Ein Segen für Alles.

Jesu, ich will aufstehen; Jesu, du wollest mitgehen; Jesu, schließ mein Herz in dein Herz hinein, laß dir mein' Leib und Seel' befohlen seyn. Gekreuziget ist der Herr. Behüte mir Gott meine Sinnen, daß mich die bösen Feind' nicht überwinden, im Namen Gottes des Vaters, des Sohnes und des Heiligen Geistes. Amen.

145. Zum Spielen, daß einer allezeit gewinnen muß.

Binde mit einem rothen seidenen Faden das Herz einer Fledermaus an den Arm, womit du auswirfst, so wirst du alles gewinnen.

146. Für das Verbrennen

Unser lieber Herr Jesus Christ gieng über Land, da sah er brennen einen Brand; da lag St. Lorenz auf einem Rost. Kam ihm zu Hülf' und Trost; Er hub auf seine göttliche Hand, und segnete ihn, den Brand; Er hub, daß er nimmer tiefer grub und weiter um sich fraß. So sey der Brand gesegnet im Namen Gottes bis Vaters, des Sohnes und des Heiligen Geistes. Amen.

147. Ein anderes für das Verbrennen.

Weich aus Brand und ja nicht ein; du seyest kalt oder warm, so laß das Brennen seyn. Gott behüte dir dein Blut und dein Fleisch, dein Mark und Bein, alle Aederlein, sie seyen groß oder klein, die sollen in Gottes Namen für den kalten und warmen Brand unverletzet und bewahret seyn, im Namen Gottes des Vaters, des Sohnes und des Heiligen Geistes. Amen.

148. Dem Vieh einzogeben für Hexerey und Teufelswerk.

S A T O R
A R E P O
T E N E T
O P E R A
R O T A S

149. Wunden zu verbinden und zu heilen, sie mögen seyn wie sie wollen.

Sprich also: Die Wunde verbinde ich in drey Namen, dass du an dich nimmst, Gluth, Wasser, Schwinden, Geschwulst, und alles, was der Geschwulst Schaden mag seyn, im Namen der Heiligen Dreyfaltigkeit. Und das muß dreymal gesprochen werden. Fahre mit einem Faden dreymal um die Wunde herum, leg es unter die rechte Ecke gegen der Sonne, und sprich: Ich lege dich dahin, † † † daß du an dich nimmst Gliedwasser, Geschwulst und Eiler, und alles, was der Wunde Schaden mag seyn. Amen. Bete ein Vater unser und das Walt' Gott.

150. Die Schmerzen zu nehmen an einer frischen Wunde.

Unser lieber Herr Jesus Christ hat viele Beulen und Wunden gehabt, und doch keine verbunden. Sie jähren nicht, sie geschähren nicht; es gilt auch kein Eiter nicht. Jonas war blind, sprach ich das himmlische Kind, so wahr die heiligen fünf Wunden seyn geschlagen. Sie gerinnen nicht sie geschwären nicht. Daraus nehm' ich Wasser und Blut; das ist vor alle Wunden, Schaden gut. Heilig ist der Mann, der allen Schaden und Wunden heilen kann. † † † Amen.

151. So der Mensch Würmer im Leibe hat.

Petrus und Jesus fuhren aus gen Acker, akkerten drey Furchen, akkerten auf drey Würmer. Der eine ist weiß, der andere ist schwarz, der dritte ist roth. Da sind alle Würmer todt, im Namen † † † Sprich diese Worte dreymal.

152. Für alles Böse.

Herr Jesu deine Wunden roth, stehen mir vor dem Tod.

153. Vor Gericht und Rath Recht zu behalten.

Jesus Nazarenus, Rex Judeorum.

Zuerst trag diesen Character bey dir in der Figur, alsdann sprich folgende Worte: Ich N. N. trete vor des Richters Haus; da schauen drey todte Männer zum Fenster heraus; der eine hat keine Zung', der andere hat keine Lung', der dritte erkrankt, verblindt und verstummt.

Das ist, wenn du vor's Gericht gehest oder Amt, und eine Rechtssache hast, dagegen dir der Richter nicht günstig ist, so sprich, wann du gegen ihn gehest, den schon oben stehenden Segen.

154. Blutstillung, so allezeit gewiß ist.

Sobald als du dich geschnitten oder gehauen, so sprich: Glückselige Wunde, glückselige Stunde; glückselig ist der Tag, da Jesus Christus geboren war im Namen † † † Amen.

155. Ein anderes.

Schreib die vier Hauptwasser der ganzen Welt, welche aus dem Paradies fließen, auf einen Zettel, nämlich Pisan, Gihon, Hedekiel und Pheat, und aufgelegt. Im ersten Buch Mose des zweyten Kapitels, Vers 11, 12, 13, allda kannst du es aufschlagen. Es hilft.

156. Ein anderes dergleichen.

Oder hauche den Patienten dreymal an, bête das Vater unser bis dahin auf Erden, und das dreymal, so wird das Blut bald stehen.

157. Eine andere, ganz gewisse Blutstillung.

Wenn einem das Blut nicht stehest will, oder eine Aderwunde ist, so leg den Brief darauf, dann steht es von Stunde an. Wer es aber nicht glauben will, der schreibe, die Buchstaben, auf ein Messer, und steche ein unvernünftiges Thier; es wird nicht bluten. Und wer dieses bey sich trägt, der kann vor allen seinen Feinden bestehen: l. m. I. K. I. B. I. P. a. x. v. ss. Ss. vas I. P. O. unay Lit. Dom mper vobism. Und wenn eine Frau in Kindsnöthen liegt, oder sonst Herzeleid hat, so nehme sie den Brief zu sich; es wird gewiss nicht mislingen.

158. Ein besonderes Stück, sowohl die Menschen als auch das Vieh zu verstehen.

Wenn du dich wehren mußt, so trage dies Zeichen bey dir:

In Gottes Namen greif' ich an. Mein Erlöser wolle mir beystehen. Auf die heilige Hülfe Gottes verlaß ich mich von Herzen grausam sehr;

auf die heilige Hülfe Gottes, und auf mein Gewehr, verlaß ich mich von Herzen grausam sehr. Gott mit uns allein; Jesu Heil und Segen.

159. *Schutz und Beschirmung des Hauses und Hofes.*

Unter deinen Schirmen bin ich vor den Stürmen aller Feinde frey. J. J. J. Die drey J. bedeuten dreymal Jesus.

160. *Eine Anweisung zum Beysichtragen.*

Trage diese Worte bey dir, so kann man dich nicht treffen: Annania, Azaria und Misael, lobet den Herrn; denn er hat uns erlöset aus der Höllen, und hat uns geholfen von dem Tode, und hat uns erlöset aus dem glühenden Ofen, und hat uns im Feuer erhalten; also wolle es, Er, der Herr, kein Feuer geben lassen.

I.

N. I. R.

I.

161. *Alle Feinde, Räuber und Mörder zu stellen.*

Gott grüß' euch, ihr Brüder; haltet an, ihr Dieb', Räuber, Mörder, Reuter und Soldaten, in der Demuth, weil wir haben getrunken Jesu rosenfarbes Blut. Eure Büchsen und Geschütz seyn euch verstopfet mit Jesu Christi heiligen Blutstropfen; alle Säbel und alle Gewehr' seyn auch verbunden, mit Jesu heiligen fünf Wunden. Es stehen drey Rosen auf Gottes Herz; die erste ist gültig, die andere ist mächtig, die dritte ist sein göttlicher Will'. Ihr Diebe, müßt hiemit darunter stehen, und halten still, so lang' ich will. Im Namen Gottes des Vaters, des Sohnes und des Heilgen Geistes, seyd ihr gestellet und beschworen.

162. *Eine Festigkeit für alle Waffen.*

Jesus, Gott und Mensch, behüte mich N. N. vor allerley Geschütz, Waffen, lang oder kurz, Gewehr von allerley Metall und Geschütz; behalt dein Feuer, wie Maria ihre Jungfrauschaft behalten hat, vor und nach ihrer Geburt. Christus verbinde alles Geschütz, wie Er sich verbunden hat in der Menschheit voll Demuth; Jesus vermache alle Gewehr' und Waffen, wie Maria, der Mutter Gottes Gemahl, vermachet gewesen; also behüte

die heiligen drey Blutstropfen, die Jesus Christus am Oelberge geschwitzt hat; Jesus Christus behüte mich vor Todschlag und brennendem Feuer: Jesus laß' mich nicht sterben, vielweniger verdammt werden, ohne Empfang des heiligen Abendmahls. Das helf' mir Gott der Vater, Sohn und heiliger Geist. Amen.

163. Schußwaffen und Darstellung

Jesus gieng über das rothe Meer, und sah in das Land; also müßen zerreißen alle Strick' und Band', und zerbrechen und unbrauchbar werden alle Rohrbüchsen, Flinten und Pistolen, alle falsche Zungen verstummen. Der Segen, den Gott that, da er den ersten Menschen erschaffen hat, der gehe über mich allezeit; der Segen, den Gott that, da er im Traum befohlen, daß Joseph und Maria mit Jesu in Egypten fliehen sollte, der gehe über mich allezeit, seye lieb und werth das heilige † in meiner rechten Hand. Ich gehe durch die Frey des Landes, da keiner wird beraubt, todtgeschlagen oder ermordet; sogar mir niemand etwas Leid thun kann; daß mich überdies kein Hund beiß', kein Thier zerreiß'. In allen behüte mich mein Fleisch und Blut, vor Sünden und falschen Zungen, die von der Erde bis an den Himmel reichen, durch die Kraft der vier Evangelisten, in Namen Gottes des Vaters, Gottes des Sohnes und Gottes des Heiligen Geistes. Amen.

164. Ein anderes.

Ich, N.N. beschwöre dich, Geschütz, Säbel und Messer, eben alle Waffen, bey dem Speer; der in die Seite Gottes gegangen ist und geöffnet, daß Blut und Wasser herausgeflossen, daß ihr mich als einen Diener Gottes nicht verletzen lasset im † † † Ich beschwöre dich bey St. Stephan, welchen die Juden gesteiniget, dass sie mich als einen Diener Gottes nicht betrüben können im Namen † † † Amen.

165. Eine Versicherung vor Schießen, Hauen und Stechen.

Im Namen J. J. J. Amen. Ich N. N. Jesus Christus ist das wahre Heil; Jesus Christus herrschet, regieret, verbricht und überwindet alle Feind; sichtbare und unsichtbare; Jesus sey mit mir in allweg, immer und ewiglich auf allen Wegen und Stegen; auf dem Wasser und Land,

in Berg und Thal, in Haus und Hof, in der ganzen Welt, wo ich bin, wo ich steh', lauf', reit' oder fahr', ich schlaf oder wach', eß' oder trink', da sey du, O Herr Jesu Christ, allezeit früh und spät, alle Stund' und Augenblick', ich gehe aus oder ein. Die heiligen fünf Wunden roth, o Herr Jesu Christe, die seyen mir allezeit gut für meine Sünden, sie seyen heimlich oder öffentlich; daß sie mich nicht meidet, ihr Gewehr mich nicht verletzen noch beschädigen könne, das helf' mir † † † Jesus Christus, mit seiner Beschützung und Beschirmung, behüte mich N. N. allezeit vor täglichen Sünden, weltlichem Schaden und vor Ungerechtigkeit, vor Verachtung, vor Pestilenz und andern Krankheiten, vor Angst, Marter und Pein, vor allen bösen Feinden, vor falschen Zungen und alten Plappertaschen; dass mich kein Geschütz an meinen Leib beschädige, das helf' mir † † † und ja kein Diebsgesind, weder Zigeuner, Straßenräuber, Mordbrenner, Hexerey oder allerley Teufelsgespenst, sich zu meinen Haus und Hof einschleichen, ja vielweniger einbrechen können: das bewahre alles die liebe Frau Maria, auch alle Kind', so bey Gott im Himmel sind, in der ewigen Freud, und Herrlichkeit Gottes des Vaters erquicke mich, die Weisheit Gottes des Sohnes erleuchte mich, die Tugend und Gnade Gottes des Heiligen Geistes stärke mich zu der Stund' bis in Ewigkeit. Amen.

166. Gewehr- und Waffenstellung.

Der Segen, der vom Himmel kam, da Jesus Christus geboren war, der gehe über mich N. N. Der Segen, den Gott der Herr gethan hat, da Er den ersten Menschen erschaffen hat, der gehe über mich; der Segen, so erfolgte, da Christus gefangen, gebunden, gegeißelt, so bitter übel gekrönet und geschlagen worden, dadurch am Kreuz den Geist aufgab, gehe über mich; der Segen, den der Priester gab über den zarten, frohen Leichnam unsers lieben Herrn Jesu Christi, gehe über mich. Die Beständigkeit der heiligen Maria und aller Heiligen Gottes, die heiligen drey Könige, Caspar, Melchior und Balthasar, seynd mit mir; die heiligen vier Evangelisten, Matthäus, Marcus, Lucas und Johannes, seynd mit mir; die Erzengel, St Michael, St. Gabriel, St. Raphael und St. Uriel, seynd mit mir; die heiligen zwölf Bothen der Patriarchen

und das ganze himmlische Herr, sey mit mir; die sämmlichen Heiligen, deren unausprechlich viel, seynd mit mir. Amen.

Papa, R. tarn, Tetragrammaten Angen.

Jesus Nazarenus, Rex Judeorum.

167. Daß mich kein böser Mensch betrügen, verzaubern noch verhexen könne, und daß ich allezeit gesegnet sey.

Als der Kelch und Wein und das heilige Abendbrod, da unser lieber Herr Jesus Christus am grünen Donnerstage seinen lieben Jüngern bot, und daß mich allezeit, weder Tag noch Nacht, kein hund beiß', kein wildes Their zerreiß', kein Baum fäll', kein Wasser schwell', kein Geschütz treff', keine Waffen, Eisen oder Stahl kann schneiden, kein Feuer verbrenn', und vor falschem Urtheil, kein falsche Zunge beschwör', kein Schelm erzürne, vor allen bösen Feinden, vor Hexerey und Zauberey, davor behüte mich, o Herr Jesu Christ. Amen.

168. Ein anderes.

Es behüte mich die heilige Dreyfaltigkeit; die sey und bleibe bey mir N. N. zu Wasser und zu Land, im Wasser oder Feld, in Städten oder Dörfern, in der ganzen Welt, oder wo ich bin. Der Herr Jesus Christus behüte mich vor allen meinen Feinden, heimlich oder öffentlich; also behüte mich die ewige Gottheit durch das bittere Leiden Jesu Christi. Sein rosenfarbes Blut, das Er am Stamme des heiligen Kreuzes vergossen hat, das helfe mir. J. J. Jesus ist gekreuziger, gemartert worden und gestorben. Das seyn wahrhaftige Worte; also müßen auch alle Worte bey ihrer Kraft seyn, die hier geschrieben, und von mir gesprochen und gebetet werden. Das helfe mir, daß ich von keinem Menschen gefangen, gebunden oder überwunden werde. Vor mir sollen alle Gewehr' und Waffen unbrauchbar und ohne Kraft seyn. Geschütz, behalte dein Feuer in Gottes allmächtiger Hand. Also sollen alle Geschütz verbannet seyn. † † † Als man dem Herrn Jesu Christo seine rechte Hand an das Kreuzholz band. Gleichwie der Sohn seinem himmlischen Vater gehorsam war bis zum Tod des Kreuzes: also behüte mich die ewige Gottheit, durch sein rosenfarbes Blut, durch die heiligen fünf Wunden, welche Er am Stamme des heiligen Kreuzes vergossen hat; also muß ich gesegnet

und so wohl bewahret seyn, als der Kelch und Wein, und das wahre, theure Brod, das Jesus seinen zwölf Jüngern bot an dem grünen Donnerstag Abend. J. J. J.

169. Ein anderes.

Gottes Gnad' und Barmherzigkeit, die gehe über mir N. N. Jetzo will ich ausreiten oder ausgehen; ich will mich umgürten, ich will mich umbinden mit einem sichern Ring, will's Gott der himmlische Vater, der wolle mich bewahren, mein Fleisch und Blut, alle meine Aederlein und Glieder, auf dem heutigen Tag und Nacht, wie ich's vor mir hab'; und wie viel Feind' meiner wären, so sollen sie verstummen, und alle werden wie ein schneeweißer todter Mann, dass mich keiner schießen, hauen noch werfen kann, noch überwinden mag, er habe gleich Büchsen oder Stahl in seiner Hand, von allerley Metall, wie alle böse Wehr und Waffen seyn genannt. Meine Büchse soll abgehen wie der Blitz vom Himmel, und mein Säbel soll hauen wie en Scheermesser. Da gieng unsere liebe Frau auf einer sehr hohen Berg; sie sah hinab in ein sehr finsteres Thal, und ihr liebes Kind unter den Jüden stehen, herb, so herb, daß Er gefangen so herb, daß Er gebunden so hart, daß behüte mich der liebe Herr Jesus Christus, vor allein, was mir schädlich ist. † † † Amen.

170. Ein anderes dergleichen.

Da schreit' ich aus auf diesen heutigen Tag und Nacht, daß du alle meine Feind' und Diebsgesind' nicht lässest zu mir kommen, sie bringen mir denn sein rosenfarbes Blut in meinen Schooss [?]; sie mir aber das nicht bringen, was auf dem heiligen Altar gehandelt wird. Den Gott der Herr, Jesus Christ, ist mit lebendigem Leib gen Himmel gefahren. O Herr, das ist mir gut auf den heutigen Tag und Nacht † † † Amen.

171. Ein anderes dergleichen.

In Gottes Namen schreit' ich aus. Gott der Vater sey ob mir, Gott der Sohn sey vor mir, Gott der Heilige Geist neben mir. Wer stärker ist, als diese drey Mann, der soll mir sprechen mein' Leib und Leben an; wer

aber nicht stärker ist, denn diese drey Mann, der soll mich bleiben lan. J. J. J.

172. Eine richtige und gute Schußstellung.

Der Friede unsers Herrn Jesu Christ sey mit mir N. N. O Schuß, steh' still, in dem Namen der gewaltigen Propheten Agtion und Eliä, und tödte mich nicht! O Schuß, steh' still! ich beschwöre dich durch Himmel und Erde, und durch des jüngsten Gerichts willen, daß du mich, als ein Kind Gottes, nicht beleidigen wollest. † † † Amen.

173. Ein anderes dergleichen.

Ich beschwöre dich, Schwerdt, Degen und Messer, was mir schad't und verletzlich ist, durch des Priesters aller Gebet, und wer Jesum in den Tempel geführet hat und gesprochen, ein schneidiges Schwerdt wird durch deine Seele dringen, daß du mich als ein Kind Gottes nicht beleidigen lässest, J. J. J.

174. Eine sehr geschwinde Stellung.
Ich N. N. beschwöre dich, Säbel und Messer, und eben alle Waffen, bey dem Speer, der in die Seite Jesu gegangen ist und geöffnet, daß Blut und Wasser heraus geflossen, daß Er mich als einen Diener Gottes nicht beleidigen lasse, † † † Amen.

175. Eine gute Stellung für Diebe.
Es stehen drey Lilien auf unsers Herrn Gottes Grab: die erste ist Gottes Muth, die andere ist Gottes Blut, die dritte ist Gottes Will. Steh still, Dieb! So wenig als Jesus Christus von dem heiligen † gestiegen, eben so wenig sollst du von der Stelle laufen; das gebiet' ich dir bey den vier Evangelisten und Elementen des Himmels, da im Fluß oder im Schuß, im Gericht oder Gesicht. So beschwör' ich dich bey dem jüngsten Gericht, daß du still stehest und ja nicht weiter gehest, bis ich all' die Stern' am Himmel sehe, und die Sonn' giebt ihren Schein. Also stell'

ich dir dein Laufen und Springen ein; das gebiete ich dir im Namen † † † Amen.

Dieses muß dreymal gesprochen werden.

176. Ein besonderes Stück, gestohlene Sächen wieder herzuzwingen.

Beobachtet es wohl, wo der Dieb hinaus zu der Thür, oder sonsten wo; da schneid' drey Spänlein in den drey höchsten Namen ab, alsdann geh mit den drey Spänlein zu einem Wagen, aber unbeschrauen, thue ein Rad ab, thue die drey Spänlein in die Rad-Nab hinein, in den drey höchsten Namen, alsdann treib uns Rad hinter sich, und sprich: Dieb, Dieb, Dieb! kehre wieder um mit der gestohlnen Sache. Du wirst gezwungen durch die Allmacht Gottes; † † † Gott der Vater rufet dich zurück; Gottes Sohn wendt dich um, dass du mußt gehen zurück; Gott der Heilige Geist führet dich zurück, bis du an dem Ort bist, wo du gestohlen hast. Durch die Allmacht Gottes mußt du kommen; durch die Weisheit Gottes des Sohnes habest du weder Rast noch Ruh', bis du deine gestohlene Sache wieder an seinem vorigen Ort hast; durch die Gnade Gottes des Heiligen Geistes mußt du rennen und springen, kannst weder rasten noch ruhen, bis du an den Ort kommst, wo du gestohlen hast. Gott der Vater bindt dich, Gott der Sohn zwingt dich, Gott der Heilige Geist wend't dich zurück. Treib das Rad nicht gar zu stark um. Dieb, du mußt kommen; † † † Dieb, du mußt kommen; † † † Dieb, du mußt kommen, † † † Wenn du allmächtiger bist, Dieb, Dieb, Dieb, wenn du allmächtiger bist, als Gott, so bleibe, wo du bist: Die zehn Gebote zwingen dich, du sollst nicht stehlen; deswegen mußt du kommen. † † † Amen.

177. Eine rechte approbirte Schußstellung.

Es seynd drey heilige Blutstropfen Gott dem Herrn über sein heiliges Angesicht geflossen; die drey heiligen Blutstropfen sind vor das Zündloch geschoben. So rein als unsere liebe Frau von allen Männern war, eben so wenig soll ein Feuer oder Rauch aus dem Rohr gehen. Rohr, gieb du weder Feuer, noch Flamm', noch Hitz'. Jetzt geh' ich aus; denn

Gott der Herr geht von mir hinaus, Gott der Sohn ist bey , Gott der Heilige Geist schwebt ob mir allezeit. Amen.

178. Noch ein Stück für böse Leute.

Es heißt, wenn man einem nichts Gutes zutrauete, und derjenige säße auf einem Stuhl, und man thäte eine neue Schuhmacher-Seil unten in den Stuhl stechen, auf den Sitz am untern Ende, so müßte dieser, der sich auf dem Stuhl befinde, brunzen, und würde in kurzer Zeit sterben; die Seil darf aber noch nicht gebraucht seyn.

179. Noch eine approbirte Schußstellung.

Glückhaftig ist die Stund', da Jesus Christus geboren war; glückhaftig war die Stund', da Jesus Christus gestorben war; glückhaftig ist die Stund', da Jesus Christus von den Todten auferstanden ist; glückhaftig sind diese drey Stunden über dein Geschütz verbunden, dass kein Schuß gegen mich soll gehen, meine Haut und mein Haar, mein Blut und mein Fleisch nicht soll verletzet werden, mit keinem Bley noch Pulver, Eisen, Stahl, oder sonst Metall gar nicht bleßirt werden, so wahr, als die liebe Mutter Gottes keinen andern Sohn gebähren wird. † † † Amen.

180. Ein besonderes Stück, einen Mann zu zwingen, der sonst Vielen gewachsen.

Ich N. N. thue dich anhauchen; drey Blutstropfen thue ich dir entziehen, den ersten aus deinem Herzen, den andern aus deiner Leber, den dritten aus deiner Lebenskraft; damit nehme ich dir deine Stärke und Mannschaft.

Hbbi Mafsa danti Lantien. I. I. I.

181. Eine bewährte Kunst, die Erdflöhe zu vertreiben.

Nimm die Spreu, worauf die Kinder in der Wiege gelegen haben, oder nimm kurzen Pferdemist, und streue ihn aufs Land; so thun die Erdflöhe keinen Schaden.

182. Dass ein Anderer kein Wild schießen kann.

Sprich dessen Namen, nämlich Jakob Wohlgemuth; schieß, was du willst; schieß nur Haar' und Federn mit, und was du den armen Leuten giebst. † † † Amen.

183. Ein Segen für und wider alle Feinde.

Christi Kreuz sey mir N. N. Christi † überwindet mir alle Wasser und Feuer; Christi † überwindet mir alle Waffen; Christi † ist mir ein vollkommen Zeichen und Heil meiner armen Seel'. Christus sey bey mir und meinen Leib, zu meinem Leben, Tag und Nacht. Nun bitte ich N. N. Gott den Vater durch des Sohnes willen, und bitte Gott den Sohn durch des Vaters willen, und bitte Gott den Heiligen Geist durch des Vaters und Sohnes willen. Gottes heiliger Leichnam segne mich vor allen schädlichen Dingen, Worten und Werken. Christi † öffne mir auch alle Glückseligkeit; Christi † vertreibe von mir alles Uebel; Christi † sey bey mir, ob mir, vor mir, hinter mir, unter mir, neben mir und allenthalben, und vor allen meinen Feinden, sichtbar und unsichtbar; die fliehen alle vor mir, so sie mich nur wissen oder hören. Enoch und Elias, die zween Propheten, die waren nie gefangen, noch gebunden, noch geschlagen, und kamen nie aus ihrer Gewalt: also muß mich keiner meiner Feinde an meinem Leib und Leben beschädigen, verletzen und angreifen können, im Namen Gottes des Vaters, des Sohnes und des Heiligen Geistes. Amen.

184. Ein anderer Segen für Feinde, Krankheit und Unglück.

Der Segen, der vom Himmel, von Gott dem Vater, kommen ist, da der wahre lebendige Sohn Gottes geboren ward, der gehe über mich allezeit; der Segen, den Gott that dem menschlichen Geschlecht, der gehe über mich allezeit. Das heilige † Gottes, so lang und breit, als Gott seine so gebenedeyete, bittere Marter davor gelitten hat, segne mich heut' und allezeit. Die heiligen drey Nägel, die Jesu Christo durch seine heiligen Hände und Füsse geschlagen worden, die segnen mich heute und zu allen Zeiten. Die bittere Dornenkrone, die Christo Jesu durch sein heiliges Haupt gedrückt worden, segne mich heut' und allezeit. Das Speer, durch welches Jesu Christo seine heilige Seite

geöffnet worden, segne mich heut' und allezeit. Das rosenfarbe Blut, das sey mir vor alle meine Feinde gut, und vor alles, was mir Schaden thut, an Leib und Leben oder Hofgut. Segnen mich allezeit die heiligen fünf Wunden, damit alle meine Feinde werden vertrieben oder gebunden, da Gott alle Christenheit mit hat umfangen. Das helf' mir Gott der Vater und der Sohn und der Heilige Geist. Amen.—Also muß ich N. N. so gut und so wohl gesegnet seyn, als der heilige Kelch und Wein, und das wahre, lebendige Brod, das Jesus den zwölf Jüngern an dem grünen Donnerstag Abend gab. Alle, die dich hassen, müßen mir alle stillschweigen; ihr Herz sey gegen mich erstorben; ihre Zunge verstumme, daß sie mir ganz und gar nicht zum Haus und Hof, oder sonst Schaden thun können. Auch Alle, die mich mit ihrem Gewehr oder Waffen wollen angreifen und verwunden, die seyen vor mir unsieghaft, lach und unwehrsam. Das helfe mir die heilige Gottes-Kraft, die macht alle Waffen und Geschütz unbrauchbar. Alles im Names Gottes des Vaters, des Sohnes und des Heiligen Geistes. Amen.

185. Der Talisman

Es heißt: wer auf die Jagd geht, und denselben in seiner Jagdtasche bey sich trägt, dem kann es nicht fehlen, selbigen Tag etwas Wichtiges zu schießen und heim zu bringen.

Ein alter Einsiedler fand einst einen alten, lahmen Jäger im Thüringer Walde am Wege liegen und weinen. Der Einsiedler frug ihn: warum er so traurig sey? Ach, Mann Gottes! sagte er, ich bin ein armer, unglücklicher Mensch: ich muß meinem Herrn jährlich so viel Hirsche, Rehböcke, Hasen und Schnepfen liefern, als ein junger, gesunder Jäger kaum auftreiben kann, sonst jagt er mich aus dem Dienst; nun bin ich alt und lahm, das Wild ist rar dazu, und ich kann ihm nicht mehr recht nach; ich weiß nicht, wie mir's noch gehen wird. Hier konnte er vor Traurigkeit kein Wort mehr reden. Der Einsiedler zog hierauf ein keines Papier heraus, auf welches er das hier folgende Zettelchen mit einem Bleystift schrieb, es dem Jäger gab, und sagte: Da, Alter, stecke das in deine Jagdtasche; so oft du nach Wild ausgehst, und es bey dir trägst, wird es dir nicht fehlen, selbigen Tag

etwas Wichtiges zu schießen und heim zu bringen; gieb aber Acht, daß du nie mehr schießest, als du nothwendig brauchst, und es auch keinen lernst, als nur den, der keinen Mißbrauch davon zu machen verspricht, wegen dem hohen Sinn, der in den Worten liegt. Der Einsiedler gieng nun seines Weges, und nach einer Weile stand der Jäger auch auf, und gieng, ohne an etwas zu denken, in den Busch; aber kaum war er hundert Schritte weit gegangen, als er schon einen so schönen Rehbock schoß, als er seit langer Zeit nicht gesehen hatte. Dieser Jäger war nach diesem, so lange er lebte, alle Tage glücklich der Jagd, und man hielt ihn deswegen für den besten Waidmann im ganzen Lande.

Ut nemo in sese tentat, descendere nemo,

At praecedenti spectatur mantica tergo.
Man thut am besten, und probirt es.

186. Daß einer das gestohlene Gut wieder bringen muß.

Gehe des Morgens früh, vor Sonnenaufgang, zu einem Wachholderbusch, und bieg ihn gegen der Sonne Aufgang mit der linken Hand, und sprich: Wachholderbusch, ich thu' dich bucken und drucken, bis der Dieb dem N. N. sein gestohlen Gut wieder an seinen Ort hat getragen. Du mußt einen Stein nehmen, und diesen auf den Busch legen, und unter den Stein, auf dem Busch eine Hirnschale von einem Uebelthäter thun. † † † Du mußt aber Achtung geben, wenn der Dieb das gestohlene Gut wiedergebracht hat, daß du den Stein wieder an seinen Ort trägst, wo und wie er gelegen, und den Busch wieder los machst.

187. Eine Kugeln-Anweisung

Die himmlischen und heiligen Posaunen, die blasen alle Kugeln und Unglück von mir, und gleich und gleich von mir ab. Ich fliehe unter den Baum des Lebens, der zwölferley Früchte trägt. Ich stehe hinter dem heiligen Altar der Christlichen Kirche. Ich befehle mich der Heiligen Dreyfaltigkeit. Ich N. N. verberg' mich hinter des Fronleichnams

Jesu Christi. Ich befehle mich in die Wunden Jesu Christi, daß ich von keines Menschen Hund werde gefangen noch gebunden, nicht gehauen, nicht geschossen, nicht gestochen, nicht geworfen, nicht geschlagen, eben überhaupt nicht verwundet werde; das helf' mir N. N.

188. Wer dieses Büchlein bey sich trägt, der ist sicher vor allen seinen Feinden, sie seyen sichtbar oder unsichtbar, und so auch der, welcher dieses Büchlein bey sich hat, kann ohne den ganzen Fronleichnam Jesu Christi nicht ersterben, in keinem Wasser ertrinken, in keinem Feuer verbrennen, auch kein unrecht Urtheil über ihn gesprochen werden. Dazu hilf mir † † †

189. Unglückliche Tage,

Wie solche in jedem Monat sich befinden.

Januar 1. 2. 3. 4. 6. 11. 12.	Julius 17. 21.
Februar 1. 17. 18.	August 20. 21.
März 14. 16.	September 10. 18.
April 10. 17. 18.	October 6.
May 7. 8.	November 6. 10.
Junius 17.	December 6. 11. 15.

Wer auf einen dieser Tage geboren wird, ist unglücklich und leidet Armuth. Auch wer auf einen der vorgemeldeten Tage krank wird, bekommt selten seine Gesundheit wieder; und wer sich verlobt oder heirathet, kommt in große Armuth und Elend. Man soll auch nicht ziehen aus einem Hause in das andere. Auch soll man nicht reisen, nichts handeln, und keine Prozesse anfangen.

NB. Am Tage der Verkündigung Mariä, Simon und Judä, und Apostel St. Andreä, soll man keine Ader lassen.

Die Zeichen des Zodiaci sollen nach dem Lauf des Monats beobachtet werden, wie sie täglich in dem gemeinen Kalender verzeichnet sind.

Wenn eine Kuh im Zeichen der Jungfrau kälbert, so lebt dasselbe Kalb kein Jahr; fällt es im Scorpion, so stirbt es noch ehender: darum soll man keines in diesem Zeichen, wie auch im Steinbock und Wassermann, abgewöhnen; so bekommen sie nicht leichtlich das tödtliche Feuer.

Nur dies obengemeldete einzige Stücke ist aus einem hundertjährigen Kalender, der aus Deutschland kommt, gezogen worden, und es erhält bey Vielen Glauben.

Hohman.

190. Zum Schluß wird noch das hier folgende Morgenbet geliefert, welches man sprechen muß, so man über Land gehet. Es bewahret den Menschen vor allem Unglück.

O Jesu von Nazareth, ein König der Juden, ja ein König über die ganze Welt, beschütze mich N. N., diesen heutigen Tag und Nacht, beschütze mich allezeit durch deine heiligen fünf Wunden, daß ich nicht werde gefangen noch gebunden. Es beschütze mich die heilige Dreyfaltigkeit, daß mir kein Gewehr, Geschoß, noch Kugel oder Bley, auf meinen Leib sollen kommen; sie sollen lind werden, als die Zähren und Blutschweiß Jesu Christi gewesen seyn, im Namen Gottes des Vaters, und des Sohnes, und des Heiligen Geistes. Amen.

APPENDIX A

A1. *Anhang*

Folgendes Mittel wider die Fallende-Krankheit wurde in den Lancaster Zeitungen bekannt gemacht, ins Jahr, 1828.

An die leidende Menschheit.

Wir selbst wissen von manchem Unglücklichen der mit der fallende Sucht behaftet ist—allein welche Menge mag wohl noch in unserm land vorhanden seyn; und viele vielleicht schon ihr Vermögen geopfert um davon befreyet zu werden—aber umsonst. Wir haben nun eine Nachricht erhalten die uns ein Mittel liefert das ganz untrüglich seyn, und von den berühmtesten Aerzten Europas anerkannt und durch viele angestellten Proben höchst bewährt befunden worden seyn soll—und allgemein in Europea angewendt wird. Man soll nämlich dem Kranken eine Bettstelle auf dem Kuhstalle errichten, und sorgen daß er sich meistens auch bey Tage da aufhalten könne. Dieses läßt sich sehr leicht bewerckstellingen, indem man sich ja eine Wohnstube darauf bauen kann. Nun sorge man, daß eine gute Oeffnung an der Decke des Kuhstalls beliebe, damit sich die Ausdünstung aus demselben in die Stube ziehe und von dem Kranken eingeathmet, auch von der Kuh die Ausdünstung des Kranken eingeathmet werden könne. Letztere wird nach und nach die ganze Krankheit an sich ziehen, die gichterischen Anfälle bekommen, und wenn der Mensch sie verloren hat, wird die Kuh todt zur Erde fallen. Der Stall darf nicht ausgemistet, sondern mit frischem Stroh versehen werden—u. es versteht sich, daß die Milch der Kuh, so lang sie noch geben wird, als unbrauchbar weggeschüttet werde.

Lancaster Adler

A2. Salben zur Heilung von Wunden

Nimm Toback, grün oder dürre; ist er grün eine gute Hand voll; ist er dürre, 4 loth. Dazu eine gute Hand voll Holderblätter, dieses in Butter wohl gesotten, drucke es durch ein Tuch, und gebrauche es als eine Salbe die Wunde ist in wenig Stunden geheilet.

Oder Gehe an einen weiß Eichenbaum der ziemlich allein stehet, und schabe auf der ostlichen Seite des Baumes die rauhe Kinde hinweg, als dann ziehe die feine Kinde davon, zerhaue sie klein, und koche sie bis alle Säfte daraus gekommen sind, dann seihe es durch ein Stück leinewand und koche es wieder bis es so dick wird wie Theer, dann nimm davon heraus so viel du willt, und thue eine gleiche Quantität Schaafunschlitt, Rasem und Wachs hinzu, reibe es durch einander bis es zur Salbe wird, und bestreiche alsdann einen leinen lappen dünn damit, und lege es auf die Wunde und fahre damit fort bis die Wunde geheilt ist.

Oder: nimm eine Hand voll Petersilien, zerstoße ihn fein, und thue als dann so viel ungesalzene Butter hinzu als du Petersilien hast, und mache eine Salbe daraus; Diese Salbe läßt kein faules Fleisch entstehen und heilet schnell.

A3. Pfirsich

Die Blüte von den Pfirsichen wie Salat bereitet und gegessen, bringet den Stuhlgang, und ist den Wassersüchtigen nützlich.

Sechs oder sieben geschälte Pfirsich-Kerne eingenommen treiben den Stein; sollen auch die Trunkenheit verhindern, so man sie vor dem Essen gebrauchet.

Welchem das Haar ausfallet, der stoße Pfirsich-Kerne, mache mit Essig daraus ein Sälblein, oder Müßlein, und schmiere damit den kahlen Ort.

Das aus der Pfirsich-Blüte destillirt Wasser larirt die jungen Kinder, und tödet bey ihnen die Würmer.

A4. Baumöhl.

Das Baumöhl hat sehr viele Tugenden, daher zu rathen wäre, daß sich eine jeder Hausvater solches allezeit im Haus halten möchte, damit

es im Fall der Noth bey der Hand wäre. Hier folgen also einige der vorzüglichsten Tugenden.

Es ist ein sicheres Mittel innerlich und äußerlich in allerley hitzigen Entzündigungen für Menschen und Vieh.

Innerlich wird es gegeben in heftigen Brennen des Magens, wann er von starkem Getränk oder durch starke Purgirungen oder giftige Arzeneyen entzündet ist: ja wann auch einer wirklich puren Gift sollte in Leib bekommen, so soll er nur ein Glas voll Baumöhl über das andere trinken bis es zu einem Brechen kommt so führt es das Gift wieder ab, wann es anderst noch nicht gar zu lang im Leib gewesen ist; und nach dem Erbrechen muß dann noch immer fortgefahren werden alle Stund einen Löffelvoll Baumöl einzunehmen, bis der Brand, den das Gift erregt hat, gänzlich gelöscht ist.

Wer von einer Schlange oder sonst giftigen Thier oder von einem bösen Hund gebissen ist und nimmt gleich warm Baumöhl, und wascht damit die Wunde aus, und legt einen 4- oder 6-doppelten Lumpen darauf, welcher in Baumöhl naß gemacht ist, alle 3 Stunden frisch, und trinkt auch alle 4 Stunden ein paar Löffel voll etliche Tage lang, wird erfahren was für eine Kraft im Baumöhl ist, dem Gift zu wiederstehen.

In der rothen Ruhr ist das Baumöhl gleichfalls vortrefflich gut, wenn man erst den Leib durch Rhebarbara oder eine andere dazu dienenende Larierung ausfegt, und hernach alle 3 Stunden ein paar Löffel voll Baumöhl einnimmt; hierzu aber sollte das Baumöhl erst wohl gekocht seyn, und etwas gebrannt Hirschhorn darein gethan werden; dieses gekochte Oehl ist auch gut in allerley Arten des Bauch-Grimmens und der Kolik, und sonderlich mann jemand gefallen ist und hat sich inwendig weh gethan, der nehme alle 2 Stunden ein paar Löffel voll dieses gekochten Oehls ein: es stillet Schmerzen, zertheilt das geronnene Geblüt, wehret aller Entzündung und heilet sänftiglich.

Äußerlich ist es gut bey allerley Geschwulsten; es ist erweichend, schmerzstillend und wehret den Entzündungen.

Baumöhl und Bleyweiss unter einander klein gerieben giebt eine vortreffliche Haus-Salbe; sie ist dienlich gegen allen Brand, es sey

durch Wasser oder Feuer gebrannt; diese Salbe ist vortrefflich gut gegen alle Vergiftungen von Gift-Kraut oder giftigen Wassern, wenn man den vergifteten Ort damit gleich schmieret, so bald man es gewahr wird.

Wenn man Baumöhl in ein groß Glas thut, und füllt es über die Hälfte damit, und thut darnach von den Blumen vom St. Johannis-Kraut hinein, daß es beynahe, voll werde, stopft es zu, und hängt es an die Sonne, und läßt es etwa 4 Wochen hängen und destilliren, so bekommt man ein solches gute Wund-Oehl für allerley frische Wunden an Menschen und Vieh zu heilen, daß es schwerlich jemand glauben kann, der es nicht selbst erfahren hat. Hiermit sollte sich gleichfalls ein guter vorsichtiger Hausvater vorsorgen, daß er es allezeit zur Vorsorge im Hause hätte. Auf die vorgemeldete Weise kann man auch von weißen Lilien ein Oehl machen, welches auch sehr nützlich ist in Brandschäden und harten Geschwulsten, sie zu erweichen, auch die böse Brüste der Weiber zu heilen.

A5. Wider die Wassersucht.

Wassersucht ist eine Krankheit aus kalter Feuchtigkeit, so die Glieder durchläuft, dergestalt, daß sie entweder alle oder etliche aufschwellet. Die gemeinen Zeichen und Vorläufe jeglicher Wassersucht sind anfänglich Geschwellen und Auflaufen der Füße und Schenkel, nachmals des Angesichts; auch Verwandlung natürlicher Farbe in Weiße, großer Durst, Unlust zum Essen, Verhaltung des Stuhlgangs, Schweiß, Auswurf, und dergleichen Ueberflüssigkeiten, wenig Harnen, Trägheit und Verdrossenheit zu allen Sachen.

Es werden von den Aerzten dreierlei Arten der Wassersucht insonderheit benennt, als Anasarca, wenn das Wasser zwischen Haut und Fleisch, durch den ganzen Leib alle Glieder, auch das Angesicht dringet, und die aufschwellet. 2. Ascites, da der Bauch und Schenkel aufschwellen, hingegen die oberen Glieder verdorren. 3. Tympanites entstehet mehr aus Wind als Wasser, und der Bauch läuft davon hoch auf, der Nabel bolzet weit herfür, die andern Glieder werden alle mager, der Bauch wird dermaßen aufgeblasen, daß, wo man darauf klopft, er einen hellen Hall, wie eine Pauke gibt, daher dann auch der Name gekommen.

Der ganze Zweck, die Wassersucht insgemein zu vertreiben, stehet auf diesen drei Punkten, nämlich:

1. Die Härte der Geschwulst, so in den Gedärmen und anderswo liegt, zu erweichen. 2. Sich solcher Sachen zu befleißen, so die Feuchtigkeiten zertheilen; und 3, zu trachten, dieselbe durch den Stuhlgang, und vornehmlich mit den Harn, auszuführen.

Die vornehmsten Mittel hierzu haften darin: so viel als nur möglich vor allem Getränke sich hüten, nur trockne Kost geniessen, sich gelinde üben, viel schwitzen und auch purgiren.

Wo einer sich der Wassersucht beforget, oder dieselbe noch im ersten Angriff wäre, der gebrauche fleißig den Erdrauchzucker, denn dieser reinigt das Geblüt, und der Augentrostzucker öffnet die Berstopfung.

A6. Unsehlbare Kur wider die Wassersucht.

Nimm einen Steinern oder irdenen Krug, in diesen gieße vier Quart starken gesunden Seider, nimm eine doppelte Hand voll Petersilien-Wurzel sammt dem Kraut und schneide es fein, ein Hand voll geschabten Meerrettig, 2 Suppenlöffel voll zerquetschten Senfsamen, eine halbe Unze Meerzwiebeln, und eine Unze Wachholderbeeren; diese alles thue zusammen in den Krug, und lasse denselben 24 Stunden bei dem Feuer stehen, damit der Seider beständig warm bleibe, und schüttele es oft; dann siehe es durch ein Tuch und hebe es auf zum Gebrauch. Einem erwachsenen Menschen gibt man dreimal des Tages auf einen nüchternen Magen ein halbes Weinglas voll. Man kann aber, wenn es nöthig ist, die Dose vermehren, nur muß man, nachdem das Wasser abgeführt ist, wenig trinken, nor trockene Kost genießen, und sich gelinde üben, wie schon früher gemeldet. Dieses Mittel hat schon Vielen geholfen und unter andern einer fast 70jährigen Frau, welche die Wassersucht so schlimm hatte, daß sie sich nicht getraute aufzustehen, aus Furcht, die Haut möchte zerspringen, und wo Jedermann dafür heilt, daß sie nur noch wenige Tage leben würde. Diese gebrauchte es der Vorschrift nach und in weniger als einer Woche war

das Wasser abgetrieben: die Geschwulst ihres Leibes siel gänzlich und in etlichen Wochen war sie wieder vollkommen gesund.

Oder: Trinke für einige Tage lang recht starken Bohea-Thee und iß auch dieselben Blätter. Dieses geringe Mittel hat, wie es heißt, schon einige Personen in Zeit von 3 bis 4 Tagen von allem Wasser und der Geschwulst befreit, wo die Krankheit schon in den höchsten Grad gestiegen war.

Oder: Nimm 3 Löffel voll Rübsamen und auserlesener Myrrhen, nach Gutdünken, zusammen in einer Quart guten alten Weins über Nacht, wohl zugedeckt, in der Stube stehen lassen. Hiervon werden, eine Stunde nach dem Nachtessen, vorm Schlafengehen, 2 Löffel voll eingenommen, so der Mensch bei Jahren ist; wenn er aber halb gewachsen, oder je nachdem er sich bei Kräften befindet, mehr oder minder, und hiermit fortgefahren.

Oder: Nimm Sprußpein-Aeste, haue sie klein, und fülle einen großen Kessel damit an, dann gieße Wasser darüber und laß es eine Zeit lang kochen, hernach gieße es in einen großen Zuber, ziehe deine Kleider aus und setze dich darüber und laß einen Teppich über dich und den Zuber hängen, damit der Dampf nicht entfliehen kann; wenn das Wasser anfängt kalt zu werden, so laß heißgemachte Backsteine hinein thun, und wann du diesem Schweiß eine Zeit lang abgewartet hast, so behalte den Teppich noch immer um dir, und gehe damit zu Bett. Wenn diese für mehrere Tage wiederholt wird, so wird man dadurch von allem Wasser befreit.

APPENDIX S

Vorrede.

Der Verfasser glaubt nicht, daß es nothwendig ist, ein nützliches Buch durch eine lange Vorrede zu empfehlen, welche doch nur die mehrste Zeit von den Lesern überblättert und gewöhnlich gar nicht gelesen wird; um aber doch dem gewöhnlich Gebrauche Genüge zu leisten, und um zugleich den Leser über die geheimen Mittel und Künster welche in diesem Buche enthalten sind, und vielleicht bei manchen Gewissensscrupel erregen könnten zu unterrichten, hält es derselbe für zweckmäßig, eine kleine Vorrede dem Werkchen vorauszusetzen.

Viele Leute scheuen sich, in Fällen der Noth, Mittel anzuwenden, bei welchen heilige oder wie man gewöhnlich zu sagen pflegt: hohe Worte gebraucht werden; doch diese Grundsätze und Meinungen, konnen bei Anwendung dieser im Buche enthaltenen Mittel nicht berücksichtigt werden. - Es besteht unstreitig in der Wahrheit, daß viele, sehr viele Mittel und Künste in diesen Buche enthalten sind, bei deren Anwendung die Namen heiliger Personen, heiliger Dinge und selbst die drei höchsten Namen vorkommen; aber, kann dieses Sünde sein? Zwar sagt das Göttliche Gesetz deutlich: "Du sollst den Namen Gottes deines Herrn nicht unnütz und vergeblich führen." Dieses Gesetz kann aber nicht berücksichtiget werden, bei Anwendung von Mitteln und Künsten zum Wohle der Menschen; denn Niemand wird wohl auf den Einfall kommen, dergleichen Mittel und Künste zu gebrauchen, wenn er nicht wegen Noth derselben bedürftig ist. Es heiß't deutlich in 50sten Psalm, wie das Motto dieses Buchs sagt: "Rufe mich an in der Noth, und ich will dich erretten und du sollst meinen Namen preisen." Folglich kann

215

der Gebrauch hoher Worte keine Sünde sein, sondern muß im Gegentheile Gott, dem obigen Schriftsatze gemäß, angenehm sein.

So gehe den hin du liebes Büchlein in die Welt, kehre bei jeden friedlichen Manne ein, und bringe Segen und Hülfe welche dein Inhalt verkündet; und beglücke deine Inhaber, führe sie nicht den Weg des Laster sondern zum Heile. Diese ist dein einziger Beruf, zu welchen du geschrieben bist, und das er erfüllt werden möge, wünscht herzlich;

Der Verfasser.

Geschrieben, zu Skippacksville, in Pennsylvanien, Im September 1837.

S1. Mittel wieder die Kornwürmer

Bestreiche die Fruchtkisten mit Kiehnöl, und sie verschwinden in ein paar Tagen nach dem Überstreichen.

S2. Unschädliches Mittel, daß die jungen Mädchen einem gewogen bleiben.

Trage auf der linken Seite im Hemde genäht oder befestigt, ein Stück vom Schwanze eine Maus und zwei lange Pfefferkörner. Es ist gewiß sehr gut.

S3. Mittel, um die Mücken zu vertreiben.

Koche Kürbis in Wasser, und besprenge damit die Zimmer, oder räuchere mit Kürbisblättern und halte die Fenster zu, so krepiren sie sicherlich.

S4. Mittel gegen dem Brand in Waizen.

Nimm Seifensieder-Salzlauge und benetze damit den Waizen welcher gesäet werden soll. Auch kann man dazu etwas ungelöschen Kalk nehmen.

S5. Mittel die Flöhe der Hunde zu vertreiben.

Wische Anisöhl auf eine solche Stelle des Körpers, die der Hund nicht belecken kann, und in kurzer Zeit sind die Flöhe verschwunden.

S6. Ein Mittel gegen den Pips der Hühner.

Schneide ein Stück Brod in kleine Würzel, tunke solche in Essig, trockne sie hernach ein Wenig und gieb den Hühnern drei Mal täglich davon.

S7. Mittel wieder das Aufschwellen des Viehes nach dem Genuße des jungen Klees

Man nimmt Tabaksabfall oder sonst gemeinen Tabak, gies't gemeinen Whiskey darauf und läßt es solange stehen bis es so braun wie Bier ist. Ist ein Stück Vieh vom Klee aufgeschwollen, so nimmt man ein Stück Seife wie eine Wallnuß gros, steckt es dem Vieh in den Hals und giest eine Theetasse voll von dem Tabaksertrakt nach, und das Aufschwellen verschwindet auf der Stelle.

S8. Ein feuerfester Kitt um Oefen zu verkleben.

Man nehme Eisenseilspäne, ungelöschten Kalk und Salz; mache diese 3 Theile mit dem Weißen von Eiern zu einem Teige an, und verschmiere damit die Ritzen der Oefen. Man laße die beschmierten Stellen an der Luft trocken werden, und heize hernach den Ofen anfangs nicht zu heiß; so wird man finden, daß dieser Kitt so lange, wie der Ofen selbst; hält.

S9. Mittel, um Flöhe zu fangen.

Man nehme einen Schuß von einem Hollunder-strauch, ziehe die grüne Schaale ab, und befreie ihn von dem Marke (Pettig), wische mit einer Feder etwas Honig hinein, und lege ihn Abends bei sich im Bette, am andern Morgen sind die Flöhe am Honig fest und also gefangen.

S10. Ein großer Vortheil beim Brodbacken

Koche fünf Pfund Kleie, mit dem davon abgegoffenen Wasser menge 56 Pfund Mehl, mache wie sonst gewöhnlich den Teig und backe ihn zu Brod. Durch dieses Kleiwasser erhält man ein fünftheil Zuwachs an Brod, das Brod wird fein und schmackhast, und die Kleie bleibt zum Verfüttern gut. Bei dem Backen kleinerer Quantitäten, kann man beides, Mehl und Kleie, in Verhältniß die Hälfte, das Drittel oder Viertel nehmen.

S11. Mittel für aufgesprungene, gefrorne Glieder.

Lasse für 4 Cent Wallrath, (Speremaceti Oel) für 4 Cent süßes Mandelöl und ein Stück weißes Wachs von der Größe einer kleinen Ruß schmelzen, und schmiere die Wunden damit; so werden die Wunden in einigen Tagen völlig und gut geheilt sein.

S12. Mittel für tollen Hund-Biß.

Wenn man das Unglück hat, von einem tollen Hunde gebissen zu werden, so bedine man sich des folgenden Mittels. Man bürste die Wunde öfters und sehr stark mit Salzwasser aus und lege auf ein Stück mit Butter beschmiertes Brod Anagalis, welches man in der Apotheke erhält und esse es. Ist der biß am Fuße oder an der Hand, so stecke sie in frische aufgegrabene Erde.

S13. Mittel gegen die Wasser-Sucht

Nimm 1 Unze blaue Lilienzwiebeln
- 1—Gewürznägelein und
- 2—klein Rosinen.

Diese Theile koche in zwei Peint Wasser und etwas Wein; sodann getrunken und das Uebrige gegessen. Schon sehr viele Menschen sind durch dieses wohlfeile Mittel geheilt, und deshalb ist es allen, an dem gefährlichen Uebel liedenden, nicht genug zu empfehlen.

S14. Sicheres Mittel zu machen, daß ein Anderer mit seiner Flinte kein Wild schießen oder tödten kann

Nimm Cuculi Arambosti, pp. für 6 Cent Werth, rühre dieses zwischen frisches Haasenfett und wische von dieser Salbe in den Gewehrlauf, und nie wird er ein Thier todtschießen können.

S15. Mittel das dem Andern das Gewehr stets versage.

Ziehe die linke Hosentasche heraus, lege beide Hände in Kreutz darüber, doch so, daß die Daumen sich einander begegnen und sprich, wenn der Andere abdrücken will, die folgenden Worte:

RACCE, BALCE, VELUTI, ARMA.

S16. Mittel wenn die Kühe Statt Milch, Blut geben.

Gieb den Kühen täglich unter ihr Futter folgendes:

Gedörrete Gerste 1 Buschel,

CRINIS FULVAE eine halbe Unze geschnitten und

SANCTA SIMPLEX für 1 Cent.

Alles dieses wohl untereinander gemischt.

S17. Ein sehr erprobtes Mittel wider den Sonnenbrand.

Brate ein Pfund weiße Lilienzwiebeln in heißer Asche, stoße sie im Mörser, und thue 4 Unzen seinen Candiszucker hinzu, mache es zu einer Salbe, und lege es auf die verbrannten Stellen.

S18. Mittel wider die Wanzen.

Man bestreiche das Holzwerk täglich einigemal mit Bierhäfen, und laße er darauf trocknen, so vergehen die Wanzen gewiß in ein paar Tagen.

S19. Mittel wider die Auszehrung.

Man koche geraspeltes Hirschhorn, lasse es zu Gallert werden, und gebe dem Kranken täglich davon zu essen. Dieses Mittel, welches lange geheim gehalten wurde, diente schon sehr Vielen an dieser Krankheit leidenden auf dem besten Erfolge.

S20. Daß ein Pferd gegen den Willen des Treibers still stehe.

Sehr viele und geheime Mittel, waren bis jetzt für diese Kunstückchen schon bekannt; um aber auch denjenigen Leuten, welche an dergleichen übernaturliche Mittel nicht glauben oder sich scheuen Gebrauch davon zu machen, eine Gelegenheit zu geben um dasselbe auf eine natürliche Art zu bewirken, so diene hier folgendes natürliche und untrügliche Mittel. Mische nämlich folgende Theile zusammen:

Eine halbe Unze Quarilaserum,

Eine viertel do. Putandrum longum und

Eine do. do. Succus leritarium.

Und streue es über den Weg, wo der Gault stehen bleiben soll; und er wird nicht weiter geben bis der Stoff welcher ihm hindert hinweg genommen ist. Hat aber der Treiber das linke Ohr von einer Maus bei sich, so hilft es nicht.

S21. Mittel wenn ein Gaul nicht Stallen kam.

Rühre dem Schaafmist auf, und stelle darauf den Gaul, so wird er in kurzer Zeit Stallen können.

S22. Daß das Haar schnell wächst, und selbst an Stellen wo keine waren oder dieselben ausgefallen sind.

Nimm ein halb Pfund Sweineschmalz,
Eine halbe Unze Lindenbluthensaft,
Eine viertel Unze Assa fötida pulver und
Ein do. do. Schneckenfett.

Alles wohl unter einander gemischt und mit der daraus enstandenen Salbe die haarleren Stellen geschmiert.

S23: Ein Mittel, das Blut zu stillen.

Lege die zwei ersten Finger der rechten Hand auf die Wunde, und sprich; Christus und Petrus gingen über die Fluth, da nahm Christus die Ruth und schlug in die Fluth, da stillt sich das Blut.

† † †

S24: Noch ein anderes dergleichen.

Lege ebenfalls die zwei ersten Finger der rechter Hand auf die Wunde, und sprich: Blut, halt ein, zwischen Mark und Bein; daß die Wunde soll wieder geheilet sein.

† † †

220

S25: Ein geheimes, aber natürliches Stück, wenn irgend einer von einem Hause oder Familie verreiset oder lange abwesend ist, zu erfahren ob er lebendig oder todt sei.

Hierzu dient das Kraut Telepium item Grasula auf Deutsch genannt, Wundenkraut, Donnerkraut, Fette-Henne, oder auch Knableinskraut; doch ist es kein Orchis oder Specis Satiri, welches oft in Kräuter-Büchern Knabenkraut genannt wird. Es wacht mehrentheils an dürren magern Orten, etwa eine Spanne hoch, hat grüne, dick und fette Blätter, hellrothe Blüthen und an den Wurzeln viele Knoten.

Ist nun jemand aus einem Hause verreiset, sei der Vater, der Sohn oder die Tochter, nur muss derjenige Antheil am Hause haben, und man weiß nicht ob er lebendig oder tod sei, so bricht man von den obengemeldeten Kraut, ohne weiter etwas zu thun oder zu sagen, einen Stengel ab, und steckt denselben unter des Hauses Dach, in welches der Abwesende gehört, zwischen die Latten und Schindeln oder Ziegel. Ist der abwesende Mensche tod, so wird der Krautstengel bald verwelken und verdorren, ist er aber noch am Leben, so wird derselbe nicht allein grün bleiben, sondern fortwachsen und neue Sprossen treiben. Dieses Stück ist schon vor mehreren hundert Jahren, von dem original Verfasser (einem Araber) erprobt, und nach der Zeit von vielen Andern als untrüglich befunden werden.

S26: Eine Kur wenn ein Pferd steif und hinfällig wird, welches ganz ohne Rachtheil ist, dasselbe davon zu befreien.

Nimm ein Peint Schweinefett, thue es in eine Pfanne und schmelze es, dann schütte es in ein anderes Geschirr und rühre ein halbes Peint frisch gemolkene Kuhmilch darunter, hierauf gieb des dem Pferde ein. Diese Kur sollte angewendet werden, sobald man ausfindet, daß das Pferd mit obiger Krankheit befallen ist. Wer dieses beobachtet, der kann das Pferd einspannen oder brauchen, wie gewöhnlich, und es wird ihm weiter keinen Schaden thun.

S27: Eine der besten Kuren welche jemals gebraucht wurde, für ein Pferd das in Gefahr ist blind zu werden.

Schneide ein Stück neues Linnen, von der Größe eines Viertelthalers, ziehe durch dasselbe eine Nadel mit einen starken Faden, so daß man es damit zusammen ziehen kann, denn thue drei lebendige Spinnen hinein, welche von drei Ecken des Hauses genommen werden müssen, zieh es zusammen und mache drei Knoten hinein, hernach binde es vorne an des Pferdes Kopf, aber so, dass es gerade über des Pferdes Auge hängt, und laß es hängen bis es von selbst abfällt. Wenn das Auge noch nicht völlig tod ist, so wird dieses Mittel unfehlbar dasselbe kuriren.

S28: Ein Pferd zu kuriren welches überhitzt ist.

Wenn ein Pferd hinfällt und überhitzt ist, so gieb ihn ein halbes Peint Flach-Saamen-Oel und ein halbes Peint Schweinefett unter einander gemischt ein, und wasch das Pferd mit frischen Wasser.

S29: Mittel um das Aufschwellen und Springen der Kühe beim Genusse des Klees zu vermeiden.

Nimm Rainfarn, gereiebenes Epheu und Alaun, zerstoße es wohl, und gieb davon dem Viehe jeden Mittwoch und Freitag Morgen, unter Salz zu fressen.

S30: Ein Pferd welches Wunden von Drücken oder auf andere Art erhalten, in zwei oder drei Tagen zu kuriren.

Koche eine Handvoll innere Weißeichen-Rinde und etwas Wallwurz in drei Quart guter Lauge, bis es zu zwei Quart eingekocht ist; dann nimm es vom Feuer und gieße es ab in einen irdenen Topf, und thue vier Unzen Waun hinein; nun lass es stehen bis es lauwarm ist, dann rühre es wohl um und wasch das Pferd dreimal das Tages damit, vermittelst eines Schwammes miche etwas Spik-Oel und Stein-Oel zusammen und schmiere das Pferd damit, jedesmal nach dem Waschen.

S31: Eine Kur für die Ausfallen der Tragt einer Kuh.
Wenn die Tragt einer Kuh ausgefallen ist, so nimm etwas reine Asche, streue sie über dieselbe, und bringe sie wieder an ihren rechten Platz, dies macht sie bleiben.

S32: Ein Rezept, Seider-Fässer zu reinigen.
Spüle das Faß erst wohl mit heissen Wasser aus, als dann schütte das Wasser heraus, und thue eine Pfund ungelöschten Kalf durch das Spundloch mit neun oder zehn Gallonen kochenden Wasser; mache es wohl zu und schütte es aus, schwenke das Faß wohl, mit kalten Wasser und fulle es mit kalten Wasser auf, und lass es 24 Stunden liegen, dann schütte das Wasser heraus, schwenke das Faß aber mals und laß das Wasser völlig heraus laufen, schütte ein Quarte Aepfel-Whiskey hinein, schwenke es wohl damit und laß es hernach liegen bis du es gebrauchen willst. Dies kann man mit allen Fässern thun, welche man willens ist mit Seider zu füllen.

S33: Ein Rezept guten Wein von Seider zu machen.
Koche 2 Barrel Seider bis auf ein Barrel ein, gieb Acht und schäume ihn wohl während dem Kochen, thue ihn kochend heiß in ein Barrel, vermache es wohl und laß es bis zum nächsten März Monat liegen, dann zapfe ihn an einen hellen Tage im Vollmond ab, schwenke das Bärl mit kalten Wasser wohl aus, thue eine Gallone guten Lissabon-Wein und eine Gallone guten Aepfel-Whiskey hinein, ehe du es wieder auffullest, hernach fülle es auf, vermache es wohl und leg es auf. Je alter es wird desto besser wird es sein, aber es wird keinen regulären Wein-Geschmack haben, bis zwei Jahre verflossen sind, doch ist es auch während dieser Zeit ein liebliches Getränk. Wenn er zwei Jahre alt ist so wird er weit besser sein wie der importirte Wein.

S34: Ein Rezept guten Seider zu machen, der nicht gehrt.
Stelle einen Zubber so hoch, daß du einen Eimer darunter stellen kannst, thue den Seider hernach hinein, und rühre gute fuße Häfen darunter, in Proportion von einer Gallone Häfen zu drei Barrel Seider. Nachdem es durchgehends gewirkt hat, so zapfe es unten ab in die

gereinigten Barrels, und laß es zwei Monat liegen, dann zapfe ihn an einem hellen Tage im Vollmond ab, spüle die Barrels mit kalten Wasser wohl aus, und thu in jedes Barrel ein Peint guten Aepfel-Whiskey und fülle den Seider hernach wieder hinein, vermache es wohl und laß es liegen so lange du willst, es wird gewiß nicht verderben. Dieses untrügliche Mittel ist nicht allein wegen seiner Billigkeit sondern auch wegen seiner Güte zu empfelen.

S35: Seider-Oil zu machen.

Wenn du wunschest Seider-Oil zu machen, so thue in das Barrel, sobald es gereinigt ist, zwei Gallonen Aepfel-Whiskey, fulle es auf mit Seider, und wenn du es, wie im vorhergehenden Stücke gesagt ist, abzapfest, so thue abermals eine Gallone Whiskey in jedes Barrel. Drei Gallonen sind hinsanglich, um ein Barrel Seider-Oil zu machen.

S36: Ein anderes Rezept um guten Seider zu machen.

Nimm ein reines Orhoft, mit einen Boden, bohre Löcher in den Boden und thue sauber gewaschenes Roggen-Stroh in das Orhoft, etwa 6 Zoll hoch, ebenfalls zwei Buschel gewaschenen Sand, hernach thue den Seider hinein und laß ihn durch ziehen in einen Zubber, Wenn der Seider auf diese Weise prepparirt ist, wird er nicht gehren und fort während süß schmecken, aber das Stroh und der Sand mussen alle Tage gewaschen werden während dem Seidermachen, weil es sonst sauer wird und der Seider verdirbt.

S37: Ein Mittel, die Kornwürmer (Weavils) zu vertreiben.

Kehre deine Scheuer recht sauber aus am dritten Tage im neuen Mond vor der Erndte, dann nimm eine handvoll Hopf und drei handvoll Andorn oder Marrubium, eine gleiche Quantität Camille und eine volle Quart frischen Schaaf-Mist, thue es alle in einen Kessel voll Wasser und koche es wohl, zuletzt thue es in ein anderes Geschirr, und besprenge durch eine Seihe deine ganze Scheuer damit über, und ebenfalls die Ecken wo sich die Weavils aufhalten. Ohne dies laß der Frau einige Kuchen in Schweinefett backen am Fastnachts-Tage, bewahre das Fett bis der Erndte, wenn die Frucht heimgefahren wird

so beschmiere den Wagen und die Gabeln damit. Wenn du dieses thust so wirst du ebensowenig mit Mäuse wie mit Weavels geplagt sein.

S38: Ein Kur für den Schorf (Letter).

Nimm die Wurzel von Indian Pen, [diese Pflanze wächst im Walde, nur allein in Kaltstein Boden, hat beinahe runde aber gebogene Blätter, und trägt weiße Blumen im April. Die Wurzel ist von rothgelber Farbe, weich, und nicht tief unter der Oberfläche der Erde,) zerstoße es ein wenig, thue es in ein Geschirr und schütte etwas scharfen Essig dazu, nachdem laß es einige Zeit stehen, und leg es hernach auf, den Schorf, laß es ungefahr drei Stunden liegen, dann nimm es ab und wasch den Schorf mit deinem eigenen Urin, alsdann mache einen neuen Umschlag auf und laß ihn für die ganze Nacht darauf liegen. Des Morgens, sobald on aufstehst nimm es ab und wasche die Stelle wieder mit Urin und leg einen frischen Umschlag auf. Wenn dein eigener Urin nicht stark genug ist, so nimm den Urin von einen Knaben der noch nicht sieben Jahre alt ist. Dies Kur wird nicht fehlschlagen den gewunschten Erfolg hervorzubringen.

S39: Eine Kur für den Schlangebiß.

Wenn du von einer Schlange gebissen wurdest, nach so geschwind wie möchlich, daß du an fließendes Wasser kömmst, und wasche die Wunde bis das Folgende bereitet ist. Eine handvoll Wegbreit-Blätter, von der kleinen Sorte, müßen ein wenig zerdrückt und eine kleine Quantitat Fünf-Fingerkraut dazu gethan werden, dann thue es in ein Pfanne und thue ein Peint frischgemolkene Kuhmilch dazu, wenn solche zu haben ist, und koche es wohl, nachdem wird es aufgelegt so warm wie du es vertragen kannst. Wenn der Biß von einer sehr giftigeu Schlange war, so nimm einen frischen Umschlag eine Stunde nachher, und alle zwei Stunden nimm ein wenig Brand-Pulver ein.

S40: Ein anderes.

Koche etwa zwei Pfund Kristanien Blätter mit ebensoviel Eschen Blätter in guter Lauge, dann leg es auf deine Hand oder Fuß sobald es

hinlänglich abgekühlt ist. Ist es ein Thier welches gebissen, so binde ein gutes Bündel von den Blättern auf die Wunde.

S41: Noch eine anderes.
Nimm Berenklau, theile es den breiten Weg in zwei Theile und binde es auf die Wunde.

S42: Eine Kur gegen das giftige Kraut welches in Wiesen wächst.
Zerstoße etwas Ruß aus dem Schornsteine zu Pulver und ruhre es zu einer Salbe mit süßen Rahm, streiche diese Salbe auf Wegbreit Blätter und leg es auf die giftige Stelle, und in zwölf Stunden wird das Gift getödtet sein.

S43: Eine Beschreibung aller Krankheiten an Pferden.
Wenn du die Natur der Krankheit deines Pferdes ausfinden willst, so drehe seine Ober-Lippe, auf solche Art, daß du dieselbe genau unter-suchen kannst; hat dieselbe ein weißes und knopfiges Ansehen, so ist dieses ein Zeichen von Würmern; ist sie roth und knöpfig, so hat das Pferd die Batz; wenn die Lippe roth und voll von Adern ist, so hat das Pferd die Wind-Kolik; ist die Lippe roth ohne volle Adern, so hat es nur allein die Kolik, Ich habe versucht, in diesem Buche alle die verschiedenen Kuren zu beschreiben. Die folgenden Regeln mögen beobachtet werden, gleich nachdem man die Krankheit kennt. Reite oder führe das Pferd für eine kurze Zeit herum, dann nimm einen starken Mistgabel-Stiel, stecke ihn unter des Pferdes Bauch durch, laß einen andern Mann an der entgegengesetzten Seite anfassen und so reibe das Pferd nichtig nach den hintern Theile zu, aber nicht auf-wärts nach der Brust, und halte auf diese Art jedesmal drei Minuten an. Diese Operation mag alle Stunde erneuert werden so lange bis die Krankheit des Pferdes vorüber ist.

Wenn ein Pferd Würmer hat, so gieb ihm ein volles Peint Flachssa-men-Oel ein, und verfahre weiter wie oben gesagt ist.

S44: *Eine Kur für die Batz.*

Schütte dem Pferde ein halbes Peint süßen Oel ein. Dieses ist das beste Mittel welches für die Batz gebraucht werden kann. Ein Tschill Terpentin-Spiritus ist ebenfalls gut für die Batz, aber süßer Oel ist das allerbeste Mittel.

S45: *Eine Kur für die Wind-Colik der Pferde.*

Schlag ein schwarzes Huhn nieder mit dem dicken Ende einer Peitsche (Wipp) u. zerreiße es so schnell wie möchlich in Stücke, aber wenn du es nicht zerreißen kannst so schneide es offen und nimm das ganze Eingeweide heraus, dann stopfe es dem Pferde ins Maul und stoße es mit dem Hendel von deiner Wipp in den Halse hinunter. Dieses wird die Wind-Colik so vollkommen kuriren, daß das Pferd nie mehr damit befallen werden wird.

S46: *Eine Andere.*

Thue eine gute Handvoll Espen-Rinde in einen eisernen Topf mit zwei Quart Wasser, und koche es bis auf eine Quart ein, dann gieße es ab in ein anderes Geschirr und laß es stehen bis es Milch warm ist. Alsdann magst du es dem Pferde eingeben und die Regeln welche oben gegeben sind beobachten.

S47: *Eine Andere.*

Thue in halbes Peint Whiskey in eine Flasche, ein wenig Essig und ein wenig geschabte Kreide dazu, dann blasé den Rauch einer brennenden Cigarre in die Flasche hinein, halt die Hand fest darüber und schütte es, wiederhole dieselbe Operation bis die Cigarre beinahe ganz verbrannt ist, gieb aber Acht und halt die Hand fest auf die Flasche damit der Rauch nicht heraus geht und schüttle es wohl. Nachdem es milchwarm geworden so gieb es dem Pferde ein.

S48: *Eine Kur für den Magen und Reinigung des Geblüts.*

Nimm Genzian-Wurzel, Ginseng-Wurzel, Hollunder Rinde, Hollunder-Wurzel, die Rinde von Sassafrass-Wurzeln, Andorn, Kletten, von jedem eine halbe Unze, und Rosin von Pein-Holz soviel wie eine Hickory-Nuß

gros, thue es alle zusammen in eine Flasche und gieße ein Quart guten Kornbranntewein dazu. Wenn es 24 Stunden gestanden hat so ist es zum Gebrauche gut.

Eine erwachsene Person von starker Natur und Körperbau, kann einen Theelöffel voll zur Zeit davon nehmen, und es ist leicht auszufinden ob mehr oder weniger sein muß um gehörig zu wirken. Es ist zu nehmen dreimal des Tages, Morgens vor dem Essen, Mittags und Abends.

S49: Ein anderes Mittel zur Reinigung des Geblüts und Stärkung des Magens.

Nimm Muskatenblüthe, Blumen von Sulphur, Gewürznägelein, Zimmet-Rinde, von jeden ein halbe Unze, für elf Pens Werth Saffran und etwa eine halbe Unze kleine Schlangenwurzel, thue es zusammen in eine Flasche und gieße ein Quart guten Wein dazu, lass es 24 Stunden stehen und es wird zum Gebrauch gut sein. Ein Theelöffel voll mag davon des Morgens vor den Essen genommen werden oder auch dreimal des Tages.

S50: Eine Kur für die Auszehrung.

Nimm von dem Kraut Herz-Zunge, Lungenkraut, Leberkraut, Sarsaparillen-Wurzel und Fluellin, von jeden eine kleine Handvoll, thue das Ganze in einen neuen, saubern irdenen Topf, thue 2 Quart guten Wein dazu und koche es uber einem gelinden Kohlfeuer. Der Topf muß zugedeckt gehalten werden, aber die Mixture muß alle fünf Minuten umgerührt werden mit einem saubern Schüppchen von Peint-Holz. Von der Zeit wenn es anfängt zu kochen, laß es eine halbe Stunde dann nimm es ab, laß es stehen bis es Milchwarm ist, seihe es durch ein rein linnenes Tuch, thue es in eine Flasche und vermach es wohl. Eine erwachsene Person mag davon einen Esslöffel voll Morgens vor dem Essen nehmen, und nachher alle drei Stunden dieselbe Dosis. Es ist ebenfalls gut, daß der Kranke alle Tage etwas Löffelkraut oder Brunnenkreste zu sich nehme. Jede Art Speisen kann dabei genossen werden ausgenommen Schweinefleisch und scharfer Essig.

S51: Eine andere Kur für die Auszehrung.
Sammle das Kraut und die Blüthen von Veilchen, im Monat Mai, und trockne sie im Schatten. Dann stopfe es in die Pfeife und rauche es.

S52: Eine andere Kur für die Auszehrung.
Nimm ein frischgelegtes Hühnerei, am dritten Tage im neuen Mond des Morgens vor dem Essen, schlag es in ein Glass und rühre es wohl mit einem Schüppchen von Peint Holz, dann thue ein Tschill guten Wein dazu und trink es für sieben oder neun Tage. Französicher Klee (Haasenkiee) ist ebenfalls sehr gut für die Auszehrung, wenn all Tage ein wenig davon gegessen.

S53: Eine Kur für die Verstopfung des Urins.
Irgend eine Person welche ihr Wasser nicht lassen kann, nehme ein wenig Fünf-Finger Kraut, einige Wegbreitblätter mit der Wurzel und ein wenig Schaaf Mist, und trinke Thee davon. Thee von Nesseln gemacht, ist ebenfalls ein gutes Mittel für die obengenante Beschwerde.

S54: Eine Kur für die Warzen oder andere Auswüchse.
Am dritten Tage im zunehmenden Mond, Abends, wenn du den neuen Mond zum ersten Mal siehst, dann nimm den Kranken hinaus, leg deine Finger der rechten Hand auf die Warze und blicke nach dem Monde, dann sprich wie folgt: Dasjenige darauf ich sehe ist zunehmend, und Dasjenige was ich jetzt anfasse ist abnehmend nachdem du dieses dreimal wiederhohlt hast, gehe in das Haus zurück.

S55: Eine Anweisung, Brandpulver zu machen.
Nimm ein viertel Pfund gewöhnliches Schießpulver, ein viertel Pfund Schwefel und ein Pfund Alaun, thue alles zusammen in einer Mörser und stoße es so fein wie Staub. Von diesen Pulver kann ein Mensch von starken Körper und Natur soviel wie auf einem elfpens Stück liegen kann, in einen kleinen Eßlöffel voll starken Essig nehmen. Eine schwächere Person nach Verhältniß weniger. Es ist alle zwei Stunden zu nehmen.

Dieses Pulver bewahret vor dem kalten Brand und ist gleichzeitig gut für das Sanct Antonis Feuer.

S56: Einer der besten Umschläge für den Brand.

Wenn dieser Umschlag angewendet und etwas von den obigen Pulver gleichzeitig genommen wird, so ist kein Schaden weiter zu befurchten.

Nimm eine Handvoll Haber und eine Handvoll roth Ceder Sproßen, mit den kleinen Aestchen an welche die Nadeln gewachsen sind, schneide die Letzteren fein und thue es mit dem Haber zusammen in eine Pfanne und röste es auf dieselbe Art wie Caffee gewöhnlich geröstet wird und mahle das Ganze in einer Caffee-Mühle, dann thue es wiederum in eine Pfanne und ein Peint süßen Ram dazu, backe es zu einen Kleister, schlage ein Ei dazu hinein und ruhre es wohl untereinander, dann nimm es vom Feuer, streiche es auf einen reinen linnen Lappen und lege es auf die Wunde so warm wie du es vertragen kannst.

S57: Wie man süsses Oel reinigen kann.

Nimm soviel Schrot als sonst zu zwei Flintenladungen erforderlich ist, thue denselben in eine Flasche voll süßen Oel und er wird so klar werden wie Wasser.

S58: Ein unschätzbares Mittel das Gehör wieder zu erlangen wenn es verloren ist.

Nimm Pfeffermünz, etwas Pfefferwurz und den Kopf von einer Ratze, senge die Haare davon und koche ihn mit dem Pfefferwurz in einen vollen Peint März-Schnee-Wasser, thue ebenfalls drei Köpfe von Hopfen hinein, alsdann vermische es mit einem Peint Flauer und mache einen Teig davon, mache soviel Pfeffermünz (welches vorher ganz fein geschnitten werden muß) in den Teig wie möglich ist, den backe einen Kuchen davon, und des Abends befor du ins Bett gehst spalte ihn in der Mitte, binde die eine Halfte auf das linke und die andere auf das rechte Ohr, und halte es darauf bis zum nächsten Morgen, alsdann magst du es abnehmen, und drei Tropfen von gereinigten Oel in jedes Ohr thun. Das Fett einer Rattel-Schlange ist ebenfalls sehr gut für

Taubheit, angenommen, wenn eine Schlange zu haben ist, welche sich nicht selbst gebißen hat, welches nicht wohl verhütet werden kann, ausgenommen man schiesst den Kopf ab ehe das Thier beginnt bös zu werden. Der Körper ist nicht giftig, ausgenommen er ist gebißen, und wenn du eine auf die beschriebene Art bekommen kannst, so thue von dem Fett alle neun Tage einen Tropfen in jedes Ohr.

S59: Pillen für Zahnschmerzen.

Thue etwas braunen Zucker in eine Pfanne, und brate ihn über dem Feuer bis er zu Blasen wird, dann thue soviel gemahlten Pfeffer dazu wie Zucker da ist, nimm es von Feuer und rühre es zusammen, hernach mache Pillen davon in der Größe daß man sie in einem hohlen Zahn theun kann.

S60: Eine Kur für das Seitenstechen.

Nimm eine kleine Handvoll Hagedorn-Blüthe, soviel Distelblumen, ein wenig Catnip, eine kleine Handvoll Knospen von einen peruanischen Palmbaume, (diese Knospen mussen im Anfange des Marz Mondes gebrochen werden), und, ein wenig Andorn, thue es alle zusammen in eine Flasche und thue ein Quart Kornbranntewein dazu. Diese Medizin hat nicht eher ihre volle Kraft, bis sie ein Jahr alt ist, wo es durch ein Stuck neues Linnen gesiehet und in eine saubere Flasche gethan werden muß. Eine starke Person kann einen Theelöffel voll alle zwei Stunden nehmen so lange bis die Plage vorüber ist.

S61: Eine approbirte Kur für die Mutterkrankheit.

Nimm eine Unze Bergamotte, eine gleiche Quantität Catnip, etwa einen Eßlöffel voll den Weißen von trockenen Hühner-Mist, und brenne drei Welschkorn-Grutzen zu Asche, thue das Ganze zusammen in eine Flasche und thue ein Quart Spiritus von Kornbranntenwein dazu, dann stelle die Flasche neun Tage, in die Sonne und schüttle sie alle Tage einmal, nach diesen siehe es durch im abnehmenden Mond und thue es aber mals in eine Flasche. Wenn sich ein Satz zeigt, so gieße das Klare ab, bis es ganz klar wird. Eine Frau welche mit der Mutterkrankheit geplagt ist, kann von achtzehn bis dreißig Tropfen alle

zwei Stunden nehmen, und einem Kinde, welches die Colik hat, giebt man von ein bis sieben Tropfen, gemäß seines Alters. Ist das Kind ganz klein so kann diese Medizin in der Mutter-Milch gegeben werden.

S62: Ein Mittel gegen das Erbrechen der Kindbetterinnen.

Nimm ein wenig Catnip und laß es der Kindbetterin als Thee trinken. Dieses wird das Erbrechen stillen.

S63: Eine Kur wenn ein Kind die Colik hat.

Wenn ein Kind mit der Colik geplagt ist, wenn es auch so schlimm ist, daß es auf keine Weise zu lindern wäre, so nimm ein wenig Garten-Knoblauch, zerquetsche es und drücke den Saft durch einen reinen linnen Lappen. Von diesen Extract mische einen Tropfen mit einen Tropfen Spiritus von Kornbranntwein für ein ganz junges Kind, und gieb es demselben in der Mutter Milch. Für ein Kind welches drei Monat alt ist mögen drei Tropfen von jeden in der Mutter Milche gegeben werden.

S64: Eine Kur für den wehen Mund der Kinder.

Nimm die Blätter von rothen Fallrosen, weiße Lilien und Salbei, von jeden eine Handvoll, thue alles in eine Flasche mit einer Quart guten Kornbranntewein und laß es drei Tage stehen. Wenn du es für den wehen Mund der Kinder gebrauchen willst, mische einen Theelöffel voll von den obigen Liquer mit einem halben Tschill Marz-Schnee-Wasser und einen Theelöffel voll Honig in eine Thee-Tasse, dann rühre es mit einem Stuckchen Alaun bis der Alaun soviel als eine Messerspitze verschwunden ist, hernach wickle einen saubern linnenen Lappen um deinen Finger und wasche des Kindes Mund ein oder zweimal des Tages mit der obigen Preparation. Dieses wird es bald heilen.

S65: Eine Mittel für die rothe Ruhr oder Colik.

Nimm etwa eine Unze innere Weißeichen Rinde, ein wenig von dem Kraut Krausemünze, eine Unze Knotengraß und ein Tschill Heidelbeeren [whortleberries], thue es alle in eine Flasche, mit einer

Quart Franzbranntewein und laß es drei Tage stehen, dann mag eine erwaschene Person einen Theelöffel voll dreimal des Tages nehmen, aber ein Eßlöffel voll süßes Oel muß des Morgens eine halbe Stunde vor dem Einnehmen der Medizin genommen werden.

S66: Ein Oel zu bereiten, welches jede Art Wunden heilet.

Thue eine Handvoll weiße Lilien, eine Handvoll rothe Fallrosen-Blätter und ein Tschill peruanische Balsam-Knopfen [die Knopfen müßen im Anfang des Marz-Monds gebrochen werden,] in eine Flasche mit einem Peint guten Kornbranntewein, ein Peint Brändi und eine Unze Kampher, stelle es drei Tage in die Sonne, dann nimm ein Peint von diesen Liquer und mische es in eine Flasche mit einen halben Tschill Terpentin-Spiritus, einer halben Unze Spiek-Oel, einen Eßlöffel voll braunen Zucker und eine halbe Unze Stein-Oel, stelle die Mixtur wiederum drei Tage an die Sonne und schüttle die Flasche alle Tage. Dieses giebt ein vortreffliches Oel zur Heilung für alle und jede Art vom Wunden.

S67: Eine Salbe zu machen, welche alle andere übertrifft.

Nimm drei rothe Welschkorn-Gruzen und brenne sie ganz fein zu Pulver, etwa drei Unzen von den Excrementen eines Mannes, (das letztere muß auf eine Schaufel gethan und zu ganz feinen Pulver gebrannt werden), eine halbe Unze Drachenblud und eine Unze Silberglätte; stoße es alle zu feinem Pulver, alsdann nimm ein halbes Tschill Mullein Blumen, ein halbes Tschill junge Hollunder-Aestchen, eine gleiche Quantität Peterzilien, ein wenig Wallwurz-Wurzeln, etwas Alantwurzel und eine kleine Handvoll stinkende Nachtschatten-Blumen, thue alle die Kräuter zusammen in ein Tuch und zerquetsche sie ein wenig, dann thue sie in eine Pfanne, thue nahe zwei Pfund frische ungesalzene Butter dazu und eine halbe Unze Rosin, brate es wohl denn nimm es ab und siehe es wohl durch ein Tuch in eine Bowl, hiernach thue eine Unze Bienen-Wachs dazu, und laße es eine kleine Weile so stehen, zuletzt rühre d. Pulver hinein mit einen Schüppchen von Peintholz, thue 1 halbe Unze Campher u. rühre es wohl bis es kalt wird. Wenn du Wunden hast, so streiche etwas von der obigen Salbe auf

233

einen Lappen von einen linnenen Hemde, leg es auf und laß es für einen halben Tag darauf liegen, dann nimm es ab, wasch die Wunde mit etwas Marz-Schnee-Wasser, mit etwas von dem im vorgehenden Stücke beschriebenen Oele vermischt, und wärme es ein wenig, leg ein anderes Pflaster auf und fahre fort wie vorhin. Dieses wird es schnell heilen.

S68: Eine anderes Mittel Wunden zu heilen.

Thue ein Pfund ungelöschten Kalk in eine Bowl mit etwa ein Peint März-Schnee-Wasser, lass es 12 Stunden stehen, dann gieße das Klare ab in ein anderes Geschirr und thue ein wenig süßen Oel oder Flachs-samen-Oel dazu. Dieses macht eine sehr gute Salbe für Brand-Wunden. - Und wenn du ein halbes Tschill von dem im vorletzten Stücke beschriebenen Oele vermischest und die Wunde damit wäschest, so wirst du gute Wirkung davon ausfinden.

S69: Ein herrliches Mittel für ersrorne Füße.

Nimm ohngefähr 6 Quart Huhnermist und rühre ihn auf mit etwa 2 Gallonen kochenden Wasser, in einen Eimer, dann lege ein kleines Brett daruber, auf welches du die Füße stellst und bedecke sie solange bis die Mixture so kalt ist, daß du die Füße hinein thun kannst, thue sie dann solange hinein bis es ganz kalt ist.

ENDNOTES

1. Owen Davies, *Wall Street Journal*, August 16, 2009.
2. For example, see Stokker, Kathleen. *Remedies and Rituals: Folk Medicine in Norway and the New Land*. St. Paul, MN: Minnesota Historical Society Press, 2007, 79–82.
3. Thanks to my sister Cathy for sending me this.
4. The title given here is slightly inaccurate, as the word "Verborgene" is closer to "hidden" in meaning, which bears different connotations. Nonetheless, I have decided to employ the more common title in this work.
5. For more on the grimoire tradition in general, see Owen Davies, *Grimoires: A History of Magic Books* (Oxford: Oxford University Press, 2009).
6. Margo M. Lambert, *Francis Daniel Pastorius: An American in Early Pennsylvania, 1683–1719/20* (doctoral dissertation).
7. Steven M. Nolt, *Foreigners in Their Own Land: Pennsylvania Germans in the Early Republic* (University Park: Pennsylvania State University Press, 2002), 112.
8. Frederick S. Weiser, "Piety and Protocol in Folk Art: Pennsylvania German Fraktur Birth and Baptismal Certificates," *Winterthur Portfolio* 8 (1973).
9. Don Yoder, "European Chapbook Literature in Pennsylvania German Culture," in *The Harold Jantz collection: proceedings of a conference to introduce the collection to specialists in German-American literary relations*, ed. Leland R. Phelps and Duke University Center for International Studies (Durham, NC: Duke University, Center for International Studies, 1981).
10. Thomas Royce Brendle and Claude W. Unger, *Folk Medicine of the Pennsylvania Germans: The Non-occult Cures*, Pennsylvania-German Society, 45, 2 (Norristown, PA: Soc., 1935), 289–290.
11. Larry L. Burkhart, *The Good Fight: Medicine in Colonial Pennsylvania*, ed. Stuart Bruchey, Garland Studies in Historical Demography (New York: Garland Publishing, 1989), 72–73.
12. Edith Birch, "Barrick Mariche: Mountain Mary," *Historical Review of Berks County* 4, no. 1 (1938); Ned D. Heindel, *Hexenkopf: History, Healing & Hexerei* (Easton, PA: Williams Township Historical Society, 2005), 17–22.
13. Philadelphia Passenger Lists, 1800–1950.
14. Allan Kulikoff, *From British Peasants to Colonial American Farmers* (Chapel Hill: University of North Carolina Press, 2000), 194–95.

15. William J. Buck, *Local Sketches and Legends Pertaining to Bucks and Montgomery Counties, Pennsylvania* ([Philadelphia, PA: Printed for the author, 1887). This work contains some inaccurate statements with regard to Hohman, possibly due to confusing him with another individual.

16. Mayor of Philadelphia, *Registry of redemptioners* (1785), 287.

17. Ibid., 283.

18. Don Yoder, *The Pennsylvania German Broadside: A History and Guide* (University Park PA: Penn State University Press for the Library Co. of Philadelphia and the Pennsylvania German Society, 2005), 212.

19. Wilbur H. Oda, "John George Homan: Man of Many Parts," *The Pennsylvania Dutchman* 1, no. 16 (1949).

20. Joh Geo Homan, "Schöne Bücher," *Der Readinger Adler*, 1813.

21. Oda, "John George Homan: Man of Many Parts."

22. *The First Century*, vol. 2, 875.

23. Edward H. Quinter and Charles L. Allwein, *Most Blessed Sacrament Church, Bally, Pennsylvania: originally known as St. Paul's Chapel of Goshenhoppen, Berks County, Pennsylvania* (Bally, PA: Most Blessed Sacrament Church, 1976).

24. Oda, "John George Homan: Man of Many Parts."

25. Weiser, "Piety and Protocol in Folk Art: Pennsylvania German Fraktur Birth and Baptismal Certificates," 8.

26. Wilbur H. Oda, "John George Homan," *Historical Review of Berks County* 13(1948), 66.

27. Yoder, *The Pennsylvania German Broadside: A History and Guide*, 212–215.

28. Ibid., 22.

29. Oda, "John George Homan: Man of Many Parts."

30. Gerd-J. Bötte et al., *The first century of German language printing in the United States of America: a bibliography based on the studies of Oswald Seidensticker and Wilbur H. Oda*, 2 vols. (Göttingen: Niedersächsische Staats- und Universitätsbibliothek Göttingen, 1989), vol. 2, 640.

31. Ibid., vol. 2, 735.

32. Ibid., vol. 1, 358.

33. Brendle and Unger, *Folk Medicine of the Pennsylvania Germans: The Non-occult Cures*, 239.

34. Weaver has speculated that the term "Freund" is a familiar or magician's tool. The discovery of the other *Freunds* makes this derivation less likely. See William Woys Weaver, *Sauer's Herbal Cures: America's First Book of Botanic Healing, 1762–1778* (New York: Routledge, 2001), 23.

35. Homan, "Schöne Bücher."

36. John George Homann, "An das Publikum," *Der Readinger Postbothe und Berks, Schuykill und Montgomery Caunties Adverteiser*, November 23, 1816.

37. John George Homan, "Bekanntmachung," *Der Readinger Postbothe und Berks, Schuykil und Montgomery Caunties Adverteiser*, 1820.

38. Oda, "John George Homan: Man of Many Parts."

39. Ibid.

40. Heindel, *Hexenkopf: History, Healing & Hexerei*, 46; *Der Readinger Adler*, April 22, 1845.

41. Morton L. Montgomery, J. H. Beers, and Co., *Historical and biographical annals of Berks County, Pennsylvania, embracing a concise history of the county and a genealogical and biographical record of representative families, comp. by Morton L. Montgomery* (Chicago: J. H. Beers & Co., 1909), 1302.

42. Solomon and S. L. MacGregor Mathers, *The Key of Solomon the King (Clavicula Salomonis)* (York Beach, ME: Samuel Weiser, 2000), 3.

43. Albertus, *Albertus Magnus. Being the approved, verified, sympathetic and natural Egyptian secrets; or, White and black art for man and beast* (Chicago: Egyptian Pub. Co., 1930), i.

44. For folktales about witches from this region, see: Don Yoder, *Discovering American folklife: studies in ethnic, religious, and regional culture*, American material culture and folklife (Ann Arbor, MI: UMI Research Press, 1990); Frederick Starr, "Some Pennsylvania German Lore," *The Journal of American Folklore* 4, no. 15 (1891).

45. George Lincoln Burr, *Narratives of the Witchcraft Cases, 1648–1706* (New York: Barnes and Noble, 1946), 87, 88.

46. Some of Hohman's charms for witchcraft have been phrased so as to obscure that association. I call attention to such charms in the notes.

47. See Charm 123.

48. David L. Cowen, "The impact of the materia medica of the North American Indians on professional practice," in *Botanical drugs of the Americas in the Old and New Worlds: invitational symposium at the Washington-congress, 1983 = Amerikanische pflanzliche Arzneien in der Alten und Neuen Welt: Einladungs-Symposium anlässlich des Kongresses in Washington, 1983*, ed. Wolfgang Hagen Hein, *Veröffentlichungen der Internationalen Gesellschaft für Geschichte der Pharmazie e.V., n.F., Bd. 53* (Stuttgart: Wissenschaftliche Verlagsgesellschaft, 1984), 52–53.

49. Burkhart, *The Good Fight: Medicine in Colonial Pennsylvania*, 77.

50. Adolf Spamer and Johanna Nickel, *Romanusbüchlein; historisch-philologischer Kommentar zu einem deutschen Zauberbuch* (Berlin: Akademie-Verlag, 1958), 25.

51. Don Yoder, "Hohman and Romanus: Origins and Diffusion of the Pennsylvania German Powwow Manual," in *American Folk Medicine: a Symposium*, ed. Wayland Debs Hand, et al. (Berkeley: University of California Press, 1976).

52. Isabelle Draelants and Albertus, *Le Liber de virtutibus herbarum, lapidum et animalium: (Liber aggregationis); un texte à succès attribué à Albert le Grand*, Micrologus' library, 22 (Firenze: SISMEL, Ed. del Galluzzo, 2007).

53. Joseph A. M'Jimsey, "Cure of the Hydrophobia," *Niles' Weekly Register*, October 11, 1817.

54. Davies, *Grimoires: A History of Magic Books*, 215–224.

55. Paul Bolmer, *Eine Sammlung von neuen Rezepten und erprobten Kuren für Menschen und Thiere* (Deutschland: Gedruckt für den Käufer, 1831).

56. Johann Georg Hohman, *John George Homan's Pow-wows, or, Long lost friend: a collection of mysterious and invaluable arts and remedies for man as well as animals; with many proofs of their virtue and efficacy in healing diseases, the greater part of which was never published until they appeared in print for the first time in the United States in the year of eighteen hundred and twenty* (Chicago: De Laurence, 1924), 2.

57. Letitia Humphreys Wrenshall, "Incantations and Popular Healing in Maryland and Pennsylvania," *The Journal of American Folklore* 15, no. 59 (1902).

58. Lee R. Gandee, *Strange Experience; the Autobiography of a Hexenmeister* (Englewood Cliffs, NJ: Prentice-Hall, 1971), 120.

59. Earl F. Robacker, *Arts of the Pennsylvania Dutch* (New York: Castle Books, 1965). 213.

60. Heindel, *Hexenkopf: History, Healing & Hexerei*, 51.

61. Scott Francis Brenner, *Pennsylvania Dutch, the Plain and the Fancy* (Harrisburg, PA: Stackpole Co., 1957), 70.

62. Earl F. Robacker, "Long-Lost Friend," *New York Folklore Quarterly* (1956).

63. ———, *Arts of the Pennsylvania Dutch*, 213.

64. Barbara L. Reimensnyder, *Powwowing in Union County: A Study of Pennsylvania German Folk Medicine in Context* (New York: AMS Press, 1989), 117, 129.

65. Richard H. Shaner, "Recollections of Witchcraft in the Oley Hills," *Pennsylvania Folklife* 21, Folk Festival Supplement (1972), 41.

66. Those interested in these unofficial actions against witches might start with the following sources: Adam Ashforth, *Madumo: A Man Bewitched* (Chicago: University of Chicago Press, 2000); Jeanne Favret-Saada, *Deadly Words: Witchcraft in the Bocage* (Cambridge [Eng.]: New York: Cambridge University Press, 1980); T. J. Knab, *A War of Witches: A Journey into the Underworld of the Contemporary Aztecs* (Boulder, CO: WestviewPress, 1995).

67. I have seen reports of such a copy in newspaper stories, but attempts to contact the owners have not been successful.

68. David W. Kriebel, *Powwowing among the Pennsylvania Dutch: a Traditional Medical Practice in the Modern World*, Publications of the Pennsylvania German Society (Pennsylvania State University Press, 2007), 23.

69. "Modern American Charms," *Otago Witness*, April 3, 1907.

70. Harry Middleton Hyatt, *Hoodoo—conjuration—witchcraft—rootwork; beliefs accepted by many Negroes and white persons, these being orally recorded among blacks and whites* (Hannibal, MO: Printed by Western Pub.; distributed by American University Bookstore, Washington, 1970); For specific instances, see Daniel Harms, "The Role of Grimoires in the Conjure Tradition," in *Journal for Academic Study of Magic* no. 5 (2008) 40–68.

71. Hortense Powdermaker, *After Freedom: A Cultural Study in the Deep South* (New York: Viking Press, 1939), 295.

72. Lyle Saxon, Edward Tallant, and Robert Dreyer, *Gumbo Ya-Ya* (Boston: Houghton Mifflin, 1945), 259. Examination of the early catalogues has failed to turn up any advertisement for the *Friend*.

73. Loudell F. Snow, *Walkin' over Medicine* (Boulder: Westview Press, 1993), 64.

74. Catherine Yronwode, "Hoodoo: African-American Magic," http://www.luckymojo.com/hoodoohistory.html.

75. Manly Wade Wellman, *The Old Gods Waken* (Garden City, NY: Doubleday, 1979); ———, *After Dark* (Garden City, NY: Doubleday, 1980); ———, *The Lost and the Lurking* (Garden City, NY: Doubleday, 1981); ———, *The Hanging Stones* (Garden City, NY: Doubleday, 1982); ———, *The Voice of the Mountain*, Doubleday science fiction (Garden City NY: Doubleday, 1984); Manly Wade Wellman and John Pelan,

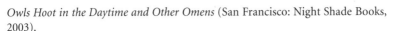

Owls Hoot in the Daytime and Other Omens (San Francisco: Night Shade Books, 2003).

76. Jesse Glass, *Man's Wows* (Madison, WI: Black Mesa Press, 1983).

77. Brian Keene, *Dark Hollow* (New York; Enfield: Leisure: Publishers Group UK [distributor], 2008); ———, *Ghost Walk* (New York; Enfield: Dorchester; Publishers Group UK [distributor], 2008).

78. RavenWolf, *HexCraft: Dutch Country Pow-wow Magick* (St. Paul, MN: Llewellyn, 1997).

79. Robin Artisson, *The Horn of Evenwood: A Grimoire of sorcerous operations, charms, and devices of Witchery* (Los Angeles: Pendraig Publishing, 2007), 103.

80. C. R. Bilardi, *The Red Church or The Art of Pennsylvania German Braucherei* (Sunland,CA: Pendraig Publishing, 2009).

81. *"Call upon me ... "*: Psalms 50:15. This is also a reference to Hohman's previous publication, *Der Freund in der Noth*. Not only does that work quote the same passage word for word on the title page, it also notes that the numbering of the Psalm is different in the Catholic Bible.

82. *Panting ... hideboundness*: The German terms refer to a disorder unplaceable in modern medicine, which might refer to pleurisy and rickets, with Hohman 1846 translating the terms into the colloquial "Livergrow." Brown has here "disease of the heart, gunshots." Hohman 1846 has "Livergrow."

83. Brown has here "smallpox."

84. *Mother-fits*: Either hysteria or a disorder of the female reproductive system. See below.

85. Most likely Peter Heilbron, a former soldier and Capuchin who arrived in Philadelphia with his brother James in 1787. Appointed to a congregation in Goshenhoppen, Berks County upon arrival; he was later sent to Holy Trinity in Philadelphia, where he became involved in a parish dispute that caused him to leave in 1799. He was noted while in Philadelphia for his horsemanship. He ministered in Unity Township from his departure from Philadelphia until his death in 1816. Joseph L. J. Kirlin, *Catholicity in Philadelphia from the Earliest Missionaries Down to the Present Time* (Philadelphia: J. J. McVey, 1909); Andrew Arnold Lambing, *A History of the Catholic Church in the Dioceses of Pittsburg and Allegheny from Its Establishment to the Present Time* (New York: Benziger Bros., 1880).

86. Brown and Hohman 1846 both omit this list of illnesses.

87. This sentence is omitted from Brown.

88. The rest of the preface is omitted in Brown.

89. It is not known what books Hohman means here, as few books of magical remedies have appeared from American publishers at this time.

90. *Rosenthal*: Rose Valley, an area in Alsace Township between Egelman and Pendora Parks. The area was supposedly named after the small roses that bloomed on the valley's slopes at one time. Its most prominent feature was the Mineral Springs Hotel, which capitalized on the supposed health-producing effects of the local spring.

91. The German adds, "Who stops the blood?"

92. In Pennsylvania Dutch Braucherei, many practitioners insist that the person seeking healing believe in Christianity and the practice to be healed. See David

W. Kriebel, *Powwowing Among the Pennsylvania Dutch: A Traditional Medical Practice in the Modern World*, Publications of the Pennsylvania German Society (Pennsylvania State University Press, 2007). Hohman actually reverses the usual argument—the recipes work, and this is proof of the validity of the Christian cosmology.

93. Brown notes that the following passage appears here in the 1863 edition: "Gebrauchs-Anweisung: In allen Krankheiten, wo man mit Worten braucht, legt man die Hand auf die blosse Haut, während man die Wort spricht."—"Instructions for use, in all illness, which one tries for it with words, place one's hand on the bare skin when one speaks the words."

94. *Benjamin Stout*: German: Benjamin Staubt (1785–1825), son of Daniel and Sophia Staudt. Daniel Staudt, born in 1754 in Upper Pflaz, served as the schoolmaster at Trinity Lutheran until passing away in 1820, having taught for thirty-four years. Jacob Fry, *The History of Trinity Lutheran Church, Reading, Pa, 1751–1894* (Reading, PA: The Congregation, 1894), 108.

95. *Henry Jorger*: German: Heinrich Jorger.

96. *John Bayer*: Bayer was a common name in this area. One candidate might be Jacob K. Boyer, a Reading area merchant who engaged Hohman in a lawsuit in 1826, ultimately leading to the loss of his property in 1828. Boyer was convicted of passing a counterfeit note in 1829.

97. *Landlin Gottwald*: German: Landlin Gottwalt. The 1820 census lists a Landerling Gadwald, living in Lebanon Township.

98. *Catherine Meck*: German: Catharina Meck. A Catharina Meck, daughter to Dewald and Maria Meck, was born on March 10, 1807, and christened at Zion Spies' Church in Alsace Township on August 16 of the same year. Frank Hale and Joyce Marks Hale, *Descendants of the Jacob Meck Family, Berks Co. Pa* (n. p.: Frank & Joyce Marks Hale, 2001), 13.

99. *Mr. Silvis*: The 1820 census lists a "John and Widow Silvis" living in Reading's north ward.

100. *Brewery of my neighbor*: Brewing was a major industry in the Reading area. The brewery in question has not been placed.

101. *Anna Snyder*: German: Anna Schneider. Snyder was a common name in Alsace in the 1820 census.

102. *Michael Hartman, Jr.*: The 1820 census lists Michael Hartman, Jr., as head of a household in Alsace.

103. *John Bingemann*: German: Johann Bingemann;" Brown has "John Zingeman."

104. *My wife came to that place…*: Hohman's wife was apparently a braucher in her own right. Notably, this incident takes place earlier than the rest mentioned herein.

105. Hohman 1846 has "a very sore leg with a cold." Nonetheless, the German supports the version given above.

106. *Susanna Gomber*: A Peter Gombert is listed as living with two women between 26 and 44 in Lower Bern, Berks County in the 1820 census.

107. *The wife of David Brecht*: The most likely candidate is Catharine Hottenstein Brecht, wife of David Brecht or Bright (1771–1846), a farmer, tanner, and hotel owner who later became a county comissioner and treasurer. Brown has "David

Beech." Pam Harden, *Brecht: Descendants of Kuntz Brecht* (Kutztown, PA: Berks County Genealogical Society, n. d.), 18.

108. *John Junkin's daughter and daughter-in-law*: German: Johann Junken. Hohman 1846 has "John Yunken." A John Younkin is listed as residing in Nockamixon, Bucks County, with three adult women.

109. *Cheek*: Brown has back, but the German is "cheek."

110. *Nackenmixen*: Likely Nockamixon Township. The original adds that it is near "Heckack" (Hohman 1846: "the Hickack"), which is likely Haycock Township.

111. *Four*: five.

112. *Daughter of John Arnold*: The Census of 1820 lists John Arnold and a girl of 10–15 years in Lebanon.

113. *Lebanon*: Brown has "Solomon," which he labels as a misprint.

114. In the German, Hohman provides the year for the Arnold curing after this statement, suggesting that he might have been particularly concerned as to whether the Arnolds would express agreement with him.

115. *Jacob Stouefer*: German: Jacob Staufer. The census lists a Jacob Stover living in Haycock, with five children under 16.

116. *A book containing the 25 letters*: Likely a reference to the SATOR square, for which see below. It is quite possible that the book in question is *Der Freund in der Noth*, which includes such a square and which Hohman is believed to have published in 1813.

117. *Henry Frankenfield*: An individual of this name is listed a few entries below Jacob Stover in the census for Haycock Township.

118. *A letter to cure rheumatism*: Charms such as this were often sold as broadsides. The exact broadside in question has yet to be located, but Hohman reprinted the charm as Item 114. Given that Hohman's book sold for seventy-two cents, his work was quite the bargain for a potential buyer.

119. *John Allgaier*: German: John Algaier. The census lists the family of John Allgaier in Reading's South Ward.

120. This could be a reference to either the *Romanusbüchlein*, based on a mistaken etymology of its title, or to another book, whether real or invented. Hohman 1846 has "Gipsey Chief."

121. This statement is likely rhetorical; Hohman seems to have made extensive use of the materials that he had immediately at hand for his book.

122. Hohman's inclusion of readers of both sexes should be noted.

123. This sentence is omitted in Hohman 1846.

124. The German "Mutterkrankheit" can signify either hysteria, a condition thought at the time to be caused by an illness in the womb, or any disorder of the female reproductive system.

125. *to be used…*: Omitted in Hohman 1846.

126. *the small bone…*: The xiphoid process, at the base of the sternum.

127. Addressing diseases or body parts is common in medical charms from across the globe. In medieval times, the "wandering womb" was thought to be a separate being living in a woman's body which might attack her. See Jeffrey Spier, "Medieval Byzantine Magical Amulets and Their Tradition," *Journal of the Warburg and Courtauld Institutes* 56(1993). The motif of speaking to the uterus to remind it that

its life and that of the person are linked dates to the twelfth century in Germany (Hanns Bächtold-Stäubli, Eduard Hoffmann-Krayer, and Gerhard Lüdtke, *Handwörterbuch des Deutschen Aberglaubens* (Berlin und Leipzig: W. de Gruyter & Co., 1927), vol. 5, 84.) Such beliefs might explain why the healer places his or her hand in the area defined.

128. This word, as with the one in the German, is likely nonsensical and inserted to maintain the rhyme.

129. A version of this remedy was collected in Lebanon and York counties in the early twentieth century. Edwin Miller Fogel, *Beliefs and Superstitions of the Pennsylvania Germans*, ed. Marion Dexter Learned, *Americana Germanica* (Philadelphia: American Germanica Press, 1915), 268, 286 (coryza), 304.

130. *rightly pronounced*: Hohman 1846 has "distinctly spoken."

131. This, or a similar phrase, often appears at the end of rituals conducted by today's powwowers. Whether this originates with this charm is unknown. See Kriebel, *Powwowing among the Pennsylvania Dutch: A Traditional Medical Practice in the Modern World*, 141, 263.

132. *falling away*: "withering away." Later editions add "oder abnimmt," "or declines."

133. *in perfect soberness*: The German can also be interpreted as "fasting."

134. One source stipulates that these be the red ants found in pine forests. Oskar Hovorka and Adolf Kronfeld, *Vergleichende Volksmedizin: Eine Darstellung Volksmedizinischer Sitten und Gebräuche, Anschauungen und Heilfaktoren, des Aberglaubens und der Zaubermedizin* (Stuttgart: Strecker & Schröder, 1908), vol. 2, 39–40.

135. This charm was especially popular around Mecklenburg, but it was known even as far south as France. One version stated that the egg must come from a black hen, and that anyone who uncovered the egg would receive the disease. Jacob Grimm and Leopold Kretzenbacher, *Deutsche Mythologie* (Graz: Akademische Druck- und Verlagsanstalt, 1968). vol. 3, 465. Other versions, used for impotence, stated that the urine should be half boiled away, and that leaving the egg at the anthill must be done in silence. A molehill was on occasion substituted for the anthill. Felix Liebrecht, des *Gervasius von Tilbury Otia Imperialia in Einer Auswahl Neu Herausgegehen* (Hannover: Rümpler, 1856), 237; Karl Bartsch, *Sagen, Märchen und Gebräuche aus Meklenburg* (Wien: Braumüller, 1879). vol. 2, 354; Hohn, H. Volksheilkunde 1. 90. 94. 99; Hovorka and Kronfeld, *Vergleichende Volksmedizin: Eine Darstellung Volksmedizinischer Sitten und Gebräuche, Anschauungen und Heilfaktoren, des Aberglaubens und der Zaubermedizin*, vol. 2, 39–40; Franz Xaver von Schönwerth, *Aus der Oberpfalz—Sitten und Sagen* (Augsburg: Rieger, 1859). vol. 3, 258–59.

136. *Without having conversed…*: The translation of the word "unbeschrauen" is one of the most baffling elements in *The Long-Lost Friend*. The converse of the word, beschrauen, can mean casting a spell, accusing a person in court, shouting, or slandering, bringing together many of the negative functions of language, both social and supernatural. A good translation seems to be "in silence," though this could mean the one performing the charm should either be silent or avoid conversation.

137. A procedure similar to that of the witch-bottle, a container in which a bewitched individual's urine was placed to reverse the charm. Though they might have parallels in some German and Dutch traditions, the bottles are an exclusively Brit-

ish phenomenon brought to the New World, making this a foreign addition to Hohman's usual German repertoire. Though Hohman does not state this explicitly, the admonition against giving a key to another likely indicates that the illness was caused by a witch who sought to obtain the bottle to free himself or herself from enchantment. Ralph Merrifield, "Witch Bottles and Magical Jugs," *Folklore* 66, no. 1 (1955).

138. A variant on the charm-type "Job sedebat in sterquilino," a traditional charm against worms believed to date back to the twelfth century. This one is notable for its substitution of Mary for Job as its main figure. Jonathan Roper, *English Verbal Charms*, Ff Communications, No. 288 (Helsinki: Suomalainen Tiedeakatemia, 2005), 111–12.

139. *not less… three minutes*: Hohman 1846 has "no more than three minutes."

140. The German here is "beschrauen." See Item 4.

141. According to the German, the shirt should be put on again once inside-out.

142. According to the German, this should be done three times.

143. The days of the week were sometimes invoked to drive off fever in Germany, though Sunday and Friday, days with more Christian associations, were more common. In other examples of this charm, only the "day" or "beloved" was addressed. Bächtold-Stäubli, Hoffmann-Krayer, and Lüdtke, *Handwörterbuch des Deutschen Aberglaubens*, vol. 2, 1464; Anton Birlinger, *Volksthümliches, Aus Schwaben. Herausgegeben von Dr. Anton Birlinger* (Freiburg im Breisgau: Herder, 1861), vol. 1, 209; G. Sello, "Ein Fiebersegen Kurfürst Joachims I von Brandenburg," *Zeitschrift für Deutsches Alterthum und Deutsche Literrratur* 23(1879); Theodor Wolff, "Volksglauben und Volksgebräuche an der Oberen Nahe," *Zeitschrift des Vereins für rheinische und westfälische Volkskunde* 2(1905), 289; Adolf Wuttke and Elard Hugo Meyer, *Der Deutsche Volksaberglaube der Gegenwart* (Berlin: Wiegandt & Grieben, 1900), 13. Personification of days of the week occurred in other contexts; one Pennsylvania Dutch custom required that part of the ear of a calf born on Wednesday be dedicated to that day. Fogel, *Beliefs and Superstitions of the Pennsylvania Germans*, 174–75.

144. German sources often give a number of the various types of fever and other conditions, with seven, seventy-seven, and ninety-nine being the most common. Bächtold-Stäubli, Hoffmann-Krayer, and Lüdtke, *Handwörterbuch des Deutschen Aberglaubens*, vol. 2, 1448; Wuttke and Meyer, *Der Deutsche Volksaberglaube der Gegenwart*, 320. The seventy-seven fevers refer to a frequently recurring fever. Max Höfler, *Deutsches Krankheitsnamen-Buch* (München: Piloty & Loehle, 1899), 144.

145. Brown and Hohman 1846 have "the Creed."

146. *until after sunrise*: The German states that no speech at all should occur at any time during the period.

147. *nor eat pork*: This likely reflects the Biblical prohibition on eating this meat (Leviticus 11:7, Deuteronomy 14:8).

148. A folkloric remedy usually associated with witches and spirits, not with ill individuals. Bächtold-Stäubli, Hoffmann-Krayer, and Lüdtke, *Handwörterbuch des Deutschen Aberglaubens*, vol. 2, 1687–88. According to one Hessian folk belief, however, crossing a stream when a spirit was following a person would cause him or her to fall into its power. Theodor Bindewald, *Oberhessisches Sagenbuch, aus*

dem Volkskunde Gesammelt (Frankfurt a.M.: Heyder und Zimmer, 1873), 166–67. Another possibility is that running water will break the healing charm itself (Chris Bilardi, personal communication).

149. The address is actually to the colic itself, addressed as a personality.

150. The same charm was used to make cattle used to a new owner. Wuttke and Meyer, *Der Deutsche Volksaberglaube der Gegenwart*, 435.

Hohman advertised for the return of a missing dog in the supplement to *Der Readinger Adler* for January 28, 1823. Wilbur H. Oda, "John George Homan," *Historical Review of Berks County* 13(1948), 70.

151. The divining-rod. References to these items in the German literature date back to the fifteenth century. William Barrett and Theodore Besterman, *The Divining-Rod; an Experimental and Psychological Investigation* (New Hyde Park, N.Y.: University Books, 1968), 6–7.

152. The German adds, "and such things."

153. Divining rods were often cut on a particular day, with Christmas Day being a typical choice in western Germany. Bächtold-Stäubli, Hoffmann-Krayer, and Lüdtke, *Handwörterbuch des Deutschen Aberglaubens*, vol. 9, 831.

154. This differs from the traditional divining rod, which merely points to the substance in question.

155. *Archangel Gabriel*: An angel who bore messages to the Prophet Daniel and the Virgin Mary (Daniel 8:15–27, 9:20–27, Luke 1:26–38). It might be that he is connected with the rod here as it plays a similar role of bringing "news" to the user.

156. *Hide-bound*: See note 82.

157. Numerous versions of this incantation appear in Pennsylvania Dutch lore, often accompanied with the application of motherwort and spittle. Thomas Royce Brendle and Claude W. Unger, *Folk Medicine of the Pennsylvania Germans: The Non-Occult Cures*, Pennsylvania-German Society, 45,2 (Norristown, PA: Soc., 1935), 196–98.

158. The German word "Fledermaus" is a bat.

159. Similar charms involved burning the entire bat to powder and then inserting the powder into the barrel, or inserting the blood, heart, or liver into the lead ball when cast. Hanns Bächtold, "Volkskundliche Mitteilungen aus dem Schweizerischen Soldatenleben: Proben aus den Einsendungen Schweizerischer Wehrmänner," *Schweizerisches Archiv für Volkskunde* 19(1915), 227; Albertus, *Bewährte und Approbierte Sympathetische und Natürliche Ägyptische Geheimnisse für Menschen und Vieh,* (Leipzig: Bohmeier, 2008), 203; Fogel, *Beliefs and Superstitions of the Pennsylvania Germans*, 369; Alois John, *Sitte, Brauch und Volksglaube im Deutschen Westböhmen, von Alois John* (Prag: J. G. Calve, 1905), 326–28.

160. *A young mule (just foaled)*: The German calls for "a mole."

161. Brown's translation.

162. Brown translation. For another example, see Victor Lommer, *Volksthümliches aus dem Saalthal* (Orlamünde: Heyl, 1878), 50.

163. Other versions have the tongue as a possibility. Whether such an attribution is a corruption of the next charm, calling for houndstongue, or vice versa, is unknown. Anton Birlinger, *Aus Schwaben Sagen, Legenden, Aberglauben, Sitten, Rechts-*

bräuche, Ortsneckereien, Lieder, Kinderreine, Neue Sammlung, von Anton Birlinger (Wiesbaden: H. Killinger, 1874), vol. 1, 435.

164. Another version requires the person to hold the heart, transfixed with the hound's tooth, in the left hand. C. M. Blaas, "Kleine Beiträge zur Mythologie," *Germania: Vierteljahrsschrift für Deutsche Alterthumskunde,* 22(1877), 261. Another adds the stipulation that the hound be black. Adolf F. Dörler, "Die Tierwelt in der Sympathetischen Tiroler Volksmedizin," *Zeitschrift des Vereins für Volkskunde* 8(1898), 39. Yet another involves both the heart and the tongue, thus bridging this charm and the one following. Oswald von Zingerle, "Segen und Heilmittel aus Einer Wolfsthurner Handschrift des XV. Jahrhunderts," *Zeitschrift des Vereins für Volkskunde* 1(1891), 324.

165. "Dogs run away from one who carries a dog's heart..." Pliny and W. H. S. Jones, *Natural History, Libri XXVIII—XXXII,* (Cambridge, MA: Harvard Univ. Press, 1975), 247; Bächtold-Stäubli, Hoffmann-Krayer, and Lüdtke, *Handwörterbuch des Deutschen Aberglaubens,* vol. 4, 475; August Engelien and Wilhelm Lahn, *Der Volksmund in der Mark Brandenburg: Sagen, Märchen, Spiele, Sprichwörter und Gebräuche* (Berlin: Schultze, 1868), vol. 1, 275.

166. Houndstongue: *Cynoglossum officinale.*

167. "... [dogs] indeed do not bark if a dog's tongue is placed in the shoe under the big toe." Pliny and W. H. S. Jones, *Natural History, Libri XXVIII—XXXII,* (Cambridge, Mass.: Harvard Univ. Press, 1975), 247. Pseudo-Albertus Magnus: "And if thou shalt have the aforenamed herb [houndstongue] under thy foremost toe, all the Dogs shall keep silence, and shall not have power to bark." (Best and Brightman p. 9) See also Paul Drechsler, *Sitte, Brauch und Volksglaube in Schlesien* (Leipzig: B.G. Teubner, 1903), vol. 2, 97.

168. *Mule-foal:* The German has "mole."

169. Another version requires the areas that will be turned white to be shaved, and the mole bodies and fat to be strained out before use. J. Staricius, *Geheimnissvoller Heldenschatz, Oder der Vollständige Egyptische Magische Schild* (1750), 279–80.

170. "If any man will bind the right eye of a Wolf on his right sleeve neither men nor Dogs may hurt him." (Best and Brightman, 61)

171. The German indicates that these people are officials or lords.

172. *Five-finger grass:* The European plant most often connected with healing was the creeping cinquefoil (*Potentilla reptans*), but the dwarf cinquefoil (*P. canadensis*) seems to have been better known among the Pennsylvania Dutch. D. E. Lick and Thomas Royce Brendle, "Plant Names and Plant Lore among the Pennsylvania-Germans," *The Pennsylvania-German Society* 33, no. 3 (1923), 101.

173. "Moreover if any man will ask any thing of a king or prince, it giveth abundance of eloquence, if he have it with him, and he shall obtain it that he desireth." (Best and Brightman, 21) The German adds here that the herb is good for the dysentery, a usage supported by the medical literature.

174. "Take the grain or corn of [the rose], and the corn of Mustard seed and the foot of a Weasel; hang up these in a tree, and it will not bear fruit after. And if the aforesaid thing be put about a net, fishes will gather there." (Best and Brightman, 16–17)

175. *Ironweed*: A term for several species of the genus *Vernonia*. Although this is a literal translation of the German "Eisenkraut," that term actually refers to the vervain plant (genus Verbena), so called due to its ability to heal wounds inflicted by iron or its ability to cause iron to be tempered. Lick and Brendle, "Plant Names and Plant Lore among the Pennsylvania-Germans," 92. Plants in both genuses have medicinal uses, though the correspondence to Hohman's suggested usages is slight.

176. Hohman 1846 has "the Quincy, or Kings-evil."

177. The German adds, "in the home."

178. "The root of this herb put upon the neck healeth the swine pox, impostumes behind the ears, and botches of the neck, and such as can not keep their water. It healeth also cuts, and swelling of the tewel, or fundament, proceeding of an inflammation which growth in the fundament; and the haemorrhoids. If the juice of it be drunken with honey and water sodden, it dissolveth those things which are in the lungs or lights. And it maketh a good breath ... If any man put it in his house or vineyard, or in the ground, he shall have abundantly revenues, or yearly profits ... And infants bearing it shall be very apt to learn, and love learning, and they shall be glad and joyous." (Best and Brightman, 22–23) Omitted from Hohman's work are its uses for love, purgatives, and driving demons.

179. "Kalten und heissen Brand" can cover a wide variety of conditions, ranging from fever to erysipelas to cancer, but the context seems to indicate moist and dry gangrene. Brendle and Unger, *Folk Medicine of the Pennsylvania Germans: The Non-Occult Cures*, 150.

180. *Sanct Itorius*: No figure named "Saint Itorius" is known. The best candidate might be "St. Isidorus," though none seem to be associated with gangrene. Brown has "Sanctus Storius."

181. The German states this must be over the spot of the affliction.

182. The German adds, "The single N. means the first name, but two N. N. mean the first and last names of the one who is tried for. That is the meaning of the single N. through the entire book. Everyone should be careful." Brown and Hohman 1846 include this line.

183. The German here, "böse Leute," signifies witches. See Johannes Dillinger, *"Evil People": A Comparative Study of Witch Hunts in Swabian Austria and the Electorate of Trier* (Charlottesville: University of Virginia Press, 2009).

184. A version of this charm was used in the Ozarks against witchcraft. Vance Randolph, *Ozark Magic and Folklore* (New York: Dover Publications, 1964), 286.

185. *Pontio, Pilato*: Pontius Pilate, the Roman official who authorized the crucifixion of Jesus (Matthew 27:11–26). This might be a corruption of the Latin "sub Pontio Pilato," which appears in the Apostles' Creed. It might also include a punning reference to "pons," Latin for bridge (Chris Bilardi, personal communication).

186. Another version of Roper's "Job sedebat in sterquilino" charm-type. See Item 6.

187. Brown has "mount and ride him to a certain distance and back three times."

188. *Pollevil*: An inflammation of the bursa where the nuchal ligament meets the vertebrae, near the top of a horse's head.

189. Brown (1904, 145) cites a use of a similar charm among the Pennsylvania Germans for blisters on the tongue.

190. Cherries were very popular with German settlers in the New World. The use of the cherry tree to transfer many ailments from a sufferer is well known in Germany; Bächtold-Stäubli, Hoffmann-Krayer, and Lüdtke, *Handwörterbuch des Deutschen Aberglaubens*, vol. 4, 1430–1432.

191. *The eaves*: Symbolically the eaves are a liminal area, on the boundaries of a habitation, in which transactions of power might occur.

192. The German states the twigs must be laid down at midnight.

193. Excrement, human or otherwise, was a common ingredient in folk remedies for wounds and other ailments. Bächtold-Stäubli, Hoffmann-Krayer, and Lüdtke, *Handwörterbuch des Deutschen Aberglaubens*, vol. 5, 342.

194. This final line seems to have been added in this edition.
A similar charm for blisters on the tongue was found in Pennsylvania Dutch country in the late nineteenth century. W. J. Hoffman, "Folk-Lore of the Pennsylvania Germans II," *The Journal of American Folklore* 2, no. 4 (1889).

195. Compare to "Mother's milk and Christ's blood / Is for the red rose good." Charms with similar wording are often used for erysipelas. Determining the transformations of a charm over time is a risky business, but the additional material might indicate that this is a former rhyming charm expanded and repurposed for other ailments. Carly Seyfarth, *Aberglaube und Zauberei in der Volksmedizin West-Sachsens* (Leipzig: Wilhelm Heims, 1913), 117–118

196. The German adds, "To treat the wildfire both at wounds and a sore limb also."

197. *Dragon*: The term "Drache," among the Pennsylvania Dutch, is also a term that applied to the will-o'-the-wisp, the mysterious lights seen in the swamp. See Hoffman, "Folk-Lore of the Pennsylvania Germans II" 35.

198. *Wagon*: Though "wagon" does rhyme with dragon, the word "Bach" in the original means "stream."

199. *Skeated*: vanished.

200. This is an example of a charm tradition known from Saxony and Thuringia, in which a disease and a dragon appear over a stream. In many versions, the dragon drowns and the disease likewise vanishes. See Bächtold-Stäubli, Hoffmann-Krayer, and Lüdtke, *Handwörterbuch des Deutschen Aberglaubens*. vol. 2, p. 389–390. Among the conditions for which a similar charm was used were syphilitic buboes and ulcers: A. Birlinger, "Besegnungen Aberglauben," *Alemannia: Zeitschrift für Sprache, Litteratur und Volkskunde des Elsaszes Oberrheins und Schwabens.* 17(1889), 243; Elard Hugo Meyer, *Badisches Volksleben im Neunzehnten Jahrhundert* (Strassburg: Trübner, 1900), 574, respectively. Another version, used to cure disease of the udders in cows, should be spoken three times, each time stroking the animal from head to tail, followed by an invocation of the Trinity. Adalbert Kuhn, *Sagen, Gebräuche und Märchen Aaus Westfalen: und Einigen Andern, Besonders den Angrenzenden Gegenden Norddeutschlands* (Leipzig: F A. Brockhaus, 1859), vol. 2, 211; Wuttke and Meyer, *Der Deutsche Volksaberglaube der Gegenwart*, 443.

201. "and dry": Added in this edition.

202. Variants of this particular charm, involving rubbing a wart with a piece of meat and disposing of it, are relatively common. See James Hardy, "Wart and Wen Cures," *The Folk-Lore Record* 1, 271.

203. The German "Hinkelfusse" signifies a young chicken's feet. See Fogel, *Beliefs and Superstitions of the Pennsylvania Germans*, 322.

204. *Under the eaves*: A popular place to leave or find items that could take away warts. A. Jäckel, "Aphorismen über Volkssitte, Aberglauben und Volksmedicin in Franken, mit Besonderer Rücksicht auf Oberfranken," *Abhandlungen der Naturhistorischen Gesellschaft zu Nürnberg* 2(1861), 229.

205. Fogel, *Beliefs and Superstitions of the Pennsylvania Germans*, 338–39.

206. *which has cured…*: Omitted from Brown and Hohman 1846.

207. The German has "ohne beschrauen" (see Item 4). Brown renders this as "without washing."

208. Thrusting a person through a blackberry bush three times has been a common cure for many ailments across both Europe and America. Wayland D. Hand, *Magical Medicine: The Folkloric Component of Medicine in the Folk Belief, Custom, and Ritual of the Peoples of Europe and America: Selected Essays of Wayland D. Hand* (Berkeley: University of California Press, 1980), 140. For another German language charm, see Paul Hirzel, "Aberglauben im Kanton Zürich," *Schweizerisches Archiv für Volkskunde* 2(1898), 260–61.

209. *Compulsive fevers*: German: "Kamp-Fieber." Hohman 1846 has "Hectic fever."

210. *AbaxaCatabax*: Likely a variant of the charm word "Abracadabra," first attested in the *Liber medicinalis* of the physician Quintus Serenus Sammonicus (212 AD). See Quintus Serenus Sammonicus, *Liber Medicinalis* (Paris: Presses universitaires de France, 1950). LI, 4. The word has become a staple of both charms and stage magic. Intriguingly, the purpose and usage of this word are almost the same in both Sammonicus and Hohman. See also Steve Miller Band, *Abracadabra* (Los Angeles: Capitol Records, 1982).

211. *Rye whiskey*: The German "Kornbranntwein" might also signify corn brandy, but Hohman 1846 has "rye whiskey."

212. *Tobacco*: Leaves from plants of the *Nicotiana* genus. A New World plant, tobacco became associated with a wide variety of folk remedies. Other uses of tobacco in colic remedies can be found in the Ozarks and Kentucky. Katharine T. Kell, "Tobacco in Folk Cures in Western Society," *The Journal of American Folklore* 78, no. 308 (1965).

213. Apples and apple trees were often incorporated into toothache preventatives and remedies in Germany. Bächtold-Stäubli, Hoffmann-Krayer, and Lüdtke, *Handwörterbuch des Deutschen Aberglaubens*, vol. 2, 519–520. The intent here is to transfer the condition to the tree.

214. The idea here is one of transference. Similar charms, also using blood from an aching tooth, were used to transfer the toothache to a tree, wooden cross, or other object. Jäckel, "Aphorismen Über Volkssitte, Aberglauben und Volksmedicin in Franken, mit Besonderer Rücksicht auf Oberfranken," 178; Otto Knoop, *Volkssagen, Erzählungen, Aberglauben, Gebräuche und Märchen aus dem Östlichen Hinterpommern* (Posen: J. Jolowicz, 1885), 162; Albertus, *Albertus Magnus. Being the Approved, Verified, Sympathetic and Natural Egyptian Secrets; or, White and Black Art for Man and Beast* (Chicago: Egyptian Pub. Co., 1930), 24, 56.

215. *Knot-grass*: The term here actually means *Plantago media*, or hoary plantain. This was a common remedy, usually taken internally but sometimes used as an amulet,

for fever since late Antiquity (Pliny, *Historia Naturalis* 26, 24). Bächtold-Stäubli, Hoffmann-Krayer, and Lüdtke, *Handwörterbuch des Deutschen Aberglaubens*, vol. 9, 219–221. Elsewhere, Hohman states that this term refers to the "Säuohren," a term used to refer to the *Plantago major*, or common or greater plantain. Johann Georg Hohman, *Die Land- und Haus-Apotheke, Oder, Getreuer und Gründlicher Unterricht für den Bauer und Stadtmann, Enthaltend Die Allerbesten Mittel, Sowohl für Die Menschen Als für Das Vieh Besonders für Die Pferde. Nebst Einem Grossen Anhang von der Aechten Färberey* (Reading, PA: Gedruckt bey Carl A. Bruckmann, 1818), 51.

216. *Potmat sineat*: The origin of this phrase is unknown.

217. Éva Pócs has referred to such phrases as "impossibility formulas," which place a condition on a particular event that is impossible. The second son for the Virgin Mary appears repeatedly in Hohman's work. See Éva Pócs, "Miracles and Impossibilities in Magic Folk Poetry," in *Charms, Charmers and Charming: International Research on Verbal Magic*, ed. Jonathan Roper, *Palgrave Historical Studies in Witchcraft and Magic* (Hampshire, England; New York: Palgrave Macmillan, 2009).

218. This sentence is an addition to the text.

219. Hohman 1846: "A good cure to stop one from moving." This is not indicated in the German.

220. The German indicates the first and last name should be used here.

221. A line from the German hymn, "Gott Lob! Es geht nunmehr zum ende."

222. *White swelling*: Synovitis.

223. Brown has "who had sought half of the doctors."

224. *Tobacco*: See Item 34 above.

225. The German simply states the mixture should be boiled and strained.

226. *White vitriol*: Zinc sulfate. The German has "Callinenstein," which might be a misreading of "Galitzenstein." Bächtold-Stäubli, Hoffmann-Krayer, and Lüdtke, *Handwörterbuch des Deutschen Aberglaubens*. vol, 3, 269. This substance can cause irritation in the eyes.

227. *Spicewort (Calamus root)*: The German "Kalmen," likely indicates caraway, an ingredient in other eye salves (e.g. Christof Wirsung and Peter Uffenbach, *Ein New Artzney Buch Darinn Fast Alle Eusserliche unnd Innerliche Glieder dess Menschlichen Leibs Sampt Ihren Kranckheiten und Gebrechen von Dem Haupt an Biss zu der Fussolen und Wie Man Dieselben Durch Gottes Hülff und Seine Darzu Geschaffene Mittel Auff Mancherley Weiss Wenden und Curieren Soll* (Ursel: Durch Cornelium Sutorium, 1605), 37. Spicewort was a term for *Acorus calamus*, or sweet flag, at this time.

228. *Cloves*: *Syzygium aromaticum*, a common spice with medicinal uses. Applying to the eyes is not recommended.

229. Brown adds "(Nose-Bleed?)"

230. Fogel, *Beliefs and Superstitions of the Pennsylvania Germans*, 304.

231. Hohman, *Die Land- und Haus-Apotheke.*, 50.

232. *Flaxseed oil*: The type of oil is an addition to this translation. Its usage for this purpose is unknown.

233. The German here echoes the last words of Jesus on the cross (John 19:30). A written charm with these words was also used to stop bleeding in Brütz. Bartsch, *Sagen, Märchen und Gebräuche aus Meklenburg*, vol. 2, 376.

234. The original adds "in silence." See Item 4.

235. The original adds, "and the thread should have no knots."

236. *Tie a rag … the first time*: i. e., the first bandage used to dress the wound.

237. *Copperas*: Iron(II) sulfate. The original indicates copper(II) acetate, or verdigris.

238. Not in Hohman 1846.

239. This seems to be a guess on the part of the translator for "unbeschrauen." It most likely means "in silence." See Item 4. Brown has "before making your toilet."

240. *Albertus Magnus*: (c. 1193–1280) Dominican theologian and philosopher. Hohman's passages attributed to the man largely derive from the *Liber Aggregationis*, a likely apocryphal work on the natural virtues of stones, herbs, and animals composed after his death. See Isabelle Draelants and Albertus, *Le Liber de Virtutibus Herbarum, Lapidum et Animalium: (Liber Aggregationis); Un Texte à Succès Attribué à Albert Le Grand*, Micrologus' Library, 22 (Firenze: SISMEL, Ed. del Galluzzo, 2007); Michael R. Best, Frank Brightman, and Albertus, *The Book of Secrets of Albertus Magnus of the Virtues of Herbs, Stones and Certain Beasts, Also a Book of the Marvels of the World*, Series of Studies in Tudor and Stuart Literature (Oxford [Eng.]: Clarendon Press, 1973).

241. "Isidorus seemeth to say, that the ashes of a great Frog, borne at a woman's girdle, restraineth greatly the coming of a woman's natural purgation … Also, if it be tempered with water, and the head or another place be anointed with it, hair will no more grow there." (Best and Brightman, 61). The reference would seem to be to Isidore of Seville, author of the *Etymologies*, though no corresponding recipe might be found in that work. Isidore and Stephen A. Barney, *The Etymologies of Isidore of Seville* (Cambridge; New York: Cambridge University Press, 2006).

242. "*Milvus*, a Kite or Glede, is a bird sufficiently known … There is a certain stone found in the knees of this bird, if it be looked craftily, which if it be put into the meat of two enemies, they shall be made friends, and there shall be made very good peace among them." (Best and Brightman, 58).

243. *Vulture*: Brown has "hawk." Albertus Magnus cites the kite, an Old World predatory bird of the genus *Milvus*.

244. *Fits or Convulsions*: Brown states that Gichter is gout, though Brendle and Unger state that this refers specifically to convulsions among infants.

245. In the original, this was not part of the incantation.

246. *77-fold fits*: Numerous seizures. See Item 8 above for the significance of the number 77.

247. Brown has, "You take three shots; at each shot you button one button." Tying three twigs or switches into knots are found in other versions of the charm; see Wuttke and Meyer, *Der Deutsche Volksaberglaube der Gegenwart*, 328.

248. *Decrease of the moon*: A typical time for charms causing a condition to diminish, as with the moon. Ibid, 323–24.

249. Most likely "in silence." See Item 4.

250. Many such charms in Germany involved transferring the gout to a tree. Although an exact replica of this charm has not been found, elements such as the 77-fold

gout and the timing on Friday before sunrise can be found in other charms. Bächtold-Stäubli, Hoffmann-Krayer, and Lüdtke, *Handwörterbuch des Deutschen Aberglaubens*, vol. 3, 845–846; K. E. Haase, "Volksmedizin in der Grafschaft Ruppin und Umgegend," *Zeitschrift des Vereins für Volkskunde* 7(1897), 167.

251. The advertisement Hohman wrote for the book states this will be effective in two to three minutes.

252. Brown: "So I conjure thee by the Holy Virgin."

253. Three hairs were a common component of Pennsylvania Dutch magic. Scott Francis Brenner, *Pennsylvania Dutch, the Plain and the Fancy* (Harrisburg, PA: Stackpole Co., 1957), 74–75. Many charms involving the transfer of cattle from buyer to seller involve the use of hair to 'hold' the cow in place (Wuttke and Meyer, *Der Deutsche Volksaberglaube der Gegenwart*), 438–39. The same charm was used so that a cow would not miss her calf. Fogel, *Beliefs and Superstitions of the Pennsylvania Germans*, 169.

254. *Hessian fly*: *Mayetiola destructor*, an Old World insect destructive of wheat crops that came to the States in the late eighteenth century.

255. i.e., put it through a leaching process to create a solution.

256. *Martinmas*: St. Martin's Day, November 11. Cherries are typically in season in early summer, so this would be quite a feat.

257. *Mulberry tree*: The mulberry tree blooms in late spring or summer.

258. *Stinging nettle*: *Urtica dioica*.

259. *Millifolia*: Likely common yarrow (*Achillea millifolia*). Brown has "arsesmant, and also caraway," which is not in the German.

260. *Hemlock*: A mistranslation of "Hauswurzel," or houseleek (genus *Sempervivum*), a reading confirmed in Hohman 1846. As houseleek is native to Southern Europe and the Fertile Crescent, locating it for this recipe would have been quite difficult.

261. The German adds, "and in the cracks."

262. This is another formula from Albertus Magnus' *Book of Secrets*. "He that holdeth this herb in his hand, with an herb called Milfoil, or Yarrow, or Nosebleed, is sure from all fear and fantasy, or vision. And if it be put with the juice of Houseleek, and the bearer's hand be anointed with it, and the residue be put in water; if he enter in the water where fishes be, they will gather together to his hands, and also ad piscellum. And if his hand be drawn forth, they will leap again to their own places, where they were before." Best, Brightman, and Albertus, *The Book of Secrets of Albertus Magnus of the Virtues of Herbs, Stones and Certain Beasts, Also a Book of the Marvels of the World*, 6.

263. According to the *Book of Secrets*, Hohman's source, the author is incorrect on the equation of these two flowers. The correct plant is likely *Heliotropium europaeum*. Hohman 1846 has here, "Sun- or Choke-weed."

264. The German adds, "and to discover the unfaithfulness of a woman."

265. The German adds, "If the abovementioned thing is placed around a place, where many women are, namely in a church, so those that broke their marriage between them, cannot sooner go from the place, until it is taken away again." This line seems to have been removed from later German editions, and the only translation appears in Brown. Other German versions omit this as well, e.g. Dörler, "Die Tierwelt in der Sympathetischen Tiroler Volksmedizin," 40.

266. "The virtue of this herb is marvellous: for if it be gathered, the Sun being in the sign of *Leo*, in August, and be wrapped in the leaf of a Laurel, or Bay tree, and a Wolf's tooth be added thereto, no man shall be able to have a word to speak against the bearer thereof, but words of peace. And if any thing be stolen, if the bearer of the things before named lay them under his head in the night, he shall see the thief, and all his conditions. And moreover, if the aforesaid herb be put in any church where women be which have broken matrimony on their part, they shall never be able to go forth of the church, except it be put away. And this last point hath been proved, and is very true" (Best and Brightman, 4–5).

267. Brown: "brown." Hohman 1846: "the mumps."

268. A name applying to any number of plants, with greater celandine (*Chelidonium majus*) being the most likely here, based on Best and Brightman, as well as Hohman 1846. Its use to treat eye conditions is traditional, but the herb is now known to be toxic and should only be administered in prescribed dosages. The German name came about due to the knotting of the roots. Lick and Brendle, "Plant Names and Plant Lore among the Pennsylvania-Germans," 215.

269. "This herb springeth in the time in which the Swallows, and also the Eagles, make their nests. If any man shall have this herb, with the heart of a Mole, he shall overcome all his enemies, and all matters in suit, and shall put away all debate. And if the before named herb be put upon the head of a sick man, if he should die, he shall sing anon with a loud voice, if not, he shall weep" (Best and Brightman, 7). The rest is not found in the Latin or the English translation. Draelants and Albertus, *Le Liber de Virtutibus Herbarum, Lapidum et Animalium: (Liber Aggregationis); Un Texte à Succès Attribué À Albert Le Grand*, 266–68.

270. *A dirty plate*: A common Pennsylvania Dutch cure for a sty. Fogel, *Beliefs and Superstitions of the Pennsylvania Germans*, 299–300.

271. In his advertisement for the book, Hohman claimed this charm would be effective in twenty-six or twenty-seven hours.

272. This particular incantation lacks the Trinitarian elements usually found in such ceremonies. Bächtold-Stäubli, Hoffmann-Krayer, and Lüdtke, *Handwörterbuch des Deutschen Aberglaubens*, vol. 9, 840–841.

273. *As before directed*: In Item 11.

274. *At the very first hour*: This section is a bit of poetic license on the part of the translator, to provide a rhyme to the charm.

275. *Tape Worm*: The translation here obscures the large number of diseases attributed to worms that existed in Pennsylvania German folk healing, ranging from felons to acne to insanity. Brendle and Unger, *Folk Medicine of the Pennsylvania Germans: The Non-Occult Cures*, 178.

276. Similar charms, moving an affliction from the bones outward through the body to the natural world, date from the ninth century and on. William D. Paden and Frances Freeman Paden, "Swollen Woman, Shifting Canon: A Midwife's Charm and the Birth of Secular Romance Lyric," *PMLA: Proceedings of the Modern Language Association* 125, no. 2 (2010).

277. An example of the "Tres boni fratres" charm. Roper, *English Verbal Charms*, 127–130.

278. *Increase… cease*: German "eat in… eat out."

279. Yoder finds a similar charm with the thrice-repeated phrase "zian dein güft" ("draw out the poison") in a manuscript. Don Yoder, "Hohman and Romanus: Origins and Diffusion of the Pennsylvania German Powwow Manual," in *American Folk Medicine: A Symposium*, ed. Wayland Debs Hand, et al. (Berkeley: University of California Press, 1976).

280. For a German parallel, see Friedrich Losch, "Deutsche Segen, Heil- und Bannsprüche," *Württembergische Vierteljahrshefte für Landesgeschichte* 13(1890), 162. This charm appears in the film *Apprentice to Murder* (1988), though Sutherland's character ignores the admonition regarding remaining out of the dog's sight.

281. *Hollow horn*: A folk explanation for illness in cattle. Some farmers were unaware that these horns were naturally hollow, only checking inside when the cow was sick. This cure, though ineffectual, was less harmful than the use of turpentine. Ray Douglas Hurt, *American Agriculture: A Brief History* (West Lafayette, IN: Purdue University Press, 2002), 282.

282. *Use a syringe…*: An extrapolation by the translator. See also Fogel, *Beliefs and Superstitions of the Pennsylvania German*, 163.

283. *The Bots*: Infestations of worm larvae.

284. Another example of Roper's "Job sedebat in sterquilino" charm-type. Oddly, it appears that none of the variants in Hohman include the Biblical figure Job himself.

285. *And do you good*: The German has, "and anger pus."

286. *Words are always to have an interval*: A general instruction as to how the charms should be used. The last sentence here is omited in Hohman 1846.

287. Similar charms includes the word "gekreuzigt," or "crucified," here. Bartsch, *Sagen, Märchen und Gebräuche aus Meklenburg*, vol. 2, 448; Losch, "Deutsche Segen, Heil- und Bannsprüche," 229. The other translators have tried their best— Hohman 1846 "Which Christ, the Lord has build"; Brown, "Which Christ, the Lord, has borne."

288. A similar charm was used for the purpose of fighting toothache. Hirzel, "Aberglauben im Kanton Zürich," 259. *Egyptian Secrets* stipulates that this is to be used for horses, for whom the hands should be run over the back three times and its left side tapped. Albertus, *Albertus Magnus. Being the Approved, Verified, Sympathetic and Natural Egyptian Secrets; or, White and Black Art for Man and Beast*, 40.

289. *Bittany/Betony*: Likely wood betony, or *Stachys officinalis*. As with the birch, it is not known to have any effect on this condition

290. *St. John's wort*: *Hypericum perforatum*. This herb has a number of side effects, and findings on its effectiveness for fatigue are inconclusive.

291. Before having…: Hohman 1846: "when sober."

292. White oak: *Quercus alba*. Teas or decoctions made from white oak bark was a common treatment among the Pennsylvania Dutch for a variety of disorders. Lick and Brendle, "Plant Names and Plant Lore among the Pennsylvania-Germans," 251.

293. The German does not mention destroying rodents, and neither does the charm itself. Nonetheless, it is part of a broader tradition of charms that also center around leaving three sheaves of grain in the barn, often in a cross pattern, with

an incantation that does call for the deaths of the mice. Most of these end with an invocation of the Trinity. Bächtold-Stäubli, Hoffmann-Krayer, and Lüdtke, *Handwörterbuch des Deutschen Aberglaubens*, vol. 6, 61; Albertus, *Bewährte und Approbierte Sympathetische und Natürliche Ägyptische Geheimnisse für Menschen und Vieh*. p. 203; John, *Sitte, Brauch und Volksglaube im Deutschen Westböhmen*, 188; Birlinger, *Volksthümliches, aus Schwaben*, vol. 1, 120–21; Meyer, *Badisches Volksleben im Neunzehnten Jahrhundert*, 423; F. Ohrt, *Danmarks Trylleformler* (Kbh.: Gyldendal, 1917), 314–319; Drechsler, *Sitte, Brauch und Volksglaube in Schlesien*, vol. 2, 75; Elard H. Meyer, *Deutsche Volkskunde mit 17 Abbildungen und 1 Karte* (Strassburg: K. J. Trübner, 1898), 228–232; Richard Wossidlo, *Erntebräuche in Mecklenburg* (Hamburg: Quickborn, 1927), 29–30.

294. The idea here seems to be that the ailment will be transferred to the bone. Johann Adolf Heyl, *Volkssagen, Bräuche und Meinungen aus Tirol* (Brixen: Katholisch-politischer Pressverein, 1897), 801; Albertus, *Albertus Magnus. Being the Approved, Verified, Sympathetic and Natural Egyptian Secrets; or, White and Black Art for Man and Beast*, 120; Fogel, *Beliefs and Superstitions of the Pennsylvania Germans*, 169. The same technique was also used to cure bone spurs and warts. Fanny D. Bergen and William Wells Newell, *Current Superstitions Collected from the Oral Tradition of English Speaking Folk* (Teddington, Middlesex: Echo Library, 2007), 96; Johann Pollinger, *Aus Landshut und Umgebung: Ein Beitrag zur Heimat- und Volkskunde* (München: Oldenbourg, 1908), 287–88; Schönwerth, *Aus der Oberpfalz—Sitten und Sagen*, vol. 3, 235; Else Roediger, "Allerlei aus Bärwalde, Kr. Neustettin, Pommern," *Zeitschrift des Vereins für Volkskunde* 13(1903), 99.

295. *White vitriol*: See Item 40.

296. *Sugar of lead*: Lead(II) acetate. This substance is also harmful.

297. Rosewater was a common ingredient in eye-water in Saxony. Bächtold-Stäubli, Hoffmann-Krayer, and Lüdtke, *Handwörterbuch des Deutschen Aberglaubens*, vol. 7, 779.

298. This final sentence is an addition of the translator.

299. *Without being able...*: Brown substitutes "It is the Best Charm for this Purpose in the Book," and omits the following sentence.

300. *Oh Peter... bound*: A reference to Peter's power granted by Christ (Matthew 16:19). Given this Scriptural reference, it is unsurprising that we see Peter in many charms to still thieves, e.g. Hirzel, "Aberglauben im Kanton Zürich," 264–65.

301. This is the same opening as that of a thief-charm found by Otto Heilig in a recipe book found in Handschuhsheim near Heidelberg, written in 1818, two years before Hohman's book appeared. See Otto Heilig, "Segen aus Handschuhsheim," *Zeitschrift des Vereins für Volkskunde* 5(1895).

302. *Young or old*: Omitted in Brown.

303. *Your articles of faith*: Brown and Hohman 1846 have "the creed."

304. It is curious that Peter is not invoked here once again to loose as he is bound, and it might be that other versions of this charm will be found substituting him here.

305. The German states that the choice of pronoun should be based on whether one or more thieves are affected.

306. *Sweeney*: Atrophy of the shoulder muscles in a horse.

307. *Piece*: German "pound."

308. *Pumpkins*: Weaver (2001) takes the term Kürbiss to mean squash in a more general sense, though this attribution is by no means certain. This is, however, one of the few instances in which a plant native to the New World and not the Old is used in a Hohman recipe.

309. *Five … water*: Omitted in Brown.

310. Ginger: The German "gelben Ingwer" indicates turmeric (*Curcura longa*).

311. Molasses beer had been a popular recipe in the early days of the colony of Pennsylvania. "Our Beer was mostly made from Molosses, which well boyld, with Sassafras or Pine infused into it, makes very tolerable Drink …" William Penn, "A Further Account of the Province of Pennsylvania, by William Penn, 1685," in *Narratives of Early Pennsylvania, West New Jersey and Delaware, 1630–1707*, ed. Albert Cook Myers (New York: C. Scribner's Sons, 1912), 267.

312. The German adds, "It is then good beer."

313. Hohman, *Die Land- und Haus-Apotheke, oder, Getreuer und Gründlicher Unterricht für den Bauer und Stadtmann, Enthaltend die Allerbesten Mittel, Sowohl für die Menschen Als für das Vieh Besonders für die Pferde. Nebst Einem Grossen Anhang von der Aechten Färberey*, 50.

314. *Turtle dove*: Birds of the genus Streptopelia, none of which are native to the New World.

315. *Die Land- und Haus-Apotheke* adds that the blood must be warm, and that the treatment has already aided some sufferers.

316. *White lily*: *Lilium candidum*. It has been traditionally used as a topical treatment for pain relief.

317. *Southernwort*: The German *Ebenkraut* applies to the genus Epilobium. Some of its species, most notably fireweed (*E. angustifolium*), have been used to treat topical afflictions. The translator might have read this as "Eberraute," or *Artemisia abrotanum*, known as southernwood. Lick and Brendle, "Plant Names and Plant Lore among the Pennsylvania-Germans," 38. Brown has "common thistle" (*Cirsium vulgare*); Hohman 1846 has "Carline thistle" (*Carlina vulgaris*), which has no known medical effects but was used as a folk remedy to treat wounds.

318. *As long as …*: Hohman 1846 omits this.

319. *Capuchin powder*: This substance was a common apothecary's cure for lice. After its use for a poisoning, it was banned in Saxony, with various remedies substituted therefore. See Friedrich Küchenmeister, *On animal and vegetable parasites of the human body*, vol. 2, 79.

320. *Cammock*: Rest harrow (*Ononis spinosa*), a European plant not known for its insect repellent qualities. Brown has "cowslip," a name that describes various plants, none of which have the desired effect.

321. The German adds that the paper must be dunked in pounded alum first.

322. *Seven*: Brown has "forty-seven."

323. *Peach stones*: Peaches (*Prunus persica*) were brought to the New World in the seventeenth century. The pits include amygdalin, which can lead to cyanide poisoning.

324. *Several*: German "a few"

325. *The person …*: The German indicates that this was a woman. Brown has "my wife." Hohman 1846 omits the sentence entirely.

326. Hohman, *Die Land- und Haus-Apotheke, oder, Getreuer und Gründlicher Unter-richt für den Bauer und Stadtmann, Enthaltend Die Allerbesten Mittel, Sowohl für die Menschen Als für das Vieh Besonders für die Pferde. Nebst Einem Grossen Anhang von der Aechten Färberey*, 50.

327. The German text has here "increasing moon." This includes a curious twist; generally one would associate a diminishing growth with a waning moon, but the language of the charm reverses the traditional linkage. A charm for goiter using similar language circulated among the Pennsylvania Dutch in the late nineteenth century. See J. G. Owens, "Folk-Lore from Buffalo Valley, Central Pennsylvania," *The Journal of American Folklore* 4, no. 13 (1891), 124.

328. A similar charm for warts was used throughout Pennsylvania Dutch country. Fogel, *Beliefs and Superstitions of the Pennsylvania Germans*, 324.

329. Albertus, Aristotle, and John Baumann, *Kurzgefasstes Weiber-Büchlein* ([Ephrata, PA]: Gedruckt [bey G. Baumann?], 1799), 62; Werner Manz, "Volksglaube aus dem Sarganserland," *Schweizerisches Archiv für Volkskunde* 24(1922–23), 305.

330. The first part appears in Hohman's *Land- und Haus Apotheke*, 7, including the curious distinction between five and eight roots that appears in the German.

331. August 24 in the calendar of the Western church.

332. The German has "eight."

333. Dandelion: *Taraxacum officinale*, an Old World import. It has various medicinal properties, though none related to the eyes are noted. Brown and Hohman 1846 include various words derived from the German.

334. The German is unclear as to where the roots should be hung. In both Brown and Hohman 1846, around the neck as the proper position.

335. *Tape*: A strip of cloth, instead of the modern sticky-sided office supply.

336. Weaver 2001, 82: "Cotton, moistened with a few drops of distilled oil of cam-phor and then laid upon an aching tooth, will stop the pain. The same preparation inserted into the ears will strengthen weak hearing and heal buzzing and ringing of the same."

337. See Item 102 for pertinent safety issues.

338. Fogel, *Beliefs and Superstitions of the Pennsylvania Germans*, 310–11.

339. Theodor Zwinger, *Theodori Zuingeri Theatrum Botanicum* (Basel: In Verie-gung Hans Jacob Bischoffs, 1744), 217: "Wider das Würgen, Erbrechen und den Durchlauf des Magens, so von Kälte verursacht wird; Nimm eine Schnitte gebähet Brod, nässe sie in Malvasier, bestreue sie mit ein wenig gestossener Nelcken, und nutze also dieselbige." The calmative effects of cloves on the stomach have been noted elsewhere.

340. Zwinger lists "Malvasia wine" instead, a vintage originating on Madeira which is usually white.

341. The German "Fahnenkraut" is *Lathyrus vernus*, or the spring pea.

342. Zwinger, *Theodori Zuingeri Theatrum Botanicum*, 217: "Morgens nüchtern zwey Tröpflein ein einem Lössel voll weissen Wein eingenommen. Auf gleiche Weise dienet es auch wider die kalte Gebresten der Mutter und Därmen, vertreibet daher das Bauch-Grimmen. Über das ist es auch dem kalten Magen sonderlich gut, stärcket und erwärmet denselbigen, und stillet das Erbrechen. Ein paar Tröpflein

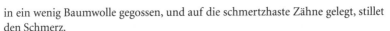

in ein wenig Baumwolle gegossen, und auf die schmertzhaste Zähne gelegt, stillet den Schmerz.

"Die Nelcken-Oel wird auf folgende Weise destilliert: Nehmt einen guten Theil der Gewürz-Nelcken, stosst sie zu einem dicken Pulver, giesst laues Wasser darüber, lasst es also vier Tage in warmen Sand stehen, destilliert es hernach aus einem zinnernen oder kuyfernen Kolben, und sonderet das Oehl mit Baumvolle; oder durch ein Separier-Glas davon ab. Auf gleiche Weise wird auch aus Zimmet, Muscaten-Blüthe, Muscatnuss, Psesser und Zittwen-Wurtzen das Oehl bestillierer und separiret."

343. The German adds, "The clove oil is distilled in this manner: Take a good amount of cloves, pound it into a thick powder, pour a half ounce of water over it, leave it thus to stand for four days in warm sand, distill it after that into a pewter or copper flask, and separate the oil from it with cotton or a separating-glass."

344. Zwinger, 625, for *Muscus arboreus*: "Welche mit der rothen Ruhr oder dem Durchlauf behaftet sind, denen soll man Baum-Moos in Wasser oder rothem Weine stehen, und zu trincken geben."

345. Zwinger gives the plant's Latin name as *Usnea officinarum*, a lichen that grows on the branches of trees.

346. Zwinger also includes water as a possibility.

347. Club moss (*Lycopodium clavatum*) has been used in a tea as a diuretic, but this is the exact opposite of the desired effect for someone in these conditions.

348. Not present in Hohman 1846.

349. *Blue vitriol*: Copper sulfate ($CuSO_4$). A recent study showed that the use of copper sulfate in conjunction with a fluoride toothpaste lowered the rate of tooth decay—see A. Z. Abdullah et al., "The Effect of Copper on Demineralization of Dental Enamel," *Journal of Dental Research* 85, no. 11 (2006). Nonetheless, this is a highly toxic substance.

350. Current medical knowledge supports Hohman on both of these assessments. The German adds that those with the mother-fits cannot abide the smell.

351. *Mr. Valentine Kettering*: A man of this name died in Dauphin County in 1836, but this does not seem to be consistent with the stay in America given below.

352. *Fifty years*: German: "sixty years."

353. *And that he ... States*: Omitted in Hohman 1846.

354. *Chick-weed*: *Stellaria media*, another European plant. It has been both taken internally as a laxative and used as a poultice for a number of conditions, though its efficacy in cases of rabies is dubious.

355. *Gauchheil*: *Anagallis arvensis*, or scarlet pimpernel. It seems that two plants have been confused here. Some editions have *Gauchneil*.

356. *Table-spoonful*: Brown has "a small egg-glass full." Hohman 1846 has "a tea spoon ful."

357. This might be confusing the Reverend Henry Muhlenberg (1711–1787), a prominent figure in the Pennsylvania Lutheran Church, with his son, the botanist Gotthilf Hunrich Ernst Muhlenberg (1753–1815). Whether either had any actual connection to this recipe is unknown.

358. *Four times a day ... whole week*: Hohman 1846 has "four times a day for a whole week."

359. Henry William Stoy (1726–1801), a former minister and doctor later known for his sale of "Stoy's Drops" and a hydrophobia cure. Francis R. Packard, in his article on Stoy in *A cyclopedia of American medical biography*... (1114), comments as following on the latter:

> Whether Dr. Stoy's success in curing the disease was due to the remedy or to the fact that possibly only a small per cent of the so-called rabid dogs are afflicted with rabies, we are unable to say, but from the ingredients it contained we are led to believe there was not much virtue in it. The remedy consisted of one ounce of the herb, red chick-weed, four ounces of theriac and one quart of beer, all well digested, the dose being a wine glassful. Red chickweed is supposed to be antivenomous, nervine, and stimulating.

360. Ellis, *A Compleat System of Experienced Improvements*...

361. Hohman 1846 has instead, "I notice one time"

362. Ellis, 378–9: "*A Flock of Sheep had more Wool than ordinary on them, by their Bodies being rubb'd over with Butter-Milk as soon as shorn, &c.*—In June, 1745, I was inform'd of a Farmer that was Owner of a Flock of large, coarse-wool'd Sheep, that prosper'd very well, partly because that, as soon as they were shorn, he having a Tub of Butter-Milk standing by him, rubb'd some over Part of each Sheep's Body; for you must know that Butter-Milk is what will cause Wool to grow apace on Sheep, and Hair on any Beast; or, if you have not Butter-Milk, mix only a little Milk with much Salt and Water, and rub this Liquor on your new-shorn Sheep, and I do assure you, if you manage this right, you will kill the Breed of Ticks, or Sheep-Lice, heal all Scabs and Wounds, prevent Sheep catching Cold, and cause their Wool to grow thick and quick; for these Vermin are frequently so thick, both in Lambs and Sheep, that after they are shorn, the Jack-Daws, and other Field-Fowls, will get on their Backs and pick them off."

363. *A gill of lard*: The German stipulates that "Küchlein" must have been cooked therein. Brown has "chickens"; Hohman 1846 has "cakes." Either one could be correct.

364. *Rue*: *Ruta graveolens*, a plant native to Southern Europe. Though it is employed in homeopathic remedies for sprains and topical injuries, it is highly toxic. A similar topical remedy, involving both eggs and rue, was used to ease childbirth (Dörler, "Die Tierwelt in der Sympathetischen Tiroler Volksmedizin," 171).

365. *Cloth*: Hohman 1846 stipulates a linen cloth.

366. Cross-gender transmission of powwowing was common, but cross-gender healing requirements are barely present in the corpus.

367. *Wormwood*: *Artemisia absinthium*, or other members of the *Artemisia* genus. Originally from the Old World, its only known topical use is as an insect repellent.

368. *Medels/Medeln*: Hohman gives "Meldy" in his translation, likely indicating "Melde," or goosefoot (Genus *Atriplex*), an herb used topically for menstruation and cramps. Brown (1904) suggests "Middel," or common quaking grass (*Briza media*).

369. *Sheepripwort*: The German "Schafrippen" refers to *Achillea millefolium*, or yarrow. Brown (1904) has "quaking-grass" (*Briza media*).

370. *Pointy plantain*: The German "spitzigen Wegrich" is likely "Spitzwegerich," or *Plantago lanceolata* (English plantain). Omitted in Brown.

371. Omitted in Hohman 1846.

372. *White turpentine*: Turpentine made from the yellow pine (*Pinus* subgenus *Pinus*). Weaver (2001, 330) notes that the most common source for this in Pennsylvania was the Carolinas.

373. German "Klauenfett," a substance skimmed off when the stomach and hooves of cattle are boiled.

374. *Rub*: German "fry."

375. *Wells*: Brown has "flowers." See below.

376. *Courage ... good*: Brown has "might ... height," likely to preserve the rhyme.

377. The similarities between this and the "Three Flowers" charm (Item 109) are notable. It might be that this charm is the result of a misreading of "Blumen" (flowers) as "Brunnen" (wells).

378. Albertus, *Albertus Magnus. Being the Approved, Verified, Sympathetic and Natural Egyptian Secrets; or, White and Black Art for Man and Beast*, 97. Omitted in Hohman 1846, save for the final line.

379. *valued ... rulers*: Brown has "all-pervading."

380. *and the third says*: Omitted from the German, but restored to its original intent in the English.

381. An example of the "Drei Blumen" charm, first recorded in Switzerland in 1429 and common in the German literature. It might be derived from the "Drei Frauen" charm, of which Item 134 is an example. Roses are the most common flower to appear therein, possibly due to their apotropaic effects against the Devil and witchcraft, with lilies following closely. Bächtold-Stäubli, Hoffmann-Krayer, and Lüdtke, *Handwörterbuch des Deutschen Aberglaubens*, vol. 2, 422–425.; Oskar Ebermann, *Blut- und Wundsegen in Ihrer Entwicklung* (Berlin: Mayer & Müller, 1903), 97.

382. This line omitted in Brown.

383. *Job*: The protagonist of the Biblical Book of Job, whom Satan afflicted with sores at the behest of God, who later cured him.

384. *Did meet*: Brown has "blessed."

385. *Name*: The German stipulates the first and last name.

386. The version in the *Romanusbüchlein* indicates the teeth, gums, and tongue as well, as well as a reference to Jesus Christ, who was not a contemporary of Job.

387. *Romanusbüchlein* 4, Spamer 1958, 46, discussion, 76–94. Spamer believes this to be a variant on a famous charm for toothache and sore throat which usually features St. Peter. Other sources feature St. Jacob as the protagonist. J. Ph. Glock, "Lieder und Sprüche aus dem Elsenztal. aus dem Munde des Volks Gesammelt.," *Alemannia: Zeitschrift für Sprache, Litteratur und Volkskunde des Elsaszes Oberrheins und Schwabens*, 25(1898), 239. See also: Manz, "Volksglaube aus dem Sarganserland," 298–99. Hohman 1846 lists "scrofula" as the condition treated.

The *Romanusbüchlein* adds that an adult patient should use water in which alum has been dissolved as a mouthwash three times after each of the names of the Trinity. The omission of this passage accounts for the curious reference to the rite being for children at its end, which was not mentioned before in the charm. Other versions simply include a glass of water placed at the mouth. Losch, "Deutsche Segen, Heil- und Bannsprüche," 223.

388. Throughout German-speaking lands and beyond, placing herbs or characters within a shoe in hope of warding off ill effects has been common. See Bächtold-Stäubli, Hoffmann-Krayer, and Lüdtke, *Handwörterbuch des Deutschen Aberglaubens*, vol. 7, 1314–1315.

389. *Desh*: German "Deisch," Hohman 1846 "Deish." The meaning of this word is unclear. Similar words with a broad variety of names exist in many German dialects, and it also turns up as a place name. Ralf Oderwald suggests that the structure indicates a different meaning might be intended for each appearance of the word (private correspondence).

390. This portion of the charm is printed in a broadside from Joseph Hartman's press in Lebanon circa 1818. Russell D. Earnest, Corinne P. Earnest, and Edward L. Rosenberry, *Flying Leaves and One-Sheets: Pennsylvania German Broadsides, Fraktur, and Their Printers* (New Castle, DE: Oak Knoll Press, 2005), 169.

391. *8*: German, "9."

392. *Civit, (musk)*: Civet likely refers to the secretions of the civet, a mammal native to Africa and Asia. Musk is technically the secretions of the musk deer (genus *Moschus*), but the term might also be used in a broader sense to refer to the civet secretions. Both were noted for their strong scent and used in the manufacture of perfume.

393. *Castorium*: German "Biebergail," English "castoreum."

394. *Where … warm*: German, "in the sun."

395. *Net*: Hohman 1846 has "line." The German could favor either explanation.

396. *Not quite*: Hohman 1846 has "not under."

397. *And the cloth … age*: Brown omits these instructions.

398. Most likely "in silence." See Item 4.

399. *On the first … moon*: Hohman 1846 has "on the last Friday in the last Quarter."

400. *Articles of Faith*: Brown has "the Creed."

401. *And immediately … repeated*: Not in the 1820 German, which has instead "The author of this letter has also been taught that, when the finished letter is folded together, three ends of the same page must be by each other."

402. *Whom God did love …* : The German suggests instead that God should be loved.

403. *Through the burning oven …* : Likely a confused reference to Daniel's three companions thrown in the fiery furnace (Daniel 3). This sentence and the previous one are repeated in this charm in Brown.

404. *Raving convulsions*: Apparently gout with stabbing pains.

405. *Yellow convulsions*: The German "gelb Gicht" could possibly mean gout accompanied by jaundice.

406. *White convulsions, red convulsions*: Unknown, and possibly included to complement the others rather than as references to actual conditions.

407. *Black convulsions*: The German "schwarz Gegicht" might signify a disease in which the limbs display black markings.

408. *Reins*: veins.

409. *Pensses Blum*: "Penseebloem," or *Viola tricolor*. Brown (1904) gives "Flower of Prusse."

410. The German adds that no other book on the topic includes this remedy.

411. *Asbestos*: The German has "Aspect," the meaning of which is unknown. Hohman 1846 leaves the term untranslated.

412. *Ley*: Soapsuds.

413. The German adds that the wick should be dried in the sun.

414. *Seven rings*: Possibly a reference to *The Mystical City of God*, a text attributed to divine vision by a seventeenth-century nun. Madre Maria de Jesús de Agreda and George John Blatter, *City of God, the Coronation; the Divine History and Life of the Virgin Mother of God, Manifested to Mary of Agreda for the Encouragement of Men* (Hammond, IN: W. B. Conkey, 1914), vol. 1, 341. Another version has "seven eyes." Manz, "Volksglaube aus dem Sarganserland," 293.

415. *Save me...*: Brown has "Protect me, O God, this day."

416. *Than the...Jesus*: Omitted from Brown.

417. *Ave Maria*: A traditional Catholic prayer in honor of the Virgin Mary. The German states that this must be repeated three times.

418. *Romanusbüchlein* 1, Spamer 1958, 45.

419. God as creator is often invoked in German fire charms. Bächtold-Stäubli, Hoffmann-Krayer, and Lüdtke, *Handwörterbuch des Deutschen Aberglaubens*, vol. 2, 1435.

420. This section is an example of the Flum Jordan charm (Roper, *English Verbal Charms*) 104–109). The original version of this story appears in the Apocryphal Chronicum Paschale, dating from the seventh century (Owen Davies, "Healing Charms in Use in England and Wales 1700–1950," *Folklore* 107(1996), 21). Typically found in charms for stilling blood, it also exists in the German literature as a charm to stop fires. For more variants, see Drechsler, *Sitte, Brauch und Volksglaube in Schlesien*, vol. 2, 141.

421. Fire charms invoking the virginity of Mary were common in Germany. The use of "Damen," or "women," instead of "Namen," or "name," indicates that this particular version is of late origin. Grimm and Kretzenbacher, *Deutsche Mythologie*, vol. 3, 500. Birlinger, "Besegnungen Aberglauben," 239; Drechsler, *Sitte, Brauch und Volksglaube in Schlesien*, vol. 2, 142; Otto Weinrich, "Eine Bewährter Feuersegen," *Hessische Blätter für Volkskunde* 9(1910), 141.

422. This phrase also appears as a solitary charm. See H. Prahn, "Glaube und Brauch in der Mark Brandenburg," *Zeitschrift des Vereins für Volkskunde* 1(1891), 190.

423. Many versions of this charm are attributed to a Gypsy, though at least one seems to be tied to a king of the West Indies. Weinreich, "Eine Bewährter Feuersegen."

424. *Anno 1740...*: The German edition has 1714. Brown has the first of June.

425. *Ten minutes*: German: "half of a quarter hour." Hohman 1846: "5 minutes."

426. *and the General...*: Hohman 1846 omits this.

427. The German edition has 1715.

428. This places the charm into the category of the Himmelsbrief, or protective letter. Oddly enough, the instructions describe its use both in that capacity and as a verbal charm.

429. This was a common charm at this time, that appeared not only in books but in broadsides. The earliest version of the charm itself, sans the surrounding tale, appears in 1617. (Ferdinand Mencik, "Ein Erprobter Feuersegen," *Zeitschrift des Vereins für Volkskunde* 8(1898).) Versions of this charm circulated in broadside

form and were believed to ward off fire if posted in a house; see Yoder 2005: 221–222. One version was to be written three times and placed in three corners in the three highest names (Birlinger, *Volksthümliches, Aus Schwaben. Herausgegeben von Dr. Anton Birlinger)*, vol. 1, 201–2. Others were to be said while passing around the fire three times (e.g. Losch, "Deutsche Segen, Heil- und Bannsprüche, 161–62). For other examples, see Georg Althaus, "An Eighteenth-Century Gypsy Charm," *Journal of the Gypsy Lore Society* Series 3, 38(1959); Bartsch, *Sagen, Märchen und Gebräuche Aus Meklenburg*, vol. 2, 357–8; Drechsler, *Sitte, Brauch und Volksglaube in Schlesien*, 143–44; J. Löbe, "Aberglaube und Volksmittel aus dem Altenburg-schen," *Mitteilungen der Geschichts- und Altertumsforschenden Gesellschaft des Osterlandes.* 7(1874), 453–454; Franz Weinitz, "Zwei Segen," *Zeitschrift des Vereins für Volkskunde* 21(1911), 340. A broad comparison of several versions can be found in Herbert Freudenthal, *Das Feuer im Deutschen Glauben und Brauch* (Berlin; Leipzig: W. de Gruyter & Co., 1931), 551–556. For a discussion of variants of this charm, see Weinreich, "Eine Bewährter Feuersegen," 139–142.

430. *Black chicken*: An Estonian custom dispenses with most of this and simply has the chicken thrown into the fire. Johann Wolfgang Boecler, *Der Ehsten Abergläubische Gebrauche, Weisen und Gewohnheiten, von Johann Wolfgang Boecler, ... Mit auf die Gegenwart Bezüglichen Anmerkungen Beleuchtet, von Dr. Fr. Kreutzwald* (St. Petersburg: Eggers, 1854), 125.

431. *During her terms*: Menstrual blood, often considered a substance with mystical power. The *Egyptian Secrets* has "gold quartz" here instead, though the German agrees with Hohman. Albertus, *Albertus Magnus. Being the Approved, Verified, Sympathetic and Natural Egyptian Secrets; or, White and Black Art for Man and Beast*, 23; ———, *Bewährte und Approbierte Sympathetische und Natürliche Ägyptische Geheimnisse für Menschen und Vieh*, 36.

432. *Romanusbüchlein* 7, Spamer 1958, 47. Not present in Hohman 1846. The combination of an egg laid on Maundy Thursday, Good Friday, or Easter with menstrual blood and a black hen is a common one in Germany. Bächtold-Stäubli, Hoffmann-Krayer, and Lüdtke, *Handwörterbuch des Deutschen Aberglaubens*, vol. 2, 1424; Birlinger, *Aus Schwaben Sagen, Legenden, Aberglauben, Sitten, Rechtsbräuche, Ortsneckereien, Lieder, Kinderreine, Neue Sammlung, von Anton Birlinger*, vol 1, 435; Grimm and Kretzenbacher, *Deutsche Mythologie*, vol. 3, 491; Karl Huss and Alois John, *Die Schrift "Vom Aberglauben" von Karl Huss nach dem in der Fürstlich Metternichschen Bibliothek zu Königswart Befindlichen Manuskripte Herausgegeben*, Beiträge zur Deutsch-Böhmischen Volkskunde, 9,2 (Prag: Calve, 1910), 34; Albertus, *Albertus Magnus. Being the Approved, Verified, Sympathetic and Natural Egyptian Secrets; or, White and Black Art for Man and Beast*, 23; Johann Wilhelm Wolf, *Beiträge zur Deutschen Mythologie* (Leipzig; Göttingen 1852), vol. 1, 236. This particular variant first appears in a book of remedies compiled by Michael Schorno, Landaman of the Swiss canton of Schwyz, between 1629 and 1670. This particular remedy was acquired from one Caspar Betz, who claimed he received it from a Gypsy. See A. Dettling, "Aus Dem Arzneibuch des Landamanns Michael Schorno von Schwyz, + 1671," *Schweizerisches Archiv für Volkskunde* 15(1911), 90.

433. This latter operation is not in the *Romanusbüchlein*, but it nonetheless dates back to the seventeenth-century Swiss canton's book already mentioned. As Winstedt observes, the use of menstrual blood in the charm makes it unlikely that this is

a Gypsy charm. E. O. Winstedt, "German Gypsies and Fire," *Journal of the Gypsy Lore Society* Series 3, 12(1933), 58–60. Another version lists the bedsheet from a childbed as an alternative. Huss and John, *Die Schrift "Vom Aberglauben" von Karl Huss nach dem in der Fürstlich Metternichschen Bibliothek zu Königswart Befindlichen Manuskripte Herausgegeben*, 34. The piece of cloth might also be tied around a rock and thrown into the fire. Staricius, *Geheimnissvoller Heldenschatz, Oder der Vollständige Egyptische Magische Schild*. See also Drechsler, *Sitte, Brauch und Volksglaube in Schlesien*, vol. 2, 140. Manz, "Volksglaube aus dem Sarganserland," 303.

434. "Trotterkopf" might be another form of "Trudenkopf," a term used to correspond to a nightmare or a witch. Such a spirit might enter the stable, leaving horses exhausted and with matted manes. Mahr has speculated that the spell was originally intended to drive off a nightmare, keeping it busy with various activities until the morning, and only later became connected with witchcraft in general. August C. Mahr, "A Pennsylvania Dutch 'Hexzettel'," *Monatshefte für Deutschen Unterricht* 27, no. 6 (1935); Birlinger, *Aus Schwaben Sagen, Legenden, Aberglauben, Sitten, Rechtsbräuche, Ortsneckereien, Lieder, Kinderreine, Neue Sammlung, von Anton Birlinger*, vol. 1, 457. Spamer sees the phrase as derivative of the medieval Latin "trotare," "to trot." The *Egyptian Secrets* has here "Bedgoblin" (German: "Bettzairle") and employs the rite on its own and as part of a longer ritual for inflicting harm upon a witch. Albertus, *Albertus Magnus. Being the Approved, Verified, Sympathetic and Natural Egyptian Secrets; or, White and Black Art for Man and Beast*, 5, 55.

435. *Premises*: Brown: "court."

436. Breathe on me: The German might be translated as "comfort."

437. The *Egyptian Secrets* have here the impossibility formula, "until that beloved day arrives when the mother of God will bring forth her second son," adding that the formula should be said three times aloud. Albertus, *Albertus Magnus. Being the Approved, Verified, Sympathetic and Natural Egyptian Secrets; or, White and Black Art for Man and Beast*, 5.

438. *Romanusbüchlein* 8, Spamer 1958, 47, discussion and bibliography, 95–108. The earliest known variant of this incantation dates to the early seventeenth century. A. Birlinger, "Besegnungen aus dem XVII Jahrhundert," *Alemannia: Zeitschrift für Sprache, Litteratur und Volkskunde des Elsaszes Oberrheins und Schwabens*. 14(1886), 74. This spell was a staple in powwowing. Such charms were among those brought into evidence at the Hageman trial ("Further Evidence in Hageman Case," *North American*, March 12 1903, 11; "Witnesses Heard in Hageman Case," *North American*, March 13, 1903, 13; Bertolet, *New York Herald*, January 14, 1900). Mahr located copies of it inserted into an antique sofa, likely to bring its owner protection. Mahr, "A Pennsylvania Dutch 'Hexzettel'." Such charms have been considered one of the main three types of written charms used to protect barns in Pennsylvania Dutch country. Thomas E. Graves, "The Pennsylvania German Hex Sign: A Study in Folk Process" (s.n., 1990), 150–162. See also Manz, "Volksglaube aus dem Sarganserland," 307.

439. Witches. See Item 24.

440. See Item 106.

441. *Gith*: The common corn-cockle (*Agrostemma githago*). The German here calls for black cumin (*Nigella sativa*), a common ingredient in anti-witchcraft remedies. See

Bächtold-Stäubli, Hoffmann-Krayer, and Lüdtke, *Handwörterbuch des Deutschen Aberglaubens*, vol. 7, 1455.

442. *Five-finger weed*: Cinquefoil. See Item 20.

443. *Assafoetida*: *Ferula assafoetida*. The pungent smell of this Old World plant made it a common ingredient in recipes for driving off evil spirits; e.g. Joseph H. Peterson, *The Lesser Key of Solomon: Lemegeton Clavicula Salomonis: Detailing the Ceremonial Art of Commanding Spirits Both Good and Evil* (York Beach, ME: Weiser Books, 2001), 52. Its usage was prevalent until the mid-twentieth century among the Pennsylvania Dutch; Donald Roan, "Deivels-Dreck (Asafoetida) Yesterday and Today," *Pennsylvania Folklife* 14, no. 2 (1964).

444. A German variant has "six Pfennige." Bächtold-Stäubli, Hoffmann-Krayer, and Lüdtke, *Handwörterbuch des Deutschen Aberglaubens*, vol. 9, 499.

445. *Horse-beans*: The fava bean (*Vicia fabia*).

446. *Salt*: A substance often used in magical procedures for protection and cleansing.

447. *Lignum vitae wood*: Genus *Guaiacum*. German: Lit. "Ivory-wood." Schramek gives two possibilities: *Rhamnus fangula* (alder buckthorn) and black alder. Josef Schramek, *Der Böhmerwaldbauer: Eigenart, Tracht und Nahrung, Haus- und Wirtschaftsgeräte, Sitten, Gebräuche und Volksglaube. Nebst Einem Anhange: Der Böhmerwaldholzhauer*, Beiträge zur Deutsch-Böhmischen Volkskunde, Xii. Bd. (Prag: J. G. Calve (R. Lerche), 1915), 264. The latter is given in another version: Hirzel, "Aberglauben im Kanton Zürich," 272. Another version of this spell (Löbe above) lists "Drachenholz"—"Dragon wood," possibly referring to the black cherry (*Prunus serotina*).

448. *Romanusbüchlein* 9, Spamer 1958, 48. See also Löbe, "Aberglaube und Volksmittel aus dem Altenburgschen." A manuscript found near Rendsburg has a similar charm: "Wenn einer besorgt, dass böse Leute sein Vieh unterhaben, geräuchert mit Teufelsdreck, weissem Kampfer, Dillsamen, schwarzen Köhm (Kümmel) weissen Arand. Auch muss etwas den Boden gebohrt werden und mit einem Erbbohrer und mit einem Pflaumenbaum-Pfropf geschlossen." H. Handelmann, "Volksmedizin. Zauber- und Heilsprüche Udgl.," *Am Ur-Quell* 1(1890). See also John, *Sitte, Brauch und Volksglaube im Deutschen Westböhmen, von Alois John*, 320; Manz, "Volksglaube aus dem Sarganserland," 307. Other versions mention that the items should be placed while speaking the names of the Trinity. Hirzel, "Aberglauben im Kanton Zürich."

449. One source stipulates a tin plate. Löbe, "Aberglaube und Volksmittel aus dem Altenburgschen," 447.

450. Bächtold-Stäubli, Hoffmann-Krayer, and Lüdtke, *Handwörterbuch des Deutschen Aberglaubens*, vol. 2, 1423; John, *Sitte, Brauch und Volksglaube im Deutschen Westböhmen, von Alois John*, 274; Schönwerth, *Aus der Oberpfalz—Sitten und Sagen*, vol. 2, 85. P. Amand Baumgarten, *Aus der Volksmässigen Ueberlieferung der Heimat 1 zur Volkthümlichen Naturkunde* (Linz: Oberösterr. Musealverein, 1862), 23–24. This belief was so prevalent that, in 1742, Duke Ernst August of Saxe-Weimar ordered all mayors and judges to keep on hand wooden plates inscribed with the words "An Gottes Allmach liegts; Consumatum est," so they might be tossed into blazes. William L. Evenden, *Deutsche Feuerversicherungs-Schilder = German Fire Marks* (Karlsruhe: VVW, 1989), 18. Its most recent known use was in 1858 near Landshut. Pollinger, *Aus Landshut und Umgebung: Ein Beitrag zur Heimat-*

und Volkskunde, 159–60. One version of the charm states it may also be carried to guard against dog bites and witchcraft; Löbe, "Aberglaube und Volksmittel aus dem Altenburgschen," 447–78.

451. SATOR square. Its first known instance appearing in the ruins of , the square has been used for a wide variety of magical purposes over a vast range of geography and time. It has been hypothesized that the square's words are a permutation of the Latin "Pater Noster" and the Greek alpha and omega. Its use in Germany to stop fires was ubiquitous. See Drechsler, *Sitte, Brauch und Volksglaube in Schlesien*, vol. 2, 142. A. Haas, "Feuersegen," *Blätter für Pommersche Volkskunde* 3, no. 2 (1894), vol. 3, 26.

452. *Romanusbüchlein* 6, Spamer 1958, 47–48. See also Manz, "Volksglaube aus dem Sarganserland," 303.

453. *Sarah*: Likely the wife of Abraham and the mother of Isaac. This charm usually features God or Jesus as the individual carrying the brand. Such examples from the Germanic corpus date back to at least 1596. Freudenthal, *Das Feuer im Deutschen Glauben und Brauch*, 394, 396–7.

454. Another "impossibility formula"; see Item 37.

455. Brown omits these instructions.

456. A slight variant of this charm seems to have been used as part of evening prayers for children, e.g. Johannes Thäter, *Selbstbiographie Eines Alten Schulmeisters: Nach dem Tode des Verfassers für Seine Freunde Herausgegeben* (Nürnberg: Sebald, 1866), 5.

457. *Sadrach and his companions…*: Shadrach, Meschach, and Abednego. These three figures were often seen in German fire charms. Bächtold-Stäubli, Hoffmann-Krayer, and Lüdtke, *Handwörterbuch des Deutschen Aberglaubens*, vol. 2, 1435. Birlinger, *Volksthümliches, Aus Schwaben. Herausgegeben von Dr. Anton Birlinger*, vol. 1, 199.

458. *Romanusbüchlein* 5, Spamer 1958, 46. See also Manz, "Volksglaube aus dem Sarganserland," 303; Löbe, "Aberglaube und Volksmittel aus dem Altenburgschen," 446–47; Losch, "Deutsche Segen, Heil- und Bannsprüche," 237.

459. *Three false… bound thee*: A reference to the power of speech to create misfortune via witchcraft, opposed by the three tongues of the Trinity in the next statement.

460. *Three holy tongues*: Another version has "five holy wounds." Schramek, *Der Böhmerwaldbauer: Eigenart, Tracht und Nahrung, Haus- und Wirtschaftsgeräte, Sitten, Gebräuche und Volksglaube. Nebst Einem Anhange: Der Böhmerwaldholzhauer*, 264.

461. *The holy Ciprian*: Saint Cyprian (-304), a possibly mythical magician turned Christian bishop who was eventually martyred. Traditions linking him with magic are strong in both Scandinavia and the Hispanic world.

462. *Servant*: Brown: "knight."

463. *Led you astray*: Brown "run away."

464. *I bless…*: Brown: "I bless thee before thou art destroyed."

465. *And all the Jews*: The context of this makes it clear that Jesus is the one trembling, though the wording is unclear.

466. *Itch*: The German "Ritter," or knight, is likely a misreading of "Ritt," the shivering that accompanies a fever. Brown takes the former translation.

467. The end of this charm parallels that of Crux Christi, an English charm from the eighteenth and nineteenth century for cure of the ague (Jonathan Roper and Fellows Folklore, *English Verbal Charms*, Ff Communications, No. 288 (Helsinki: Suomalainen Tiedeakatemia, 2005), 101–103). The event is an apocryphal occurrence, likely inspired by the earthquake at Jesus' death (Matthew 27:51). Similar charms in Germany date back to 1373; Bächtold-Stäubli, Hoffmann-Krayer, and Lüdtke, *Handwörterbuch des Deutschen Aberglaubens*, vol. 3, 842; Grimm and Kretzenbacher, *Deutsche Mythologie*, vol. 3, 497. It seems that the latter material was added due to the mistaking of the word "Ritter" for "Ritt," or fever. It has been hypothesized that this is at least two separate charms run together; Löbe, "Aberglaube und Volksmittel aus dem Altenburgschen," 444–45.

468. *Romanusbüchlein* 10, Spamer 1958, 48, discussion, 109–157. See also Manz, "Volksglaube aus dem Sarganserland," 307; Löbe, "Aberglaube und Volksmittel aus dem Altenburgschen," 444–445.

469. The version in *Romanusbüchlein* omits this letter, though it is likely it should be included.

470. *You must write...*: Not in the German.

471. *Romanusbüchlein* 11, Spamer 1958, 48. A shepherd in Brütz used the same charm to help animals who had not been eating by hanging it from the tail or in the stable. Bartsch, *Sagen, Märchen und Gebräuche Aus Meklenburg*, vol. 2, 447. See also Manz, "Volksglaube aus dem Sarganserland," 307.

472. *Romanusbüchlein* 12, Spamer 1958, 49. See also Losch, "Deutsche Segen, Heil- und Bannsprüche," 252; Manz, "Volksglaube aus dem Sarganserland," 303.

473. The derivation of this phrase is unknown, but it dates back to at least the seventeenth century, and often appears as a charm against illness and theft. For a full range of variants, see Adolf Spamer and Johanna Nickel, *Romanusbüchlein; Historisch-Philologischer Kommentar Zu Einem Deutschen Zauberbuch* (Berlin: Akademie-Verlag, 1958), 159; Manz, "Volksglaube aus dem Sarganserland," 303. For a similar phrase in this work, see Charm 180.

474. *Romanusbüchlein* has "I. N. R. I." Hohman's version seems to have been changed to promote symmetry.

475. The German indicates "for" should be inserted here.

476. *Be silenced...*: Brown reads these traits as applying to the speaker of the chant and not the slanderers.

477. *Romanusbüchlein* 13, Spamer 1958, 49, discussion, 158–166. See Manz, "Volksglaube aus dem Sarganserland," 303. The content of the charm indicates it is intended to protect one from slander. Versions of the latter portion date back to the fourteenth century and are applied as charms in a wide variety of contexts; see Spamer *supra*.

478. The Roma did come to the New World with other colonists, and many took up their previous mode of life. See Henry W. Shoemaker, *Gipsies and Gipsy Lore in the Pennsylvania Mountains: An Address [to the] Civic Club, Huntingdon, Pennsylvania, December 5, 1924* (Altoona, PA: *Times Tribune*, 1924).

479. *the prophet Jonas... whale*: Jonah 1:17–2:10. The "type of Christ" likely refers to a similar period of three days in an "underworld" setting.

480. *Romanusbüchlein* 14, Spamer 1958, 49. Also Albertus, *Albertus Magnus. Being the Approved, Verified, Sympathetic and Natural Egyptian Secrets; or, White and Black Art for Man and Beast*, 183.

481. The reference is to Job 19:25, with the quote here being taken directly from Luther's translation of the Bible. The passage has been interpreted as prophesying the coming of the Messiah, which was likely why it was identified as a passage granting magical protection. The context suggests that the next verse, "Und werde darnach mit dieser meiner Haut umgeben werden, und werde in meinem Fleisch Gott sehen," should be included with it when written.

482. *Romanusbüchlein* 15, Spamer 1956, 49.

483. *Hoarse*: Brown: "rough." The German supports both readings.

484. *Romanusbüchlein* 16, Spamer 1958, 49. See also Löbe, "Aberglaube und Volksmittel aus dem Altenburgsche," 450. Omitted from Hohman 1846. A variant of Roper's "Tres Mariae" charm (130–131) or the "Drei Frauen" charm (Ebermann, *Blut- und Wundsegen in Ihrer Entwicklung*, 80–95), a charm usually used for stopping blood. Versions of this charm date back to the year 400, in the writings of Marcellus of Bordeaux, who recorded two charms used for intestinal complaints. After 1500, it was employed for a wide range of purposes. Who the three pure Virgins might be, and if they are of Pagan or Christian origin, is still debated; Ebermann connects them with the three women who visited Jesus' tomb (Mark 16:1), the Norns, and the Valkyries. Similar versions of this charm have turned up in southern Germany and Austria (——, *Blut- und Wundsegen in Ihrer Entwicklung*, 94.) See also Losch, "Deutsche Segen, Heil- und Bannsprüche," 168; Seyfarth, *Aberglaube und Zauberei in der Volksmedizin West-Sachsens*, 116; Staricius, 154.

485. An apparent reference to Isaiah 9:6.

486. *Romanusbüchlein* 17, Spamer 1956, 49. See also Losch, "Deutsche Segen, Heil- und Bannsprüche," 252.

487. German has "first."

488. Brown states this should be "Blutmalen," but it is most likely "Blutmelken."

489. Brown adds here, "If any one asks thee what thou hast done with the milk, say…"

490. *Nimmfrau*: Brown gives "Nunnefrau." The 1863 edition has "milk-maid" here, while Brown (1904) suggests "Wet-nurse." Another version cites a "shepherd" who is driven out as the culprit. Jäckel, "Aphorismen über Volkssitte, Aberglauben und Volksmedicin in Franken, mit Besonderer Rücksicht auf Oberfranken," 204. The implication here is that a witch has taken away the cow's milk, causing it to give blood instead. Other versions of the charm spell give this as the cause; see Raimund Friedrich Kaindl, "Ein Deutsches Beschwörungsbuch: Aus der Handschrift Herausgegeben." *Zeitschrift für Ethnologie* 25(1893), 28.

491. *Romanusbüchlein* 18, Spamer 1956, 49. See also Manz, "Volksglaube aus dem Sarganserland," 308. This charm is omitted from Hohman 1846.

492. *Skull of a criminal*: The remains of a criminal are common magical ingredients. Bächtold-Stäubli, Hoffmann-Krayer, and Lüdtke, *Handwörterbuch des Deutschen Aberglaubens*, vol. 5, 207–8, 212.

493. *Romanusbüchlein* 19, Spamer 1956, 50. See also Manz, "Volksglaube aus dem Sarganserland," 308.

494. *Romanusbüchlein* 20, Spamer 1956, 50. Omitted in Hohman 1846. See also: Jäckel, "Aphorismen über Volkssitte, Aberglauben und Volksmedicin in Franken, mit Besonderer Rücksicht auf Oberfranken," 192; Werner Manz, "Volksglaube aus dem Sarganserland," *Schweizerisches Archiv für Volkskunde* 25(1924–25), 65–66. (includes variant).

495. A Franconian version of this charm includes the instruction to walk around the property three times at a distance of three paces, following the same path each time. Jäckel, "Aphorismen über Volkssitte, Aberglauben und Volksmedicin in Franken, mit Besonderer Rücksicht auf Oberfranken," 192.

496. *Thirty-three angels*: Spamer indicates that the number of angels here was likely three in the charm's original form (176).

497. *Speak to*: German: "sit with."

498. *Daniel*: The presence of Daniel here seems incongruous, but it is a common element of the many different versions of this charm. Other anti-theft charms include three figures—Daniel and two angels—suggesting that "Daniel" might be an angel instead of the prophet. Bartsch, *Sagen, Märchen und Gebräuche aus Meklenburg*, vol. 2, 335–336; Jäckel, "Aphorismen über Volkssitte, Aberglauben und Volksmedicin in Franken, mit Besonderer Rücksicht auf Oberfranken," 193. Ohrt (Bächtold-Stäubli, Hoffmann-Krayer, and Lüdtke, *Handwörterbuch des Deutschen Aberglaubens*, vol. 2, 242) links it to the shared revelation of Daniel and John of Patmos of the horned dragon who, in Revelation 12, attempts to steal the new child from the woman who wears the sun. A Franconian version simply mentions a conversation between Mary and the thirty-three angels, omitting both Daniel and Peter; another from Wurttemberg features Peter and the angels helping Mary; a Pomeranian charm includes only Peter and Mary, trying to keep Jesus away from the angels (Spamer considers this a mistaken transcription); and *Egyptian Secrets* only mentions Peter and Mary. These are only representative examples. Jäckel, "Aphorismen Über Volkssitte, Aberglauben und Volksmedicin in Franken, Mit Besonderer Rücksicht Auf Oberfranken," 192; Losch, "Deutsche Segen, Heil- und Bannsprüche," 162–63; Knoop, *Volkssagen, Erzählungen, Aberglauben, Gebräuche und Märchen aus dem Östlichen Hinterpommern*, 170; Albertus, *Albertus Magnus. Being the Approved, Verified, Sympathetic and Natural Egyptian Secrets; or, White and Black Art for Man and Beast*, 88.

499. *Some*: The number of thieves varies in other versions of the charm. See Spamer, 185.

500. In the German, Mary asks St. Peter to bind, and he speaks the words that follow. Although St. Peter is the most common binding agent in the other charms, other figures sometimes substitute for him (Spamer, 186–87).

501. *In the orchard*: Brown: "in tree, and plant, and garden."

502. *Or wherever…*: Omitted in Hohman 1846.

503. *Stake*: Brown: "block." Hohman 1846: "staff." The "Stock/Bock" rhyme could also show up in other charms as a key component. See Losch, "Deutsche Segen, Heil- und Bannsprüche," 161.

504. *Command…*: Hohman has "command you and all the spirits of them who knows the master of tricks."

505. The German adds, "while you my eyes do not see."

506. *Romanusbüchlein* 21, Spamer 1958, 50–51, discussion, 167–218. Variant: Albertus, *Albertus Magnus. Being the Approved, Verified, Sympathetic and Natural Egyptian Secrets; or, White and Black Art for Man and Beast*, 77–78, 88, 90; Bächtold-Stäubli, Hoffmann-Krayer, and Lüdtke, *Handwörterbuch des Deutschen Aberglaubens* (vol. 2, 241) dates this particular charm back to circa 1400. Some versions include a "Flum Jordan" variant (Item 119) or an invocation of the cross to reverse it, instead of St. John. Knoop, *Volkssagen, Erzählungen, Aberglauben, Gebräuche und Märchen aus dem Östlichen Hinterpommern*, 170; Drechsler, *Sitte, Brauch und Volksglaube in Schlesien*, vol. 2, 47.

507. *Like Jesus…*: Brown omits this.

508. Another example of the Flum Jordan charm, usually found for stilling blood. See Item 119. Staricius 157; Grimm and Kretzenbacher, *Deutsche Mythologie*, vol. 3, 505.

509. *To release…*: Brown: "and he destroyed the power of the old-father of hell."

510. Some versions of this charm elsewhere include a mirroring motif of Jesus leaving the Jordan after being baptized for freeing the thief. Bächtold-Stäubli, Hoffmann-Krayer, and Lüdtke, *Handwörterbuch des Deutschen Aberglaubens*, vol. 2, 243.

511. *Romanusbüchlein* 22, Spamer 1958, 51, discussion, 219–222. See also Albertus, *Albertus Magnus. Being the Approved, Verified, Sympathetic and Natural Egyptian Secrets; or, White and Black Art for Man and Beast*, 183–84; Losch, "Deutsche Segen, Heil- und Bannsprüche," 237. Omitted in Hohman 1846. Other sources include the same stipulations that appear at the beginning or ending of Charm 139 apply, or that the person must go in silence to the place they believe a theft could occur.

512. *Hats*: German "care."

513. *Romanusbüchlein* 23, Spamer 1958, 51. See also: Albertus, *Albertus Magnus. Being the Approved, Verified, Sympathetic and Natural Egyptian Secrets; or, White and Black Art for Man and Beast*, 184; Löbe, "Aberglaube und Volksmittel aus dem Altenburgschen," 452–53; Manz, "Volksglaube aus dem Sarganserland," 67.

514. *Will*: German: "sanctuary."

515. *Romanusbüchlein* 23a, Spamer 1958, 51. See also: Albertus, *Albertus Magnus. Being the Approved, Verified, Sympathetic and Natural Egyptian Secrets; or, White and Black Art for Man and Beast*, 184; Löbe, "Aberglaube und Volksmittel aus dem Altenburgschen," 453. Manz, "Volksglaube aus dem Sarganserland," 67.

516. Pears were a popular fruit among the Pennsylvania Dutch, who had numerous varieties thereof.

517. *Nails out of a coffin*: Even in the Classical era, nails have often been used in magical contexts. Silvia Alfayé Villa, "Nails for the Dead: A Polysemic Account of an Ancient Funerary Practice," in *Magical Practice in the Latin West: Papers from the International Conference Held at the University of Zaragoza, 30 Sept.–1 Oct. 2005*, ed. Richard Gordon and Francisco Marco Simón, *Religions in the Graeco-Roman World* (Leiden [etc.]: Brill, 2010), 132, 141–42. For German usage, see Spamer, p. 229–30; Bächtold-Stäubli, Hoffmann-Krayer, and Lüdtke, *Handwörterbuch des Deutschen Aberglaubens*, vol. 7, 956–57; Albertus, *Bewährte und Approbierte Sympathetische und Natürliche Ägyptische Geheimnisse für Menschen und Vieh*, 67; Hermann Leberecht Strack, *Das Blut im Glauben und Aberglauben der Menschheit*.

Mit Besonderer Berücksichtigung der "Volksmedizin" und des "Jüdischen Blutritus",
Schriften des Institutum Judaicum in Berlin, Nr. 14 (München: Beck, 1900), 51.

518. *Romanusbüchlein* 24, Spamer 1958, 51–52, discussion, 223–276. See also: *Der
Freund in der Noth, Oder Geheime Sympathetische Wissenschaft, Welche Nie Zuvor
im Druck Erschienen. aus dem Spanischen Übersezt* (Offenbach [?]: Calendar-Fabrike, 1790), 6–7; Albrecht Wünsch Richard Dieterich, *Kleine Schriften* (Leipzig:
Berlin, B.G. Teubner, 1911), 197; Albertus, *Albertus Magnus. Being the Approved,
Verified, Sympathetic and Natural Egyptian Secrets; or, White and Black Art for Man
and Beast*, 184–85; Bächtold-Stäubli, Hoffmann-Krayer, and Lüdtke, *Handwörterbuch des Deutschen Aberglaubens*, vol. 2, 221, 224; Ernst John, *Aberglaube, Sitte und
Brauch im Sächsischen Erzgebirge: E. Beitr. zur Dt. Volkskunde* (Annaberg: Graser,
1909), 27; Hirzel, "Aberglauben im Kanton Zürich," 265; Manz, "Volksglaube aus
dem Sarganserland," 66–67; M. Lambelet, "Prièures et Recettes," *Schweizerisches
Archiv für Volkskunde* 15(1911), 185. A similar charm from Oberviechtacht calls
for five nails—one for each limb and one for the head. Schönwerth, *Aus der Oberpfalz—Sitten und Sagen*, vol. 3, 213.

519. *I will arise*: Brown: "I am about to undertake (such a thing)."

520. *Romanusbüchlein* 26, Spamer 1958, 52.

521. *Heart of a bat*: Brown: "heart of a field mouse."

522. *Right*: An addition to the German. Brown adds, "with which you throw."

523. *Romanusbüchlein* 27, Spamer 1958, 52. In Reichenbach, Franconia, and Pennsylvania Dutch country, luck in gambling could be obtained with the dried heart of a
bat. Johann August Ernst Köhler, *Volksbrauch, Aberglauben, Sagen und Andere Alte
Ueberlieferungen im Voigtland: Mit Berücksichtigung des Orlagau's und des Pleissnerlandes: Ein Beitrag zur Kulturgeschichte des Voigtlandes* (Leipzig: Fleischer, 1867,
417; Fogel, *Beliefs and Superstitions of the Pennsylvania Germans*, 359, 377–78;
Jäckel, "Aphorismen über Volkssitte, Aberglauben und Volksmedicin in Franken,
mit Besonderer Rücksicht auf Oberfranken," 189. Other versions add that this is
only effective when the wearer sits with his face toward the setting moon; sitting
in the opposite direction causes loss. C. Kleeberger, *Volkskundliches aus Fischbach
I. D. Pfalz* (Kaiserslautern: H. Kayser, 1902), 50. Variants call for three pulverized
hearts or the head of a bat: e.g. John, *Sitte, Brauch und Volksglaube im Deutschen
Westböhmen, von Alois John*, 319. This formula was strongly adopted among practitioners of Hoodoo, with plastic bats still being found in small conjure bags for
the purpose of luck at gambling. Catherine Yronwode, "Pow-Wows: The European
Influence on Hoodoo," http://www.luckymojo.com/powwows.html.

524. *St. Lorenzo*: Saint Lawrence, deacon of the Roman Catholic Church who died
in 258. The apocryphal story of his martyrdom has him burning to death on a
gridiron.

525. *Romanusbüchlein* 28, Spamer 1958, 52, discussion, 277–290. Omitted from
Hohman 1846. Also: J. Dillman, "Alte Äberglaubische Mittel," *Zeitschrift des Vereins
für rheinische und westfälische volkskunde* 6, no. 4 (1909), 289; Herman Haupt, "Aus
Karl Bernbecks Sammlungen zur Oberhessichen Volkskunde," *Hessische Blätter für
Volkskunde* 1(1902), 17.

526. *Artery*: German: "small veins." Brown: "vines."

527. *Amen*: Omitted in Hohman 1846.

528. *Romanusbüchlein* 29, Spamer 1958, 53.

529. Another example of the SATOR square. See Item 123.

530. *Romanusbüchlein* 25, Spamer 1958, 52. See also Albertus, *Albertus Magnus. Being the Approved, Verified, Sympathetic and Natural Egyptian Secrets; or, White and Black Art for Man and Beast*, 185; Manz, "Volksglaube aus dem Sarganserland," 307.

During his fieldwork in West Virginia, Gerald Milnes found an example of this charm in a barn where cattle were kept, as well as above every window in the nearby house. He links this to *The Long-Lost Friend*, but those who used it seems to derive from a different tradition, given its limited scope and instructions for use here. It should be noted that the German does not instruct that the square be fed to cattle, though it also does not suggest it be used in one's house. Gerald Milnes, *Signs, Cures, & Witchery: German Appalachian Folklore* (Knoxville: University of Tennessee Press, 2007), 175–180.

531. *Some good hymn*: Hohman specifies "Das Walt' Gott," a musical arrangement by Daniel Vetter from 1713.

532. *Romanusbüchlein* 30, Spamer 1958, 53. The German adds, "be they as they want." See also: Manz, "Volksglaube aus dem Sarganserland," 296.

533. This phrase is not in Spamer's *Romanusbüchlein*. It, and a line below, are examples of Ebermann's charm "Sie quellen nicht...," which dates back to Anglo-Saxon times. Ebermann, *Blut- und Wundsegen in Ihrer Entwicklung*, 52–64.

534. Romanus adds "sie geschwellen nicht," "nor does it swell."

535. *Jonas was blind*: This is another statement at variance with Biblical accounts. Ebermann states that other variants substitute Tobias, John, or Thomas here, suggesting that the original reference might have been to Longinus, the centurion who stabbed Jesus who was, according to some accounts, blind. Ibid., 61.

536. The original adds, "They did neither coagulate nor fester. From them I take water and blood, that is for all wounds and pains good. Holy is the man, who all injury and wounds can heal. † † † Amen." Dillman, "Alte Äberglaubische Mittel," 290; Albertus, *Albertus Magnus. Being the Approved, Verified, Sympathetic and Natural Egyptian Secrets; or, White and Black Art for Man and Beast*, 53.

537. *Romanusbüchlein* 31, Spamer 1958, 53. See also Dieterich, *Kleine Schriften*, 197–9; Albertus, *Albertus Magnus. Being the Approved, Verified, Sympathetic and Natural Egyptian Secrets; or, White and Black Art for Man and Beast*, 185; Kleeberger, *Volkskundliches Aus Fischbach I. D. Pfalz*, 54; Löbe, "Aberglaube und Volksmittel aus dem Altenburgschen," 452; Manz, "Volksglaube aus dem Sarganserland," 296.

538. *Against Worms*: The German indicates that these are worms in one's body. A slight variant of this charm, however, was used in Franconia to remove earthworms from an area—not the best idea for a farmer, in retrospect. Jäckel, "Aphorismen über Volkssitte, Aberglauben und Volksmedicin in Franken, mit Besonderer Rücksicht auf Oberfranken," 200.

539. Romanus has four here.

540. Roper's "Job sedebat in sterquilino" charm-type once again, this time with Peter and Jesus substituting for Job.

541. Romanus adds, "with it lay the right hand on the stomach."

542. *Romanusbüchlein* 32, Spamer 1958, 53. Discussion, 291–316. See also: Kuhn, *Sagen, Gebräuche und Märchen aus Westfalen: und Einigen Andern, Besonders den Angrenzenden Gegenden Norddeutschlands*, vol. 2, 207; Kleeberger, *Volkskundliches aus Fischbach I. D. Pfalz*, 52.

543. *Romanusbüchlein* 33, Spamer 1958, 53. A copy of this spell was found in the papers of the schoolmaster Wilhelm Munster, who was active circa 1800 in Sohren, Rhineland-Palatinate. Dillman, "Alte Äberglaubische Mittel." It was also found as a charm to protect from a hostile judge in the same area. Kleeberger, *Volkskundliches Aus Fischbach I. D. Pfalz*, 55.

544. *Romanusbüchlein* 34, Spamer 1958, 54. Discussion, 317–330.

545. *Jesus Nazarenus, Rex Judeorum*: The words placed above Jesus' head on the cross (Matthew 27:37).

546. On December 20, 2007, a piece of paper bearing this phrase, along with a list of individuals, was released to the public during a court proceeding to remove alleged crime boss Vincent "Vinny Gorgeous" Basciano from solitary confinement. The paper had been found in Mr. Basciano's right shoe during his 2006 trial for murder and racketeering. Defense lawyers for Mr. Basciano were said to have claimed it was a ritual connected with Santería. Stephanie Cohen, "Vinny 'Gorgeous' Winds up Doing Time for a 'Spell,'" *The New York Post*, December 21, 2007. John Marzulli, "Hit List? Nah, Just a Silly Li'l Curse, Sez Mob Boss," *Daily News*, December 21 2007.

547. Brown adds, "and you have a just cause."

548. Kleeberger adds this charm instead: "Lord Jesus thine wounds red, stand with me in front of death." Kleeberger, *Volkskundliches Aus Fischbach I.D. Pfalz.* p. 55. Another version states that this should be spoken when passing over the threshold to the courthouse. Losch, "Deutsche Segen, Heil- und Bannsprüch," 163.

549. An example of the charm-type "Glückselige Wunde," which is found, with slight amendments, across Germany. Ebermann, *Blut- und Wundsegen in Ihrer Entwicklung*, 74.

550. *Romanusbüchlein* 35, Spamer 1958, 54. See also Albertus, *Albertus Magnus. Being the Approved, Verified, Sympathetic and Natural Egyptian Secrets; or, White and Black Art for Man and Beast*, 185; Löbe, "Aberglaube und Volksmittel aus dem Altenburgschen," 451. Another version states that a Pater Noster must be said after breathing between each stanza. Losch, "Deutsche Segen, Heil- und Bannsprüche," 220.

551. *Pison…*: The four rivers of Eden, from Genesis 2:11–14. *Romanusbüchlein* has Phrath as the final river.

552. Homan has added this last phrase to the *Romanusbüchlein* charm, indicating that he used it successfully.

553. *Romanusbüchlein* 36, Spamer 1958, 54. Omitted from Hohman 1846. See also Losch, "Deutsche Segen, Heil- und Bannsprüche," 252; Manz, "Volksglaube aus dem Sarganserland," 297.

554. *Romanusbüchlein* 37, Spamer 1958, 54. Romanus adds another charm here: "Say: Jesus Christ carries his cross, why, around it, because he wants, blood stay still. 9 times in the name of † † †."

555. Likely derived from. "Sit Dominus semper vobiscum"—Bächtold-Stäubli, Hoffmann-Krayer, and Lüdtke, *Handwörterbuch des Deutschen Aberglaubens*, vol. 2, 306. Other versions give "I. m. I. K. I. B. L. P. a. X. V. ss. St. vus. I. P. Q. unny Lütt. Domm. Per. vobism." Jäckel, "Aphorismen über Volkssitte, Aberglauben und Volksmedicin in Franken, mit Besonderer Rücksicht auf Oberfranken," 212. The same phrase was used by soldiers from the Simme River Valley to withstand one's enemies. Bächtold, "Volkskundliche Mitteilungen aus dem Schweizerischen Soldatenleben: Proben aus den Einsendungen Schweizerischer Wehrmänner," 218; Kleeberger, *Volkskundliches Aus Fischbach I. D. Pfalz*, 54.

556. *Romanusbüchlein* has "I, m. I. K. I. B. I. P. a, x. v.st. St. vas I. P. Q. unay, Lit. Dommper vocism."

557. *Romanusbüchlein* 38, Spamer 1958, 54. See also: Manz, "Volksglaube aus dem Sarganserland," 297.

558. *Romanusbüchlein* has, "Helchen," likely an improper rendering of "Zeichen."

559. *Depend...*: German: "I rely on my cruel heart." The meaning is unclear.

560. This sentence is not in Spamer's *Romanusbüchlein*.

561. *Romanusbüchlein* 39, Spamer 1958, 55. Omitted from Hohman 1846.

562. This sentence is another insertion into the *Romanusbüchlein* charm.

563. *Romanusbüchlein* 40, Spamer 1958, 55. See also Manz, "Volksglaube aus dem Sarganserland," 303. This phrase appears in Johann Franck's hymn, "Jesu, meine Freude," which later became the text of a motet by Johann Sebastian Bach.

564. *Annania, Azaria, and Misael*: Better known as Shadrach, Meshach, and Abednego, whom King Nebuchadnezzar cast into a fiery furnace but found them unburnt. (Daniel 3) These three names are also used in a written charm to remove a birthmark. Bartsch, *Sagen, Märchen und Gebräuche aus Meklenburg*, vol. 2, 358.

565. The passage to this point is a German translation of the apocryphal *Song of the Three Young Men*, an apocryphal hymn of thanksgiving often inserted into Daniel 3 and dating to at least 100 B.C. Though the Biblical narrative that accompanies it is striking, the passage seems much more appropriate for a charm to avoid fire rather than one to avoid harm in general. Spamer's *Romanusbüchlein* omits "and he has... furnace," which is present in the *Apocrypha*.

566. *I. N. R. I.*: Abbrevation for "Iesus Nazarenus, Rex Iudaeorum," or "Jesus of Nazareth, King of the Jews," the words Pilate affixed to Jesus' cross (John 19:19).

567. *Romanusbüchlein* 41, Spamer 1958, 55. See also: Albertus, *Albertus Magnus. Being the Approved, Verified, Sympathetic and Natural Egyptian Secrets; or, White and Black Art for Man and Beast*, 186; Manz, "Volksglaube aus dem Sarganserland," 67. This also appears to be a repurposed charm originally intended to protect against fire, and other versions are labeled as such. e. g. Kleeberger, *Volkskundliches aus Fischbach I. D. Pfalz*, 54.

568. *Guns*: German "cannons." This likely indicates that the charm was intended for use to protect during warfare.

569. *Beneficent*: German "valid."

570. *There are three roses...*: See the discussion of the "Drei Blumen" charm at Item 109.

571. *Romanusbüchlein* 42, Spamer 1958, 55. Variants: Jäckel, "Aphorismen Über Volkssitte, Aberglauben und Volksmedicin in Franken, mit Besonderer Rücksicht

auf Oberfranken," 195–96; Albertus, *Albertus Magnus. Being the Approved, Verified, Sympathetic and Natural Egyptian Secrets; or, White and Black Art for Man and Beast*, 53, 70–71.

572. *Fire*: German "virginity."

573. *The three holy drops…*: Sweated in the Garden of Gethsemane, on the lower slopes (Luke 22:43–44).

574. *Romanusbüchlein* 43, Spamer 1958, 55–56. See also: Albertus, *Albertus Magnus. Being the Approved, Verified, Sympathetic and Natural Egyptian Secrets; or, White and Black Art for Man and Beast*, 186; Manz, "Volksglaube aus dem Sarganserland," 68.

575. *Jesus… Red Sea*: The Bible does not record such an event. A similar charm from Franconia substitutes Moses for Jesus. Jäckel, "Aphorismen Über Volkssitte, Aberglauben und Volksmedicin in Franken, Mit Besonderer Rücksicht Auf Oberfranken," 196.

576. *Romanusbüchlein* adds here: "the blessing that God works, go over me at all times."

577. *Jesus*: Brown: "James."

578. *when he ordered… Egypt*: Matthew 2:13–15.

579. *Romanusbüchlein* 44, Spamer 1958, 56, discussion, 331–351. See also: Albertus, *Albertus Magnus. Being the Approved, Verified, Sympathetic and Natural Egyptian Secrets; or, White and Black Art for Man and Beast*, 186–87; Manz, "Volksglaube aus dem Sarganserland," 69.

580. *Blood and water*: A reference to John 19:34, blood and water are often mentioned magically in the "Blut und Wasser" charm, a later version of the "Longinus" charm usually applied to bleeding instead of avoiding injury. Ebermann, *Blut- und Wundsegen in Ihrer Entwicklung*, 64–71.

581. *Saint Stephan… virgin*: The German here states that the Jews stoned Stephen, which more accurately reflects the Biblical story (Acts 6:5–7:60) .

582. *Romanusbüchlein* adds the obvious "Gottes des Vaters, Gottes des Sohnes und Gottes des heiligen Geistes" ("God the Father, God the Son, and God the Holy Spirit.").

583. *Romanusbüchlein* 45, Spamer 1958, 56. Omitted from Hohman 1846.

584. *Name*: The German indicates both the first and last names are to be used here.

585. The German adds here "which are always good to me for my sins." These sins are likely the subject of the following line regarding "secret or public," not the firearms.

586. *Name*: Once again, the first and last names.

587. *Romanusbüchlein* 46, Spamer 1958, 56–57. See also Manz, "Volksglaube aus dem Sarganserland," 69.

588. *Name*: First and last names.

589. *The blessing…*: Another occurrence not in the Biblical accounts.

590. *And all the saints of God*: Omitted in Hohman 1846.

591. *The three holy kings… Balthasar*: The three wise men who visited Jesus as an infant.

592. *Romanusbüchlein* omits Michael.

593. *Saint Michael … Saint Uriel*: Uriel is not technically a saint. One version omits all of these save Uriel: Manz, "Volksglaube aus dem Sarganserland," 68.

594. *Romanusbüchlein* has "Rapa. R. tarn. Tetragrammaton Angeli." Tetragrammaton is a name substituting for the Holy Unspeakable Name of God, Yod-He-Vau-He. "Angeli" means "of the angels." The rest of the passage is of unknown meaning. The same phrase appears in the beginning of another charm against weapons— Kleeberger, *Volkskundliches aus Fischbach I. D. Pfalz*, 61.

595. See Item 153.

596. *Romanusbüchlein* 48, Spamer 1958, 57.

597. *Romanusbüchlein* 47, Spamer 1958, 57. Omitted from Hohman 1846.

598. The German instructs that the person's first and last names be inserted here.

599. *In the water or in the fields*: Omitted in Hohman 1846.

600. *Secret or public*: Omitted in Hohman 1846.

601. *This shall assist*: Omitted in Hohman 1846.

602. *Fire-arms, hold …*: Omitted in Hohman 1846.

603. *Romanusbüchlein* 49, Spamer 1958, 58.

604. *Romanusbüchlein* 50, Spamer 1958, 58.

605. The German adds, "they bring to me for his rosy blood in my bosom."

606. *Romanusbüchlein* 51, Spamer 1958, 58–59.

607. *With*: German "above."

608. A reference to God the Son is an obvious omission here. The *Romanusbüchlein* adds, "God the Son be before me."

609. An "impossibility formula"; see Item 37.

610. *Romanusbüchlein* 52, Spamer 1958, 59. This charm was found in Aischgrund, where it was used by soldiers before battle. Jäckel, "Aphorismen über Volkssitte, Aberglauben und Volksmedicin in Franken, mit Besonderer Rücksicht Auf Oberfranken," 185.

611. *Name*: First and last name.

612. *Agtion and Elias*: Agtion appears to be a corruption of the Greek αγιον, or "holy." Another charm gives it as "Agian" (Jäckel, "Aphorismen über Volkssitte, Aberglauben und Volksmedicin in Franken, mit Besonderer Rücksicht auf Oberfranken," 186). Elias is the Hellenized form of Elijah.

613. *Romanusbüchlein* 53, Spamer 1958, 59. See also Albertus, *Albertus Magnus. Being the Approved, Verified, Sympathetic and Natural Egyptian Secrets; or, White and Black Art for Man and Beast*, 187; Manz, "Volksglaube aus dem Sarganserland," 68.

614. *Gone*: German: "led Jesus." This might relate to his appearances there as a boy (Matthew 2).

615. *Romanusbüchlein* 54, Spamer 1958, 59. Omitted in Hohman 1846.

616. *Blood and water*: See Item 164.

617. *Romanusbüchlein* 55, Spamer 1958, 59. See also Jäckel, "Aphorismen über Volkssitte, Aberglauben und Volksmedicin in Franken, mit Besonderer Rücksicht auf Oberfranken," 186; Manz, "Volksglaube aus dem Sarganserland," 68.

618. *Courage*: Brown "spirit"; Hohman "Heroism." All are possible translations.

619. This is another example of the "Drei Blumen" charm—see Item 109 above.

620. *Romanusbüchlein* 56, Spamer 1958, 59–60, discussion, 352–360; Albertus, *Albertus Magnus. Being the Approved, Verified, Sympathetic and Natural Egyptian Secrets; or, White and Black Art for Man and Beast,* 53–54.

621. German: "or where otherwise," i.e. if they exited another way.

622. *Unbeschrewedly*: See Item 4.

623. *Backwards*: Omitted in Brown.

624. *The Father*: Omitted in Brown.

625. Other sources stipulate that, if this is not done, the thief will run himself to death or have his or her feet blistered and feel pain unto death. A. Haas, "Diebsglaube in Pommern," *Blätter für Pommersche Volkskunde* 4, no. 9 (1896), 139; Albertus, *Albertus Magnus. Being the Approved, Verified, Sympathetic and Natural Egyptian Secrets; or, White and Black Art for Man and Beast,* 37.

626. *If thou art more almighty...*: Another impossibility formula. See Item 37.

627. *Romanusbüchlein* 58, Spamer 1958, 60, discussion, 375–378. Omitted from Hohman 1846. This charm, in which three chips are placed on a wagon wheel and turned while speaking the names of the Trinity and an incantation, was a common one in Germany. Bächtold-Stäubli, Hoffmann-Krayer, and Lüdtke, *Handwörterbuch des Deutschen Aberglaubens,* vol. 2, 221; Georg Conrad Horst, *Zauber-Bibliothek: Oder, von Zauberei, Theurgie und Mantik, Zauberern, Hexen und Hexenprocessen, Dämonen, Gespenstern und Geistererscheinungen* (Freiburg i.Br.: Aurum-Verlag, 1979), vol. 4, 172; Wolf, *Beiträge zur Deutschen Mythologie.* vol. 1, 257–58.

628. *Touch-hole*: Brown has "sinner."

629. *Neither fire*: Brown "neither fire, nor smoke, nor flame, nor hiss."

630. The German adds, "Amen."

631. *Romanusbüchlein* 61, Spamer 1958, 61; Bächtold, "Volkskundliche Mitteilungen aus dem Schweizerischen Soldatenleben: Proben aus den Einsendungen Schweizerischer Wehrmänner," 229. Albertus, *Albertus Magnus. Being the Approved, Verified, Sympathetic and Natural Egyptian Secrets; or, White and Black Art for Man and Beast,* 52–53.

632. Witches. See Item 24. The English translation is from Brown.

633. *Shoemaker's wax-end*: A thread covered in wax with a bristle at the end, used to sew together holes in leather.

634. According to the German text, this should read "... in which Jesus Christ died."

635. *No kind...*: German: "no lead nor powder, iron, steel, or other metal."

636. *Romanusbüchlein* 62, Spamer 1958, 61.

637. *Name*: First and last name.

638. *Hbbi*: Hohman 1846: "Hobbi."

639. *Massa*: German: "Mafsa." Brown: "Mofsy."

640. *Romanusbüchlein* has here "Habi Massa denti Lantien. I. I. I." A similar phrase, "H bbi Masra danti Santien," is found in a Palatinate magical manual dated 1814 in a charm intended to ward off slander, attacks, and witchcraft. Kleeberger, *Volkskundliches Aus Fischbach I. D. Pfalz,* 51. The phrase is "Hbbi Matsu dnnti Lnntien" in the Franconian charm described below.

641. *Romanusbüchlein* 60, Spamer 1958, 61, discussion, 379–387. An early version of this charm dates to Biel, Switzerland, in 1647. One source described therein states that the phrase should be written on a piece of paper, which is burned and the ashes swallowed. Brown: "A Charm to Constrain a Man from Growing too Large." See also: Albertus, *Bewährte und Approbierte Sympathetische und Natürliche Ägyptische Geheimnisse für Menschen und Vieh*, 69; Kuhn, *Sagen, Gebräuche und Märchen aus Westfalen: und Einigen Andern, Besonders den Angrenzenden Gegenden Norddeutschlands*, vol. 2, 191. Another version of this charm, without the final words, can be found in other sources. Albertus, *Albertus Magnus. Being the Approved, Verified, Sympathetic and Natural Egyptian Secrets; or, White and Black Art for Man and Beast*, 52. This charm was used in Franconia for bringing back a cheating husband. Jäckel, "Aphorismen über Volkssitte, Aberglauben und Volksmedicin in Franken, mit Besonderer Rücksicht auf Oberfranken," 185.

642. *Spring-tails or Ground Fleas*: The German "Erdflöhe" points to a different pest: the leaf beetles of the genus *Psylliodes*.

643. *The dung of horses*: The German specifies that this must be "short," or free of straw or other detritus.

644. *Jacob Wohlgemuth*: Other versions do not include this name; e.g. Birlinger, *Aus Schwaben Sagen, Legenden, Aberglauben, Sitten, Rechtsbräuche, Ortsneckereien, Lieder, Kinderreine, Neue Sammlung, von Anton Birlinger*. vol. 1, p. 457; Kuhn, *Sagen, Gebräuche und Märchen Aus Westfalen: und Einigen Andern, Besonders den Angrenzenden Gegenden Norddeutschlands*, vol. 2, 196 ("Jakob Klein").

645. *Romanusbüchlein* 59, Spamer 1958, 61.

646. The German includes the first and last names here.

647. This phrase is omitted in Spamer's *Romanusbüchlein*.

648. *For the soul's sake*: German: "through the Son."

649. *Enoch and Elias*: Two prophets who did not die, but ascended into heaven (Genesis 5:24, 2 Kings 2:11). Some believe them to be the two witnesses who will return before the apocalypse, sending fire out of their mouths to destroy those who attempt to stop them (Revelation 11:5).

650. *Imprisoned*: Brown: "taken, bound and slain."

651. *Romanusbüchlein* 63, Spamer 1958, 61–62.

652. *N.*: The German indicates the first and last name.

653. The German follows this with "twelve."

654. *My premises*: Brown: "court."

655. *Romanusbüchlein* 64, Spamer 1958, 62. Omitted in Hohman 1846.

656. The German adds, "Thuringian," which might indicate the origin of the charm.

657. *Deer...*: German: "deer, roe deer, hares and snipes."

658. *On account...*: Omitted from both Brown and Hohman 1846.

659. *Yards*: German: "paces."

660. Persius, *Satires* IV:23–24: "Ut nemo in sese termat descendere? Nemo./ Sed praecedenti spectatur mantica tergo." Translation: "Not a soul is there—no, not one—who seeks to get down into his own self; all watch the wallet on the back that walks before!" (Juvenal and Persius, *Juvenal and Persius. With an English Translation by G.G. Ramsay* (Cambridge: Harvard University Press, 1965), 361. Aulus Persius Flaccus (34–62) was a first-century satirist. It is likely that Persius' dig at those

examining the packs of others instead of themselves was used for satirical purposes, later being taken seriously and inserted into the magical corpus.

661. *The best argument...*: German: "Man thut am besten, und probirt es."

662. *Juniper tree*: A tree that is treated as powerful and having apotropaic powers in German tradition. Other versions of the same charm call for elder, thistle, or nettle to be used.

663. *Bend and squeeze*: Brown: "Bow and stoop."

664. This phrase is not present in Spamer's *Romanusbüchlein*.

665. *Skull of a malefactor*: See Item 137. Other versions substitute a stone. Wilhelm Mannhardt and Walter Heuschkel, *Wald- und Feldkulte* (Berlin: Gebrüder Borntraeger, 1875), vol. 1, 68–69; Wolf, *Beiträge zur Deutschen Mythologie*, vol. 1, 258.

666. *Romanusbüchlein* 65, Spamer 1958, 62–63, discussion, 388–394. Omitted from Hohman 1846. Most examples of this charm appear in the south of Germany and date after the appearance of the *Romanusbüchlein*. Kuhn, *Sagen, Gebräuche und Märchen aus Westfalen: und Einigen Andern, Besonders den Angrenzenden Gegenden Norddeutschlands*, vol. 2, 194. See also Jäckel, "Aphorismen über Volkssitte, Aberglauben und Volksmedicin in Franken, mit Besonderer Rücksicht auf Oberfranken," 191; Albertus, *Albertus Magnus. Being the Approved, Verified, Sympathetic and Natural Egyptian Secrets; or, White and Black Art for Man and Beast*, 54; Ferdinand Andrian-Werburg, *Die Altausseer; Ein Beitrag zur Volkskunde des Salzkammergutes* (Wein: A. Hölder, 1905), 157. Another version adds that this should not be done for unimportant matters. Manz, "Volksglaube aus dem Sarganserland," 66.

667. *Trumpet*: Brown: "sackbuts." Hohman 1846: "Trompunes" [sic]. The exact brass instrument referred to is uncertain in the German.

668. *The hand of no man...beat me*: Brown: "may not be sized by the hand of any man, nor bound, nor cut, nor shot, nor stabbed, nor thrown down, nor slain, and especially may not be wounded." Hohman 1846: "no mans hand shall take me, bind, cut, shoot, stab or whip and conquer."

669. *Romansbuchlein* 66, Spamer 1958, 63. Albertus, *Albertus Magnus. Being the Approved, Verified, Sympathetic and Natural Egyptian Secrets; or, White and Black Art for Man and Beast*, 187.

670. *Is safe...*: Omitted from Hohman 1846.

671. *Nor can any unjust...*: Hohman 1846: "and none can say ought about it."

672. This, the most famous passage from this book, appears at the end of the previous charm in the *Romanusbüchlein*. It has been broken out here due to its influence and importance upon the history of the book. As it is not the last charm in the book, however, it might suggest that Spamer's text represents a later stage of editing, in which additional charms have been added to the work. It is often repeated in the beginning matter of later editions, beginning with the 1828, or on the cover thereof.

673. Lists of such days were known since the New Kingdom in Egypt. Lists of so-called "Egyptian Days" turn up in medieval literature, but none of these I have examined parallels the list given here. Robert Steele, "Dies Aegyptiaci," *Proceedings of the Royal Society of Medicine* 12(Supplement)(1919).

674. *And those who engage*: Omitted in Hohman 1846.

675. The German includes the following line here: "On the days of Mary's Annunciation, Simon, Jude, and the Apostle St. Andrew, one should let no blood." The days in question are March 25, October 28 (for both Simon and Jude), and November 30.

676. *Der Hundertjährige Calender, auf das Gegenwärtige Jahr-Hundert nach Christi Geburt, von 1799 bis 1899* (Baltimore: Samuel Saur., 1799), 41–42

677. *There are many who believe it*: Given Hohman's expressed certainty about so many charms, this expression seems to indicate some question as to its efficacy, whether in Hohman's mind or in those of his readers.

678. The German inserts the first and last names here.

679. *Romanusbüchlein* 2, Spamer 45. See also Manz, "Volksglaube aus dem Sarganserland," 67.

680. This appeared first in the 1828 edition. Files of the *Lancaster Eagle* are too fragmentary to state in which issue this charm might have originally appeared.

681. *Elder leaves*: Probably from the black elder (*Sambucus nigra*). Its use to heal wounds is a folk remedy that has not been proven.

682. *In a short time*: German: "In a few hours."

683. On the use of the bark of the white oak, see Item 74 above.

684. *That stands…*: Omitted in Hohman 1846.

685. *Strength*: German: "sap."

686. Weaver 2001 (238) states that German settlers preferred *Petroselinum crispum tuberosum*, or "Hamburg parsley," a variant known for its thick roots like those of a parsnip.

687. *Pound it fine*: Omitted in Hohman 1846.

688. *Open the bowels…*: Hohman 1846: "eat physics mildly and is useful for person which have the dropsey."

689. *Six or seven peeled kernels*: See Item 90 above.

690. See Zwinger, *Theodori Zuingeri Theatrum Botanicum*, 50.

691. A mild vegetable oil, such as olive oil. Hohman 1846 glosses over much of the following.

692. *Rhubarb*: Weaver 2001 (260) links this to *Rheum officinale*, a more toxic plant than the *Rheum x hybridum* that is cultivated for food today.

693. *Hartshorn*: The shavings of the horn of the red deer (*Cervus elaphus*), a common remedy for this condition.

694. *White lead*: Basic lead carbonate $(PbCO_3)_2Pb(OH)_2$. Its use is not recommended.

695. *St. Johnswort*: *Hypericum perforatum*, a plant with many medicinal uses.

696. Three lilies plucked on St. John's Day were inserted in olive oil and blessed by the priests of the church of Maria Bildstein to create a safe burn remedy. Otto Stoll, "Zur Kenntnis des Zauberglaubens, der Volksmagie und Volksmedizin in der Schweiz," *Jahresberichte der Geographisch-Ethnographischen Gesellschaft in Zürich* 9(1908–09), 89.

697. *Fumatory*: Plants from the genus *Fumaria*. Their usage for edema is unknown.

698. *Euphrasy sugar*: Plants from the genus *Euphrasia*. The given effects have not been documented.

699. *Squills*: *Scillae bulbus* or *Scilla maritima*. Its use for dropsy is unknown.

700. *Bohea tea*: Tea from China's Wu-I hills, or black tea in general.

701. *Rape seed*: Brassica napus. No known benefits for edema are noted.

702. *Gum myrrh*: Commiphora molmol. No known benefits for edema are noted.

703. *Spruce pine*: Picea species. Its usage for this condition is unknown.

704. *Broom-corn*: Sorghum vulgare.

705. *Red cabbage leaves*: Brassica oleracea. No known effects from topic use are known.

706. *Onion*: Allium cepa. This is a common folk remedy for an insect sting.

707. *Madder compound*: A substance that could be purchased at drugstores.

708. This, the following recipe, and A15 may be found in the *The New Genesee Farmer* 2, no. 10 (October 1841), 153.

709. *Lac dye*: Dye made from parasitic insects from eastern Asia and Mexico.

710. *Gargling oil*: Merchant's Gargling Oil was a nineteenth century patent medicine used as a topical treatment for livestock.

711. *Sulphate of zinc*: Zinc sulfate ($ZnSO_4$).

712. *Corrosive sublimate*: Mercury(II) chloride ($HgCl_2$).

713. *Spirit of salt*: Hydrochloric acid (HCl).

714. *Venetian soap*: Soap made from a base of olive oil instead of tallow.

715. *Sal prunella*: Saltpeter heated to high temperatures.

716. *Sweet spirits of nitre*: Ethyl nitrite in an alcohol solution.

717. *Calamus*: Acorus calamus. This is considered unsafe to consume.

718. *Sulphate of potasso*: Likely sulfate of potassium (K_2SO_4).

719. *Tartar emetic*: Antimony potassium tartrate ($K(SbO)C_4H_4O_6$), a highly toxic substance.

720. *Liver of sulphur*: Sulfurated potash. Some versions have flour of sulfur, or sulfur that has been heated and ground.

721. *Stramonium (Jamestown weed)*: Datura stramonium. It is not noted for topical use and has toxic properties.

722. *Wind-broken*: A respiratory ailment of horses.

723. Peregrine Montague, *The Family Pocket-Book or, Fountain of True and Useful Knowledge. Containing the Farrier's Guide; ... The Good Housewife's Daily Companion; ... Compiled ... By Peregrine Montague* (London: printed for George Paul, 1762), 32.

724. *Elecampane*: Inula Helenium, used among the Pennsylvania Dutch for coughing of horses, among other causes. Lick and Brendle, "Plant Names and Plant Lore among the Pennsylvania-Germans," 181.

725. *Sulphur squills*: Likely these two ingredients should have had a comma between them.

726. *Cinnabar of antimony*: Cinnabar (red mercuric(II) sulphide).

727. *Aurum mosaicum*: Tin(IV) sulfide, SnS_2.

728. *Sulphuric ether*: Ethyl ether, $C_2H_5OC_2H_5$.

729. *Sal-Soda*: Sodium carbonate, used as a cleanser.

730. *Gum guiacum*: Lignum vitae.

731. *Whitning*: Substance made of finely pulverized chalk.

732. *Aqua ammonia*: Ammonia dissolved in water.

733. *Iodide of potassium*: Potassium iodide (KI). This was used in contemporary formulae for asthma; see A. B. Hoyt, "Case of Asthma Treated by Iodide of Potassium," *The Boston Medical and Surgical Journal* 53, no. 16 (1855).

734. *Tincture of lobedia*: *Lobedia inflata*, a potentially toxic herb from the New World used to treat respiratory disorders.

735. *Syrup of senega*: An extract of the *Polygala senega* root, another New World plant, used in cases of bronchitis. The substance is harmful in high doses.

736. *Hydrate of potassium*: KHO, or potash.

737. *Pips*: A respiratory infection in chickens, the most recognizable symptom at this time being a dried-out tongue.

738. *Cuculi arambosti*: Unknown.

739. *Crinis fulvae*: "Yellow hair." The exact substance is uncertain.

740. *Sancta simplex*: Significance unknown.

741. *Bierhäfen*: Likely "Bierhefe," or brewer's yeast.

742. *Quarilaserum*: Possibly derived from *Cyclanthera pedate*, or stuffing cucumber.

743. *Putandrum longum, Succus leritarium*: Unknown.

744. St. John's wort.

745. *Knabenkraut*: A name applied to genera of orchids.

746. *Tansy*: *Tanacetum vulgare*, a toxic substance.

747. *Ivy*: Another toxic plant.

748. *Uterus*: German: Tragt.

749. *Lisbon wine*: A white table wine from Portugal.

750. *Sweet earth*: Ballmer has "sweet yeast."

751. *Marrubium*: Horehound.

752. *Indian pen*: Corresponds in description to bloodroot (*Sanguinaria canadensis*).

753. *Fire-powder*: See S50 for the recipe.

754. Possibly stinging nettles (*Urtica dioica*), as most other plants causing adverse topical reactions grow in shady areas.

755. Definitely not recommended.

756. *Elder bark, elder root*: This is toxic.

757. *Rye whiskey*: As with the recipes in the main body of the work, the German "Kornbranntwein" could also signify corn schnapps.

758. *Flower of sulphur*: Likely flour of sulphur.

759. *Small snake's root*: Either jack in the pulpit (*Arum maculatum*) or creeping jenny (*Lysimachia nummularia*).

760. *French clover*: Plants of the genus *Anthyllis*.

761. Postage stamp: The German "elfpens Stück" might indicate a coin.

762. *Mint*: Ballmer indicates this is pennyroyal, but the German labels it mint.

763. *Knotengrass*: Multiple possibilities exist here: Velvetgrass (*Avena elatior*/*Holcus avenaceus, Panicum verticillatum*), tall oat-grass (*Arrhenatherum elatius*), common meadow-grass (*Poa trivialis*), knotgrass (*Polygonum aviculare*), bristly foxtail (*Setaria verticillata*), or creeping wheat (*Triticum repens*/*Agropyrum repens*). Ballmer chooses knotgrass.

764. *Stinking Nachtschatten*: Possibly henbane, but possibly one of eight different plants. Ballmer has "stinky Tom flowers."

INDEX

283

bread, 67, 69, 71, 90, 95, 119–120

breasts, curing sore, 102

breath, 51, 56, 59, 66

Brecht, Catharine Hottenstein, 240

Brecht, David, 43, 150, 240

Breiten Wegrich, 54, 161

brewer's yeast, 111, 281

bricks, 104, 112, 123

bristly foxtail, 281

Brooklyn NY, 29

broom-corn (sorghum vulgare), 104

Brown, Carleton, xiv, 22, 31

Bruckman, Carl A., 9–10

bruises, 57

Buck, Nicholas, 6

burdock, 128

burns, 52, 56, 67, 83, 101–102, 134

butter, unsalted, 71, 133

buttermilk, 69, 112

buttermilk pop, 112

C

cabbage, 104

cabbage leaves, red, 104, 280

calamus root, 108

calomel, 106, 114

cammock, 65

camphor oil, 110, 133

spirits of camphor, 105, 110, 113, 132–133

canning fruit, 114

cape aloes, 106

Capricorn, 97

Capuchin powder, 65

carbolic acid, 115

castile soap, 106, 108

castorium, 71

cattle, not giving milk, 80

cattle, swelling of, 55–56, 71, 119, 123

catnip, 131–132, 231–232

cayenne pepper, 105, 115

cedar, sprouts of red, 130

celandine, 252

Centennial almanac, 98

chair, 26, 93

chalk, 105, 107, 128

Chambersburg PA, 20

chamomile, 125

Champagne, making false, 111

charcoal, 58

charms and charming, 4, 13, 20–21, 141

cheese, 58

chemic blue, 106

cherries, 58

chestnut, leaves of, 126

chicken cholera, 114

chicken feet, 134

chickens, 60, 114, 119

chickens, pips in, 217

chickweed, 176

childbirth, help in, 86, 132, 258

chips from door, 92

chloroform, 110

Christmas, 11, 49

Chronicum Paschale, 261

Kettering, Valentine, 19, 68–69, 176

key, 8, 13, 22, 48, 141

Key of Solomon, 13, 22, 141

Knabenkraut, 122, 221

Knableinskraut, 122, 221

Knopp, Emma, 25–26

knot-grass, 54

Kriebel, David, 28, 35, 139

L

lac dye, 106

Lancaster Eagle, 99

hog's lard, 65, 108

Last Supper, 89

laudanum, 105, 110

laurel leaf, 59

lawsuit, success at, 71, 97

leaves, pressing, 114

Lebanon, 43

lemonade, 109

lemons, 109, 113

Leo, 252

Lewis, Arthur, 24

Liber Aggregationis, 19, 34, 137

licorice, 107–108

lilies, 101–102, 132–133

lily bulbs, 120–121

limbs, 62–63, 67, 90, 102, 120

lime, 56, 58, 66, 110–111, 118–119, 122, 124, 134

lime water, 56, 58, 66, 110–111, 119, 124, 134

linen, unbleached, 53, 56

liniment, 110, 133

linseed oil, 107, 110

liver, disorders of, 104

liver of sulphur, 107–108

Liverpool, 105

liverwort, 129

lobelia, 114

lockjaw, 21

Lord's Prayer, 64, 72, 74, 77, 83–85

Louisiana, 29, 36

love, 72

Lovecraft, H. P., 30

Luke, Apostle, see St. Luke

lungwort, 129

Luther, Martin, 39

lye, 58, 74

M

madder, 105–106

madder compound, 105–106

Maine, 109

male fern, 67

maple syrup, 112

March snow water, 131–132, 134

Marietta, 25

Mark, Apostle, see St. Mark

marrubium, 125, 224

Martinmas, 58

Maryland, 23, 37

Maundy Thursday, 76, 89

meadow-grass, common, 281

Mertz Church, Dryville PA, 6

mice, destroying, 60, 94

milk, 14, 49, 52, 61, 69, 99, 112, 126, 128–129, 132

milk, blood instead of, 120, 122

milk taken from cow, 80, 123

millifolia, 58, 165

mint, 133

misael, 86, 195

molasses, 64–65, 69, 107

mole, heart of, 59

moon, 56, 63–64, 66, 70, 72, 97, 124–125, 129–130, 132

mortification, 4, 39–42, 44, 69, 84, 100

moss, 68

mother-fits, 39, 44, 47, 68

mother-pains, 67

Mount of Olives, 87

Mountain Mary (see Jung, Anna Maria)

mouse, 118, 121

mouth, sore, 42, 132

Muhlenberg, Gotthilf, 257

Muhlenberg, Rev. Henry, 69, 257

mulberry tree, 58

mule, young, 50

mullein, 133, 233

mullen, 113

mumps, 252, 267

Munster, Wilheim, 272

musk, 71

muslin, 53

mustard, 51, 103

myrrh, 103, 114

Mystical City of God, 261

N

Nachtschatten, 58, 133, 233, 251, 281

Nackenmixen PA, 43

nails, coffin or horseshoe, 82, 269

neatsfoot oil, 70

Nebuchadnezzar, King, 373

needle, 48, 54, 123

net, 51, 71

nettle, stinging, 58, 251, 281

neuralgia, 112

New York Evening Post, 105

New Zealand, 29

Newbold, Samuel, 6

nightmare, 263

nightshade, 133

Niles' Weekly Register, 19, 35

ninny, 80

nitric acid, 114

Noll, Emma, 25–26

nomina barbara, 16

Norristown PA, 24, 34, 136

nutmeg, flower, 128

O

oak, white, 63, 100, 124, 133

oats, 64, 130

Obed Rego, 78

olive oil, 104

onion, 105

opium, camphorated tincture of, 114

ore, 49–50

P

Paganism, 30
pains, 53, 57, 110
Palatinate region of Germany, 2
palpitation, heart, 39, 50
panting, 39
paper, 3, 53–54, 56, 62, 65–66,
    79–80, 84–85, 95–96, 105, 114
parsley, 100, 103, 133, 279
Pater Noster (Our Father) prayer,
    265, 272
patriarchs, 89
Paul, Apostle, 72
peaches, 66
pear tree, 82
Penn, William, 141
Pennsylvania Dutch/German,
    1–3, 22–23, 32, 35–36, 139–
    140
Pensses Blum, 73, 181
pepper, black, 111,131
peppercorn, 118
peppermint, 131
pestilence, preventing, 74–75, 80
Peter, Apostle, see St. Peter
Petit Albert, 29
petroleum, 109
Pheat, river, 85, 194
Philadelphia PA, 2, 22, 34, 36–37,
    137, 139
piles, 51
pimpernel bread, 68, 120
Pimpernel, scarlet, 357
Pimpton, Tom, 29
pine oil, resinous, 118

pine, yellow, 259
pipe, white clay, 54
Pison, river, 85
plantain, 70, 126–127, 129, 249,
    258
plaster, 55–56, 65, 67, 69–70, 113,
    134
plate, dirty, tin, 60, 252
pleurisy, 131
poisoning, curing, 255
pollevil, 52
Polygala senega, 281
Pontius Pilate, 246
pork, 49, 129
pot (kitchen utensil), 43, 47, 56,
    65, 70,76, 80
Potmat sineat charm, 55
Powdermaker, Hortense, 29, 36,
    238
powwowing, 1, 4, 7, 25, 30, 36,
    139
Prussia, 75
Psalm, 50th, 239
pumpkins, 64
Putandrum longum, 121, 219

Q

quaking grass, common, 258
quarilaserum, 121, 219
quinsey, 59

R

rabbits, 60, 67
rag, 52, 53, 54, 56, 66,67,
    101

raisins, small, 120
rape seed, 103, 280
rats, 63
rattlesnake, fat, 131
RavenWolf, Silver, 36
Reading PA, 1, 3, 9, 30, 41, 43, 137
Readinger Adler, 3, 7
Readinger Postbothe, Der, 8–10, 35
reboam, 13
red pimpernel, 68
Red Sea, 15, 87
Rehmeyer, Nelson, 24–26
Rehmeyer's Hollow PA, 25
Reichenbach, Germany, 270
Reimensnyder, Barbara, 24, 36, 238
resin, 111
rest harrow, 255
rheumatism, 4, 43, 72, 111
rhubarb, 101, 105, 279
rickets, 239
Ritter, John and Company, 7
rivers of paradise, 85
Robacker, Earl, 36
rock-candy, 113
Roman Catholicism, 270
Romanusbüchlein (Romanus-Book), 18
rose water, 51, 63
rosemary, oil of, 63
Rosenthal PA 41
Rose Valley PA, 239
roses, 132, 239

rosin, pine, 128, 133
Rother Heuhnerdam/Meyer, 68, 76, 176
Royal Publishing Company, 22
Ruby, Heinrich, 20
rue (*ruta graveolens*), 69, 70, 258
Ruscombmanor PA, 42
rye straw, 125
rye whiskey, 54, 62, 64, 131–133

S

Sadrach (Shadrach), 78, 186, 265
saffron, 108, 128
sage, leaves, 71, 132
St. Anthony's fire, 130
St. Cyprian (Ciprian), 78, 187, 265
St. Gabriel, 89, 197
St. Isidorus, 246, 250
St. Itorius, 15, 51, 158, 246
St. Jacob, 259
St. John, 34, 62, 64
St. John's Day (June 23), 279
St. John's wort, 62, 253, 281
St. Lawrence, 270
St. Lorenzo, 83, 270
St. Luke, 72, 89, 244, 274, 281
St. Mark, 192
St. Matthew, 87, 246, 254, 266, 272, 274, 275
St. Michael, 89, 136, 197
St. Peter, 6, 81, 122, 189, 268, 271
St. Peter's Catholic Church, 6
St. Raphael, 89, 197